Border Wars

BORDER WARS

The Civil War in Tennessee and Kentucky

Edited by Kent T. Dollar, Larry H. Whiteaker,

and W. Calvin Dickinson

THE KENT STATE UNIVERSITY PRESS

Kent, Ohio

Library of Congress Catalog Card Number 2014049701
ISBN 978-1-60635-241-0
Manufactured in the United States of America

Library of Congress Cataloging-in-Publication Data
Border wars : the Civil War in Tennessee and Kentucky / edited by Kent T. Dollar, Larry H. Whiteaker, and W. Calvin Dickinson.
pages cm
Includes bibliographical references and index.
ISBN 978-1-60635-241-0 (hardcover : alk. paper) ∞
1. Tennessee—History—Civil War, 1861–1865—Campaigns. 2. Kentucky—History—Civil War, 1861–1865—Campaigns. 3. Tennessee—History—Civil War, 1861–1865—Biography. 4. Kentucky—History—Civil War, 1861–1865—Biography. I. Dollar, Kent T. II. Whiteaker, Larry H. (Larry Howard), 1946– III. Dickinson, W. Calvin.
E470.4.B67 2015
976.8'04—dc23
2014049701

19 18 17 16 15 5 4 3 2 1

Contents

Part II: Leaders

Preface and Acknowledgments

The idea for this book has been on our minds for some time. Indeed, as we were working on *Sister States, Enemy States: The Civil War in Kentucky and Tennessee* (2009), we recognized that because it focused exclusively on the political, economic, and social aspects of the conflict, a second, follow-up volume would be necessary, for there was much more to say about the war in these two states, particularly regarding military matters. The book is divided into two parts—Part I: "Battles, Skirmishes, and Soldiers" and Part II: "Leaders"—and promises to help fill a gap in the existing scholarship on Kentucky and Tennessee during the Civil War period. The state of Tennessee is second only to Virginia in the number of battles fought on its soil, and Kentucky, because of its geographical location, became a state vital to both the Union and the Confederacy. But these two states have not received the attention by scholars that they deserve, and few works have dealt exclusively with these two important states. However, attention is now shifting to the Civil War in Tennessee and Kentucky with Benjamin Franklin Cooling's important studies, *Fort Donelson's Legacy: War and Society in Kentucky and Tennessee, 1862–1863* (1997), *Forts Henry and Donelson: The Key to the Confederate Heartland* (2003), and more recently *To the Battles of Franklin and Nashville and Beyond: Stabilization and Reconstruction in Tennessee and Kentucky, 1864–1866* (2012), as well as our own *Sister States, Enemy States.*

We wanted to avoid a retelling of the major battles that occurred in Kentucky and Tennessee that both scholars and enthusiasts know so well and focus instead on other aspects of the war there. However, one never knows what direction a project such as this will go when it is undertaken, but we are delighted that the chapters in this volume include a wealth of material not previously published and offer new perspectives on the conflict in these two states.

Anyone who has published a book knows that it is a collaborative effort that involves many different people at many different levels. First of all, we would like to thank the scholars who contributed chapters. Although quite busy with their own projects, they were enthusiastic about this endeavor from the beginning and, believe it or not, met the deadlines we set. It has been a pleasure to work with each and every one of them.

We would also like to express our gratitude to The Kent State University Press, which embraced the project from day one. In particular, we would like to thank Joyce Harrison, Will Underwood, Mary Young, Christine Brooks, Darryl Crosby, Carol Heller, Valerie Ahwee, and Susan Cash, as well as other members of the staff. Without their support, expertise, and guidance, there would be no book. We are grateful to Frank Cooling, James Ramage, and Ken Noe, who read the manuscript and offered their feedback on it and the project as a whole. Their constructive comments made the book much better than it would have been otherwise. We are also indebted to our cartographer, Mary Eggart. The maps she designed for this volume are superb, and she was an absolute pleasure to work with.

We would also like to thank our colleagues in the History Department at Tennessee Tech University. We very much appreciate their interest in and support of our work on this volume.

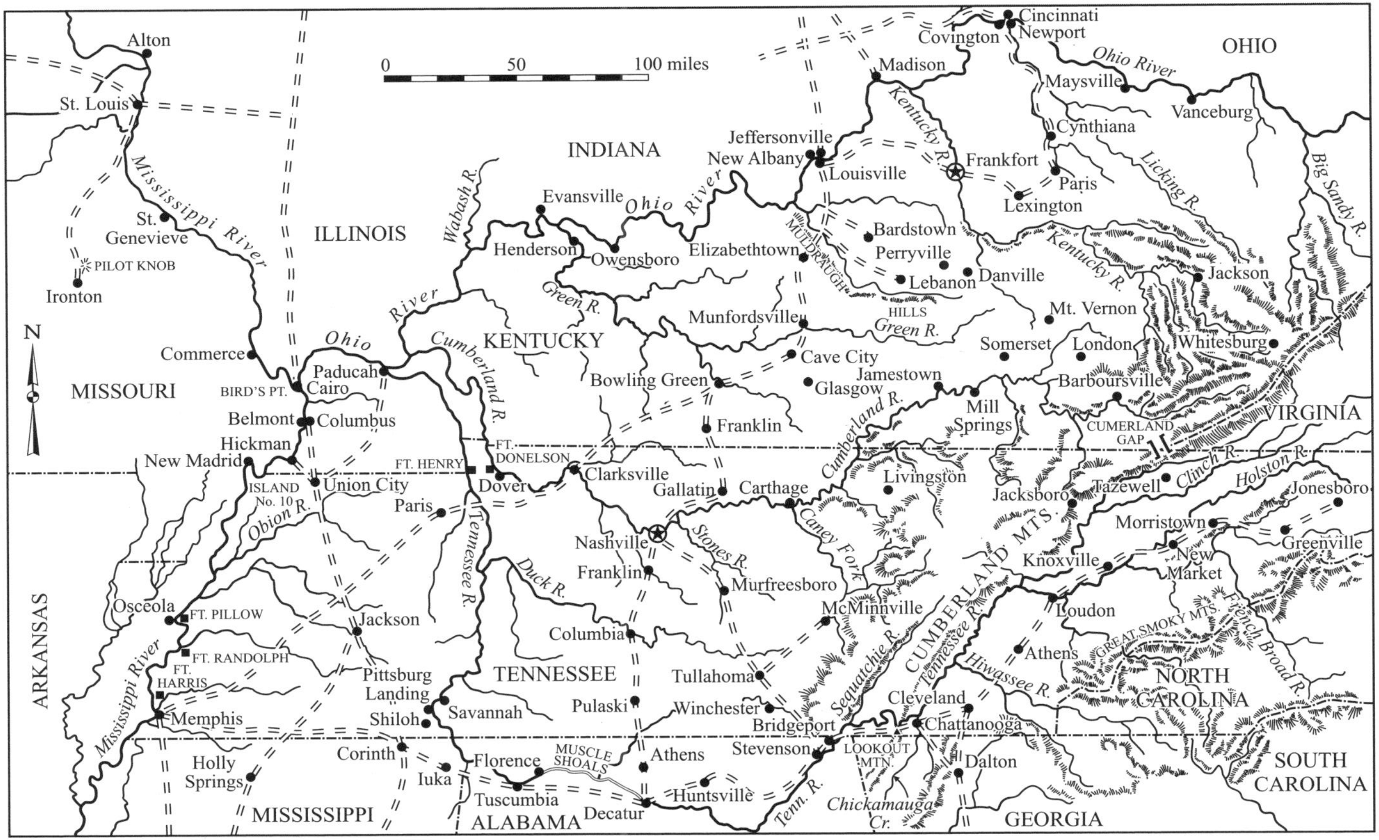

Civil War–era Tennessee and Kentucky.

Introduction

Kent T. Dollar and Larry H. Whiteaker

When the Civil War erupted in the spring of 1861, the sister states of Kentucky and Tennessee assumed enormous importance to both the Union and the Confederacy. The side that controlled the two states would control the Ohio and Tennessee valleys and, for all practical purposes, the upper reaches of the Mississippi Valley. Because the nation's canal network and burgeoning railroad system already linked the Northern states to one another and to ports on the Atlantic, the internal rivers were less important than they once had been, but they were still of vital importance to the national and regional economies, especially to the Confederacy, where canals and railroads were relatively sparse. Furthermore, as Jefferson Davis and his new government well knew, Kentucky and Tennessee were highly diversified agricultural states that at the war's start already supplied vast quantities of pork, beef, wheat, corn, and other comestibles that the Lower South, with its cotton-oriented economy, desperately needed. Also, the South had long neglected industry, and many of its factories were in Tennessee and Kentucky. If either state remained in the Union, the Confederacy would suffer a major blow. The new nation needed Tennessee and Kentucky, and it needed its northern border to be the Ohio River.

Abraham Lincoln's oft-cited statement that he hoped God was on his side but that he had to have Kentucky aptly sums up the importance to the Union of the trans-Appalachian region. The prospect of a Confederate Kentucky—and perhaps even a Confederate Missouri—no doubt gave Lincoln and any other Northern strategist grave concern. An enemy state on the south side of the Ohio River would have threatened Pennsylvania, Ohio, Indiana, and Illinois, and, more than likely, would have made it impossible to keep Missouri in the Union. Southern Illinois, with its large population of Confederate sympathizers, would have perhaps become fertile ground for further secession agitation. To Northern war planners, Kentucky had to be kept in the Union, and Tennessee had to be—if not kept in the Union—occupied and neutralized as soon as possible.

So the lines were drawn by the summer of 1861, and the games began in Tennessee and Kentucky to determine where the border of the Confederate States of America would be. The Fort Sumter battle in April 1861 had shattered any hope for a peaceful separation of the South from the North, so where the boundary would be—and who would determine it—became a major focus of the ensuing war. Kentucky and Tennessee. Tennessee and Kentucky. Sister states. Would they now be enemy states?[1]

From the 1770s, when settlers from Virginia and North Carolina began to move into the lush valleys of East Tennessee and central Kentucky, these two states would be linked—whether the residents wished this or not—in the national consciousness. Even with many similarities—terrain, climate, settlers' background, religion, to name a few—there would always be major differences. By the 1820s, for example, a huge political rift would develop, pitting the followers of Kentucky's Henry Clay against Tennessee's followers of Andrew Jackson. The ultimate difference would come in 1861.

In 1792, Kentucky, with Virginia's acquiescence, became the fifteenth state. In 1796, after a brief existence as a territory, Tennessee entered the Union as the sixteenth state. Early Kentuckians and Tennesseans had much in common, including their similar paths toward statehood. Most of the settlers in both states had migrated from Virginia and North Carolina and were largely English, Scots-Irish, or German in background. In religion, most were Presbyterians, Baptists, or Methodists, but the region also contained Catholics, Episcopalians, Lutherans, and members of smaller denominations. English was certainly the dominant language, even if spoken with a frontier twang. As late as 1860, schools were scarce in the two states, but each had them as well as several private colleges within their borders.

Economically the two states shared a largely agricultural way of life. After the initial lure of abundant game brought hunters, the permanent settlers came because of the rich soils, temperate climate, and excellent water sources. In Kentucky, farmers raised the usual food crops such as corn, but also planted large amounts of hemp, flax, and tobacco. Tennessee farmers subsisted on corn and other vegetables and raised, for commercial purposes, tobacco and—in the middle and western sections—cotton. Both states produced enough cattle and hogs not only to satisfy their own needs but to export some to adjacent states. By 1860 some development of coal mining had occurred in the region as well as the development of small industries, but agriculture still dominated the states' economies.

Raising tobacco, hemp, or cotton involved intensive labor and required large acreage. To meet these needs, Kentucky and Tennessee farmers—at least the large landowners—brought African slaves into the region. The first, of course, arrived with the original settlers. Virginia and North Carolina had long ago established a slavery-based agricultural system, and thus as the western migration began the slaves went with their owners. As the wilderness gave way to farms and plantations, commercial crops demanded more slaves. In 1800, Kentucky, more agriculturally developed than its sister state, had 40,343 slaves while Tennessee had only 13,584. After the purchase of western Tennessee territory from the Chickasaws in the late 1810s, cotton cultivation greatly expanded and with it Tennessee's slave population. By 1840, Kentucky had 182,258 slaves and Tennessee 183,059. Tennessee's slave population continued to increase at a faster rate than its neighbor to the north, as is revealed by the 1860 census: Tennessee slaves—275,719, Kentucky slaves—225,483. By this time approximately one in five Kentuckians was a slave, while in Tennessee the ratio was closer to one in four.[2] Although there were many other reasons why Tennesseans joined the Confederacy in 1861, their commitment to slavery and to cotton cultivation certainly tied them to the lower Southern states—the Cotton Belt—in ways that many Kentuckians did not share.

Political developments in the two states both bound and separated them. Initially the vast majority of the region's voters were die-hard Jeffersonians, with the rival Federalists being virtually nonexistent. Further, both states enthusiastically supported the War of 1812, with war hawks such as Henry Clay of Kentucky and Felix Grundy of Tennessee leading the way. By the 1820s, however, the growing rivalry between Clay and Andrew Jackson would split the two states' political allegiances. Calling Clay the "Judas of the West" in 1825 when he supported Jackson's rival, John Quincy Adams, in the presidential election, Jackson and his supporters became even more furious with Clay when he accepted the secretary of state position in Adams's administration. This rivalry played a huge role in just a few years in the emergence of two new political parties: the Democrats and the Whigs. (Personal animosity between Clay and Jackson led Clay to remark about Jackson that killing two thousand British soldiers at New Orleans certainly did not qualify him to be president, and caused Jackson allegedly to claim that one of his major regrets as a politician was that he had not been able to "shoot Henry Clay.")

The differences between Clay's political program and Jackson's went far beyond personality. Both men were staunch nationalists, but Clay's American System put much more emphasis on the development of industry and government-sponsored internal improvements than did Jackson's program of limited, frugal government. With the founding of the Whig Party in 1834—a party that incorporated most of Clay's goals—the Whigs would have a vigorous and popular presence in Kentucky and, somewhat surprisingly, Tennessee. In 1836, the first Whig presidential contest, Whig William Henry Harrison carried Kentucky and Whig Hugh Lawson White outpolled Martin Van Buren in Tennessee. Until 1856—even when Tennessee's own James Knox Polk ran in 1844—Kentucky and Tennessee gave their electoral votes to the Whig candidates. At the state and local levels as well, the states' Whigs maintained active and successful opposition to the Democrats. Not until 1856 did the states' voting majority choose the Democratic candidate—James Buchanan—and by then the Whig party had collapsed and the Democrats were beginning to have great difficulty in maintaining national unity.

Beginning with the Wilmot Proviso in 1846, the sectional crises that wracked the nation during the next fifteen years ripped apart the political parties, created new ones, and eventually resulted in civil war. Kentuckians and Tennesseans alike participated in the turmoil that the crises caused and saw their own political allegiances twisted and in some instances redefined. A major blow for the Whigs in both states was the collapse of the national Whig Party after the 1852 election, a collapse that sent Whigs everywhere searching for a new party. Some dabbled with the upstart and nativist American ("Know Nothing") Party, but its anti-immigrant stance and lukewarm attitude toward slavery failed to gain much support from Kentucky and Tennessee voters. After the 1856 election, its national existence ended as well. By the end of the decade former Whigs would find a more attractive party in the short-lived Constitutional Union Party.

The states' Democrats and Whigs did agree on one thing during the 1850s, however: they hated the newly emergent Republican Party. Joining with their fellow Southerners, they condemned the Republicans as not only being wrong in opposing slavery's expansion but for being closet abolitionists (at least in the minds of many Republican opponents). The prospect of a Republican victory in the 1856 presidential election played a large role in Kentucky and Tennessee voters opting for James Buchanan. Though thwarted in that election for the presidency, the Republicans made significant gains in Congress and at state and local levels, engendering fear and anger throughout the South, and opening the door once again for a South-wide debate over secession.

Thus, these two states, Kentucky and Tennessee, entering the Union as part of the New West, serving as the home of national political figures such as Henry Clay and Andrew Jackson, boasting of folk heroes such as Daniel Boone and David Crockett, waited to see how the nation's leaders would deal with the sectional crises.[3]

The election of Republican Abraham Lincoln in 1860 brought everything to a head. Just weeks after his election, South Carolina seceded from the Union, followed by six other Lower South states; and on February 4, 1861, the Confederate States of America was formed. Eight other slave states, however, remained in the Union for the time being.

Tennessee and Kentucky took different paths during the secession crisis. Kentucky, after much deliberation, proclaimed its neutrality on May 20, 1861, while Tennessee's general assembly that same month declared its independence. Kentuckians were divided over secession, and many, in fact, preferred outright neutrality. Initially reluctant to embrace secession, Beriah Magoffin, the pro-Southern governor of Kentucky, attempted to mediate the crisis and sought to rally support for a Peace Conference to resolve the sectional dispute. He compiled a list of six proposals (some offered as constitutional amendments) he thought would satisfy Southerners, among them ones calling for enforcing the Fugitive Slave Act, dividing U. S. territories between slave and free, and protecting slavery where it existed. The firing on Fort Sumter in April, however, ended the effort. When President Lincoln called for volunteers to put down the Southern rebellion, Magoffin refused, declaring, "I say, emphatically, Kentucky will furnish no troops for the wicked purpose of subduing her sister Southern States." On May 20, Magoffin, with the legislature's backing, issued a proclamation of neutrality and warned both sides against violating it.[4] Meanwhile, both pro-Union and pro-South Kentuckians departed the state to enlist in Federal and Confederate armies. The issue of which side Kentucky would take was decided once and for all when on September 3, 1861, Confederate Gen. Leonidas Polk violated the state's neutrality and seized Columbus, on the Mississippi River. In response, Union Gen. U. S. Grant occupied Paducah. Outraged by Polk's actions, the pro-Unionist legislature passed a motion (over Magoffin's veto) demanding that the Confederates withdraw and aligned the state with the North. It furthermore requested assistance from the U.S. government to expel the Southern invaders. Although pro-secession Kentuckians held a convention at Russellville in November 1861 and seceded, the Bluegrass State would officially remain in the Union. Divided loyalties existed in Kentucky perhaps more than in any other state in the Union. Indeed, approximately 50,000 white Kentuckians served in the Union Army, while 35,000 fought with the rebels.[5]

Like its sister state to the north, Tennessee, too, faced divisions over secession. Tennessee's governor, Isham G. Harris, longed to align his state with the Confederacy, but the general assembly, as well as many Tennesseans, remained divided over the matter. The legislature, therefore, decided to put the issue of whether or not to secede to the voters and set February 9 as the date for a referendum. Voters were to decide for or against holding a secession convention and, if voting in favor, which delegates they would send to it. The voters narrowly rejected the call for a secession convention and voted overwhelmingly in favor of Unionist delegates. Discouraged but not deterred, secessionists in the state, particularly the western portion, went to work in an effort to deliver the state to the Confederacy. Pro-secessionist groups sprang into action, attempting to harass and intimidate Unionist citizens. They were determined that another vote would deliver a different outcome.

Although Tennessee's actions suggested that the majority of its citizens held Unionist sentiments, they were, in fact, conditional Unionists. Their Unionism was contingent on two factors: (1) that the U.S. government must refrain from interfering with the institution of slavery in the states where it existed; and (2) that the United States would not use coercion against the states that had seceded from the Union. As long as these two conditions were met, Tennessee would remain in the Union.

The Confederate bombardment of Fort Sumter on April 12, 1861, and President Lincoln's subsequent call for 75,000 volunteers to suppress the Southern rebellion changed everything. There was now war, and Tennesseans would have to decide whether to fight with or against their fellow Southerners. Governor Harris spoke for many Tennesseans when in his response to Lincoln's call for volunteers, he said, "Tennessee will not furnish a single man for coercion, but 50,000, if necessary, for the defense of our rights and those of our southern brothers."[6]

On May 6 the Tennessee general assembly declared its independence, severing all ties to the Union. The legislature also sought endorsement of its actions in another referendum set for June 8. Unlike the earlier vote, Tennesseans overwhelmingly chose to secede. The vote was 105,000 for and 47,000 against.[7] The numbers suggest that the majority of Tennesseans sanctioned separation, but the story is more complicated. Indeed, the state remained split over the issue. West and Middle Tennesseans voted overwhelmingly in favor of secession, while voters in East Tennessee rejected separation by a two-to-one margin.[8]

Like its northern neighbor, Tennessee remained divided during the conflict and saw many of its own serve in the Union ranks. Indeed, East Tennessee alone contributed an estimated 35,000 whites to the Union war effort.[9] Tennessee's actions meant that the Volunteer State would be on the front lines of the fighting in the west.

The first task for Confederate Gen. Albert Sidney Johnston, commander of the area embracing Tennessee, was to establish a defensive line to protect the state and the entire west, for that matter, from a Union invasion. Attempting to defend everywhere, Johnston had Confederate troops at Columbus, Kentucky (after the state's neutrality had been violated), to the west, through Bowling Green and on to the Cumberland Gap to the east.

Meanwhile, President Lincoln pressed his generals to liberate the beleaguered Unionists in East Tennessee. Ordered to invade and occupy the area, Gen. George Thomas advanced through Kentucky toward the state line. Informed of the planned Union invasion, East Tennesseans loyal to the Union sprang into action, organizing to assist the invaders. On November 8, they acted, burning five railroad bridges to disrupt Confederate troop movements and commerce. The Federal incursion halted, however, hampered by weather and supply problems, and Confederates cracked down on the Unionists, declaring martial law, arresting hundreds, and executing several of the bridge-burners. Weeks later, Thomas renewed his advance through the difficult terrain.

Confederate generals George Crittenden and Felix Zollicoffer sought to keep the Federals out of East Tennessee by moving their army to confront Thomas in southern Kentucky. On January 19, 1862, the Confederates attacked Thomas at Logan's Cross Roads near Mill Springs, Kentucky. Thomas's men easily repulsed the Confederate assault, which resulted not only in the collapse of the eastern portion of Johnston's defensive line, but also in the death of Zollicoffer. Fortunately for the Confederates, the Yankees were unable to capitalize on their victory; East Tennessee would not be liberated until 1863.

Meanwhile, in the western part of Tennessee, Union Gen. Ulysses S. Grant and naval Capt. Andrew H. Foote joined forces in an attempt to capture the forts guarding the Tennessee and Cumberland rivers, which, if taken, would open up Middle Tennessee to Union occupation. Fort Henry, which protected the Tennessee River and was garrisoned by three thousand rebels, was the first fort targeted.[10] Poorly located along the river, the fort routinely flooded during the winter months. On February 6, 1862, Foote's gunboats assaulted the fort. After enduring a naval bombardment for several hours, the remaining inadequately armed Confederate defenders, nearly waist-deep in water, surrendered. Most of the garrison had evacuated before the surrender and marched overland to Fort Donelson, twelve miles to the east. Grant's force, which had been put ashore several miles away and was marching toward Fort Henry, had not even participated in the fighting.

Grant then set his sights on Fort Donelson, which protected the Cumberland River. His troops marched overland to the fort on February 12 and probed its defenses, but were repulsed. Awaiting reinforcements before renewing the assault against rebel fortifications, Grant ordered the Union Navy to bombard the fort as it had done at Fort Henry. Foote's seemingly invincible gunboats were driven off by effective Confederate cannon fire, which crippled several of his boats and wounded Foote himself. After a war council held on the evening of February 14, the Confederates decided to attempt a breakout on the morning of February 15. While Grant was away conferring with Foote, the rebel defenders launched a vicious counterattack against the Union right that pushed back the Yankees nearly a mile and temporarily opened the road to Nashville. Inexplicably, the Southern troops did not follow up on their success and escape. Instead, they retreated back into their lines, and Grant's troops quickly closed the gap. After passing down command of the fort to Gen. Simon Buckner, the Confederates surrendered the fort on February 16. Some rebels were able to avoid capture. The angry and disgusted cavalry commander, Nathan Bedford Forrest, led hundreds of troops, his own as well as others, across a flooded ford and to safety. Nashville now became untenable, and the Federal forces occupied the city on February 24. Members of the general assembly and Governor Harris fled to Memphis.

Union control of the Tennessee River permitted Grant to move to his next objective: the critical railroad junction at Corinth, Mississippi. In March 1862, initial elements of Grant's force began disembarking at Pittsburg Landing along the banks of the river. By March 31, Grant had concentrated a force primarily at the landing of nearly 35,000 men with more soldiers on the way. Grant expected his force to grow to seventy thousand–plus once Gen. Don Carlos Buell's Army of the Ohio, which was advancing from Nashville, joined him.[11] With such a sizable army deep in the heart of Confederate territory, Grant felt confident he could advance on and capture Corinth. The

Confederates, however, were not waiting to be attacked. General Johnston had assembled a force of over forty thousand at Corinth and planned to launch a surprise attack against Grant's army while at Pittsburg Landing.[12] Johnston's second in command was Gen. P. G. T. Beauregard, the hero of Fort Sumter and First Manassas. On April 3, Johnston put the Army of the Mississippi in motion and began his advance toward Pittsburg Landing. The Confederate assault began on the morning of April 6. Although the surprised Northern troops fought valiantly and stubbornly, the Confederates steadily pushed back their lines to the landing. General Johnston suffered a mortal wound while reconnoitering near the front lines; Beauregard assumed command and halted the attack at dusk, confident that he could finish off the Yankees in the morning. During the evening, however, lead elements of Buell's army, as well as Gen. Lew Wallace's lost division, began arriving to reinforce Grant. With 25,000 fresh troops, Grant launched a counterattack on the morning of the April 7 and drove back the rebels all along the front.[13] After intense fighting, Beauregard ordered a retreat back to Corinth. After recuperating, the Union Army continued its advance on Corinth and captured the city in late May 1862, after the Confederates had evacuated.

During the summer and early fall of 1862, Britain and France stood on the verge of recognizing the Confederacy and, even more importantly, perhaps intervening in the conflict. A bold offensive against the North and a decisive Southern victory might indeed prompt these European powers to act. Gen. Robert E. Lee proposed an invasion of the North, and western commanders also planned similarly audacious campaigns.

After the evacuation of Corinth, President Jefferson Davis relieved Beauregard of his duties and placed Gen. Braxton Bragg in command of the Army of the Mississippi. Bragg proposed an invasion of Kentucky, which he thought would force the Federals in Tennessee to abandon the state and pursue him. Confederates also believed that beleaguered Kentuckians would rally to the Stars and Bars and join the Confederacy. As part of the invasion, Confederate Gen. Kirby Smith was to move his troops into Kentucky from East Tennessee and link up with Bragg at some point. Initially, things went well. Smith's force departed on August 13, moving through the Cumberland Mountains into eastern Kentucky, and Bragg began his advance from Chattanooga through Middle Tennessee on August 27. Smith's army quickly won a small but impressive victory against Union forces under the command of Gen. William "Bull" Nelson at Richmond on August 30. The Confederates occupied Lexington on September 2 and Frankfort on September 3, the only Union state capital to fall to the rebels. General

Buell, meanwhile, departed Middle Tennessee and pursued the Confederate invaders. Receiving poor intelligence that the Federals were moving toward Frankfort, Bragg had Smith concentrate his forces there. While occupying the Kentucky capital, the Confederates installed a pro-Southern government and proclaimed Richard Hawes governor. Hawes was inaugurated on October 4 before a large crowd, but the Confederates were forced to abandon Frankfort later that day because of Union shelling.[14]

A major engagement between the two armies took place near Perryville on October 8, 1862, the only major battle to take place in the Bluegrass State. In this strange fight, only portions of both armies battled each other. Buell, because of an atmospheric phenomenon, heard none of the fighting at his headquarters and, therefore, did not commit to the battle his entire army of fifty thousand–plus, and part of Bragg's force (Smith's command) remained near Frankfort. Thus, the Confederates at Perryville mustered just sixteen thousand men against a larger portion of Buell's army. Believing that he faced only a small Union force, Bragg ordered his men to attack. The outnumbered Confederates enjoyed good success early on against the Union left, but a fierce Yankee counterattack against the Confederate center by Gen. Philip Sheridan pushed back the rebels. The fighting was to be renewed in the morning, but Bragg, realizing that he was facing Buell's entire army after conferring with his generals, lost his nerve and withdrew from the field. The Confederates retreated back into Tennessee and concentrated near Murfreesboro.[15]

After the battle of Perryville, Union Gen. William S. Rosecrans took over command of the Army of the Ohio. The army was concentrated at Nashville. In December 1862, Rosecrans moved out of Nashville and advanced toward the Confederates at Murfreesboro. In late December, the two armies faced each other near Stones River. Early on the morning of December 31, Bragg launched a ferocious assault against Rosecrans's right and nearly wrecked the entire Federal army. Union lines were pushed back five miles, and only stubborn resistance by Union generals Sheridan and Thomas prevented the destruction of Rosecrans's entire army. Expecting Rosecrans to retreat after the fighting on December 31, Bragg awoke on January 1 surprised to discover the Federal army still in place. Against the advice of his subordinates, Bragg ordered Gen. John C. Breckinridge's division to assault the well-defended Union positions across Stones River on January 2. The Confederate attack was repulsed with heavy losses. Bragg ordered a retreat, and the Army of Tennessee (formerly the Army of the

Mississippi) retreated on January 3 and 4 and took up new positions along Duck River to the south, where the army spent the winter.

During the spring and summer of 1863, Rosecrans, commanding the newly named Army of the Cumberland, successfully flanked and maneuvered Bragg out of Middle Tennessee in what is known as the Tullahoma campaign. Indeed, the Confederates' retreat in Tennessee was so complete that by the fall of 1863, Bragg abandoned the state entirely, taking up a position near Chickamauga Creek in north Georgia. On September 19–20, 1863, the Army of Tennessee, reinforced by Gen. James Longstreet's division from the Army of Northern Virginia, won its most spectacular and only major victory during the war. Rosecrans retreated back into Chattanooga. Bragg's Confederates followed and took up positions south of the city in an attempt to besiege its Union defenders.

The Confederates occupied Raccoon Mountain to the west and Lookout Mountain and Missionary Ridge to the south and east. Thanks to Confederate Gen. Joseph Wheeler's cavalry raid north of Chattanooga in early October, Bragg cut off all lines of supply to Rosecrans's army. Union forces in Chattanooga were on reduced rations and in a desperate situation. The same month, President Lincoln placed all military departments between the Mississippi River and the Appalachian Mountains under the command of General Grant, who began traveling to Chattanooga to take personal command of the troops there. His goals were to save the Army of the Cumberland and hold the city. He also replaced Rosecrans with Gen. George Thomas.

Grant arrived in Chattanooga on October 23 and turned his attention to opening a line of supply. Union troops captured a key ferry crossing, which opened a line of supply the hungry soldiers called the "Cracker Line." Meanwhile, Union reinforcements were arriving, bringing Grant's total force to approximately eighty thousand.[16] In late November, Grant attacked. General Thomas's troops were to demonstrate in front of the Confederate center at Missionary Ridge, while Gen. William T. Sherman's troops were to attack the Confederate right at Tunnel Hill. Gen. Joseph Hooker was to assault the rebel left on Lookout Mountain. On November 24, Hooker's troops attacked Lookout Mountain and carried the position. The following day, Sherman, who was assaulting the Confederate right, became bogged down in heavy fighting against rebel forces under the command of Gen. Patrick Cleburne. Thomas's men, who were only to demonstrate against the Confederate center, wished to erase the stain of their defeat at Chickamauga, and launched an all-out assault against Missionary Ridge, easily displacing Confederates from the position. The troops at his center routed, Bragg had no choice but to withdraw into north Georgia. Bragg resigned soon thereafter, and President Davis appointed Gen. Joseph E. Johnston to take command of the Army of Tennessee. Bragg would go on to serve as a military advisor to Davis.

Bragg was heavily outnumbered during the battles for Chattanooga, a situation that was exacerbated by his sending General Longstreet's division to Knoxville in an attempt to capture the town. Gen. Ambrose Burnside and the Army of the Ohio had entered Knoxville in September 1863, achieving Lincoln's long-held goal to rescue the Unionists in East Tennessee. After sweeping aside Union troops at Campbell's Station on November 16, Longstreet slowly approached Knoxville, skirmishing with Union cavalry under the command of Gen. William Sanders, who was killed in the fighting. Union positions around Knoxville were strong. City defenses to the west were anchored by Fort Sanders, just northwest of the town. It was here that Longstreet decided to launch his assault. At dawn on November 29, Longstreet's Confederates began their attack, but became bogged down in the trenches surrounding the fort. Unable to scale the walls, the attackers were cut up badly. Longstreet called off the attack and settled on a siege of the town. The siege lasted until December 4, 1863, when Longstreet's army withdrew from Knoxville to the north and entered winter quarters. The Knoxville campaign was a dismal failure and drew troops from Chattanooga when they were needed most.

The Army of Tennessee spent the winter of 1863–64 in Dalton, Georgia. The spring was sure to see General Sherman advancing southward toward the strategic town of Atlanta; General Johnston's main goal was to prevent the capture of the city. Johnston's skillful maneuvering north of Atlanta slowed Sherman's advance considerably. President Davis, who cared little for Johnston personally, grew fearful that Johnston was willing to abandon Atlanta without a fight. Therefore, on July 17, 1864, Davis relieved Johnston of command and appointed Gen. John Bell Hood as the new commander of the Army of Tennessee. Hood possessed the reputation of a fighter and did not disappoint. In several battles for Atlanta in the summer of 1864, Hood engaged the Federals time and again only to see his efforts fail. Hood abandoned Atlanta on September 1 and Union troops entered the city the following day. Hood then proposed an audacious plan that, if successful, would change the course of the war. His army would move into Tennessee, defeat the Union armies there, and then invade Kentucky. From there, he could perhaps take the war to the Ohio River and even into the North.

Following these successes, he could then join Robert E. Lee in the East. Naturally, Hood thought that Sherman would be compelled to pursue him and have to abandon Atlanta. President Davis approved Hood's plans.

Once the Army of Tennessee had retreated out of its namesake state, the Union Army occupied virtually all of Tennessee. However, their possession was not undisputed, for Confederate Gen. Nathan Bedford Forrest's cavalry continued to operate with impunity in the state, particularly in its middle and western portions. The result of one of these raids was the attack on and capture of Fort Pillow in West Tennessee in April 1864. What transpired during the capture of the fort is controversial and has divided Americans ever since. During Forrest's assault of the fort, the Federals, nearly half of them black, fought bravely, but were overwhelmed by Forrest's troopers. Accusations that the Confederates butchered many unarmed defenders led the United States Congress's Committee on the Conduct of the War to investigate the affair and label it the Fort Pillow Massacre.

In November 1864, Hood's Confederates left Florence, Alabama, and moved into Tennessee. Hood's objective was Nashville, but Union Gen. John M. Schofield's thirty thousand–man force stood in his way at Pulaski. Hood flanked Schofield out of Pulaski and Columbia without a fight, and Schofield retreated to Spring Hill. Hood hoped to prevent Schofield from reaching Nashville, but the Union troops slipped by the Confederates during the night of November 29 and took up a strong defensive position at Franklin. Outraged that his commanders had allowed the Yankees to escape from Spring Hill, Hood was determined to do battle and discipline his army. Instead of attempting to flank Schofield out of Franklin, as some of his commanders suggested, Hood chose instead to attack him there. On the afternoon of November 30, Hood launched an assault against Schofield's center near the Carter House. The attackers were forced to cross nearly two miles of open ground before reaching the Union lines, all the while enduring the murderous fire of the defenders. Numerous assaults were launched, each repulsed with heavy losses. On the evening of November 30, Schofield's army retreated to Nashville. Hood's army, nearly crippled from the fighting at Franklin, followed.

Once Schofield's army reached Nashville, Gen. George Thomas, the commander of Union troops in the city, had approximately 65,000 men while Hood could muster only around twenty thousand.[17] The Confederates took up positions just south of the city. They were spread out and their lines weak. On December 15, Thomas attacked. After feinting against the Confederate right, Thomas hit Hood's left, where his superiority in numbers showed as Yankees overwhelmed and overran the rebel defenders. Hood retreated a few miles to the south and took up a new defensive position. On December 16, after feinting against the right, Thomas again attacked the left of the Confederate lines. The rebel lines broke, and Hood ordered the retreat of his battered army. Fewer than fifteen thousand men were left in the once mighty Army of Tennessee as it retreated into Alabama and then regrouped at Tupelo, Mississippi.[18] Hood resigned as commander of the army, and many of the survivors traveled east to the Carolinas to fight with Gen. Joseph Johnston.

In addition to the major engagements described above, numerous smaller battles and skirmishes between regulars and guerrillas occurred throughout the war in both states.

Throughout much of their history, Kentucky and Tennessee had been considered sister states. They shared many similarities, but there are also historical differences. The ultimate difference came in 1861, when Tennessee joined the Confederate States of America, and Kentucky, after a failed attempt to remain neutral, remained in the Union. Although the citizens of these states were divided and reluctant to choose sides during the secession crisis of 1860–61, both eventually did so and suffered grievously for their decision. The war visited both states early and often. In fact, there were several wars taking place simultaneously along the border. Of course, there was the war between the Union and the Confederacy in Kentucky and Tennessee, but there was also fighting between the Union occupiers and the pro-Southern civilians they encountered. Hostilities even existed between the Federal army and local Unionists in some areas, and there was conflict between some Union generals and even more between Confederate commanders in the region. It is these wars, as well as those individuals involved, that are the subject of *Border Wars: Tennessee and Kentucky in the Civil War*.

Aaron Astor begins Part I: "Battles, Skirmishes, and Soldiers" with an investigation into the role that prewar militias played in producing Confederate military units. In particular, he examines the militias in Lexington, Kentucky, and Clarksville, Tennessee, and their conversion into formal regiments, especially in the Confederate Army of Tennessee. In his chapter, "Descent into Anarchy: The Evolution of Irregular Warfare in the Lower Green River Country of Kentucky," Scott Tarnowieckyi details how the Union military's inability to establish complete military control over Kentucky's Green River country early on, coupled with a growing sense of betrayal and anger by many Kentuckians toward the Federal government, led to increasing amounts of tension and irregular warfare in the region.

Michael Toomey takes a look at the aborted attempt by the Federals to invade East Tennessee in November 1861. The author asserts that not only was the strong Unionist sentiment a key factor in encouraging the campaign, but also that the Unionists themselves played an important role in paramilitary operations that destroyed key railroad bridges in East Tennessee on the eve of the planned invasion.

Patricia Hoskins returns to the topic of guerrilla warfare in Kentucky in her chapter entitled "Guerrilla Warfare and Federal Occupation in the Jackson Purchase Region of Kentucky, 1862–64." She contends that in this pro-Southern region of the Bluegrass State, trade restrictions, penalties, and illegal commerce, along with the ever increasing amount of Federal garrisons across the area, led to tensions and a rise in guerrilla warfare in 1862 and 1863. Union occupation and the restoration of civilian government in Middle and West Tennessee is the subject of a chapter by Derek Frisby. The author maintains that Tennessee Unionists and Federal authorities became increasingly estranged due to miscommunication, mistrust, and the inadequate resources allocated to the effort. Wiley Sword wraps up Part I with an exploration of the Battle of Franklin and its impact on the Confederate veterans who survived it. To many, it was the most terrible combat experience they had endured during the war.

The focus of Part II is leadership. Confederate Gen. Felix Zollicoffer is the focus of a chapter by Brian McKnight. In this piece, he explores Zollicoffer's encounter with the rugged terrain of East Tennessee and southern Kentucky and how it shaped his fateful campaign, which ended with the battle of Mill Springs. Union Gen. Don Carlos Buell is the topic of Stephen Engle's chapter, in particular his struggle to come to terms with the changing nature of the war. Earl Hess, in his chapter entitled "Braxton Bragg and the Stones River Campaign," reexamines the often-criticized Confederate commander and maintains that a reconsideration of Bragg's generalship in this campaign is in order. The author views Stones River as one of the more successful operations of the ill-starred Confederate Army of Tennessee. Christopher Losson continues with the topic of Braxton Bragg in his chapter, "Mutual Antagonists: Braxton Bragg, Frank Cheatham, and the Army of Tennessee." He explores the relationship between Confederate Gen. Braxton Bragg and Gen. Frank Cheatham, one of Bragg's principal lieutenants. The author argues that even though neither man seriously pondered how his inability to get along with the other hindered the Army of Tennessee and its prospects for success, their feuding, in fact, proved detrimental. A comparison of Union Gen. Ulysses S. Grant and Confederate Gen. Nathan

B. Forrest is the theme of a chapter by Jack Hurst. The author asserts that common attributes of these two men helped make them the most successful generals in the Western Theater.

Tennessee Gov. Isham G. Harris's unique role with the Army of Tennessee is the topic of Sam Davis Elliott's chapter. According to the author, Harris acted as an aide to the army's commanders, had a voice at times in strategy, inspired Tennessee troops, advanced the careers of Tennessee officers, and provided a contact point between the Confederate government and the army. Finally, noted Civil War historian Benjamin Frank Cooling offers some concluding thoughts on the war in Kentucky and Tennessee and the chapters presented here.

This important collection will help fill a niche in the historiography of the Civil War in Kentucky and Tennessee. The stories of these two states are a vital part of the larger story of the Civil War. These chapters offer numerous and specific insights to aid in understanding that four-year-long struggle and demonstrate that there is much of value still to be learned about the Civil War in Tennessee and Kentucky.

Notes

1. For an excellent introduction to the Civil War in the Western Theater, see Earl J. Hess, *The Civil War in the West: Victory and Defeat from the Appalachians to the Mississippi* (Chapel Hill: Univ. of North Carolina Press, 2012), 1–17.

2. Stanley J. Folmsbee, Robert E. Corlew, and Enoch L. Mitchell, *History of Tennessee* (New York: Lewis Historical Publishing, 1960), 1:469; Lowell H. Harrison and James C. Klotter, *A New History of Kentucky* (Lexington: Univ. Press of Kentucky, 1997), 167, 176.

3. Portions of the previous paragraphs were first published in *Sister States, Enemy States: The Civil War in Kentucky and Tennessee* (Lexington: Univ. Press of Kentucky, 2009), 1–6.

4. Lowell H. Harrison, *The Civil War in Kentucky* (Lexington: Univ. Press of Kentucky, 1975), 8; Harrison and Klotter, *A New History of Kentucky,* 186–89.

5. James McPherson, *Ordeal by Fire: The Civil War and Reconstruction,* 3rd ed. (New York: McGraw-Hill, 2001), 169; Harrison and Klotter, *A New History of Kentucky,* 192.

6. John Trotwood Moore and Austin P. Foster, eds., *Tennessee: The Volunteer State, 1769–1923* (Nashville, Tenn.: S. J. Clarke Publishing Co., 1923), 1:470.

7. Thomas L. Connelly, *Civil War Tennessee: Battles and Leaders* (Knoxville: Univ. of Tennessee Press, 1979), 3.

8. Stanley J. Folmsbee, Robert E. Corlew, and Enoch L. Mitchell, *Tennessee: A Short History* (Knoxville: Univ. of Tennessee Press, 1969), 322.

9. Oliver P. Temple, *East Tennessee and the Civil War* (Cincinnati: The Robert Clarke Co., 1899), 203.

10. B. Frank Cooling, *Forts Henry and Donelson: The Key to the Confederate Heartland* (Knoxville: Univ. of Tennessee Press, 1987), 88.

11. Larry J. Daniel, *Shiloh: The Battle That Changed the Civil War* (New York: Simon & Schuster, 1997), 106, 112.

12. Ibid., 92.

13. Ibid., 261, 265, 322.

14. Kenneth W. Noe, *Perryville: This Grand Havoc of Battle* (Lexington: Univ. Press of Kentucky, 2001), 58, 104–5, 124–25.

15. Harrison and Klotter, *A New History of Kentucky,* 198–202; Noe, *Perryville,* 129, 214, 313–15, 369, 373.

16. Wiley Sword, *Mountains Touched with Fire: Chattanooga Besieged, 1863* (New York: St. Martin's Press, 1995), 360–65.

17. Wiley Sword, *The Confederacy's Last Hurrah: Spring Hill, Franklin, and Nashville* (Lawrence: Univ. Press of Kansas, 1992), 276–77, 279.

18. Ibid., 425–26, 431.

Part I

Battles, Skirmishes, and Soldiers

The Militia Spirit

Lexington and Clarksville Militias and the Making of Civil War Armies

Aaron Astor

At Camp Quarles on the outskirts of town, a group of "Clarksville ladies" presented a flag to Capt. Frank Beaumont's company. Beaumont's men, along with hundreds of others from Montgomery and nearby counties, had been drilling in the July heat and waiting for instructions to march to Virginia. In her address to the captain, "Mrs. G" proclaimed, "In all this mighty rush for freedom, none have shown more alacrity than the Clarksville Ninety-Ones, none have made greater sacrifices upon the altar of their country."[1] In thanks to the "fair hands" of Clarksville that assembled the mighty flag, Captain Beaumont signaled that the "ladies of Clarksville have given to the 'Ninety-Ones' an additional incentive to deeds of patriotic valor."[2] In short order, Captain Beaumont's Company K of the 14th Tennessee Regiment under the command of Col. William Forbes marched off to the distant hills of western Virginia. The 14th would serve the rest of the Civil War as one of the few Tennessee regiments in the Army of Northern Virginia.

Scenes like this one occurred all across the North and South in the summer of 1861 as officers in the Union and Confederate armies quickly assembled legions of volunteers into what became the Army of the Potomac, the Army of Northern Virginia, the Army of the Ohio, and the Army of Tennessee. But one piece of this particular exchange—the reference to the "Ninety-Ones"—is noteworthy for what it reveals about the men who assembled at Camp Quarles. The "Ninety-Ones" did not mark the number of a regiment in the Army of Northern Virginia or the Army of Tennessee. Nor did the "Ninety-Ones" refer to the short-lived Provisional Army of Tennessee created by Gov. Isham G. Harris in May 1861. The "Ninety-Ones" were a

Tennessee militia company based in Clarksville and only organized as such in January of that year.

Why would Captain Beaumont and the citizens of Clarksville refer to his unit by its militia number, especially as the state militia was essentially moribund less than a year earlier? Even more remarkably, the same newspaper touting the gallant soldiers of the "Old Ninety-Ones" viciously mocked the reorganized militia just a few months earlier. One of the candidates for lieutenant colonel of the Ninety-First, James Neblett, was an editor of the Clarksville *Chronicle*. And either in a spirit of self-deprecation or downright belittlement of the whole militia system, Neblett joked, "Insane, indeed, would be the temerity of any set of fellows who would set hostile foot on this dirt, when they know that we are Lieutenant-Colonel of the bloody Ninety-First. They ain't a-goin' to do it! No, sir; *nary time!* Lincoln knows US; and ah! The dread perturbations of that miserable man's day-visions and night-dreams when he shall learn that we are running for Lieutenant-Colonel of the Ninety-First!"[3]

The *Chronicle*'s mixed characterization of the militia—from laughingstock to encomium—reveals the conflicted nature of military readiness in the spring of 1861. But it also begs the question of the legacy of the militia itself. What role did militias like the Ninety-First play—as an organizational force of citizen-soldiers or merely as a symbol of service to the defense of the community—in the organization of companies and regiments in the Confederate armies? Did militias actually prepare civilians for military life? Did they stoke a community pride that could be transferred to regiments in the official Confederate and Union armies?

An equally intriguing political question emerges. Did the late-antebellum and secession-era militias politicize and mobilize Tennesseans still reluctant to secede? And what about the Kentucky militias, which were more organized and politically galvanized in the year-old Kentucky State Guard than were the newly reorganized Tennessee militias? After all, members of the "Old Ninety-First" were not the only ex-militiamen to gather near Clarksville en route to formal enrollment in the Confederate Army. Hundreds of Kentuckians had arrived for the same purpose, with many of them belonging to militias led by prominent men like John Hunt Morgan, Roger Hanson, and W. C. P. Breckinridge. The famed Kentucky Orphan Brigade would organize just outside Clarksville, as would numerous other Kentucky Confederate units drawing from secessionist State Guard militias.

Adding to the complication was the question of loyalty. Some of the late-antebellum Kentucky militias would send leaders and men to both sides, drawing howls of "traitor" and "Tory" from beleaguered citizens. A year after the fall of Fort Donelson, Nannie Haskins Williams of Clarksville recounted in her diary: "Well upon Christmas day Colonel Bruce with his 'whiskey jug' and several regiments took possession of this place and here they have been ever since. And here I am too still writing in my journal and about those detestable blue coats for whom I have such a disgust."[4] Col. Sanders Bruce was another former Kentucky militiaman, and a veteran of the State Guard. A member of Lexington's antebellum elite centered around Gratz Park, his social circle included a neighbor, John Hunt Morgan, who married Bruce's sister in 1848. Bruce's militia, the Lexington Chasseurs, once competed with Morgan's Rifles for attention from the adoring throngs of parade-goers and well-heeled ladies and gentlemen of the Bluegrass aristocracy. In 1861, Morgan's Rifles would go, almost as a unit, into the Confederate Army of Tennessee, becoming the 2d Kentucky Cavalry Regiment. Bruce's Chasseurs would send half its men to camps around Clarksville to enlist in the Army of Tennessee along with Morgan. But Bruce and many of his fellow Lexington Unionists from the Chasseurs would occupy the town of Clarksville a year after Fort Donelson and the Lower Cumberland Valley fell to the Union.

For all the bluster about defending homes, rights and the Republic, very few Kentuckians and Tennesseans were militarily prepared to do so. Social elites from Lexington and Clarksville built regiments in the Confederate Army of Tennessee and the Union Army of the Ohio (and later the Cumberland) without any real military training or experience. In many ways, it would be the preparation for and the battle of Fort Donelson where so many men from Tennessee and Kentucky would truly become soldiers—and for many, prisoners—for the first time. With the exception of a handful of Mexican War veterans, the militias would prove to be the only experience that could have prepared the civilians of Lexington and Clarksville for a life of soldiering.

But militias were, in many ways, relics of the Old West. As quasi-military agents of public order, militias were typically called up to defend the community against Indian attacks and "domestic insurrections," especially those led by slaves. As the Kentucky and Tennessee frontier settled, the militia system transformed into a theater for social performance and entertainment. While slave patrols continued in importance—and were organized along military lines—they were legally separated from the state militia.[5] As a military system, Tennessee's and Kentucky's militia had withered by the mid-1850s, with Tennessee officially dismantling its system in 1857. A historian of Tennessee's antebellum militia system concludes, "The men who mustered for the Civil War in 1861 were militiamen in name only, with no meaningful connection to the traditional militia."[6]

Still, the militia *ideal* persisted during the key recruitment months of 1861, even if the formal bureaucratic structure of the state militias was largely incapable of training citizen-soldiers for community defense. Alas, the militia came in for mockery, even from those charged with its stewardship and promotion. But as later dispatches from the field revealed, the militia ideal continued to infuse the great recruitment drive in Lexington and Clarksville. And it may have even sustained regimental morale in the Confederate Army of Tennessee in the wake of poor corps leadership and a succession of battlefield defeats.

In his classic study of the Army of Tennessee, Thomas Connelly identified a paradox at the heart of the great Confederate Army of the West. With no Lees or Jacksons to fire the imagination or sustain morale, and few victories to cheer on the boys, how was it that the Army of Tennessee survived intact as long as it did? The predecessor organization—the Provisional Army of Tennessee—was rent with political favoritism, incompetence, and poor coordination with overall Confederate leadership. After a succession of inept commanders like Gideon Pillow, John Floyd, and Leonidas Polk, the army's great savior, Albert Sidney Johnston, died at Shiloh before having a chance to turn the western army into a feared fighting force. Subsequent leadership from P. G. T. Beauregard, Braxton Bragg, Joseph Johnston, and John Bell Hood led the army toward nothing but disappointment and defeat. The only success stories were cavalry units led by men like Morgan, Nathan Bedford Forrest, and Joseph Wheeler. Legendary as those units were, they could do little to maintain morale in the infantry regiments of the Army of Tennessee. And yet, regimental accounts reveal an army keeping up the fight until the bitter end.[7] What was the source of its continued morale and commitment? As Connelly argues, the answer lay at the junior officer and regimental level. "Unlike the Virginia army, which depended for its morale upon a few individuals such as Lee or 'Stonewall' Jackson, the men of the Army of Tennessee never attained a real esprit at a corps level. Instead," Connelly maintained, "the peculiar western morale was usually most evident at the regimental or brigade level."[8] In fact, as Captain Beaumont and Mrs. G revealed, this junior-level morale drew, at least partly, from the recently reorganized militia system.

An examination of prewar militias in Lexington and Clarksville and their conversion into formal regiments, especially in the Confederate Army of

Tennessee, sheds light on just what these new warriors thought about the life of soldiering, and what their home communities thought of the soldiers recruited to protect them. The preparation, social standing, organization, and transformation of late-antebellum militias reveal both the contours of social and political life in Kentucky and Tennessee and the extent to which local leadership was prepared for a major war. As the sister cities of Lexington and Clarksville became enemy cities, local citizens transformed themselves into armed, trained, and organized soldiers prepared to fight. The militias, for all their weaknesses, were the only institutional bodies capable of preparing the citizens of the two cities for war before the Confederate Army of Tennessee and the Union armies of the West were formally developed. Company and regimental morale in the Army of Tennessee, decimated by defeat, death and poor leadership, nevertheless sustained itself for four long years of war. The unit cohesion and élan that emerged at the company and regimental level in the Army of Tennessee had its roots in the late-antebellum militia organizations—and in particular the militia spirit and ideal—in places like Lexington, Kentucky, and Clarksville, Tennessee.

Militias garnered a proud tradition in the Old West. As historian Richard G. Stone makes clear, "The Militia of Kentucky not only preceded the formation of the commonwealth, but was the midwife at its birth. The state could never have been created without its citizen-soldiers."[9] From the earliest treks of Daniel Boone and his followers down the Wilderness Road through the Cumberland Gap to the War of 1812, the Kentucky militia stood as the vanguard of white settlement in the Trans-Allegheny West. After protecting early settlements around Boonesborough and Harrodsburg, the Kentucky militia fought British-aligned Indians at Blue Licks in the Revolutionary War and over the course of the next few decades. In response to Congress's 1792 Uniform Militia Act, the newly independent state of Kentucky organized and mustered militiamen for service against actual and potential raids by Native Americans. Kentucky militiamen helped secure peace for white settlement in the commonwealth after victory at Fallen Timbers in 1794 and continued to defend the Western frontier into the new century. Its crowning moment may have been its role in the defeat of British forces at River Raisin in Michigan during the War of 1812. Not surprisingly, most of the state's early political leadership, including governors Isaac Shelby, Richard M. Johnson, and John Adair, were prominent leaders in the Kentucky militia.

Tennessee's early militia earned equally significant praise during and after the Revolution. The famed "Overmountain Men," guarding the settlements along the Watauga River in what was then western North Carolina, helped turn the tide of the Revolutionary War at King's Mountain. In subsequent wars against the Chickamaugas—a faction of Cherokee who rejected treaties to turn over valuable hunting lands to encroaching white settlers—Tennessee militia leaders like John Sevier would secure the state's growth through the Tennessee and Cumberland River valleys. Eagerness to serve in these militias culminated in the War of 1812, where Tennessee Gen. Andrew Jackson led his legions of Tennessee volunteers against the Creek Indians in 1813 and the British at New Orleans in 1815. The state nickname—the Volunteer State—reflects the importance of militia service in Tennessee's early state identity.

In the decades after the War of 1812, Kentucky and Tennessee developed more settled agricultural economies and built growing cities along the Ohio, Tennessee, Cumberland, and Mississippi rivers. With little threat from Indian attack or British, French, or Spanish invasion, Kentucky and Tennessee militias began to wither in importance. Planters and merchants replaced frontier citizen-soldiers in the political leadership class of Kentucky and Tennessee. The Kentucky militia system transformed from a universal system of citizen-soldiery into a more selective, volunteer-driven outfit. The Mexican War briefly reinvigorated the spirit of the "Corn Stalk Militia,"[10] with several Kentucky Civil War leaders gaining military experience in Mexico. Included among these veterans were future Union leaders like Robert Anderson, John Reynolds, Theophilus Garrard, Thomas Crittenden, and Speed Fry. Future Confederate Kentuckians cutting their military teeth in Mexico included John C. Breckinridge, William Preston, Humphrey Marshall, and George Crittenden. Simon Bolivar Buckner, future commander of the Kentucky State Guard, performed exceptionally well at the battle of Molino del Rey. Also in the militia tradition, Roger Hanson served as lieutenant in an Independent Kentucky Company.[11] Tennessee also sent many of its famous sons to Texas and to the Mexican War, including Sam Houston, David Crockett, Benjamin Franklin Cheatham, and Gideon Pillow.

But the militia system in both states returned to a state of dormancy after 1848. By 1857, Tennessee's legislature officially disbanded its militia system, viewing the obligation to recruit, drill, and parade as too financially burdensome in a state suffering from financial distress. Some of Kentucky's old militias would persist, including the Lexington Old Infantry. And, of course,

John Hunt Morgan created his Lexington Rifles in 1857. But the trend was clear in Kentucky and Tennessee in the late 1850s—the militia system was moribund and very few citizens experienced anything like military training, drilling, or maneuvering. Even with the troubles in Bleeding Kansas, which drew significant attention in Kentucky and Tennessee, few citizens joined Missouri-style minutemen organizations designed to fight in Kansas. Whatever sectional tensions may have developed, few people in Lexington or Clarksville imagined themselves heading toward war. But that would all change in October 1859, when John Brown led a failed slave insurrection at Harpers Ferry in Virginia.

John Brown's raid on October 16, 1859, shattered the illusion of tranquillity that had befallen Kentucky and Tennessee. It had now become a real possibility that the nation might descend into civil war. And if it did, the Upper South states of Kentucky and Tennessee would assuredly host much of the bloodiest action. However, the pro-Southern governors of the two states responded differently. In Kentucky, Gov. Beriah Magoffin created the new Kentucky State Guard, which was to be organized and led by Mexican War veteran and West Point–trained Simon Bolivar Buckner. The Guard's purpose was simply to defend the state against all transgressors—North or South—and to guard against any possible Brown-style slave insurrections.

A determination to maintain "armed neutrality" in any subsequent conflict informed much of the State Guard's preparations. That said, there was an unmistakably pro-Southern bent to the State Guard under the leadership of Buckner. Of those who would join the Confederate Army in large numbers, no militia stands out more than John Hunt Morgan's Lexington Rifles. Morgan—descendant of one of Lexington's wealthiest businessmen, and honor-obsessed paragon of Bluegrass society—founded the Lexington Rifles in 1857, and reported the first company of volunteer militia to Governor Magoffin as part of the reconstituted Kentucky State Guard in 1860.[12] Morgan was a member of Lexington's manufacturing elite, operating a hemp factory in the heart of the city. He was also an interstate slave trader, sending slave cargoes down the Ohio and Mississippi rivers to Memphis and New Orleans as late as the summer of 1861.[13] Many of Morgan's longtime associates, friends, and neighbors, like Sanders Bruce and William Bodley, remained loyal to the Union. Though the state declared its neutrality in May 1861, some Southern sympathizers headed for Camp Boone near Clarksville, Tennessee, shortly after Fort Sumter. Morgan, like most eventual Kentucky Confederates, held out until September 1861 when the state officially sided with the Union, and evaded Unionist Home Guard pickets to reach Confederate lines in occupied Bowling Green. Once in Confederate-held territory, Morgan quickly established himself as an integral component in the Confederate military command. More important than the fate of Morgan himself was his militia; all but six of Morgan's Riflemen joined the Confederacy, most of them in Morgan's own cavalry unit. In the case of the Lexington Rifles, loyalty to the captain and loyalty to the Southern cause coalesced to form a vital backbone to the Kentucky secessionist movement and to the Confederate Army.

Not all State Guardsmen or militiamen supported secession, however. Beyond the official State Guard organization, militiamen could be found expressing a wide variety of political opinions. In fact, the vast majority of militiamen across the state continued to support the Union, even after the state officially entered the war in September 1861. For example, "Anvil's Artillery" in Danville, Kentucky, and Paris's Bourbon Rangers launched national salutes and marched in defense of the Union. During the neutrality months between May 20 and September 1861, Gen. Lovell Rousseau organized a statewide Home Guard system designed to protect local communities against a potential Confederate invasion. Never a well-respected outfit, the Home Guards provided haphazard support for the Union cause. Far more important was the enrollment of official Union regiments, with many of the recruits coming from pro-Union militias.

Despite the pro-Southern leanings of the State Guard, many of the Kentucky militias exhibited no particular political orientation. The Woodford Blues, Union Greys, Jessamine Blues, Porter Guards, and Governor's Guards held nonsectional parades in towns like Versailles, Nicholasville, and other county seats in central Kentucky, entertaining vast throngs of men and women.[14] Martha McDowell Buford Jones of Versailles reported in her diary the excitement with which her daughter Lizzie presented the flag to the Woodford Blues at the parade. "All said they had a grand time today," she wrote.[15] They reinforced and performed Southern conventions of honor and manhood even if they remained technically aloof from the sectional crisis looming over the country. And they hardly imagined that they would be torn asunder by a civil war.

Members of Lexington's three main antebellum militia organizations—the Lexington Old Infantry, the Lexington Chasseurs, and John Hunt Morgan's Lexington Rifles—eventually joined both sides in the Civil War.[16] The Old Infantry, formerly the Lexington Light Infantry, launched numerous campaigns against Indians in the 1790s and served in the War of 1812. The Chasseurs were a more recent creation, appearing in Lexington only in 1860 but very quickly attracting widespread attention. According to one historian writing in the late nineteenth century, "The Chasseurs were the favorites of everybody, and the company rarely had a parade that it was not invited to partake of the hospitality of some private residence."[17] The Chasseurs, like the Old Infantry, sent nearly half its men to each side in the Civil War. Like the Woodford Blues, they served more to train soldiers for future combat and to parade for the entertainment of the masses than they did as sectional organizations. But Morgan's Lexington Rifles stood out for its military spirit and its singular dedication to the Southern cause.

In Tennessee, Gov. Isham G. Harris did not propose any military readiness bill until much later—after Lincoln's election. The quick succession of events in early 1861 created a whirlwind of preparation and organization. In January, an extra session of the legislature reorganized the Tennessee state militia. It specifically repealed the 1857 demobilization law and called for the reorganization of the state militia, with districts established numerically across the state. Though the same bill sent a secession convention bill to the voters—only to be rejected at a February referendum—it did begin the process of arming the state for a war that seemed increasingly inevitable. Sheriffs held elections for militia regimental leaders, including the positions of colonel, lieutenant colonel, and first and second major. This was the act that created the Ninety-Ones, who commanded the eastern side of Montgomery County to the north of the Cumberland River; the Ninety-Twos organized on the opposite side.

All of the men elected to militia leadership were prominent Clarksvillians, though few had any real military experience. James Neblett, editor of the *Chronicle,* admitted to his readers: "Except while running for Lieutenant-Colonel of the Militia, we have never pretended to much military genius, and we hope that the matter of our State defense is in hands competent to guard against any unexpected incursion of an enemy."[18] Still, the Ninety-Ones moved with alacrity in the weeks after Fort Sumter. Neblett, as lieutenant colonel of the militia regiment and in place of the temporarily absent Colonel Beaumont, issued a proclamation to the people of Clarksville to create two volunteer companies "in keeping with the fame of the VOLUNTEER STATE."[19] A week later, Neblett celebrated the formation of a Home Guard, "filled up, principally, by the old men."[20] Other able-bodied men had already joined regular volunteer companies. Lt. Col. Neblett did not hesitate to offer military advice, despite his lack of formal training. Noticing the proximity of Clarksville to neutral Kentucky, soon to be "humiliated" by Lincoln, Neblett warned, "If it has not already been done, every avenue of sudden approach into our State ought to be immediately and efficiently guarded by thoroughly armed soldiers."[21] It would become clear in the coming months that the Cumberland River would be the major point of entrance for Federal troops, and Clarksville would be the first major population center to face the Union Army.

With the attack on Fort Sumter, public opinion in Middle Tennessee changed dramatically. Conditional and conservative Unionists became reluctant Confederates, with many of the state's leading antebellum Unionists like John Bell and Felix Zollicoffer dedicating themselves to the Southern cause. In Clarksville, the city's dominant ex-Whig leadership under Gustavus Henry, Cave Johnson, and James Bailey pledged full and complete allegiance to the new Confederacy. Perhaps most important was William A. Quarles, Democratic politician, judge, and president of the Memphis, Clarksville & Louisville Railroad. Quarles would quickly emerge as one of the most respected military leaders in Clarksville and in Tennessee as a whole.

Governor Harris called a second extra session of the state legislature to convene on April 25, and it concluded by issuing a declaration of independence on May 6. Harris also called for a military alliance with the Confederate States of America, and established a Provisional Army of Tennessee, commanded by Gen. Gideon Pillow and answerable to the governor. Though voters would get a chance to ratify the separation vote on June 8, with many East Tennessee counties rejecting the move, volunteer enlistments after May 6 across Middle and West Tennessee made the ratification vote a mere formality. With the state's official declaration of independence in May—and ratification vote in June—Governor Harris issued a call for 25,000 active volunteers and thirty-thousand additional volunteer troops to be held in reserve. With Governor Harris's creation of the Provisional Army of Tennessee, tens of thousands of volunteers enrolled at camps across Middle and West Tennessee; resistance to Confederate recruitment in East Tennessee signified trouble for the Confederate Tennessee government that would not disappear any time soon.[22]

As witnessed in Lt. Col. Neblett's call for volunteers, the militia would play an important role in summoning and rallying civilians for military service. The organization of companies into the Provisional Army of Tennessee proceeded with remarkable speed. Laborers, farmers, clerks, students, and others gathered at the nearby fairgrounds to enlist in companies raised by prominent men in the community. Stewart College professor of mathematics, William A. Forbes, encouraged his students to fall in line and respond to Governor Harris's call; his was the first official company to enlist in Clarksville. Alongside hundreds of others forming companies across Montgomery County, Forbes's young men would convene just outside the city and be formally enrolled in the field service by William A. Quarles, who had become a colonel in the Provisional Army.[23]

By late summer Clarksville had become an armed encampment, with civilians from across the Cumberland Valley drilling at Camp Quarles, Camp Forbes, and Camp Duncan. Added to them were Kentucky Confederates, many of them from Lexington and belonging to militias of the State Guard. As they drilled at nearby Camp Boone and Camp Burnett, the future members of the famed Kentucky Orphan Brigade developed a Confederate national identity missing in their native commonwealth. By the fall and the arrival of Gen. Albert Sidney Johnston in command of all forces in the West, myriad citizen-soldier organizations in the old Kentucky State Guard and Tennessee State Militia had already built the regimental esprit de corps that would form the backbone of the Confederate Army of Tennessee.

Not all Kentucky and Tennessee militiamen joined the Army of Tennessee. A significant portion of the Kentucky State Guard, including Lexingtonian Sanders Bruce, commanded units in the Federal Army of the Ohio (later to be renamed the Army of the Cumberland). Some Federal units were organized during the neutrality months and outside of the state. But beginning in late summer, William "Bull" Nelson began organizing Union regiments at Camp Dick Robinson, about twenty-five miles south of Lexington.[24] Some of the earliest units enlisted there were actually East Tennessee Union regiments, formed by civilians escaping Confederate recruitment agents in the Upper Tennessee Valley. The outskirts of Clarksville and Lexington became, in essence, sister and enemy recruiting grounds. Kentucky Confederates, many of them militiamen in the State Guard, entered Confederate service near Clarksville, just as thousands of East Tennessee Unionists—including militiamen in mountain communities subject to North Carolina invasion—entered Federal service at Camp Dick Robinson near Lexington, Kentucky.

For those newly enrolled Confederates at Clarksville, the first regiment would be sent east to the Army of Northern Virginia. Forbes, the Stewart College math professor, would eventually be promoted to brigadier general in command of the 14th Tennessee. This regiment, enrolled mostly in Governor Harris's first call for troops, included some of the most dedicated Confederates in Clarksville. It also included Capt. Frank Beaumont's militiamen from the old Ninety-Ones. The militia spirit continued on even as the regiment was organized under the auspices of the Army of Northern Virginia. After leaving for western Virginia, Beaumont wrote home, reporting on "promotions from the ranks of the 'Ninety Ones'."[25] When tragedy struck the 14th Tennessee and Beaumont died of typhoid fever, his funeral service would be "guarded" by legions of newer volunteer Home Guards, minutemen, and other independent companies. The city still regarded Beaumont as a militiaman serving in defense of his community even though his regiment was sent so far away.

Indeed, the old militia would be tested by the absence of the 14th Tennessee from Clarksville. With Beaumont gone, the Ninety-Ones held a new election and selected Joshua Cobb as colonel. Cobb would soon command the Independent Guards of Clarksville. But if the Ninety-Ones could transition to new leadership, the militia spirit faced new challenges from the pressures of full-scale war. Designed to defend the community, the original leadership of the Ninety-Ones had already been sent off to distant Virginia. In consequence, Lt. Col. Neblett admonished Clarksvillians, "The militia may discard the delusion that they can neither be drafted or ordered out of the county because they belong to the minute men—a mere police system that never contemplated the enlistment of men beyond the number necessary for a patrol duty. Montgomery has to raise her quota of the reserve corps, and if the people do not volunteer to that extent they will be drafted. This is the plain English of it."[26] As the Federal army inched closer to the twin forts along the Tennessee and Cumberland rivers, the militia found that home defense might mean transfer to more pressing locales like Fort Henry or Fort Donelson.

In late July, Governor Harris was finally able to transfer command of the Provisional Army of Tennessee to the Confederate government, first under the leadership of Leonidas Polk and then, upon his return from California, to Albert Sidney Johnston. The loss of the 14th Tennessee to Virginia provoked serious anger among Clarksvillians as it seemed to violate the militia ideal of community defense. As it became increasingly likely that the Federal army would invade Tennessee via the Tennessee and Cumberland rivers—and not through the mountains of East Tennessee or along the bluffs of the Mississippi—residents of Clarksville felt betrayed by both state and Confederate leadership. Neblett's exasperation reflected such worry that community defense could be defined so broadly that militiamen could expect to be sent to distant battlefields where they would serve officers of other states.

As the military threat grew more serious in the winter of 1861–62, Gen. Albert Sidney Johnston called for ever more volunteer regiments to appear at Fort Donelson on the Cumberland River near Dover. This included the new members of the Ninety-Ones. It would also include the various new militias and home guards established, including the Clarksville Guards and Independent Guards. The Home Guard minutemen under Cyrus Sugg would form the nucleus of the 50th Tennessee Regiment, organized at Fort Donelson. Meanwhile, James Bailey's collection of volunteers formed Company A of the 49th Tennessee. Two other Clarksville-based regiments would be formally organized at Fort Donelson—Adolphus Heiman's 10th Tennessee and William A. Quarles's 42d Tennessee. In both cases, the myriad militias and home guard volunteer companies created in the early summer of 1861 comprised the core of the new Army of Tennessee regiments. Though the former militiamen were reorganized in new Confederate regiments and under the command of non-Tennesseans, they continued to reveal the militia spirit in defense of their homes just twenty miles upriver.

Closer to home, however, the militia spirit continued in the form of various Home Guard minutemen organizations developed throughout 1861 and early 1862. Rifle companies filled with "noble bands of patriots," many with colorful names like the "Dixie Blues," continued to form in the last months of 1861. While some of these regiments were filled with old men incapable of lengthy and vigorous service, their eagerness to serve in home defense bolstered the militia spirit of more able-bodied men. As many as fifteen hundred men had already joined Confederate units from Clarksville by the end of November, with even more men—and hired slaves—put to work and defense in December. By early December, General Johnston began to send all new enlistees to the twin forts—Fort Henry and Fort Donelson—which had been largely neglected up to that point. When Capt. James E. Bailey and his company set off for Fort Donelson, the *Chronicle* noted that the "gallant company . . . carried with them the best wishes of the entire community."[27] The best wishes would not be enough to defend the twin forts in the end, but they would help sustain morale for the thousands of men soon bound for Northern prisons.

The transition of Lexington's Confederate militiamen to the Army of Tennessee followed a more complicated path than did the Clarksville militiamen, mostly because of the state's embrace of neutrality in May 1861. The State Guard leadership trickled southwestward to the camps around

Clarksville in the summer of 1861, accelerating its self-imposed exile in September. General Polk's ill-fated and ill-conceived invasion of Columbus on September 1 shoved the commonwealth fully into the Union camp. Gen. Ulysses S. Grant immediately seized Paducah, and the Kentucky legislature—once reassured that a recent emancipation edict issued by Gen. John C. Fremont in Missouri was rescinded—cast its lot in full with the Union.[28] While thousands of pro-Confederate Kentuckians were able to skirt Home Guard pickets and make their way to the southern Kentucky and northwest Tennessee recruitment camps, they were delayed by bureaucratic conflicts in manifesting as a major fighting force. Legal complications regarding ownership of the State Guard guns and military lines of authority between top-level Kentucky Guardsmen and the still-emerging command structure under Gen. Albert Sidney Johnston hindered the development of an effective and organized fighting force.

Underneath the command confusion, however, was an effective and spirited set of Kentucky Confederate regiments. The ex-militiamen of the State Guard included among them some of the most prominent and well-regarded military minds of Kentucky—Buckner, Roger Hanson, Morgan, John C. Breckinridge, Robert J. Breckinridge Jr., and William Campbell Preston Breckinridge.[29] When locally raised cavalry units, such as Woodward's Cavalry Regiment raised at Oak Grove near Clarksville, were added to the mix, the Kentucky Confederate contribution to the Army of Tennessee proved to be formidable.[30]

Strategic miscalculation placed the energetic regiments and brigades of the Army of Tennessee in jeopardy. General Johnston was in charge of a very long, thin line from Columbus on Kentucky's Mississippi River bluff to Cumberland Gap, where Virginia and Tennessee joined the Bluegrass State in the heart of the Appalachian Mountains. Johnston concentrated his forces at Bowling Green, sending many of the newly enlisted Clarksville and Lexington Confederates out of their Montgomery County training camps and on to the central Kentucky salient. General Buckner, old commander of the Kentucky State Guard and native of the Green River country north of Bowling Green, guarded the Louisville & Nashville Railroad as well as the series of turnpikes heading into Tennessee. It was here that Morgan and his men officially enrolled in Confederate service. It was also in Bowling Green where the few effective brigade commanders in the West—Forrest, Patrick Cleburne, and William J. Hardee (an Arkansan known more for his text on infantry tactics)—converged and potentially threatened Louisville and the Ohio River. Temporarily the capital of Confederate Kentucky, Bowling

Green signified the offensive capabilities of the eager men from Clarksville and the liberating impulses of rebel Kentuckians.[31]

But Johnston's strategic miscalculations were laid bare by mid-January 1862. Confederate Gen. George Crittenden sent Felix Zollicoffer out from Knoxville to secure the Cumberland River near Somerset before Union Gen. George Thomas could unite his forces coming down from Camp Dick Robinson and Lebanon. The campaign ended in the disaster of Mill Springs, with Zollicoffer dead and Crittenden's Confederates driven out of eastern Kentucky. The far western end was equally jeopardized by Grant's maneuvering around Belmont, Missouri. Most critical, however, was the wide-open invasion path into Tennessee via the twin rivers into the heart of Middle and West Tennessee. Fort Henry, guarding the Tennessee River, lay under water after the winter rains, and Fort Heiman, across the river, was unfinished. Despite the presence of Colonel Heiman's 10th Tennessee—many of them Clarksville boys—Lloyd Tilghman was forced to surrender Fort Henry on February 6 to Union Adm. Andrew Foote.

In the next ten days, the fate of Tennessee and the old Lexington and Clarksville militiamen would be determined. A naval assault on Fort Donelson first resulted in victory for the Confederates. The 49th and 50th Tennessee, under the commander of Gen. John W. Head inside the fort, held strong against the naval assault and against the first infantry attacks against the Confederate left. The initial reports reaching Clarksville were sanguine. The last line to appear in the Clarksville *Chronicle* before the fort's fall—and Clarksville's subsequent capture—revealed the depths of delusion: "we may expect very soon to see our two rivers swept of every Yankee on them."[32] Two days later the fort's top two commanders fled and the third in command "unconditionally surrendered" to General Grant. Donelson's fall opened the door to Clarksville and Nashville.

The battle of Fort Donelson would serve as the final proving ground for the old militiamen of Clarksville and Lexington. The Clarksville-based units guarded the Confederate left and maintained the offensive for much of the fighting on February 14. But it surrendered in full on February 16. Nearly all of the Clarksville and Lexington militiamen who entered the Confederate service in the summer, fall, and winter of 1861 now boarded ships for cold prisons in the North. Those who did not surrender managed to escape and fight on through Shiloh. The captives would be released in September 1862, just as the Army of Tennessee's great Kentucky campaign began to unravel.

Perhaps the ultimate expression of the militia spirit came from the third in command at Fort Donelson, Gen. Simon Bolivar Buckner. After the cowardly escape of generals Floyd and Pillow during the surrender discussions at the Dover Hotel, Buckner agreed to seek surrender terms with Gen. Ulysses Grant. Buckner felt bound by his code of honor to surrender with his troops, facing whatever fate befell his own men. If Fort Donelson had made Grant into a Union war hero, it also confirmed Buckner as a respected citizen-soldier leader in the old militia tradition.

Historians have generally concluded that late-antebellum militias were essentially outdated institutions, utterly incapable of developing anything like a sound, modern military force. Many contemporaries certainly agreed, as witnessed by Tennessee's 1857 law dismantling the moribund system. But when John Brown's raid stoked fears of slave insurrection and possible civil war in the minds of Southerners, the militia spirit returned in force. With a tiny Federal army, soon to be split among its officer corps by the secession crisis, the various Civil War military commanders had to rely on state-based volunteer companies and regiments. In some cases, generals ably constructed large-scale, well-organized armies. In others, infighting, jealous leadership, and bureaucratic inefficiencies hindered the development of a capable fighting force. In the West, the armies of the Cumberland and the Tennessee—under Don Carlos Buell, William Rosecrans, Ulysses S. Grant, George Thomas, and William T. Sherman—proved far more effective than the Confederate Army of Tennessee. As historian Earl Hess has concluded, the Federal advantage in the West came from superior leadership, organization, and marshaling of resources.[33]

What the Confederate Army of Tennessee lacked in corps command, it made up in regiment-level élan. While many elements contributed to this remarkably persistent morale, the militia spirit of community self-defense—briefly activated by a reinvigorated late-antebellum militia organization in places like Lexington and Clarksville—helped prepare the citizenry for years of hard fighting. Late-antebellum militias did little as formal institutions to mediate the transition of civilians in Lexington and Clarksville into official military regiments capable of fighting a modern war, but they offered a proving ground for masculinity, provided rudimentary military training, solidified networks of social allegiance, and channeled political mobilization. More importantly, they cemented the bond between soldiers and the community they were charged with protecting—even when sent off to distant battlefields. By invoking the militia ideal, Tennessee and Kentucky soldiers in far-off Virginia and Pennsylvania, in prison camps in

Chicago, and in retreat through north Georgia could summon the spirit of community defense and camaraderie made manifest in 1860 and 1861.

Notes

1. Clarksville *Chronicle*, July 26, 1861.

2. Ibid.

3. Ibid., Mar. 1, 1861.

4. Nannie Haskins Williams diary. In possession of Dr. Minoa Uffelman, Austin Peay State University, Clarksville, Tenn.

5. Sally Hadden, *Slave Patrols: Law and Violence in Virginia and the Carolinas* (Cambridge, Mass.: Harvard Univ. Press, 2001), 42–51.

6. Trevor Smith, "Pioneers, Patriots, and Politicians: The Tennessee Militia System, 1772–1857" (Ph.D. diss., Univ. of Tennessee, 2003), 222–23.

7. Perhaps the most famous Army of Tennessee regimental memoir was Sam Watkins, *Company Aytch* (New York: Penguin Books, 1999).

8. Thomas Connelly, *Army of the Heartland: The Army of Tennessee, 1861–1862* (Baton Rouge: Louisiana State Univ. Press, 1967), xiii.

9. Richard G. Stone, *A Brittle Sword: The Kentucky Militia, 1776–1912* (Lexington: Univ. Press of Kentucky, 1977), 1.

10. The nickname "Corn Stalk Militia" comes from the usage of cornstalks instead of guns during military drills. The name suggested the more lax security concerns after the War of 1812.

11. Anderson Chenault Quisenberry, *General Zachary Taylor and the Mexican War* (Frankfort: Kentucky State Historical Society, 1911), 54–70.

12. William Henry Perrin, *History of Fayette County, Kentucky* (Easley, S.C.: Southern Historical Press, 1979), 444. For John Hunt Morgan's prewar life, and especially his obsession with Southern conceptions of manhood and honor, see James A. Ramage, *Rebel Raider: The Life of General John Hunt Morgan* (Lexington: Univ. Press of Kentucky, 1986), 18–39.

13. Wm. B. Richardson to Mr. Morgan, May 22, 1861, New Orleans, La., Box 15, Folder 9, Hunt-Morgan Papers, Special Collections, University of Kentucky, Lexington, Ky.

14. *Lexington Kentucky Statesmen*, June 1, 1860.

15. Mary E. Wharton and Ellen F. Williams, eds., *Peach Leather and Rebel Gray: Diary and Letters of a Confederate Wife* (Lexington, Ky.: The Helicon Company, 1986), 10.

16. J. Winston Coleman, *Lexington during the Civil War* (Lexington, Ky.: Commercial Printing Company, 1938), 9.

17. Perrin, *History of Fayette County, Kentucky*, 448–49.

18. Clarksville *Chronicle*, May 31, 1861.

19. Ibid., Apr. 19, 1861.

20. Ibid., Apr. 26, 1861.

21. Ibid., May 31, 1861.

22. Connelly, *Army of the Heartland,* 25–45.

23. William P. Titus, *Picturesque Clarksville: Past and Present* (Clarksville, Tenn.: Ann E. Alley and Ursula S. Beach, 1973), 108–10.

24. For the creation of the Federal Army of the Ohio, see Larry Daniel, *Days of Glory: The Army of the Cumberland, 1861–1865* (Baton Rouge: Louisiana State Univ. Press, 2004), and Gerald Propokowicz, *All for the Regiment: The Army of the Ohio, 1861–1862* (Chapel Hill: Univ. of North Carolina Press, 2001).

25. Clarksville *Chronicle,* Aug. 16, 1861.

26. Ibid., Sept. 6, 1861.

27. Ibid., Nov. 29, 1861.

28. On the legislative debate over joining the Union after Polk's invasion, see William C. Harris, *Lincoln and the Border States: Preserving the Union* (Lawrence: Univ. Press of Kansas).

29. On the Kentucky Orphan Brigade, see William C. Davis, *The Orphan Brigade: The Kentucky Confederates Who Couldn't Go Home* (Mechanicsburg, Pa.: Stackpole Books, 1993). For more detail on individual companies comprising the Orphans, see Ed Porter Thompson, *History of the First Kentucky Brigade* (Cincinnati: n.p., 1868).

30. Clarksville *Chronicle,* June 21, 1861.

31. Connelly, *Army of the Heartland,* 59–77.

32. Clarksville *Chronicle,* Feb. 14, 1862.

33. Earl Hess, *The Civil War in the West: Victory and Defeat from the Appalachians to the Mississippi* (Chapel Hill: Univ. of North Carolina Press), xi–xiv passim.

Descent into Anarchy

The Evolution of Irregular Warfare in the Lower Green River Country of Kentucky

Scott A. Tarnowieckyi

"What has become of our world?" No doubt such a question was being asked by many of the citizens of Owensboro, Kentucky, on that cold January evening in 1865 as they watched their prized courthouse burn to ashes. Rounded up by a Confederate guerrilla band that had swept into town earlier that day, they were forced to stand there and watch as the Daviess County Courthouse, built just a few years before, was set aflame. The following day the dazed and weary residents watched as the bushwhackers hurriedly left town when a steamboat loaded with Union infantry arrived. Their saviors, though, were not terribly welcome due to the color of their skin. Like the destruction of their courthouse, the arrival of the soldiers of the 118th U.S. Colored Infantry was a reminder of how their world had been turned upside down. The great storm of the Civil War had swept across the lower Green River valley of Kentucky and, like it did in so many other places in the United States, it left death, destruction, and a changed world in its wake. Perhaps it all could have been avoided. Perhaps another path could have been found for the people of that region. Yet, that was not the fate for the people living there. Early in the war, they watched as armies were forged and trained in their yards and fields before sweeping south, seeming to take the war with them as they marched off. The war, however, had not fully left. It would again rear its head, but in a much uglier fashion—guerrilla war. The Union military's inability to establish firm control over the lower Green River country, coupled with many Kentuckians' growing sense of betrayal by the Federal government, led to an escalation of guerrilla warfare. Indeed, during 1864 and 1865 the region devolved into almost complete anarchy due to a massive explosion in irregular warfare.[1]

When the war had broken out in the days and weeks following Fort Sumter, Kentucky had sought neutrality; yet despite their hopes, the war came. Most Kentucky people had welcomed the state government's position of neutrality, hoping that some sort of compromise could be reached. Those hopes were dashed, however, when Confederate forces under Gen. Gideon Pillow marched into the state in September 1861, occupying the town of Columbus, which commandingly overlooked the Mississippi River. In reaction to and at the request of the Unionist-controlled state legislature, Federal troops quickly seized key locations along the northern fringes of the state. Soon a rough Confederate line of defense in southern Kentucky was established stretching from Columbus in the west to the Cumberland Gap in the east with various strongpoints in between like Bowling Green and forts Henry and Donelson on the Tennessee and Cumberland rivers. At the same time, Union forces established control in northern Kentucky along the Ohio River. In between was a relative no-man's-land where the two sides sent patrols to keep a wary eye on their enemy.[2]

This was all true in microcosm in the lower Green River country. This region begins in the south, where the Barren River pours into the Green several miles southeast of Morgantown. From there the lower Green River runs for roughly some two hundred winding miles, first west and then north until opposite Evansville, Indiana, where it empties into the Ohio River. At the end of September, Confederate forces, led by Gen. Simon Buckner, marched into Hopkinsville not far from the Tennessee–Kentucky border. From there, Confederate cavalry, under the command of a newly arrived colonel named Nathan Bedford Forrest, began patrolling on the west and south sides of the Green, traveling as far as Union County along the Ohio River. At the same time, the towns of Henderson and Owensboro on the Ohio River, as well as the village of Calhoun on the Green River, began witnessing the arrival of Union forces. There Gen. Thomas Crittenden defended the critical Lock Number Two and began to raise and train recruits that included hundreds of men from the Green River country, such as the 3rd Kentucky Cavalry, and the 11th, 17th, 25th, and 26th Kentucky infantries. Just as Confederate cavalry prowled in the lands west of the Green, so too did Union troopers. Sparring between the forces became somewhat regular, most notably in a skirmish near the town of Sacramento in McLean County, where Colonel Forrest's numerically superior Confederate troops routed elements of Col. James S. Jackson's cavalry. Further minor engagements occurred in late 1861 near the river at such places as Woodbury, Morgantown, and Whippoorwill Creek. While such clashes were significant to the people of the Green River valley, it was the decisive Union victories to the west at forts Henry and Donelson that forced a Confederate withdrawal from Kentucky in February 1862. For the people of the Green River country, this seemed to signal the end of the actual war within their midst. By mid-1862 the war was off to Mississippi and southern Tennessee, far away from the rich, fertile, tobacco-producing lands of the Green River valley. The locals' belief in the war being far beyond the southern horizon and staying there, however, was not to be. Instead, with the arrival of Adam Rankin Johnson, a new type of war emerged there in the late summer of 1862—irregular war.[3]

Born and raised in Henderson, Kentucky, Adam Rankin Johnson had left the Bluegrass State for Texas in the 1850s. When the Civil War began, Johnson returned, joining Nathan Bedford Forrest's command as a scout. In the summer of 1862, Gen. John C. Breckinridge gave Johnson and his

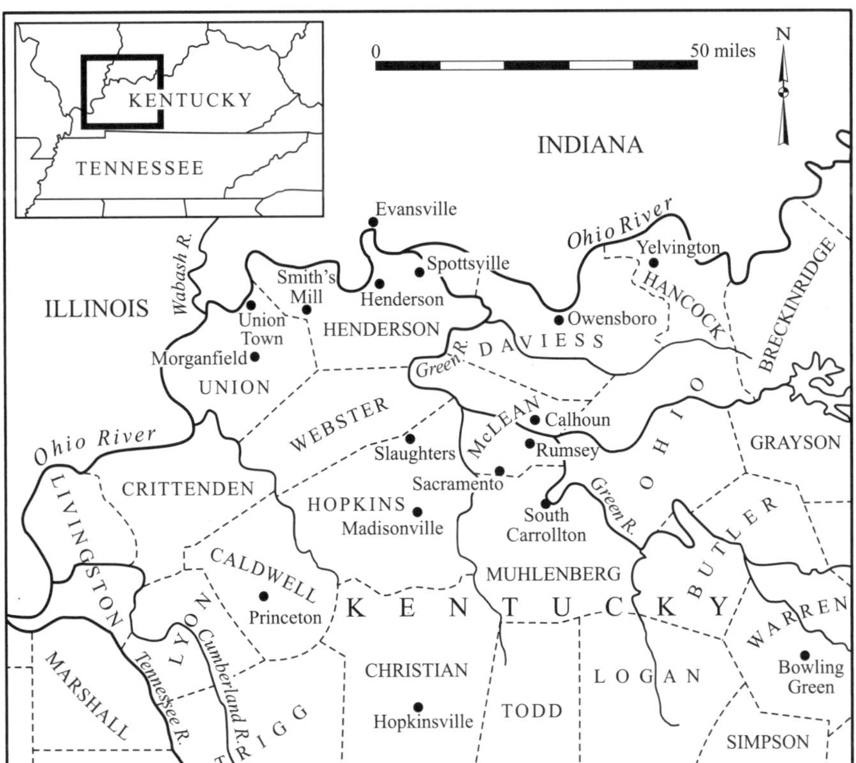

Counties, towns, and key locations in the lower Green River Valley of Kentucky during the Civil War.

close friend, Bob Martin, orders to deliver a coded top-secret message to the very wealthy David Burbank, a Confederate sympathizer in Henderson, and while there to attempt to raise troops for the Confederate cause. Delivering the message was relatively easy, but the enlistment of troops proved much more difficult. While there were many men who were Confederate sympathizers in the Green River country, some of whom had actually served in the Confederate Army and received amnesty following their capture at Fort Donelson, almost none was interested in giving up his peaceful lifestyle in order to follow a relatively unknown soldier. In order to recruit troops, Johnson needed a reputation.[4] He first attacked the provost guard in Henderson in July and followed that up with an audacious raid upon the sleepy town of Newburgh, Indiana, across the Ohio River. Such bold and successful moves accomplished his goal. By late July the newly nicknamed "Stovepipe" Johnson and his band were the toast of the lower Green River valley, at least for those who supported their cause.[5]

Johnson's successes were in no small part due to the fact that there really were no troops in that part of Kentucky who could have opposed him. When Johnson first struck in Henderson, there were hardly any soldiers stationed anywhere in the lower Green River region. The local state militia forces in Kentucky, the Home Guard as they were called, had ceased meeting as the armies moved off to the south. The same was true in Indiana. By mid-1862 the state's militia, the Indiana Legion, which had numbered in the thousands, had become largely nonexistent as few of the actual members were still assembling for training. People's assumption that the war would not return proved fortuitous for Johnson. The residents of Henderson and Newburgh were completely shocked and unprepared for any sort of attack, irregular or otherwise. The same was true farther south in the Green River country at places like Hopkinsville. While small numbers of Union forces had briefly been stationed there, mainly to ensure the victories of Unionist candidates in the state elections of August, for the most part the residents of Hopkinsville, similar to the rest of the Green River region, were on their own and unprepared for an outbreak of guerrilla warfare. That was apparent on the morning of August 16, when Johnson and his men swept into the town at dawn, easily overpowering the surprised Home Guards.[6] Johnson's early successes were not only a result of his own boldness, but also because the Federal military was simply not expecting nor prepared for any sort of serious military outburst in the Green River area. Union commanders were primarily concerned about keeping open the vital Louisville & Nashville Railroad line to the east, frequently harassed by John Morgan, and continuing to control the Tennessee and Cumberland rivers to the west. These were crucial life lines for the advancing Union armies farther south, so that was where the Union military's focus was centered, not a seeming quiet backwater area of Kentucky that had failed to demonstrate any sort of serious antagonistic attitudes toward the Union war effort and lacked any serious strategic importance for the Federal army.

While Johnson certainly enjoyed early success and raised quite a number of willing volunteers in July and August, he soon began to feel pressure as the Union military began reacting. Across the Ohio River in Evansville, brand-new, hastily raised regiments were formed, such as the 76th Indiana Infantry, which arrived in Henderson on July 21. Soon more troops from Indiana arrived, including the 55th, 65th, and 78th Indiana Infantry. Additionally, one of the leading residents of Henderson, James M. Shackelford, raised the 8th Kentucky Cavalry. Farther east, in Owensboro, another already raised regiment, the 15th Kentucky Cavalry, arrived to recruit and train. These troops did not simply sit idly by as Johnson gathered strength. Led by Col. John W. Foster of the 65th Indiana, they began pursuing him, leading to skirmishes at Morganfield, Madisonville, and elsewhere. Following Johnson's attack and capture of the recently raised 78th Indiana and its 255 men at Uniontown on September 1, 1862, Federal forces quickly moved into Union County, rousting out much of Johnson's troops. This was followed some two weeks later by another Union victory near Owensboro, where Johnson's men, commanded by Bob Martin, were defeated at Southerland's Hill. Following these defeats, as well as the failed Confederate invasion of Kentucky farther to the east that culminated in the Union victory at Perryville, Johnson ordered his men to return to their homes while he headed off to Richmond to gain official recognition for his men and regiment. After receiving it, Johnson and his regiment, the 10th Kentucky Partisan Rangers, became part of the Army of Tennessee and for two years served under John Morgan's command, far from the Green River. Johnson himself became a brigade commander. While things did not completely quiet down in the Green River country, with the presence of so many Union troops stationed at all the significant towns and the fact that Johnson had left with those men from the region who were most prone to fight for the Confederate cause (about four hundred of them), things seemed to settle down reasonably well for the remainder of the year. The Pandora's box of irregular warfare, however, had been opened in the region, and it would prove impossible for the Federal military to close it completely for the remainder of the war.[7]

On September 22, 1862, President Lincoln issued the preliminary Emancipation Proclamation. While it transformed the North's war effort from one of simply preserving the Union to one of also ending slavery in the rebel states, it alarmed the people of the lower Green River. Strong Unionists like Ellen Wallace of Hopkinsville wrote in reaction: "Lincoln's proclamation emancipating all the slaves is justly creating great indignation. The consequences of it are too awful to contemplate. The blood of women, children, and helpless aged will flow in torrents if its [*sic*] carried into effect. The vile wretch ought to suffer all the torments that could be inflicted upon him, body and soul. Then [*sic*] to place innocent women and helpless infants at the mercy of black monsters who would walk in human shape."[8]

The Unionist newspaper, the *Owensboro Monitor,* also vented its anger over the "impolitic and ill-timed Proclamation of the President," claiming that "Radicalism and fanaticism now stand at the helm of the Ship of State" and that not only was such an act unconstitutional, it would lead to even more "determined resistance" by the rebelling states and loss of life.[9] While such statements by the *Monitor*'s editor, Henry M. Woodruff, might not seem like outrage, in truth it was. Pro-secessionist newspapers in the area like the *Southern Shield* in Owensboro, the *Uniontown News,* and others had been shut down by the military and the editors arrested for voicing opinions in their papers contrary to the Union cause. Thus, for a strong Union man like Woodruff, even to dare to utter some sort of opposition to the Proclamation in his paper demonstrates the anger that Kentuckians in the region were feeling. Kentuckians' loyalty to the Union had been and still was conditional. As a state, they had refused to support secession and had assumed that President Abraham Lincoln and the U.S. government would do nothing to threaten the institution of slavery. While the Federal government had supported that position early on, as the war continued Lincoln saw his Emancipation Proclamation as an opportunity to strike at the institution he opposed, but he argued publicly that it was really just based upon wartime needs. Depriving the rebellious states of their slaves would economically injure them, thus reducing their capacity to continue to fight. Kentuckians were uninterested in such rhetoric and clearly saw the transformation of the war as the government's betrayal of them. Considering how staunch Unionists like Ellen Wallace and Henry M. Woodruff felt about the Emancipation Proclamation, one can just imagine how the rest of the people of the lower Green River valley, most of whom were at best *conditional* Unionists, felt about it. This sense of betrayal was only magnified when in 1864 Lincoln finally allowed the recruitment of African American soldiers from within the Bluegrass State itself.[10]

During the last few months of 1862 and throughout 1863, the guerrilla struggles within the lower Green River were largely contained. There was an increase in irregular activities in 1863 versus 1862, but due to the presence of large numbers of Union troops in the area, it made it difficult for the Confederates there. All of the main towns in the area—Henderson, Owensboro, Hopkinsville, Madisonville, Morganfield—had garrisons of Federal soldiers. These units were routinely marching off into the countryside in reaction to reported guerrilla activities. This in turn kept the small number of irregulars constantly on the move, denying them safe havens. Thus, while the guerrillas were out there, they were few in number, kept in check, and unable to create any sort of serious problem since the towns were adequately defended. All of that changed in 1864.

In 1864 and continuing into 1865, the lower Green River valley saw an upsurge of irregular activity that never really subsided until the end of the war. That continued chaos led to increasing anarchy throughout the area. There were a number of factors that contributed to it. One of those was the decreased presence of Federal troops in the first half of 1864. Other factors included brief raids by Adam Rankin Johnson and Hylan B. Lyon in 1864, an increasingly abusive Federal government in the minds of Kentuckians, and the arrival and recruitment of African American soldiers in the state itself.

As the winter snows began to melt in early 1864 and the roads began to dry, Gen. William Tecumseh Sherman began gathering more and more troops for his great drive toward Atlanta. Just as Gen. Ulysses S. Grant in the Eastern Theater was culling through the rear echelons for unused and unneeded troops for the big push there, the same was true in the Western Theater. While elements of various regiments had remained, scattered throughout western and central Kentucky during 1863, it was primarily Col. James M. Shackelford's 8th Kentucky Cavalry that defended the region. In September, though, the regiment's enlistment ran out and it was disbanded. At the same time that the 8th was mustered out, Edmund L. Starling of Henderson raised the 35th Kentucky Infantry (a mounted unit, but never given the official title), which was officially mustered into service in Owensboro. It would remain in the state for much of the remainder of the war. While Starling's 35th Kentucky replaced Shackelford's 8th in the Green River country, they found their role becoming more difficult as they watched other units beings shipped south. By early 1864, more and more regiments that had been garrisoning towns throughout the Kentucky were being given orders to join the armies that Sherman had assembled in Chattanooga, Tennessee. While necessary for his campaign, it stretched the abilities of the handfuls of Union forces that remained behind—like Starling's 35th—to their limits, thus providing the opportunity for irregulars to reestablish themselves.[11]

Additionally, many of the residents of Kentucky had become increasingly frustrated by a government that seemed to be betraying the people of the Bluegrass State. Censorship of their newspapers and of course the Emancipation Proclamation were clearly seen as betrayals, but that was followed by further humiliations. When the August 1863 elections in the state were approaching, the Federal government, fearing a massive electoral victory for State's Rights candidates, had issued martial law in the state weeks before and the military commander of much of Kentucky, the hated Gen. Jeremiah T. Boyle, had warned that those casting votes for non-Union party candidates would be arrested. The blatantly fraudulent elections further angered and shocked an already disgruntled population who correctly felt they were being treated as though Kentucky had seceded.[12] In 1864 this sense of betrayal was only intensified. For the first time Kentuckians were subjected to the draft. The thought of being forced into fighting against their Southern brethren upset many Kentuckians who had no desire to support a military and government that not only oppressed them, but also advocated the end of slavery. When regiments of African American troops began arriving in Kentucky, the anger was even greater. Throughout much of the war, Lincoln had worked hard at not upsetting white Kentuckian sensibilities on the issue of the use of African American soldiers or their recruitment in the state. Few things could upset white Southerners more than the presence of armed African Americans on their doorsteps and wearing the blue uniform of the United States Army. Beginning in March 1864, though, that was becoming a horrifying reality for most white Kentuckians. "Lincoln has trodden under foot the laws of our state and usurped entire control," wrote Ellen Wallace, the wife of a planter. "He has made the negro master of the white man as far as his power goes putting arms in their hands."[13] When in September 1864 the first African American regiment arrived to garrison Hopkinsville, she wrote: "the long dreaded event has at last occurred, a company of Negro troops now occupy the town." She went on to state that "The Negroes and the Yankeys [*sic*] are holding one General Jubille" and that the president, "the low born tyrant," was of course the one to blame for the loss of her family's slaves and wealth.[14] No doubt the thoughts that Ellen Wallace put down in her journal were felt by many Kentuckians. Thus, by 1864 there were already a great many factors angering the people of Kentucky, including those in the lower Green River valley.[15]

Beginning in the spring of 1864, guerrilla activity began to pick up. Jake Bennett, formally part of Adam Rankin Johnson's command, seemed to take the lead until his capture in May. Leading a small band of men, he rode throughout the countryside of Henderson, Daviess, Union, Hopkins, and McLean counties. The guerrillas attacked steamboats on the Ohio and Green rivers as well as homes and individuals. While acting as an irregular, Bennett and another guerrilla leader, William Hollis, still operated as regular soldiers and not as out and out bushwhackers. In April, Bennett and his men came across and captured James M. Shackelford near Madisonville as he was traveling to his wedding. While it had been Shackelford who had actually captured Bennett as well as much of John Hunt Morgan's command during his disastrous Ohio raid in 1863, Shackelford had resigned his command in January 1864 and returned to private life, so he was no longer a soldier. While a bushwhacker would have simply hanged or shot Shackelford on the spot, Bennett instead released him.[16] Not all of the irregulars were so inclined as to follow the rules of war. In June, a large band of men rode into Calhoun, robbing and looting the homes of known Unionists. Guerrilla fighting was breaking out everywhere. That same month, twenty-five guerrillas rode into Henderson, robbing a store before walking into a local tavern. There they were confronted with a member of the town's Home Guard, Col. Jim Poole, whom they attempted to take prisoner. In the ensuing scuffle, Poole was shot and died a few days later. Col. Edmund Starling's 35th Kentucky Infantry, while scattered from the Cumberland to the Green River, attempted to counter the growing problem. In early June, he had cornered part of William Hollis's command in Union County, capturing one wounded man. A few weeks later in a skirmish near Slaughters, Hollis fell dead, shot through the head. Yet Starling's regiment alone could not stem the tide of guerrilla activities. In early July, Henderson suffered two raids in one week alone. The first raid was led by a bushwhacker by the name of Anderson whose band of twenty included an African American who claimed loyalty to neither side. After robbing the steamboat *Gen. Halleck,* the raiders were driven off when a Union gunboat moored in the river opposite the town began firing. On July 11, another bushwhacking group, this one led by Dick Yates, rode into Henderson. Numbering roughly twenty-five, they proceeded to destroy the town's telegraph before robbing many of the businesses in the downtown. One of their victims included the prosperous and highly respected James E. Rankin, uncle of Adam Rankin Johnson. They strode into his store, demanding the keys to his safe, which he claimed he did not have. After pistol-whipping him and robbing him of $15 and a pocket watch, one of the guerrillas shot Rankin through the neck, "the ball entering one side of his neck, passing through the wind pipe and coming out at the front of the shoulder."[17] Although surviving the gunshot initially, a few days later he suffered a coughing fit that reopened the wound, causing him to bleed to death. In retaliation, the local Union commander executed two Confederate guerrillas from Yate's band who had been captured days earlier in Daviess County. Throughout the region the residents worried about this outbreak of irregular activity and the Union military's inability or unwillingness to do anything about it.[18]

In the midst of this growing crisis, Adam Rankin Johnson returned home. For almost two years he had commanded a brigade of Confederate cavalry in John Hunt Morgan's division. Only Johnson and a handful of others had managed to escape capture the previous summer during Morgan's Ohio raid, and for the next several months afterwards Johnson rebuilt the shattered division. In June 1864, Johnson received orders to take a small band of his men and return to the Green River country. Two of his orders were to raise troops and create as much of a ruckus as possible, hopefully preventing or at least delaying Gen. William G. Burbridge's planned attack upon Saltville, Virginia, and its valuable salt mines. Johnson's third and top secret order was to aid the Sons of Liberty of Indiana and Illinois in a far-fetched plan to attack two prisoner-of-war camps in the North—Camp Douglas and Camp Morton—thus freeing several thousand Confederate soldiers who, it was hoped, would then cause even more trouble. It was thought that these actions would force Grant or Sherman to send soldiers to the Midwest, thus disrupting their campaigns. When Johnson arrived, he called on the young men of Kentucky to rally to his banner:

> Your country has been overrun by lawless bands, whose depredations are only equaled by the outrages of large bands of the Federal army, who neither feel nor have any respect for submissionists, and you are plundered and robbed and murdered with impunity. How long do you intend this to continue? To what depth of degradation and shame are you to be reduced before you will cut loose the bond of slavery and assert your rights as freemen of Kentucky? Are you willing to see your families reduced to the level of your slaves? Mothers, can you realize an affiliation of your daughters to the African? Young men, can you expect to have any claim to

> manhood? Can you hope to share the smile or claim the love of the bright-eyed daughters of this famed land of beauty, while those gentle beings are subjected to the insults of Yankee hirelings and negro [*sic*] troops?[19]

Within weeks Johnson's band had quickly swelled to well above a thousand men both through volunteering and conscription.[20] At a prearranged date, Johnson was to take his men across the Ohio River at Newburgh, Indiana, there meeting with some of the Sons of Liberty. From there he would seize Evansville before advancing north. The rather ridiculous plot, however, never came to fruition. His presence and the numbers he was quickly raising did not go unnoticed by Federal commanders. Gen. Edward Hobson, with over three thousand men, rapidly advanced from Elizabethtown some eighty miles to the east to deal with Johnson, while others were preparing to move west from Paducah and Smithland.

Even before the arrival of Hobson and his troops, Johnson had begun to feel the pressure. Within days after his arrival in Henderson and Union counties, more than a thousand Federal troops, largely Indiana veterans from Evansville and Mount Vernon, Indiana, plus a battery of twelve-pounders, boarded steamboats bound for Uniontown. Just as he had in July 1862, Johnson was attempting to use Union County as a base of operations. Knowing this, Union leaders were determined to deny it to him. Troops commanded by Gen. Alvin P. Hovey landed at both Uniontown and Caseyville on August 17 and swept through the county, engaging handfuls of Johnson's command in such places as White Oak Springs south of Morganfield and Geiger's Lake. While Johnson managed largely to avoid confronting the Union troops, on August 18, Hobson's mounted infantry, including Edmund Starling's 35th Kentucky Infantry, began arriving at Calhoun on the Green River and crossing. Confronted with such overwhelming numbers from three directions that moved far more quickly than anything Johnson had anticipated, he began retreating to the southwest, hoping to put the Cumberland River between himself and the advancing Federal troops. As he withdrew, he stumbled across the numerically inferior 52d Kentucky Infantry, which numbered perhaps three hundred men, at a place called Grubb's Crossroads near the town of Princeton. While Johnson could have easily avoided them, he saw an easy victory. Plus, many of his new recruits were unarmed and in need of weapons like the ones that soldiers of the 52d were carrying. Within minutes of the attack, the Union regiment was in chaos, attempting to flee this way and that. It was at that moment that a bullet tore through Johnson's right eye and exited through his left temple, leaving him alive but completely and permanently blind. Johnson ordered his men to flee to the west while he himself was left at a nearby farm owned by Garland Simms. The following day General Hobson walked into the farmhouse and, seeing the severity of Johnson's wound, gave him his parole. As soon as he was able, Johnson was to make his way to Henderson and turn himself over to Union authorities, which he would do.[21]

With Johnson's defeat, any sort of remaining regular Confederate presence in the lower Green River region was lost. The area now crawled with armed men, many of whom had been in Johnson's force. Unable to return home for fear of being arrested, they roamed the countryside.[22] To make matters worse for the people of the Green River, Union forces under Hobson had returned to Elizabethtown to participate in General Boyle's advance east upon Saltville, Virginia. Thus, the region was once again denuded of a strong Federal military presence. Troops were sent, just not in the numbers or the type wanted by the locals. The 108th U. S. Colored Infantry, commanded by Col. John S. Bishop, arrived in Henderson on August 8, and established a fortified camp outside of town on a bluff overlooking the Ohio. The presence of African American soldiers worried many of the residents of the town, not so much out of fear of what the soldiers might do, but rather the reaction from the guerrillas. Fearing a massacre upon the citizens in retaliation, as well as hoping to avoid Johnson's conscription going on at the time, many fled, mainly across the river to Evansville.[23] Many towns in the region became depopulated as the guerrilla menace escalated. In early August, numerous residents of Hopkinsville fled when the company of soldiers who had been garrisoning the town marched off. Several days later a band of bushwhackers rode into town. While driven out by the local Home Guard, they still managed to acquire several horses.[24] The local newspapers were constantly running articles about bands of guerrillas robbing someone or other in the country and riding into small towns like Curdsville "load[ing] himself with dry goods from the stores, and obtained [money] from safes which opened at his bidding."[25] In September, guerrillas and the local Home Guard clashed in Woodbury, and the *Monitor* reported how the whole area was infested with rebels. In Hawesville, a band robbed stores of money and goods. Guerrillas struck Hebbardsville, stealing from stores and individuals from that town to nearly the outskirts of Owensboro, several miles away. Individuals traveling down country roads were accosted on an almost daily basis it seemed. Tap Maddux, a deputy sheriff of Daviess County, was attacked and almost hanged before the guerrillas decided to just leave him alive with the noose still around his neck. Guerrillas boarded the steamboat, the *Cottage,* as it was tied up to the wharf at Spottsville and stole $2,500 from the boat and its passengers. The Farmers Bank on the corner of Second and Elm streets in Henderson was robbed of $8,000, including $2,000 in gold. Another band rode into Henderson on October 30 and, before being chased off by the gunboat *Moose,* tore down an American flag and tied it to the tail of one of their horses. The stories of such incidents were never ending.[26] Towns were turned into makeshift forts by Union forces who arrived suddenly out of the blue and then departed just as suddenly. Colonel Bishop's African American regiment, who had so shocked the residents of Henderson with their arrival on August 4, stayed only two days before moving by steamboat to Owensboro, where they not only established headquarters in the county courthouse, but turned the building and the surrounding grounds into a fort. The courthouse, a recently constructed building and a point of pride throughout the county, was drastically transformed. The soldiers cut firing holes into the doors and used the wooden furniture as well as the wooden plank fence outside to board up the lower story windows. They also established crude breastworks outside. Within hours the brick building had become a formidable defensive position, especially against small bands of lightly armed bushwhackers. The troops, though, did not merely stay in their fort. Elements of the regiment were constantly patrolling throughout Daviess County, as well as the surrounding area, in search of guerrillas, engaging them in places like Yelvington, the "Charleston of Kentucky."[27] At the same time, these African American troops were actively recruiting. Hundreds of enslaved black men in the Green River country found their path to freedom by putting on the blue uniform, much to the consternation of white Kentuckians. Such actions—both the fortifying of courthouses and the like, and the recruitment of African Americans—were becoming the norm throughout the valley.[28]

On August 26, two days after the 108th U.S. Colored Infantry had departed Owensboro for Louisville, Jake Bennett's band of bushwhackers raided the town. Bennett, who had been captured in May and subsequently escaped, seemed less and less a regular soldier and more and more a guerrilla during the latter half of 1864. He and his men rode down Frederica Street, stopping in front of the courthouse, firing their guns in the air, and terrifying the townspeople. After rounding up some two hundred to three hundred residents, Bennett informed them that he was going to burn down the courthouse due to its use by African American troops. He also stated his intention of robbing all the banks and burning them as well. A number of leading citizens, though, were able to dissuade the guerrilla leader from destroying their town's buildings or robbing any of their banks. Some of his men did loot a few stores of valuables, including watches and saddles, before Bennett put a stop to it, and they set fire to a boat at the docks. The guerrillas wanted to destroy the boat because nine African American soldiers who were in town at the time of the raid were hiding in the boat. Two of the men were shot as they tried to flee, while three others managed to escape by jumping into the water and scampering up a nearby embankment. Four of the soldiers, though, were trapped inside the boat when it was set afire. After Bennett's men had left, the owner of the boat used an ax to hack open the blazing vessel, thus saving their lives. Soon after Bennett and his band had ridden off, Jim Wilson of Calhoun rode into town. A gifted guerrilla hunter, largely because he acted like one, and commander of the Daviess County militia, Wilson, upon hearing that a citizen of Owensboro during the raid had cheered for Jefferson Davis, sought the man out and shot him down before riding off in pursuit of Bennett and his men.[29] Wilson failed to catch up with the guerrillas, who struck off for Lewisport to the east, and made an attack upon Hartford, where he and his men "plundered indiscriminately," robbing the people there of more than $1,100.[30]

This pattern continued for the remainder of the war. Union troops, frequently African American units, would arrive in a given town and remain for anywhere from a few days to a few weeks. From there they would send out patrols to where guerrillas were or had been. While such tactics had worked rather well in 1862 and 1863, by 1864 the situation had changed. Previously there had been just handfuls of irregulars scattered throughout the Green River country, for the most part probably numbering little more than a one or two hundred at any given time and operating in small groups. But in 1864 the numbers were much greater than ever before, especially by the summer. The Union forces were just too few in number and normally on foot. The countryside was the domain of the mounted guerrillas, who all too often were becoming far more interested in preying upon defenseless civilians than engaging regular troops. Additionally, once those regular troops had left the town they had been guarding, the guerrillas went back there, too. For the people of the region, no place was assuredly safe. For example, an African American regiment, the 118th U.S. Colored Infantry, had arrived in Owensboro in September and remained some weeks before shipping off to Louisville aboard the *Morning Star.* Within days after their departure, twenty-five guerrillas rode into the town, relieving the stores there of some $4,500 in goods and abducting a number of prominent residents of Owensboro, including the county sheriff, whom they later released. Soon after their departure, another band of irregulars rode into town and remained in the city for two weeks. They too left when a regiment of soldiers, yet again African American, arrived. Those soldiers in turn reoccupied the courthouse.[31]

The only change in the pattern occurred in December when Confederate Gen. Hylan B. Lyon passed through the region. As Gen. John Bell Hood and the Army of Tennessee began its ill-fated march north into Tennessee that would result in the battles of Franklin and Nashville, Lyon received orders to capture Clarksville, Tennessee. Lyon, having taken command of the remnants of Adam Rankin Johnson's troops, set out in early December on his expedition. Finding Clarksville far too strong to attack, he instead swung north to weakly defended Hopkinsville, easily chasing off the African American garrison there, much to the delight of many of its residents, including even former Unionists who were weary of being occupied and ruled by African American soldiers: "To day [*sic*] at 1 o'clock the southern troops two thousand strong with four pieces of cannon took possession of the town. Oh how our hearts leaped for joy at the sight, after being subjected to Negro bayonets and black republican outrages. I could not refrain from weeping as I saw the brave heroes, half clad and half frozen pass, with a song of defiance on their lips, to their northern foes, who well fed and well clad had fled on their approach with their black hords [*sic*]."[32]

Once in Hopkinsville, Lyon sent out troops to nearby towns like Princeton and Cadiz, where the surprised and outnumbered Union forces also fled. Since it had been African American troops who had not only garrisoned those towns, but also fortified the courthouses there, Lyon burned those courthouses, as well as the one in Hopkinsville. His troops also robbed several stores in the town and the local bank. As Lyon destroyed these public buildings, Union cavalry, under the command of Gen. Edward M. McCook, began pursuing him. On December 16, a sharp fight occurred outside of Hopkinsville, forcing Lyon to retreat north. At Madisonville, Lyon stopped and set fire to the county courthouse there before heading east across Hopkins County. Lyon's men began crossing the Green River at Ashbyburg (also known as Ashby's Ferry), but just as the lead elements of his eight hundred men began to cross, Union forces arrived. Caught with his back to the river, Lyon made a delaying attack that slowed the Union advance long enough for the Confederate troops to escape. At Hartford, the county seat of Ohio County, yet another courthouse fell prey to Lyon's incendiary ways. Afterwards, Lyon continued to the east, destroying part of the Louisville & Nashville Railroad before heading to the south. It was at that time in late December, near Elizabethtown, that Lyon's men heard of Hood's terrible defeat at

Nashville. According to Lyon, some five hundred of his men deserted upon hearing the news, many of them undoubtedly making their way back to the Green River country, adding to the numbers of irregulars already roaming the countryside. Thus, by the end of the year, there were literally hundreds of men who simply could not return home and resume their civilian lives. Indeed, returning home really was not an option. Everyone in their communities knew what they had done, so back home they faced either imprisonment and/or execution for being a guerrilla. Although armed, these men were at best poorly trained and frequently under no military discipline or control at all. They were operating in a no-man's-land in a region where for months the civil and military authorities had been unsuccessful in establishing any sort of civil or military control. Worst of all, these men were desperate.[33]

Following Lyon's raid, guerrillas resumed their predatory ways. One band, led by Bill Davidson, seized the steamboat *Morning Star* at Lewisport. Almost all the Union soldiers who were on the boat jumped overboard to escape, and all, except one, drowned. One soldier was caught by Davidson's men, who riddled him with bullets before finishing him off with a point-blank shot to the head. Among Davidson's men was the six-feet six-inch Isaac Colter, who reputedly cut off the ears of all the black soldiers he killed and carried the grisly trophies in a little bag. These bushwhackers were not the only ones plaguing the region. On the morning of January 4, 1865, Davidson's gang rode into undefended Owensboro. Originally, Davidson intended to burn not only the courthouse, but also the Planter's Hotel and the homes of several known Unionists; however, he was convinced merely to set fire to the courthouse. That evening, after the records had been removed, he set fire to the building. The next day a steamboat carrying the 118th U.S. Colored Infantry arrived from Henderson, causing Davidson to flee. Unable to defend both towns, the 118th returned to Henderson, whereupon Davidson rode back into Owensboro, ordering the town to pay him $400. When the town's leaders refused, he unleashed his men, who proceeded to plunder the businesses of Owensboro of some $2,000 in goods. Again, Davidson's men fled from town when on January 11, the steamboat *Grey Eagle* arrived, carrying men of the 27th Kentucky Infantry.[34]

While Davidson was clearly a bushwhacker, not all the irregulars behaved as such. Some considered themselves part of the regular Confederate Army and refused to attack anyone or anything that was not a military target. This led to occasional clashes in the countryside between the various irregular units. Following the disintegration of Lyon's command, many of the men who had either volunteered or been conscripted into service in the Green River country began returning. Among those was Maj. Walker Taylor. Taylor was able to maintain control over his men and, recognizing bushwhackers like Davidson and his ilk for what they were—predators—would attack them. Although it is unknown, Taylor's presence may very well have had a positive influence in curbing the potential destructiveness of some of the more dangerous irregular bands who, if given free reign, could have caused even more mayhem than they did in the Green River country during the last few months of the war.[35]

While Taylor's influence cannot be fully determined, it is clear that during the months of February and March 1865, more and more Union troops were arriving in the area. While some, like the 118th U.S. Colored Infantry, were being sent by the government to help reestablish order, others were being recruited. In Henderson a new African American regiment, the 120th U.S. Colored Infantry, was being raised and trained by Lt. Col. John Glenn. Not insignificantly, hundreds of other veteran Federal soldiers were beginning to return home as their enlistments had expired. Thus, there were increasing numbers of men in the Green River country, whether current or former soldiers, capable and willing to defending their communities.[36]

Despite the increased presence of Federal troops in the Green River country, in early 1865 the irregulars were still causing problems. The guerrillas continued to operate on the fringes, carrying out quick raids, often by very small groups who would ride into a town with guns blazing, seeking some sort of quick score, and then rushing back out before the soldiers or Home Guard could react. For example, one group of guerrillas attempted to sneak into the town of Henderson with the goal of abducting Colonel Glenn, most likely intending to kill him. Their efforts were thwarted because they could not get near his headquarters due to the presence of so many soldiers. Throughout the countryside the guerrillas continued to rule. In January, Sheriff Henry C. Kerr of Henderson County was accosted and relieved of $90, his revolver, and his saddlebags. Undoubtedly, Sheriff Kerr considered himself fortunate to part with those items and remain alive. Falling into the hands of the wrong group of irregulars could easily result in death. A guerrilla band led by Ollie Steele operated out of western Henderson County and Union County. These men watched the roads, waiting to ambush unwary Federal soldiers or simply an unfortunate civilian. Of course, the Federals were pursuing the bushwhackers, and clashes were common throughout the region. Glenn's soldiers captured six guerrillas in a canebrake in far-eastern Henderson County in a place known as the Bend. Just days afterwards, Glenn's men executed the six and buried them in a mass grave. Such swift justice was commonplace.[37]

March 1865 seemed to be the tipping point for the irregulars. Throughout the month, more and more irregulars began turning themselves in to Union authorities. In many cases the men were simply allowed to take the oath of allegiance and return home, while others were taken prisoner and held for a short period. Not all were treated so kindly. John Wathan was believed to have been part of a guerrilla band who in September 1864 had hanged an African American soldier recovering from an illness. When Wathan attempted to surrender in March 1865, a squad of black soldiers seized him, knocked him to the ground with their rifle butts, and fired several shots into the man, killing him. Over the next few months the remaining irregulars, for the most part, turned themselves in and peace began returning to the people of the lower Green River.[38]

The hard hand of the Civil War had touched the Green River country of Kentucky. The burned-out husk of the Daviess County Courthouse in Owensboro was an obvious reminder to the residents there of how the conflict had affected them. Residents of Hopkinsville, Princeton, Cadiz, and Hartford, too, had watched their courthouses—visible signs of civil authority and control—destroyed by the chaos of the conflict that had raged within their midst. While the people in those towns had originally hoped to avoid conflict by refusing to take sides in 1861, they were still affected by the war. They watched the war in their region transform into a bloody, ruthless irregular conflict during 1861 and 1862, unleashed by the arrival of Adam Rankin Johnson. Small bands of guerrillas rode through the countryside, wreaking havoc and causing damage and death. However, the destructive potential of the guerrillas was largely contained in 1862 and 1863 due to the presence of so many Federal soldiers, the small numbers of irregulars involved, and the fact that when Johnson left, he took with him those men most willing to fight for the Confederate cause. However, as the number of Union troops in the area diminished along with the actions of the Federal government, which further alienated and betrayed a population of citizens, irregular warfare in the region exploded in 1864. Federal forces were clearly unprepared and slow to respond to the sheer number of guerrillas suddenly operating in the Green River and, for that matter, throughout the state. For most of the year the area spiraled down into almost complete anarchy, with many residents simply fleeing to safer areas like Evansville, and in the process abandoning homes, farms, and towns. Perhaps it was only the arrival of Adam Rankin Johnson's regular forces in the summer of 1864 that prompted the Union military into responding adequately to the threat. In December 1864 increasing numbers of Federal troops arrived in Green River country. Their presence, coupled with the fact that the war was clearly winding down, seemed to break the spirit of the irregulars, who in March began to lay down their arms and surrender. For the last two years of the war the local newspapers had regularly reported the actions of the guerrillas throughout the region, but in June 1865 the big news in the *Henderson Weekly Reporter* was: "Our city was the scene of considerable excitement yesterday morning. A dog was loose in the community. Several persons imagined the dog was afflicted with the hydrophobia. Several citizens and one or two soldiers severally fired several pistol shots at the unfortunate canine, and very severely *missed* him—Twenty or thirty shots were fired, and the dog only slightly wounded in three places. A shooting gallery is needed in this city. In this connection we would remind authorities that there are too many dogs in the city."[39]

By June 1865, the biggest story of the week in Green River country was about an afflicted dog on the loose. The Civil War and the guerrilla menace it had spawned in the lower Green River country had ended.

Notes

1. *History of Daviess County Kentucky Together with Sketches of Its Cities, Villages, and Townships, Educational, Religious, Civil, Military, and Political History; Portraits of Prominent Persons, Biographies of Representative Citizens and an Outline History of Kentucky* (Chicago: Inter-State Publishing, 1883), 175–76; Glen Hodges, "Bill Davidson's Owensboro Raid," *Daviess County Historical Quarterly* 4 (Apr. 1986): 38; Daviess County Court Order Book, Aug. 8, 1864. The last several years have seen a great expansion in the study of the irregular aspects of the American Civil War. The best and most all-encompassing is Daniel E. Sutherland's *A Savage Conflict: The Decisive Role of Guerrillas in the American Civil War* (Chapel Hill: Univ. of North Carolina Press, 2009). Sutherland's "Sideshow No Longer: A Historiographical Review of Guerrilla War," *Civil War History* 46 (Spring 2000): 5–23, provides a historiographical treatment of the subject as well as James A. Ramage's more recent "Recent Historiography of Guerrilla Warfare in the Civil War—a Review Essay," *Register of the Kentucky Historical Society* 102 (Spring 2000): 517–42. Earlier studies that at least seriously touched on the topic include Jay Monaghan, *Civil War on the Western Border, 1854–1865* (Boston: Little & Brown, 1955); Virgil C. Jones, *Gray Ghosts and Rebel Raiders: The Daring Exploits of the Confederate Guerrillas* (New York: Holt, 1956); Richard S. Brownlee, *Gray Ghosts of the Confederacy: Guerrilla Warfare in*

the West, 1861–1865 (Baton Rouge: Louisiana State Univ. Press, 1958); Albert Castel, *A Frontier State at War: Kansas, 1861–1865* (Ithaca, N. Y.: Cornell Univ. Press, 1958). More recent studies include: Phillip Shaw Paludan, *Victims: A True Story of the Civil War* (Knoxville: Univ. of Tennessee Press, 1981); Michael Fellman, *Inside War: The Guerrilla Conflict in Missouri during the American Civil War* (New York: Oxford Univ. Press, 1989); Mark Grimsely, *Hard Hand of War: Union Military Policy toward Southern Civilians, 1861–1865* (New York: Cambridge Univ. Press, 1995); Stephen Ash, *When the Yankees Came: Conflict & Chaos in the Occupied South, 1861–1865* (Chapel Hill: Univ. of North Carolina Press, 1995); Thomas Goodrich, *Black Flag: Guerrilla Warfare on the Western Border, 1861*–1865 (Bloomington: Indiana Univ. Press, 1995); Daniel Sutherland, ed., *Guerrillas, Unionists, and Violence on the Confederate Home Front* (Fayetteville: Univ. of Arkansas Press, 1999); Robert R. Mackey, *The UNcivil War: Irregular Warfare in the Upper South, 1861–1865* (Norman: Univ. of Oklahoma Press, 2004). There is also a growing historiography on irregular conflict within Kentucky itself that cannot be fully presented here, but includes: Louis De Falaise, "General Stephen Gano Burbridge's Command in Kentucky," *Register of the Kentucky Historical Society* 69 (1971): 101–27; James A. Ramage, *Rebel Raider: The Life of General John Hunt Morgan* (Lexington: Univ. of Kentucky Press, 1986); James B. Martin, "Black Flag over the Bluegrass: Guerrilla Warfare in Kentucky, 1863–1865," *Register of the Kentucky Historical Society* 86 (1988): 352–75; Benjamin Frank Cooling, *Fort Donelson's Legacy: War and Society in Kentucky and Tennessee, 1862–1865* (Knoxville: Univ. of Tennessee Press, 1997); Brian D. McKnight, *Contested Borderland: The Civil War in Appalachian Kentucky and Virginia* (Lexington: Univ. of Kentucky Press, 2006); Betty J. Gorin, *Morgan Is Coming! Confederate Raiders in the Heartland of Kentucky* (Louisville, Ky.: Harmony House, 2006).

2. The two primary published studies on the state of Kentucky during the Civil War are Thomas Speed's, *The Union Cause in Kentucky, 1860–1865* (New York: G. P. Putnam's Sons, 1907), and E. Merton Coulter's, *The Civil War and Readjustment in Kentucky* (Chapel Hill: Univ. of North Carolina Press, 1926). Lowell Harrison's *The Civil War in Kentucky* (Lexington: Univ. Press of Kentucky, 1975) is a brief overview of the war, but primarily focuses on the battles of Mills Springs and Perryville, which are examined in a somewhat cursory manner. While Speed's and Coulter's works discuss the secession crisis and Kentucky's efforts at neutrality, three dissertations have even more thoroughly examined the topics. John Alan Boyd, "Neutrality and Peace: Kentucky and the Secession Crisis of 1861" (Ph.D. diss., Univ. of Kentucky, 1999); James W. Finck, "The Secession Movement in Kentucky, 1860–1861" (Ph.D. diss., Univ. of Arkansas, 2008); Harry A. Volz III, "Party, State, and Nation: Kentucky and the Coming of the Civil War" (Ph.D. diss., Univ. of Virginia, 2007). Finck's dissertation has recently been published as *Divided Loyalties: Kentucky's Struggle for Armed Neutrality in the Civil War* (El Dorado Hills, Calif.: Savas Beatie, 2012); Ulysses S. Grant, *Personal Memoirs of Ulysses S. Grant* (Old Saybrook, Conn.: Konecky and Konecky, 1885), 218; Thomas L. Connelly, *Army of the Heartland: The Army of Tennessee, 1861–1865* (Baton Rouge: Louisiana State Univ. Press, 1967), 55–59; James M. McPherson, *Battle Cry of Freedom: The Civil War Era* (New York: Ballantine, 1988), 296–97; John H. Parks, *General Leonidas Polk, C.S.A.: The Fighting Bishop* (Baton Rouge: Louisiana State Univ. Press, 1962), 180; United States War Department, *War of the Rebellion:*

A Compilation of the Official Records of the Union and Confederate Armies (Washington, D.C.: Government Printing Office, 1880–1901), ser. 1, vol. 4, Leonidas Polk to Beriah Magoffin, Sept. 8, 1861, 185 (hereafter cited as *OR*).

3. The four locks and dams on the Green River were not only of economic importance of the people in the area, but also of local strategic importance in 1861 and early 1862. Those locks on the Green and Barren rivers made them not only navigable, but within the context of the war, invasion routes that the Union could use to threaten the center of the Confederate lines at Bowling Green. To prevent that, Confederate forces had destroyed locks Number Three and Four. Thus Crittenden's encampment at Calhoun was meant to prevent the destruction of Lock Number Two and prevent a Confederate strike at Lock Number One a few miles to the north at Spottsville. *OR,* ser. 1, vol. 4, Simon B. Buckner to W. W. Mackall, Oct. 4, 1861, 201; Ellen K. Wallace Papers, Ellen K. Wallace journal, Sept. 30, 1861, Frankfort, Ky., Kentucky Historical Society; *OR,* ser.1, vol. 4, James S. Jackson to William T. Sherman, Oct. 8, 1861, 298; ibid., Oliver D. Greene to Thomas L. Crittenden, Oct. 8, 1861, 299; ibid., A. L. Alcorn to Simon Buckner, Oct. 19, 1861, 463–65; ibid., ser.1, vol. 7; Nathan Bedford Forrest to Charles Clark, Dec. 30, 1861, 64–66; ibid., Thomas L. Crittenden to Don Carlos Buell, Dec. 30, 1861, 62–63; ibid., Jan. 3, 1862, 63; Adam Rankin Johnson, *Partisan Rangers of the Confederate States Army* (Austin, Tex.: State House Press, 1995), 42; Kentucky Department for Libraries and Archives, Public Records Division, *Report of the Adjutant General of the State of Kentucky 1861–1865* (Frankfort: Kentucky Yeoman Office, 1866); *OR,* ser.1, vol. 4, Reports on skirmishes at and near Woodbury and Morgantown, Ky., 219–26; ibid., ser. 1, vol. 7, 1; The leading and best work on the campaign revolving around forts Henry and Donelson and their importance is by Benjamin F. Cooling, *Forts Henry and Donelson: The Key to the Confederate Heartland* (Knoxville: Univ. of Tennessee Press, 1987).

4. Adam Rankin Johnson did not leave any sort of written records contemporary to his time during the Civil War; instead he had written (Johnson was blinded during the war) his memoirs, which were originally published in 1904. While of great value, they are based upon memories of events, dates, and people from thirty years in the past, and in the book Johnson and his men tend to come off more as Robin Hood and his Merry Men, so the reader must be wary. Johnson, *Partisan Rangers,* 1–43, 82–94.

5. As a result of Johnson's attack upon Newburgh, newspapers nicknamed him "Stovepipe" because he had bluffed the Newburgh militiamen into not resisting his little band because of the "cannons" across the river promising destruction. In fact, the cannons were nothing more than an old charred log and a stovepipe laid across wagon axles. Apparently "Stovepipe" sang more than "Old Charred Log" Johnson for the reporters. No doubt Johnson preferred that name over "Hospital Robber," which had just recently been applied to his name by the Evansville newspaper the *Daily Journal,* "Hospital Robber." Johnson, *Partisan Rangers,* 95–96, 104–8; *Henderson Weekly Reporter,* July 3, 1862; Ray Mulseky, *Thunder from a Clear Sky: Stovepipe Johnson's Confederate Raid on Newburgh, Indiana* (New York: Universe Star, 2005), 3–86.

6. Johnson, *Partisan Rangers,* 112; Ellen K. Wallace journal, Aug. 16, 1862, *Indiana Legion: Reports of Brigade and Regimental Officers,* Allen County Library, 19, 25, 30.

7. *Evansville Daily Journal,* July 26, 30, 31, 1862; George Washington Smith Papers, George Washington Smith diary, Aug. 2, 1862, Special Collections, Margaret I. King Library, University of Kentucky; Edmund L. Starling, *History of Henderson County, Kentucky: Comprising the History of County and City, Precincts, Education, Churches, Secret Societies, Leading Enterprises, Sketches, and Recollections, and Biographies of the Living and the Dead* (Henderson, Ky.: n.p., 1887), 748; Thomas Speed, "The Civil War Memoirs of Captain Thomas Speed," ed. James R. Bentley, *Filson Club History Quarterly* 44 (1970): 238–44; *History of Daviess County,* 161–63; Johnson, *Partisan Rangers,* 123; Richard Gildre argues within his article "Guerrilla Warfare in the Lower Cumberland River Valley," that most irregulars attempted to set up "sanctuaries" and Johnson's sanctuary was Union County. Richard Gildre, "Guerrilla Warfare in the Lower Cumberland River Valley, 1862–1865," *Tennessee Historical Quarterly* 49 (Fall 1990): 166–67.

8. Victor B. Howard, "Lincoln Slave Policy in Kentucky: A Study of Pragmatic Strategy," *The Register of the Kentucky Historical Society* 80 (Summer 1982): 299–301; Ellen K. Wallace journal, Sept. 29, 1862.

9. *Owensboro Monitor,* Oct. 1, 1862.

10. Ibid., Aug. 12, 1862; *Henderson Weekly Reporter,* Aug. 28, 1862; *OR,* Proclamation and Resolutions of the State of Kentucky, 288. The leading study on the evolution of the Federal government's move toward utilizing Union troops as well as their use during the Civil War is still Dudley T. Cornish's *The Sable Arm: Black Troops in the Union Army, 1861–1865* (Lawrence: Univ. of Kansas Press, 1987); Coulter, *The Civil War and Readjustment,* 197–206; Marion B. Lucas, *A History of Blacks in Kentucky: From Slavery to Segregation, 1760–1891* (Frankfort: Kentucky Historical Society, 1992), 151–60.

11. *Report of the Adjutant General of the State of Kentucky.* Gildre argues that the increase in irregular activities beginning in the spring of 1864 was due to plans for a Confederate offensive into the region and their need to recruit. While there clearly is some truth to that, Gildre is looking at irregular warfare and its ebbs and flows from a purely military context. Looking at the topic through such a prism can be somewhat limiting in that it ignores more local issues that might spur such actions. More recent studies by historians like Fellman, Ash, and Sutherland attempt to examine the reasons behind irregular warfare beyond the purely military perspective. Gildre, "Guerrilla Warfare in the Lower Cumberland Valley," 170–73.

12. This sort of sentiment can be seen in the personal diary of George Washington Smith, who on the day of the election wrote: "Went to the election this morning and cast my vote . . . when but sixteen men had the privilege of freeman [*sic*] the privilege which we once exercised unawed [*sic*] and unmolested of voting for the men of our choice the election was stopped by military orders and the poll book taken. . . . Ky no doubt deserves this and worse treatment we have tamely bent our necks to the yoke and invited this despotism by a base truckling to power." George Washington Smith diary, Aug. 3, 1863.

13. Cornish, *The Sable Arm;* Coulter, *The Civil War and Readjustment,* 197–206; Lucas, *A History of Blacks in Kentucky,* 151–60; Ellen K. Wallace journal, Sept. 25, 1863.

14. Ellen K. Wallace journal, Sept. 22, 1863; Howard, "Lincoln Slave Policy in Ken-

tucky," 301–3; John David Smith, "The Recruitment of Negro Soldiers in Kentucky, 1863–1865," *The Register of the Kentucky Historical Society* 72 (Oct. 1974): 364–90.

15. The leading study on how Southern civilians in the Confederacy dealt with being conquered and occupied by the invading Union armies is Stephen Ash's *When the Yankees Came.* While Kentucky never seceded, it was to a great degree still treated by Federal authorities as a seceded state, thus many of the ideas that Ash puts forth within his book are applicable. Ash, *When the Yankees Came,* 42–75, 99, 149–69; Benjamin Cooling, "A People's War: Partisan Conflict in Tennessee and Kentucky," in Sutherland, ed., *Guerrillas, Unionists, and Violence on the Confederate Home Front,* 113–32.

16. Johnson, *Partisan Rangers,* 227–78, *Evansville Daily Journal,* Apr. 6, 18, 1864; *Henderson Weekly Reporter,* Apr. 21, 1864.

17. *Henderson Weekly Reporter,* July 14, 1864, and June 29, 1864; Johnson, *Partisan Rangers,* 298–300; Starling, *History of Henderson County,* 214–15; George Washington Smith diary, July 12, 1864.

18. *Henderson Weekly Reporter,* July 28, 1864.

19. *OR,* ser. 1, vol. 39, pt. 1, Report of Alvin P. Hovey to Lorenzo Thomas, 465–67; ibid., Reports of Edward H. Hobson, 487; Johnson, *Partisan Rangers,* 163–80.

20. George Washington Smith diary, Aug. 16, 1864.

21. Ibid., Aug. 19, 1864; *Evansville Daily Journal,* Aug. 23, 27, 1864; ibid., Sept. 1, 1864; Starling, *History of Henderson County,* 717; *OR,* ser.1, vol. 39, pt. 1, Reports of Edward H. Hobson, Aug. 23, 1864, 487, Johnson, *Partisan Rangers,* 173–83.

22. *Owensboro Monitor,* Oct. 19, 1864; Gildre, "Guerrilla Warfare in the Lower Cumberland River Valley," 173.

23. *Evansville Daily Journal,* Aug. 6, 1864; Starling, *History of Henderson County,* 213, 217; George Washington Smith diary, Aug. 15, 1864.

24. Ellen K. Wallace journal, Aug. 7, 19, 1864.

25. Ibid., Aug. 7, 19, 1864; *Owensboro Monitor,* Aug. 3, 1864.

26. Ibid., Aug. 31, Sept. 14, Oct. 12, 1864.

27. Ibid., Aug. 17, 24, 1864.

28. Ibid., Aug. 24, 1864; George Washington Smith diary, Oct. 30, 1864.

29. *History of Daviess County,* 172; *Owensboro Monitor,* Aug. 31, 1864.

30. *Owensboro Monitor,* Oct. 12, 1864. This transformation of Bennett is clearly in line with Michael Fellman's ideas examining how both a region and the society there can spiral downward once this type of conflict has begun. Fellman, *Inside War,* xv–xx; in a broader context, Robert Mackey does an excellent job of breaking down the different types of irregulars in *The UNcivil War,* while James B. Martin's article "Black Flag over the Bluegrass" provides a more focused approach, including a look at James ("Jake") Bennett.

31. *History of Daviess County,* 174; *OR,* ser.1, vol. 39, pt. 1, Report of John C. Moon, Sept. 17, 1864, 492; *Evansville Daily Journal,* Sept. 3, 5, 13, 24, 1864; Starling, *History of Henderson County,* 221; *Owensboro Monitor,* Oct. 12, 1864.

32. B. L. Roberson, "The Courthouse Burnin'est General," *Tennessee Historical Quarterly* 23 (1964): 372–74; Edward M. Cofman, ed., "Memoirs of Hylan B. Lyon Brigadier General, C.S.A.," *Tennessee Historical Quarterly* 18 (1959): 48–50; *OR,* ser. 1, vol. 45, pt. 1, 803–4; Ellen K. Wallace journal, Dec. 12, 1864.

33. Robertson, "The Courthouse Burnin'est," 373–78; Cofman, "Memoirs of Hylan B. Lyon," 48–50; *OR,* ser. 1, vol. 45, pt. 1, 804–6.

34. *Evansville Daily Journal,* Dec. 26, 28, 1864; ibid., Jan. 4, 17, 31, 1865; *History of Daviess County,* 175–77; *Henderson Weekly Reporter,* Jan. 5, 1865; Glenn Hodges, *Fearful Times: A History of the Civil War Years in Hancock County, Kentucky* (Hawesville, Ky.: Hancock County Historical Society and the *Hancock Clarion,* 1986), 55–57; Daviess County Court Order Book, Aug. 8, 1864.

35. *Owensboro Monitor,* Oct. 19, 1864; *History of Daviess County,* 175.

36. *Henderson Weekly Reporter,* Jan. 12, 19, 26, 1865; ibid., Feb. 16, 1865; Starling, *History of Henderson County,* 227–28.

37. *Henderson Weekly Reporter,* Nov. 3, 1864; ibid., Feb. 16, 1865; Starling, *History of Henderson County,* 221.

38. Ibid., 229–32; Ash, *When the Yankees Came,* 226–27.

39. *Henderson Weekly Reporter,* June 15, 1865.

"There Is Shameful Wrong Somewhere"

The 1861 Campaign to Liberate East Tennessee

Michael Toomey

As the winter chill of early December brought the troubled and tragic year of 1861 to a close, United States Congressman Horace Maynard was anxious, frustrated, and angry. His circumstances were admittedly complicated as he had been elected to Congress from Tennessee, a state that, six months earlier, voted to secede from the United States and align itself with the Confederacy. Yet Maynard represented a district in East Tennessee where Unionist sentiment was overwhelming. He managed to escape from Confederate-occupied East Tennessee and take his seat in Congress, but Maynard knew that the constituents he had left behind were suffering for their loyalty. He had worked tirelessly since arriving in Washington to convince President Abraham Lincoln to move quickly and launch a military campaign to liberate East Tennessee. Maynard's efforts were rewarded in early September when Lincoln, with the endorsement of George B. McClellan, general-in-chief of all Union armies, ordered the campaign to begin. For Maynard, such high-level support seemingly ensured progress, yet three months had passed, and the campaign to liberate East Tennessee had yet to make any appreciable movement forward. A succession of commanders had shown little enthusiasm for the campaign and the troops that Maynard had expected would by now have been in East Tennessee were instead sitting idly by in eastern Kentucky. "There is shameful wrong somewhere," Maynard complained. "I have not yet satisfied myself where."[1]

Maynard's frustrations were understandable, yet the campaign that he envisioned was daunting. It was a campaign that required inadequate and inexperienced troops to contend with and overcome logistical challenges that were truly formidable. And, assuming that those problems could be resolved, the invading army would then be required to operate at the end of a long, tenuous, and vulnerable supply line, thus making resupply and reinforcement extremely difficult in the face of a certain Confederate counterattack. Moreover, Union commanders were compelled to operate under the constant criticism and scolding of elected officials (one of whom was Maynard himself), fully aware that failure would diminish any hopes for promotion and advancement, and might well ruin their careers. Mired down by inexperience, contention, and confusion, the first campaign to liberate East Tennessee was ultimately abandoned in the face of obstacles that were too overwhelming in the early chaotic months of the Civil War.

The failure of the campaign, however, did not obscure the military and political objectives that set it in motion. Indeed, it was readily apparent to anyone with a map that it was essential for the Confederate government to control the East Tennessee rail line. The line was actually owned and operated by two different companies: the East Tennessee & Georgia Railroad, completed in 1855, connected Knoxville with Chattanooga and provided access to all the markets of the Deep South. Three years later the East Tennessee & Virginia Railroad was completed, connecting Knoxville with Richmond and from there with the entire Atlantic seaboard. The completion of these two lines had already shown signs of transforming the East Tennessee economy, but of more immediate importance was its value to the Confederacy, particularly after its capital was moved to Richmond, Virginia. As the most direct rail line connecting the Confederate capital to the resources and manpower of the Deep South, the East Tennessee rail line figured prominently in the planning for both North and South.

For Abraham Lincoln, there was an additional motivation for invading East Tennessee, for he realized that the countryside surrounding the rail line was home to a predominately Unionist population. Not only would they facilitate and support an invasion, the Unionists constituted an immediate source of manpower with which to defend against a counterattack. But Lincoln also believed that he was morally obligated to come to the aid of Southern Unionists wherever possible, and no region of the South had a more visible or active Unionist population than East Tennessee. That such extensive loyalty existed within the bounds of a seceded state was seen as remarkable at the time and has continued to attract the attention of scholars and others who seek to understand the origins and motivations for Southern Unionism in general. It is clear that a number of factors were involved, but it appears that the strength of the Unionist movement in East Tennessee was among rural middle-class farmers. Few, if any, were abolitionists and, in fact, several were slave owners themselves. But their commitment to the slave-based economy was minimal and their fear of domination by the planter class of the Deep South was genuine. This attitude was aptly expressed by William G. "Parson" Brownlow, a Methodist minister turned newspaper editor. He readily accepted slavery as an institution, but that did not prevent him from attacking the plantation economy that was so clearly incompatible with the geography of East Tennessee. Brownlow no doubt spoke for many of his neighbors when he claimed that East Tennesseans "can never live in a Southern Confederacy and be made the hewers of wood and drawers of water for a set of aristocrats and overbearing tyrants."[2]

For the Confederate government, the threat from East Tennessee Unionists went well beyond Brownlow's rhetoric. Aside from the strength that came from their numbers, they were politically active and well organized. Many were former Whigs and, although that party was no longer a factor at the national level, much of the political machinery of the once-powerful Tennessee Whigs remained in place. Equally important, years of intense partisan struggles had created an effective leadership that was able to respond quickly, as they demonstrated in the early months of 1860 when Gov. Isham Harris, an avowed secessionist, called the state legislature into a special session to determine the fate of Tennessee. The legislators instead deferred the decision to the people and set a referendum for February 9 to authorize a secession convention. With just one month in which to present their case, Unionist leaders organized a statewide campaign to oppose the convention. Foremost among the leaders of Unionism in East Tennessee was Andrew Johnson of Greeneville. As a former governor and congressman, augmented by his more recent status as a United States senator, Johnson's influence was significant. He had recently enhanced his influence and gained national attention with a fiery speech on the floor of the Senate in which he denounced secession.

Johnson had not yet returned from Washington when campaigning for the February referendum began, but East Tennessee Unionists were not without other notable leaders. Among these were Oliver P. Temple, Thomas A. R. Nelson, and Horace Maynard, all of whom were prominent attorneys or businessmen. They had not always worked well together, but past differences were put aside in January 1861 and they all played a significant role in the outcome of the referendum. The final votes showed that a comfortable margin of 55 percent of voters statewide rejected Harris's call for a convention.

Unionist sentiment was particularly strong in East Tennessee, where an overwhelming 81 percent of voters stood in opposition to secession.[3]

As it turned out, however, the issue was not settled. Fort Sumter, and especially Lincoln's subsequent call for volunteers, provided Governor Harris with an opportunity to put the question of secession before Tennessee voters again. He could sense that sentiment for secession was growing and he prodded the legislature to move swiftly. The legislators complied and declared Tennessee independent of the United States, and at the same time created a military league with the Confederate Army. These measures were then to be submitted for approval to the voters on June 8 in a second statewide referendum. Like Harris, Unionists could see that enthusiasm for secession was steadily increasing, particularly in Middle and West Tennessee. It was also apparent that many former Unionists were now supporting secession, as Oliver Temple explained in a letter to T. A. R. Nelson: "We have lost a few weak kneed gentlemen, who have not been with us in heart for months, and who only acted with us for fear or selfishness." But, Temple added, "The country people especially are still firm and determined."[4] The return of Andrew Johnson from Washington brought additional energy to their efforts and there was some optimism that even though they had lost support elsewhere, their dominance in East Tennessee might yet save the state for the Union. In the final days before the votes were to be cast, Unionists convened in Knoxville to rally their supporters. More than 460 delegates from across East Tennessee and the Cumberland Plateau eventually adopted a set of resolutions that, among other things, declared secession illegal and pointed out what to them seemed obvious: Tennesseans had voted against secession in February and therefore the recent actions of the governor and legislature had clearly ignored the will of the people and should be rejected. United and harmonious, the delegates adjourned and agreed to reconvene when the results of the referendum were known.

It is doubtful that the more realistic Unionists expected to overcome the emotions generated by Fort Sumter. Still, the level of statewide support for secession was unexpected. Almost 70 percent of Tennesseans now favored secession, a dramatic increase from the 45 percent who had called for a secession convention in February. Even in East Tennessee, Unionists were shocked to see a noticeable decline in support from 81 percent to 69 percent. They still represented a clear majority in that section, almost twice the number of secessionists, but even so, Tennessee's secession was an accomplished fact, and as Unionists they were in a decidedly uncomfortable position. Their discomfort was evident when they reconvened one week later in Greeneville. Less than three hundred delegates attended and it was clear that they were no longer united. Led by T. A. R. Nelson, a militant faction gained control of the convention and called for an aggressive response to secession. The legislature had acted illegally, they claimed, and thus the results of the referendum had no legal basis. They called for the creation of militias in each county, and vowed to resist any Confederate troops who attempted to enter East Tennessee. Only with the greatest difficulty did Oliver P. Temple and other moderates convince the delegates to accept a less confrontational set of resolutions. The resolutions proposed by the moderates still condemned secession and even petitioned the state legislature to form East Tennessee into a separate state. Beyond that, however, East Tennessee Unionists promised a sort of truce—they retained the right to defend themselves, but otherwise made no threats to interfere with the Confederate government.[5]

That Temple was able to compel his fellow delegates to embrace these resolutions, which they did unanimously, was remarkable given the hostility with which the convention began. He could not have failed to detect, however, that the apparent unanimity masked a strong and unmistakable undercurrent of opposition. Several delegates remained committed to a militant response, one of whom was William Blount Carter, a former Presbyterian minister whose support for the truce that Temple and his moderates had engineered lasted no more than two weeks. Carter may have reluctantly conceded that East Tennessee Unionists were untrained, poorly armed, and no match for the growing number of Confederate troops, but he believed that a military response to secession was necessary and probably inevitable. Sometime in late June or early July, Carter slipped out of East Tennessee on a self-appointed mission to secure the arms, ammunition, and support that he believed were essential. By the end of July he was in Washington, D.C., where he met with Andrew Johnson, who had returned to take his seat in the Senate. Through Johnson's influence, Carter was able to meet with President Abraham Lincoln, but that initial meeting apparently gave Carter little encouragement that the Federal government would lend much support. In a letter written to Lincoln a few days later, Carter said, "I am now about to return to my people with but little hope," adding that he wished to make "one more effort in behalf of East Tennessee" before he left Washington. Carter then requested—as he had almost certainly done during his earlier meeting with Lincoln—that the federal government provide ten thousand stands of arms and ammunition (although he said that twenty thousand would be better) and a competent commander to provide training and overall coordination for the East Tennessee Unionists. Carter also asked for ten thousand well-drilled Union troops to protect the Unionists until their training was complete. Five days later, Carter sent yet another letter to Lincoln, this time cosigned by Andrew Johnson. But as before, there is no indication that Lincoln was willing to authorize any sort of direct military involvement or support.[6]

Lincoln was not unsympathetic to the situation in East Tennessee, and it is probable that Carter could sense that the president was genuinely touched by the plight of the Unionists. But in order to send arms and ammunition into East Tennessee, much less an army of ten thousand troops, it was necessary to move through Kentucky. Such a clear violation of Kentucky's neutrality was a risk that Lincoln was unwilling to take. Even so, there were some steps that could be taken, and in fact Lincoln had already taken those steps before he met with Carter. On July 1, at about the same time that Carter was making his way out of East Tennessee, Lt. William Nelson was ordered to Kentucky. With him he took arms and ammunition to smuggle into East Tennessee, but his more important objective was to organize and train the thousands of Kentucky volunteers, as well as the growing number of refugees who were arriving from East Tennessee.[7]

Nelson's activities did not technically infringe on Kentucky's neutrality, but they generated complaints from the Confederate government and became the cause of much concern among the Confederate forces hovering just across the border in Tennessee. Likewise, the knowledge that a Union recruiting camp was established in Kentucky caused a noticeable improvement in attitudes and morale among East Tennessee Unionists, and the change was readily apparent to Confederate authorities and sympathizers throughout the region. A semblance of calm had prevailed since the Greeneville Convention, but now, only a few weeks later, Unionist resentment and hostility were increasingly evident. Landon Carter Haynes, a former Tennessee state legislator who was then serving in the Confederate Congress, was among those who believed that "the peril of civil war in East Tennessee [is] imminent. I am looking every moment to hear that the bridges have been burned and the East Tennessee and Virginia Railroad torn up."[8]

The dual threat of a military invasion coupled with a Unionist uprising was particularly alarming to Gen. Leonidas Polk, commander of Confederate forces along the Tennessee–Kentucky border. "No time is to be lost in East Tennessee," he wrote to Confederate President Jefferson Davis. Polk recommended that ten thousand troops be stationed there and that the entire region be reorganized as a separate department under the command of Gen. Felix Zollicoffer.[9] A former newspaper editor with limited military experience, Zollicoffer was a Tennessean and had lived for a time in East Tennessee, which appeared to Polk as an advantage if there was to be any hope of reconciling the East Tennessee Unionists to the presence of the Confederate government.

Zollicoffer received his orders on August 1, and within a week he became convinced that Nelson's volunteers intended to "force a passage through the mountains into East Tennessee," and added that "the Federalists here . . . are awaiting such a movement."[10] But it was the former threat and not the latter that most concerned Zollicoffer for he was certain that in the absence of a Federal invasion, East Tennessee loyalists would eventually accept their new status as Confederate citizens. To encourage that process, he adopted a policy of conciliation. Officers who made unwarranted arrests were chastised, and reports of militant Unionist activity were dismissed as merely "mischievous." To emphasize further his commitment to conciliation, Zollicoffer issued an order that required his troops to respect the personal property of all civilians, and even encouraged all East Tennessee refugees to return to their homes.[11]

Confederate authorities were not so willing to embrace Zollicoffer's optimism, particularly after state elections in early August. East Tennesseans not only rejected the new state Confederate constitution, they voted overwhelmingly against the reelection of Gov. Isham Harris. Most disturbing of all, East Tennesseans cast a clear majority of their votes to send representatives to the United States Congress rather than the Confederate Congress. These results prompted Harris to call for "a decided and energetic policy" in East Tennessee, since he felt certain that the Federal government would now attempt to capitalize on Unionist sentiment there.[12] As it turned out, Harris's fears were not unfounded, for Union recruitment efforts were going remarkably well in Kentucky. Soon after arriving in that state, Nelson set up his headquarters on the property of Richard Robinson in Garrard County and named it Camp Dick Robinson. Within weeks he had attracted a small army of volunteers, including a large number from East Tennessee. Among these was Edward Maynard, the son of U.S. Congressman Horace Maynard. Writing to his father in early September, Edward Maynard claimed that eight hundred Tennesseans had recently arrived in a two-day period and more were arriving every day, adding to a camp that already numbered as many as six thousand recruits. All of these volunteers, he added, expected they would soon be marching into East Tennessee as part of an army of liberation.[13]

The situation changed dramatically on September 4, when Confederate Gen. Leonidas Polk ordered troops into Kentucky to seize and occupy Columbus on the Mississippi River. Union forces responded and within two days they were across the Ohio River and had begun to fortify Paducah. With Kentucky's neutrality no longer an obstacle, both sides moved quickly to send more troops into the state. Confederate troops were sent forward to Bowling Green and, on September 7, Zollicoffer received orders to fortify Cumberland Gap and then advance into eastern Kentucky.[14] Satisfied that the Gap was adequately fortified, Zollicoffer pushed forward. After establishing camp at Cumberland Ford, he moved north on the Wilderness Road and on September 19 he routed a small force of Home Guards at Barbourville.[15]

For Abraham Lincoln, these developments meant that an invasion of East Tennessee was no longer blocked by Kentucky's neutrality and he wasted no time in setting that campaign in motion. "On or about the 5th of October," he ordered, "I wish a movement made to seize and hold a point on the railroad connecting Virginia and Tennessee, near the mountain pass called Cumberland Gap." Camp Dick Robinson was designated as the base from which the campaign was to begin and on September 10 Gen. George H. Thomas was sent to assume command there.[16] At about the same time, William B. Carter arrived at Camp Dick Robinson, accompanied by Andrew Johnson and Horace Maynard. The three men presented Thomas with an interesting proposition. As a part of the overall campaign, Carter proposed to lead a covert mission into East Tennessee to recruit and coordinate a force of Unionist partisans, and then destroy several key bridges along the rail line. The bridges were thinly guarded for the most part, he claimed, and a few were unguarded altogether, so their destruction should be easy. The flames would then be the signal for an uprising of thousands of East Tennessee loyalists who would keep the few Confederate troops in East Tennessee occupied while Thomas crossed the mountains from Kentucky. The Confederate troops, cut off from reinforcements and preoccupied by the uprising of Unionists, could easily be overwhelmed and destroyed. Thomas immediately saw the merit in Carter's plan and sent him back to Washington with a letter to Gen. George B. McClellan, commander of the newly formed Army of the Potomac and a rising star among Lincoln's closest military advisors.[17]

Once back in Washington, Carter presented his plan to a meeting that included not only McClellan but also Abraham Lincoln and Secretary of State William Seward. Carter's scheme was warmly embraced by both Mc-

Clellan and Lincoln. For McClellan, the invasion of East Tennessee represented at the least a diversion that would draw Confederate attention and resources away from his own planned offensive in the East. Better yet, if the campaign was successful, the severed rail line would prevent, or at least delay, the arrival of Confederate reinforcements from the Deep South. For Lincoln, the benefits of Carter's plan, and indeed of the entire campaign, went well beyond the potential military advantages he saw as commander-in-chief. Lincoln also saw a decided political advantage in the liberation of East Tennessee. There was no other region of the Confederacy that was so heavily populated by Unionists, and their liberation would be seen by the Northern public as a major success. Moreover, it was something that Lincoln believed could be easily accomplished. After all, had not the recent Union victories in western Virginia clearly demonstrated what was possible if an army was sent to the support of a Unionist population struggling to resist Confederate occupation? East Tennessee, with an even larger Unionist population, could surely provide a similar triumph. Accordingly, Carter left Washington with the president's endorsement and $2,500 with which to finance his attack on the railroad bridges in East Tennessee.[18]

If Carter's role in the upcoming campaign was now clear, other details of the campaign itself remained vague. The invasion force was to consist of Thomas's division of about five thousand men, who would move out of Camp Dick Robinson, through Cumberland Gap, and into East Tennessee. Overall command was under Gen. Robert Anderson, a native Kentuckian and the hero of Fort Sumter, who was in command of the Department of the Cumberland, which included Kentucky and Tennessee. As the planning progressed, however, it became apparent that the ordeal at Fort Sumter had taken a toll on Anderson, and he was relieved of command on October 6. In his place was appointed William Tecumseh Sherman, an 1840 West Point graduate. Sherman, who resigned from the army in 1853, had been recommissioned just five months earlier and distinguished himself at the Battle of Manassas, but there was little indication of the remarkable career that lay ahead. Indeed, Sherman was not especially grateful for the promotion, and he embarked on his duties with little enthusiasm. He seemed particularly unenthusiastic about the East Tennessee campaign and within two days he had come to the conclusion that Nashville, not Knoxville, was the more important objective.[19]

It was Knoxville and East Tennessee, however, that were the more important objectives in Washington. For Abraham Lincoln, the liberation of the Unionists there had become almost an obsession. Aware of this fact, and perhaps hoping to ingratiate himself to the president, Secretary of War Simon Cameron decided to take a personal interest in the matter. In early October he sent orders to Gen. Ormsby M. Mitchel, commander of the adjoining Department of the Ohio, to proceed south from Cincinnati with his troops and take command of the East Tennessee campaign and to do so "with the greatest Promptitude."[20] Mitchel was an aggressive officer and a West Point graduate, but he had resigned from the army shortly after graduation. His military experience was thus limited, and he had no combat experience whatsoever; in fact, when the war began, he was better known as a scientist. But Mitchel did, apparently, have a friend in Andrew Johnson, who had come to believe that the East Tennessee campaign was progressing too slowly. Indeed, it was Andrew Johnson who personally delivered a copy of Cameron's order to Thomas. Sherman had also received a copy of those orders and quickly tried to impress upon Thomas the necessity of making some sort of movement in the direction of East Tennessee: "[I] can only say that if your men simply move, the effect will be good."[21]

As it turned out, Thomas had already ordered a few troops forward, but he had also encountered some problems. There was, he discovered, very little forage along his route and a lack of funds with which to hire wagons for transporting additional forage. Moreover, he was now convinced that an advance was impossible without at least four more regiments. Thomas's report confirmed Sherman's own doubts, for he believed that the disaster at Manassas was due to inadequate preparation and, most important, untrained soldiers. "If we could not command our men," he wrote, "we had no business to attempt invasion," and he brought that conviction with him to Kentucky.[22] Before ordering the troops forward, Sherman decided to ride to Crab Orchard and inspect Thomas's situation, and perhaps they could agree on some sort of combined action.[23]

That conference was cancelled when it was learned that Secretary of War Simon Cameron was expected to arrive in Louisville for a meeting with Sherman. Thomas was instead ordered to continue his advance and, Sherman added, not to worry about any interference from Mitchel. "General Mitchel is subject to my orders, and I will, if possible, give you the opportunity of completing what you have begun." To achieve this, Sherman dispersed the troops under Mitchel's command and effectively ended Mitchel's ability to organize an invasion of East Tennessee. Mitchel, now a general without an army, was understandably outraged and promptly submitted his resignation, which Lincoln refused.[24] Andrew Johnson was equally incensed at Sherman's interference. Years later, Frederick A. Mitchel, the general's son and a member of his staff, recalled a meeting between his father and Johnson, in which the red-faced and fiery-eyed senator bitterly complained that the real problem was jealousy: "Genl. Sherman and his subordinates would not Consent to another General operating in their territory."[25]

Thomas was now free to move forward with the invasion of East Tennessee, but those plans were abruptly postponed with the appearance of a more immediate problem. Confederate Gen. Felix Zollicoffer, after his earlier success at Barbourville in September, had assumed a defensive position at Cumberland Ford on the Cumberland River. But on October 16 his troops began advancing up the Wilderness Road toward Camp Dick Robinson. Four days later they encountered a Union regiment under the command of Col. T. T. Garrard at Wildcat Mountain, a few miles north of London. Zollicoffer made plans to attack Garrard the following morning, only to discover that Union reinforcements had arrived during the night under Gen. Albin Schoepf. Undeterred, Zollicoffer ordered his troops to attack, but Schoepf's troops were well placed in a strong defensive position and the Confederates made little headway. Repeated attacks throughout the day produced no better results, and by late afternoon Zollicoffer ordered his troops to retreat.

As soon as it became apparent that the Confederates were retreating, Schoepf secured his position and awaited orders. He was Polish-born and had extensive experience as an officer on the battlefields of Europe, but he was new to the Department of the Cumberland, having reported for duty only three days earlier. Still, as his scouts returned with their reports, Schoepf became convinced that he could scatter Zollicoffer's forces and gain possession of Cumberland Gap. Thomas concurred; he was unsure if the advance could be properly supplied with clothing and ammunition, but he nonetheless told Schoepf to prepare to move forward. Sherman, however, remained cautious. "Don't push too far," he wrote to Thomas. "Your line is already long and weak. I cannot now re-enforce you."[26] The following day, Thomas relayed those concerns to Schoepf. General Sherman, he wrote, "objects to advancing the troops too far on this route, and directs that we proceed no further than your camp at present."[27]

While Schoepf remained in place at London, Thomas prepared to move forward to Crab Orchard, where he intended to establish a supply depot for the campaign and await Sherman's order to move forward. But Sherman was still not ready to advance, and worried that Zollicoffer's advance up the Wilderness Road might have been intended to disguise a stronger attack elsewhere.[28] As the Union commanders waited, William B. Carter pressed forward with his covert mission to attack and destroy railroad bridges in East Tennessee. After leaving Washington, he had returned to Camp Dick Robinson, where he finalized his plans with the Federal commanders, although Sherman apparently required some persuasion before he gave his endorsement.[29] In mid-October, at about the same time that Zollicoffer was pushing northward on the Wilderness Road, Carter made his way through Confederate lines and back into East Tennessee. With him went Capt. William Cross and Capt. David Fry, both of whom were from East Tennessee and would provide assistance in planning and recruitment. By October 22 they were in Morgan County within a few miles of the railroad and a company of Confederate cavalry. From there Carter sent a small group of Morgan County Unionists back through the lines to contact Thomas and secure arms and ammunition with which, according to

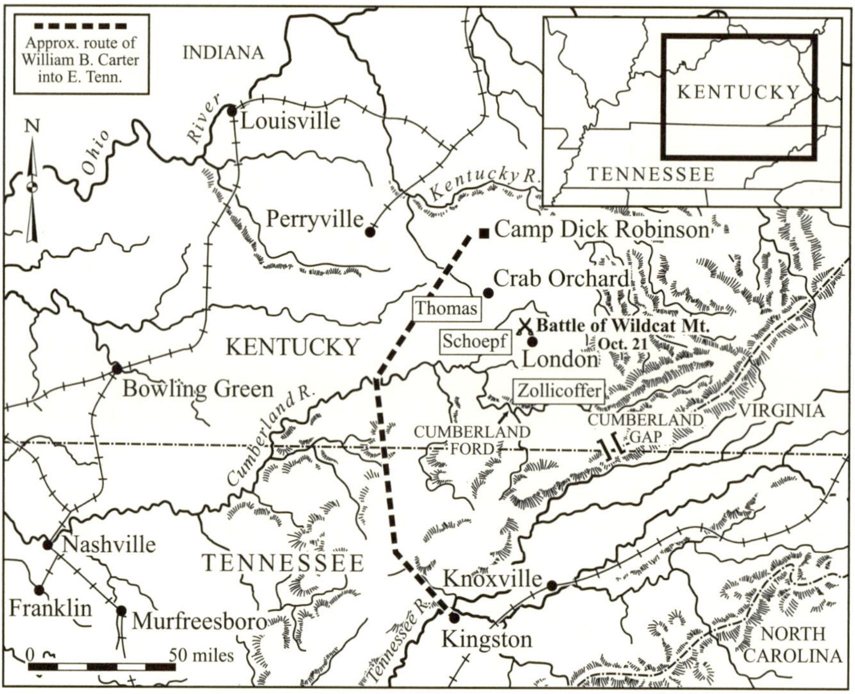

The campaign to liberate East Tennessee in the weeks that followed the Battle of Wildcat Mountain, October 21, 1861. Union Gen. Albin F. Schoepf moved to a position near London, which ultimately represented the furthest advance of any substantial Federal forces toward East Tennessee. Confederate Gen. Felix Zollicoffer retreated to the Cumberland River to protect the approach to Cumberland Gap. William B. Carter, who slipped through Confederate lines in mid-October, established headquarters near Kingston, Tennessee, and began to press forward with his secret mission to burn railroad bridges.

Carter, "they will open the war for you by routing these small bands of marauding cavalry."[30] Carter then moved to the vicinity of Kingston, where he established his headquarters. In a second letter to Thomas written a few days later, Carter explained that he was uncertain as to whether or not the bridges might be captured or if they must be destroyed. In either event, he wrote, "I beg you to hasten on to our help, as we are about to create a great diversion in General McClellan's favor."[31]

Carter did not provide the details of that diversion to Thomas, nor did he apparently share much information with anyone other than those who were recruited to participate in the attacks. That number was probably around three hundred and perhaps as high as five hundred, but there can be no doubt that most East Tennessee Unionists soon became aware that some sort of military activity was imminent.[32] The result was a visible boost in morale that alarmed Confederate authorities. Col. William B. Wood of the 16th Alabama, in command at Knoxville in Zollicoffer's absence, was particularly concerned at the increasing militancy he observed and warned that the "Unionists are talking exultingly of the approach of the Lincoln army and their intention to join it."[33] In a more pointed letter to new Secretary of War Judah P. Benjamin, Wood added that most East Tennesseans had shown no reconciliation to the Confederate government; indeed, he claimed they were "as hostile to it as the people of Ohio and will be ready to take up arms as soon as they believe the Union forces are near enough to sustain them."[34] As the Unionists became more open in their hostility, some wondered if the greatest threat to Zollicoffer was not from Federal troops in Kentucky but instead from the Unionists in his rear. Campbell Wallace, president of the East Tennessee & Georgia Railroad, expressed such a concern to Gov. Isham Harris: "I am well satisfied that there is a larger Lincoln force well-armed in East Tennessee than Zollicoffer has of Southern Men under his command. . . . They can and will be concentrated in his rear whenever they are advised of a sufficient force in his front."[35] Despite these warnings, Zollicoffer remained focused on the threat of a Union attack. From his base at Cumberland Ford, he struggled mightily to patrol the many mountain passes with a limited number of troops. As for the threat from the Unionists, Zollicoffer told Wood to remain vigilant, but added that "a few of our friends about Knoxville are unnecessarily nervous; give their expressions of apprehension only their due weight."[36]

Zollicoffer's focus on the threat of a Union invasion was not unwarranted, but it was an invasion whose forward progress was barely perceptible. Schoepf was still positioned near London, although he had moved forward slightly so as to protect the road from Richmond, Kentucky, which offered better access to supplies and reinforcements. Thomas himself was stationed at his Crab Orchard supply base, a distance of about twenty miles from Camp Dick Robinson, where he waited for the arrival of the four additional regiments he had requested earlier. Even that modest advance was possible only after Thomas made extensive improvements to the roads and then hired local wagons to transport his supplies.[37] For Sherman, these increased problems of supply and transportation caused a good deal of anxiety. He no longer saw the logic of a campaign that was intended to provide arms and supplies to support a Unionist uprising, when the invading army was itself barely armed, without adequate provisions, and woefully unprepared to fight. "Our defeat would be disastrous," he worried, "and to expect of new men who never bore arms to do miracles is not right."[38]

Yet, it was miracles that Andrew Johnson and other politicians expected, and the intense pressure on Sherman continued. To the governor of his home state of Ohio, he wrote: "All these moves take time, and the truth is adequate preparation has not been made." Requisitions had not been filled, there was no one to manage the artillery, and even the wagons arrived unassembled. "Mules are wild and horses distempered," he explained, "and worst of all no Capts., or Lieutenants to teach the details."[39] By this time Sherman had decided that it was pointless to continue, for in addition to all his other problems, "Winter is near at hand, and the roads will be almost impassable."[40] Thomas was thus instructed to do nothing more than hold his position at Crab Orchard, reassure Schoepf at London, and do his best to keep track of Zollicoffer.

Thomas was admittedly reluctant to advance without proper reinforcements and a secure supply line, but he was perhaps the only general among the Federal commanders in Kentucky who remained committed to the campaign. That commitment had recently been strengthened by the delayed arrival of William B. Carter's two letters from East Tennessee. Those letters were dated two weeks earlier and made it clear that the attack on the bridges was imminent, which implied to Thomas that he must move quickly if there was to be any benefit from Carter's attacks. He urged Sherman to send him the four additional regiments, claiming that "we can seize the railroad yet."[41] But Thomas's determination to move forward was entirely lost on the East Tennessee congressional delegation. Andrew Johnson was especially troublesome in this regard as he rode from one headquarters to another in search of a general who could be persuaded to advance. Thomas patiently explained that the logistics of the campaign were complex and could not be completed quickly or carelessly. "I have done all in my power to get troops and transportation and means to advance into Tennessee. . . . I can only say that I am doing the best I can. Our commanding general is doing the same, and using all his influence to equip a force for the rescue of Tennessee."[42] Johnson was especially irksome to Schoepf, a professional soldier with little patience for political interference. In response to Schoepf's complaints, Thomas revealed his own growing frustration: "It is time that discontented persons should be silenced both in and out of the service. . . . To make an attempt to rescue [the Tennesseans] when we are not half prepared is culpable."[43] Schoepf answered the next day and complimented Thomas on his tactful response to Johnson, then went on to note that "this outside pressure has become intolerable and must be met with firmness, or the army may as well be disbanded."[44]

While Johnson continued to push and threaten Thomas and his commanders, Horace Maynard maintained pressure on Sherman. On November 8 Sherman wrote to Thomas, complaining that "Mr. Maynard still presses the East Tennessee expedition. I do not doubt its importance but I know we have not force enough and transportation to undertake it." Sherman had by this time become concerned that his troops were badly scattered and he was making plans to concentrate his army as soon as possible. The advance into East Tennessee now seemed entirely too risky, and so on November 8, Thomas was once again directed to remain at Crab Orchard until he received further orders and to "do the best you can."[45]

Thomas remained eager to advance, but agreed with Sherman that it was unwise to do so without adequate transportation and more troops. Yet Sherman's orders to remain in place came on the very day that William B. Carter had selected to send his partisans against the bridges on the East Tennessee rail line. A total of at least ten bridges were targeted, stretching from Sullivan County southward to Bridgeport, Alabama, and Dalton, Georgia. Carter's plan was simple: after eluding or neutralizing any Confederate guards, the men were to set their fires, ensure the bridges were destroyed, and then escape without detection. Although some of Carter's partisans were sworn into Federal military service when they were recruited, none of them could claim any real training and they knew little of military discipline. Even so, Carter's "bridge-burners" were remarkably successful. Three of the bridges, it was discovered, were well guarded and could not be attacked and the same was very likely true for the bridge below Dalton. The bridge at Strawberry Plains was guarded by only a solitary watchman, but could not be destroyed because the attackers lost their matches while attempting to subdue the guard. But five other bridges were successfully fired and destroyed: one across the Holston River in Sullivan County, another at Lick Creek in Greene County, the Hiwassee River Bridge, and two bridges across Chickamauga Creek near Chattanooga. In addition, the partisans cut the telegraph lines at multiple places along the entire railroad, disrupting communications from the Virginia border to Dalton, Georgia.[46] None of the attackers was seriously injured, and all of them, for the moment at least, made their escape.

When news of the bridge burnings spread across East Tennessee, Unionists took it as a signal that the arrival of a Federal army was imminent and many began congregating at camps throughout the region. Hundreds and perhaps thousands of Unionists gathered over the next several days but, poorly armed and without any clear directives, they could do little more than wait anxiously for whatever might happen next. The initial reaction among East Tennessee Confederates was equally anxious, as they could not know if the attacks were isolated incidents or part of a larger invasion. When the true scope of the attacks became known the following day, it resulted in a brief panic. According to a subsequent account in the *Richmond Dispatch,* each community where the attacks had occurred was a scene of "wild excitement and commotion. . . . On every road could be seen citizens with their rifles and shotguns hastening to the scene of the action."[47] The military assessment was equally distressing; Richard G. Fain, colonel of the 63rd Tennessee, wrote that "a worse state of feeling never prevailed in East Tennessee than at the present."[48] Two days later an official with the East Tennessee & Virginia Railroad reported that the country remained in "great excitement and terror," but by that time it was clear that there was no Federal army on the horizon and the initial panic began to subside.[49] Another calming factor was the quick response by Confederate authorities. Additional troops began arriving within twenty-four hours, and Col. Danville Leadbetter was sent to East Tennessee to oversee repairs and coordinate the military response. Within a week it was reported that the telegraph lines had been repaired and a ferry system was in place at the burned bridges to keep the mail and essential war supplies moving.[50]

The next priority for Confederate authorities was the several camps of armed Unionists, one of which had apparently grown to include more than a thousand men and all of which represented a lingering threat to the rail lines. Indeed, reports from railroad crews indicated that several skirmishes with armed Unionists had taken place in the days since the initial attack, and "they are cutting down the telegraph wires as fast as we can put them up."[51] To this, Confederate Secretary of War Benjamin promised that "Troops are now moving to East Tennessee to crush the traitors."[52] Within a week Leadbetter located and dispersed most of the larger camps. William B. Wood, whose persistent warnings in the days leading up to the attack had been proven correct, now offered an equally perceptive and reassuring assessment of the Unionist threat in the aftermath of the attacks. Their numbers were large, he conceded, but at the same time the actual threat was negligible because they were "not yet fully organized, and have no subsistence to enable them to hold out long."[53]

Exactly how long they would be required to hold out was something that no one could answer. Unionist leaders had apparently been in Kentucky as recently as a few days prior to the attacks and returned with the assurance that "the Federal Forces under Mitchell would come to our aid," while others believed that it was Sherman who was set to cross the mountains.[54] Instead, Thomas's troops remained in place at Crab Orchard waiting for reinforcements and transportation, while Sherman became increasingly concerned about the threat of a Confederate attack and actually began to advise Thomas on his best lines of retreat.[55] But Sherman's role in the campaign was in fact at an end. His meeting with Cameron in mid-October had not gone well. The secretary came away from the meeting convinced that affairs in Kentucky were in a far worse condition than he had expected, and Sherman was reassigned in early November. His replacement was Gen. Don Carlos Buell, who arrived in Louisville on November 15, and his orders included a clear directive to attack and capture Cumberland Gap. Buell retained some discretion, as was common, but there could be no mistake that he was expected to capture Knoxville "in order to occupy the railroad at that point, and thus enable the loyal citizens of Eastern Tennessee to rise."[56]

Buell brought with him a much-needed emphasis on organization and discipline, as well as a renewed sense of optimism that the East Tennessee campaign was at last set to move forward. But, although Buell understood that he was expected to make a forward movement into East Tennessee, he quickly assessed the situation and instead concluded that Nashville was the more logical objective. Thomas was thus ordered to break up his supply depot at Crab Orchard and begin moving back toward Louisville.[57] George B. McClellan, recently promoted to general-in-chief of all armies, was not expecting such an order and again reminded Buell that "a movement into East Tennessee is absolutely necessary."[58] McClellan did not deny that Nashville offered an easier advance and that an army could be easily supplied, but he remained insistent that Knoxville should be the first objective. "First secure that," he told Buell, "and then if you possess the means carry Nashville."[59]

Johnson and Maynard were particularly frustrated with Buell's decision. They were aware of McClellan's orders and likewise aware of Lincoln's commitment to East Tennessee. They also knew that at least one of Thomas's brigade commanders, Samuel P. Carter, who was the brother of William B. Carter, was particularly anxious to advance into East Tennessee. Samuel Carter had written numerous impassioned letters to George Thomas, his commanding officer, imploring him to move forward as soon as possible.[60] Carter had also sent letters to Horace Maynard, in one of which he apparently recommended himself to lead a smaller force across the mountains into East Tennessee "to make at least an effort to save our people."[61] Maynard now sent Carter's letters to Abraham Lincoln in an attempt to get the president directly involved. Lincoln promptly forwarded these letters to McClellan, who in turn sent them on to Buell with the pointed directive to advance into East Tennessee "with the least possible delay."[62] Maynard also sent a letter to Buell, cosigned by Andrew Johnson, advising him that they had just met with Lincoln and with McClellan, and that "both concur fully with respect to the East Tennessee expedition."[63] In a separate letter to George Thomas, Maynard's frustration was more apparent. He chastised Thomas for being "further away from East Tennessee than when I left you nearly six weeks ago." The East Tennessee campaign, he added, had so far "been disgraceful to the country and to all concerned. I feel a sense of personal degradation from my own connection with it greater than from any other part of my public actions."[64]

Buell's reply to Johnson and Maynard assured them that he understood the importance of the campaign and that he would move as soon as possible. Yet, by the end of December there was still no movement forward and, as McClellan wrote to Buell, "Johnson, Maynard, etc., are again becoming frantic and have President Lincoln's sympathies excited."[65] Buell could not have been terribly surprised, then, when he received a terse letter directly from the president: "Have arms gone forward for East Tennessee? Please tell me the progress and condition of the movement in that direction. Answer."[66] Buell at last decided to admit his misgivings about the East Tennessee campaign. Arms could not be sent forward, he explained to the president, until the army itself was able to advance. He was preparing two columns for that purpose, but in truth, he said, his support for the campaign was motivated "more by my sympathy for the people of East Tennessee and the anxiety with which you and the general-in-chief have desired it than by my own opinion of its wisdom as an unconditional measure. As earnestly as I wish to accomplish it my judgment has from the first been decidedly against it."[67]

Lincoln's response was immediate and clear: Buell's reluctance to pursue the campaign, he said, "disappoints and distresses me." More specifically, he added, "My distress is that our friends in East Tennessee are being hanged and driven to despair. . . . In this we lose the most valuable stake we have in the South."[68] McClellan likewise expressed surprise when he learned of Buell's misgivings and warned him that he was underestimating the political importance of an advance into East Tennessee. "If relief is not soon afforded those people we shall lose them entirely and with them the power of inflicting the most severe blow upon the secession cause."[69]

Although Buell had plainly decided by this point that Nashville was the logical objective, he was at a loss as to how to bring his superiors to that same conclusion. He reminded McClellan again that the logistics on an East Tennessee campaign were staggering. The problems associated with resupply and reinforcements alone precluded such an attempt. Nor was Buell receptive to the proposal by Gen. Samuel Carter—whose East Tennesseans were pleading to return home at the head of a liberating army—to lead the invasion himself with five thousand mounted infantry supplied with pack mules, dismissing the idea as "in the aggregate simply ridiculous."[70] An unexpected victory at Mill Springs, however, led Buell to reassess his concerns about the East Tennessee campaign, even to the point of ordering troops forward to capture Cumberland Gap. Buell was aware that Confederate Gen. Felix Zollicoffer had shifted his forces west in November and was still looking for an opportunity to press forward into Kentucky. Zollicoffer had turned north at Jamestown and advanced to the Cumberland River across from Mill Spring, where he began to move his troops across the river. It was a slow process, and when the Cumberland River began to rise, Zollicoffer found himself with his army straddling the river, with the troops on the north bank particularly vulnerable.

Schoepf had been moving to block Zollicoffer as soon as the Confederates turned north, and by mid-December Thomas had joined him near Somerset with orders to drive the Confederates from the north side of the Cumberland. Before that attack could be launched, however, Gen. George Crittenden arrived in the Confederate camp. Crittenden had recently been appointed to replace Zollicoffer in overall command of the Department of East Tennessee, and he now assumed direct command of Zollicoffer's campaign. Alarmed at the precarious situation of the Confederate forces, Crittenden determined that a preemptive attack was his best recourse. Early in the morning of January 19, the Confederate attack began and gained some brief success before stalling. After a sharp battle that shifted back and forth throughout the morning, the Confederate forces were eventually routed. Among the Confederate dead was Zollicoffer himself.

The sudden turn of events renewed enthusiasm for the East Tennessee campaign among the Union troops, especially the East Tennesseans of Samuel Carter's command. With the total collapse of the Confederate defenders, even Buell became optimistic, and a week later he ordered Carter to "seize and hold Cumberland Gap."[71] Within hours of that order, however, Buell's misgivings had returned. In addition to the ever-present problem of horrible roads, inadequate transportation, and insufficient rations, an inordinate amount of time was suddenly required to manage the prisoners, baggage, and artillery captured at Mill Springs.[72] By the end of the month Buell had once again decided that an invasion of East Tennessee was ill advised. In a detailed letter to McClellan, Buell carefully explained the situation. It was not that he meant to abandon East Tennessee altogether, he claimed, but rather that he could more easily capture Knoxville by first capturing Nashville. To invade and hold East Tennessee first, he argued, would require a minimum of ten thousand well-trained troops, and preferably three times that number. An even greater problem, he said, were the two hundred miles that lay between his supply depot and Knoxville. There were no provisions or forage to be had along this route, which meant that his entire force would by necessity have to be supplied by at least one thousand wagons making regular trips on muddy roads across rugged terrain. Moreover, the actions of the bridge-burners, while they may have facilitated an invasion two months earlier, had served only to bring more Confederate troops into East Tennessee. Now that the railroad was repaired, it would be a simple matter for the Confederates to bring still more reinforcements should they be necessary and to keep all those troops properly provisioned and supplied. For these reasons, he concluded, "an advance into East Tennessee is impracticable at this time."[73]

Buell's reasoning apparently satisfied Lincoln and McClellan that the best line of approach into Tennessee was along the rail line between Nashville and Louisville. Given the troops at his disposal, it was simply impossible to engage in another campaign at the same time, particularly one as logistically demanding as East Tennessee. Even as Buell was listing the pitfalls associated with an invasion of East Tennessee, Ulysses S. Grant was moving his forces into position to capture Fort Henry and, soon afterward, Fort Donelson in West Tennessee. By the end of February, Nashville was also in Union hands. But if East Tennessee had ceased for the moment to be a military concern for the Union Army, it remained a very real concern for the Confederates. Their most immediate problem was to break up the armed camps of Unionists who had gathered in the immediate aftermath of the bridge-burnings. By November 19, Col. Danville Leadbetter reported to Benjamin that he had broken up a camp on the Doe River and taken thirty prisoners.[74] Eventually, more than four hundred Unionists were arrested, and Benjamin stated clearly what was to be done with the prisoners: "All such as can be identified in having been engaged in bridge burning are to be tried summarily by drum-head court martial, and, if found guilty, executed on the spot by hanging." Benjamin added that if possible, "it would be well to leave their bodies hanging in the vicinity of the burned bridges." All others were to be sent to Tuscaloosa and imprisoned for the duration of the war.[75] Three weeks after the initial attacks, Leadbetter was optimistic and reported that "we have accomplished something—have done some good." But, he cautioned, "whenever a foreign force enters this country be it soon or late three-fourths of this people will rise in arms to join them." Still, he concluded, "At present they seem indisposed to fight."[76] With the armed resistance largely at an end, Confederate authorities now turned their attention to the punishment of the bridge-burners, several of whom had been swept up with the hundreds of prisoners captured in the days after the attacks. Six individuals were eventually convicted of having been directly involved in the attacks, and all were sentenced to death. One was later pardoned, but the others, as Benjamin had ordered, were executed. The first two were hanged at Greeneville on November 30, and within two weeks the remaining three bridge-burners were executed in Knoxville.

Unionist activity in East Tennessee never died down completely, but the heavy response from Confederate authorities was effective. Leadbetter, who continued to patrol the foothills, reported in early December that many armed Unionists had retreated into the mountains, where it was virtually impossible to locate and apprehend them, but it was probably unnecessary in any event. He was making good progress toward pacification, in part because "the execution of the bridge-burners is producing the happiest effect."[77] By Christmas he was satisfied with "the favorable aspect of things generally in East Tennessee." Still, he cautioned, "the country is held by a slight tenure and the approach of an enemy would lead to prompt insurrection of an aggravated character."[78]

The Confederate hold on East Tennessee was thus secured, although it required a garrison of nearly ten thousand troops to guarantee that security.

From the Union perspective, the 1861 East Tennessee campaign revealed several problems that were not uncommon in the first year of the war: inadequate logistical support, untrained soldiers, reluctant generals, interference by local politicians, and even by the commander-in-chief, whose grasp of military logistics and procedure was still poorly developed. But two years later, Lincoln had taken steps to correct these problems. Logistics had improved dramatically and his call for 300,000 troops in July 1862 had doubled the size of the army. In early 1863 he was able to dispatch two divisions of the Ninth Corps under Gen. Ambrose Burnside to Kentucky, thus providing the necessary manpower with which to launch a second campaign to liberate East Tennessee. Perhaps most important, Lincoln had by that time achieved a better working relationship with his generals and a better understanding of military movements in general, as he revealed in a response to yet another plea for liberation from East Tennessee Unionists. They could not know, he wrote, "the difficulties of getting a Union army into that region, and of keeping it there. . . . Start by whatever route they may, their lines of supply are broken before they get half way."[79] Even as Lincoln penned his response, he knew that a second campaign to liberate East Tennessee was already underway. After two years of warfare, he and his generals were much better positioned to accomplish what had not been possible in the confusion and uncertainty of the first months of war.

Notes

1. Maynard to G. H. Thomas, Dec. 7, 1861, *Official Records of the Union and Confederate Armies* (Washington, D.C.: Government Printing Office, 1880–1901), ser. 2, vol. 1, 898 (hereafter cited as *OR*).

2. William G. Brownlow, *Knoxville Whig*, Jan. 13, 1861. There are several studies that explain the origins and characteristics of East Tennessee's Unionists. One of the earliest was written by Oliver P. Temple, who was an active participant in the Unionist movement. See Oliver P. Temple, *East Tennessee and the Civil War* (1899; Johnson City, Tenn.: Overmountain Press, 1995). See also Robert Tracy McKenzie, *Lincolnites and Rebels: A Divided Town in the American Civil War* (New York: Oxford Univ. Press, 2006), 123–28; Noel Fisher, *War at Every Door: Partisan Politics and Guerilla Violence in East Tennessee* (Chapel Hill: Univ. of North Carolina Press, 1997), 179–83; and Peter Wallerstein, "'Helping to Save the Union': The Social Origins, Wartime Experiences, and Military Impact of White Union Troops from East Tennessee," in *The Civil War in Appalachia: Collected Essays*, ed. Kenneth Noe and Shannon H. Wilson (Knoxville: Univ. of Tennessee Press, 1997), 1–29.

3. The results of the February referendum and the secession crisis in Tennessee in general are discussed in Paul H Bergeron, Stephen V. Ash, and Jeanette Keith, *Tennesseans and Their History* (Knoxville: Univ. of Tennessee Press, 1999), 132–36.

4. Oliver P. Temple to T. A. R. Nelson, Apr. 16, 1861, quoted in McKenzie, *Lincolnites and Rebels,* 72.

5. Temple, *East Tennessee and the Civil War,* 343–55.

6. William B. Carter to Abraham Lincoln, Aug. 1, 1861; William B. Carter and Andrew Johnson to Abraham Lincoln, Aug. 6, 1861, Abraham Lincoln Papers, Library of Congress, Manuscript Division (Washington, D.C.: American Memory Project, 2000–2001), http://memory.loc.gov/ammem/alhtml/malhome.html. See also Paul H. Bergeron, *Andrew Johnson's Civil War and Reconstruction* (Knoxville: Univ. of Tennessee Press, 2011), 8–12; and Hans L. Trefousse, *Andrew Johnson: A Biography* (New York: W. W. Norton and Co., 1989), 145–48.

7. Lorenzo Thomas to William Nelson, July 1, 1861, *OR,* ser. 1, vol. 4, 251–52.

8. Landon Carter Haynes to Leroy P. Walker, July 6, 1861, ibid., ser. 2, vol. 1, 824; see also L. P. Walker to Isham Harris, July 18, 1861, ibid., 828–29.

9. Leonidas Polk to Jefferson Davis, July 9, 1861, ibid., 824.

10. Felix Zollicoffer to Samuel Cooper, Aug. 6, 1861, ibid., 825.

11. Zollicoffer to Cooper, Aug. 10, 1861, ibid., 830; P. B. Lee to W. E. Baldwin, Aug. 26, 1861, ibid., 832; Zollicoffer to Colonel Baldwin, Sept. 1, 1861, ibid., 833; Orders no. 3, Aug. 18, 1861, ibid., 831.

12. Harris to Walker, Aug. 1, 1861, ibid., 1, 830.

13. Edward Maynard to Horace Maynard, Sept. 1, 1861, Horace Maynard Papers, MS.0415, University of Tennessee Libraries, Special Collections.

14. The breakdown of Kentucky's neutrality is discussed in Earl J. Hess, *The Civil War in the West: Victory and Defeat from the Appalachians to the Mississippi* (Chapel Hill: Univ. of North Carolina Press, 2012), 7–17.

15. Zollicoffer's activities associated with the East Tennessee campaign are discussed in more detail in Brian McKnight's chapter in this volume.

16. Abraham Lincoln, undated directive, *OR,* ser. 1, vol. 52, 191–92. Special Orders, Sept. 10, 1861, ibid., ser. 1, vol. 4, 257.

17. G. H. Thomas to McClellan, Sept. 30, 1861, ibid., ser. 1, vol. 4, 284; ibid., ser. 2, vol. 1, 889. For Thomas's role in the East Tennessee campaign, see Christopher J. Einolf, *George Thomas: Virginian for the Union* (Norman: Univ. of Oklahoma Press, 2007), 103–15.

18. For Lincoln's commitment to the liberation of East Tennessee and the Northern perception of East Tennessee, see McKenzie, *Lincolnites and Rebels,* 86–87, and Richard Nelson Current, *Lincoln's Loyalists: Union Soldiers from the Confederacy* (Boston: Northeastern Univ. Press, 1992), 29. For the campaign in western Virginia, see Earl J. Hess, *Field Armies and Fortifications in the Civil War: The Eastern Campaigns, 1861–1864* (Chapel Hill: Univ. of North Carolina Press, 2005), 47–58. Carter's Washington meeting is described in Temple, *East Tennessee and the Civil War,* 370–71. According to some accounts, Carter may have received as much as $20,000. See Andrew Johnson to Abraham Lincoln, Nov. 18, 1862, *OR,* ser. 1, vol. 20, 70.

19. William T. Sherman to Garrett Davis, Oct. 8, 1861, *OR,* ser. 1, vol. 4, 296. Sherman's role in the East Tennessee campaign is discussed in John F. Marszalek, *Sherman: A Soldier's Passion for Order* (New York: McMillan, 1993), 154–63.

20. G. H. Thomas to Ormsby Mitchel, Oct. 11, 1861, *OR,* ser. 1, vol. 4, 303; Mitchel to Thomas Scott, Oct. 11, 1861, ibid.

21. Sherman to G. H. Thomas, ibid., 302–3.

22. Sherman to Thomas Ewing, Sept. 15, 1861, Brooks D. Simpson and Jean V. Berlin, eds., *Sherman's Civil War: Selected Correspondence of William T. Sherman, 1860–1865* (Chapel Hill: Univ. of North Carolina Press, 1999), 137–38.

23. Sherman to G. H. Thomas, Oct. 12, 1861, *OR,* ser 1, vol. 4 305–6.

24. Sherman to G. H. Thomas, Oct. 13, 1861, ibid., 306; Mitchel to Lincoln, Oct. 27, 1861, Abraham Lincoln Papers, Library of Congress. See also Winfield Scott to Abraham Lincoln, Oct. 17, 1861, in ibid.

25. F. A. Mitchel to O. P. Temple, Dec. 22, 1898, O. P. Temple Papers, MS 0021. University of Tennessee Libraries, Special Collections.

26. Sherman to Thomas, Oct. 25, 1861, *OR,* ser. 1, vol. 4, 318.

27. Thomas to Schoepf, Oct. 29, 1861, ibid., 323. See also Thomas to Sherman, Oct. 23, 1861, ibid., 206; Schoepf to Thomas, Oct. 22, 1861, ibid., 206–7; Schoepf to Thomas, Oct. 27, 1861, ibid., 207; Thomas to Schoepf, Oct. 23, 1861, ibid., 318; Thomas to Sherman, Oct. 28, 1861, ibid., 321.

28. Thomas to Sherman, Oct. 28, 1861, ibid., 321–22; Sherman to Thomas, Nov. 1, 1861, ibid., 326.

29. Temple, *East Tennessee and the Civil War,* 375–76.

30. William B. Carter to G. H. Thomas, Oct. 22, 1861, *OR,* ser. 1, vol. 4, 889–90.

31. W. B. Carter to G. H. Thomas, Oct. 27, 1861, ibid., 890–91.

32. Temple, *East Tennessee and the Civil War,* 400–401; H. C. Young to D. M. Curtin, Dec. 19, 1861, *OR,* ser. 2, vol. 1, 859.

33. William Wood to Cooper, Nov. 4, 1861, *OR,* ser. 2, vol. 1, 837; Wood to Zollicoffer, Oct. 28, 1861, ibid., 835.

34. Wood to Judah P. Benjamin, Nov. 4, 1861, ibid., 836–37.

35. Campbell Wallace to Harris, Oct. 29, 1861, ibid., 835–36; see also Reuben Davis to Jefferson Davis, Nov. 4, 1861, ibid., 836.

36. Zollicoffer to Wood, Oct. 30, 1861, ibid., 836.

37. G. H. Thomas to Sherman, Oct. 28, 1861, ibid., ser. 1, vol. 4, 321.

38. Sherman to Lorenzo Thomas, Oct. 22, 1861, Simpson and Berlin, eds., *Sherman's Civil War,* 150–52; see also Sherman to Salmon P. Chase, Oct. 14, 1861, ibid., 148–50.

39. Sherman to William Dennison, Nov. 6, 1861, Simpson and Berlin, eds., *Sherman's Civil War,* 156–57.

40. Sherman to G. H. Thomas, Oct. 31, 1861, *OR,* ser. 1, vol. 4, 324–25; Sherman to G. H. Thomas, Nov. 5, 1861, ibid., 335–36.

41. G. H. Thomas to Sherman, Nov. 5, 1861, ibid., 338–39.

42. G. H. Thomas to Andrew Johnson, Nov. 7, 1861, ibid., 342–43.

43. G. H. Thomas to Albin Schoepf, Nov. 7, 1861, ibid., 343.

44. Schoepf to G. H. Thomas, Nov. 8, 1861, ibid., 347–48. Schoepf later became

involved in a heated argument with Johnson, during which he threatened to have the senator forcibly removed from camp, whereupon Johnson defiantly dared him to try. Thomas himself was forced to intervene. See Einolf, *George Thomas,* 113.

45. Sherman to G. H. Thomas, Nov. 8, 1861, *OR,* ser. 1, vol. 4, 347.

46. Carter's initial report claimed that he believed the bridge below Dalton had also been destroyed. See Samuel P. Carter to George Thomas, Nov. 16, 1861, ibid., ser. 2, vol. 1, 892–93. A good account of the attack on the bridges is in David Madden, "Unionist Resistance to Confederate Occupation: The Bridge Burners of East Tennessee," The East Tennessee Historical Society's *Publications* 52–53 (1981–82): 22–39. See also Temple, *East Tennessee and the Civil War,* 378–87.

47. *Richmond Dispatch,* Nov. 22, 1861, http://dlxs.richmond.edu/d/ddr/.

48. Richard G. Fain to Judah Benjamin, Nov. 9, 1861, *OR,* ser. 1, vol. 4, 231.

49. J. W. Lewis to Jefferson Davis, Nov. 11, 1861, ibid., 235.

50. *Richmond Daily Dispatch,* Nov. 11, 1861; Nov. 14, 1861.

51. Branner to Benjamin, Nov. 13, 1861, *OR,* ser. 1, vol. 4, 243.

52. Benjamin to Branner, Nov. 13, 1861, ibid.

53. Wood to Cooper, Nov. 11, 1861, ibid., 840–41.

54. C. P. Toncray to O. P. Temple, Apr. 15, 1895; A. Jobe to O. P. Temple, Sept. 20, 1899, O. P. Temple Papers.

55. Sherman to G. H. Thomas, Nov. 11, 1861, *OR,* ser. 1, vol. 4, 350.

56. George B. McClellan to Don Carlos Buell, Nov. 7, 1861, ibid., 342. Buell's role in the campaign is discussed in Stephen D. Engle, *Don Carlos Buell: Most Promising of All* (Chapel Hill: Univ. of North Carolina Press, 1999), 99–155. Sherman's meeting with Cameron was subsequently reported in various newspapers in such a way as to suggest that Sherman was mentally unstable, a charge that seemed substantiated by Sherman's pessimism and eccentric behavior. See Marszalek, *Sherman,* 161–62.

57. G. H. Thomas to Buell, Nov. 17, 1861, *OR,* ser. 1, vol. 4, 360–61.

58. McClellan to Buell, Nov. 25, 1861, ibid., ser. 2, vol. 1, 894; McClellan to Buell, Nov. 27, 1861, ibid., 895.

59. McClellan to Buell, Nov. 29, 1861, ibid., 895.

60. S. P. Carter to Thomas, Nov. 11, 1861, ibid., ser. 1, vol. 4, 350; S. P. Carter to Thomas, Nov. 16, 1861, ibid., ser. 2, vol. 1, 892–93; S. P. Carter to Thomas, Nov. 20, 1861, ibid., 893; S. P. Carter to Thomas, Nov. 24, 1861, ibid., 894; S. P. Carter to Thomas, Nov. 25, ibid.

61. S. P. Carter to Horace Maynard, Nov. 21, 1861, ibid., ser. 2, vol. 1, 896; S. P. Carter to Maynard, Nov. 25, 1861, ibid., 896–97.

62. McClellan to Buell, McClellan to Buell, Dec. 3, 1861, ibid., 895–96.

63. Andrew Johnson and Horace Maynard to D. C. Buell, Dec. 7, 1861, ibid., 897–98.

64. Maynard to G. H. Thomas, Dec. 7, 1861, ibid., 898.

65. McClellan to Buell, Dec. 29, 1861, ibid., 899.

66. Lincoln to Buell, Jan. 4, 1862, ibid.

67. Buell to Lincoln, Jan. 5, 1862, ibid., 900.

68. Lincoln to Buell, Jan. 6, 1862, ibid.

69. McClellan to Buell, Jan. 6, 1862, ibid., 900–901.

70. Buell to McClellan, Jan. 13, 1862, ibid., 901.

71. Buell to S. P. Carter, Jan. 26, 1862, ibid., ser. 1, vol. 7, 566–67.

72. G. H. Thomas to Buell, Jan. 26, 1862, ibid., 567; Buell to Lorenzo Thomas, Jan. 27, 1862, ibid., 568.

73. Buell to McClellan, Feb. 1, 1862, ibid., ser. 2, vol. 1, 900–901.

74. Danville Leadbetter to Benjamin, Nov. 19, 1861, ibid., 845.

75. Benjamin to Wood, Nov. 25, 1861, ibid., 848.

76. Leadbetter to Benjamin, Nov. 28, 1861, ibid., 849.

77. Leadbetter to Benjamin, Dec. 8, 1861, ibid., 852–53.

78. Leadbetter to Cooper, Dec. 24, 1861, ibid., 859.

79. Abraham Lincoln to John M. Fleming and Robert Morrow, Aug. 9, 1863, Abraham Lincoln Papers, Library of Congress.

Guerrilla Warfare and Federal Occupation in the Jackson Purchase Region of Kentucky, 1862–64

Patricia A. Hoskins

In early September 1864, President Abraham Lincoln received an urgent letter from Kentucky Gov. Thomas H. Bramlette complaining of Union authorities in the Bluegrass State. Lincoln had been fielding complaints from his home state since the beginning of the war. This letter, however, was different. Governor Bramlette leveled his outrage at Gen. Eleazor A. Paine, military commander of the Jackson Purchase region in southwestern Kentucky. Paine, Bramlette argued, had insulted, plundered, and oppressed the people of the region, and must be removed from his duties. Similar and more troubling complaints had also reached Gen.Ulysses S. Grant. The people of the Jackson Purchase accused Paine of banishing loyal citizens to Canada, extorting money from them, and executing and murdering nearly forty people. According to reports, his soldiers had also robbed citizens of their homes and conscripted slaves into the army. Both Grant and Lincoln had long been acquainted with Paine and moved quickly to resolve the situation. Two months later, Paine was court-martialed and relieved of command.[1]

To the people of the Jackson Purchase, Paine and his reign were the culmination of three years of chaos resulting from Federal occupation. During those three years, ordinary citizens, whose loyalty to the Union was constantly questioned, were caught in the crossfire as guerrillas raided the land and stalked the rivers. The Union Army in turn, attempted to thwart partisan efforts by raising Home Guards, curtailing trade, and fining and arresting citizens suspected of aiding the enemy. Thus by the time Paine was removed in late 1864, the Purchase had long seen the Federal army not as their salvation but as their crucible. That image would ultimately shape how the Jackson Purchase defined itself as a region, and how the Civil War was remembered in the area.

Located in the far-western corner of Kentucky, the Jackson Purchase is the smallest of Kentucky's geographic regions. Bordered in the east by the Tennessee River, in the north by the Ohio, and in the west by the Mississippi, the area in 1861 was comprised of seven counties: Ballard, Calloway, Fulton, Graves, Hickman, McCracken, and Marshall. The largest city in the area was Paducah, which served as the commercial hub for western Kentucky, southern Illinois, and northwestern Tennessee. Smaller towns such as Mayfield, Murray, Hickman, and Columbus likewise dotted the map. The area became a focal point of the war in the fall of 1861, when Confederate Gen. Leonidas Polk violated Kentucky's neutrality by occupying Columbus. Grant and the Union Army responded by occupying Paducah. Both Polk and Grant realized the strategic significance of the area's waterways, and both men recognized the fierce Southern loyalty of the population. Indeed, the Jackson Purchase was considered "Kentucky's South Carolina." The area was a Democratic stronghold and ultimately would contribute a majority of the state's Confederate soldiers. While many Kentuckians in 1861 were debating that state's position in the war, the radical secessionists in the Purchase contemplated seceding from Kentucky and joining Tennessee. This fierce loyalty to the South was noted by Grant in September 1861 after he and his men entered Paducah. Writing to his wife, he noted "secession flags flying and the citizens eagerly awaiting the arrival of the Rebel Army."[2]

From September 1861 until February 1862, the residents of the Purchase held out hope that Polk and his Confederate forces would prevail. Their hopes were dashed in February when Grant and his forces pushed out the rebels after capturing forts Henry and Donelson, located on the important Tennessee and Cumberland rivers. Polk abandoned Columbus soon after. As historian Benjamin Franklin Cooling has noted, with the fall of the forts, the heartland of Middle Tennessee, so crucial to the Confederates, fell into the hands of the Federal army, sealing the fate of West Tennessee and west Kentucky. Indeed, the Union Army would remain in the Jackson Purchase for the duration of the war. And, beginning in spring 1862, they would be joined by pro-Southern insurgents.[3]

In May 1862, Gen. Henry Halleck separated the seven counties that made up the Purchase from the rest of Kentucky and organized them into the Military District of West Tennessee, Department of the Mississippi. In addition to the garrison at Paducah, the Federals soon established bases at Columbus and Fort Heiman, located on the Kentucky–Tennessee border near forts Henry and Donelson. Just over the border of Kentucky to the south, the Federals also manned Union City, Tennessee. Over the next three years, the Union Army constructed additional outposts at the smaller towns of Hickman, Clinton, Benton, Moscow, Mayfield, and Murray.[4]

Guerrillas quickly made their presence known. In early May the Purchase narrowly escaped a raid by Col. Thomas Claiborne and the 6th Confederate Tennessee Cavalry, who planned to raid Paducah for medicines. Col. William W. Lowe of the 5th Iowa Cavalry, camped at Paducah, pursued the Confederates, and warned Hickman, Mayfield, and Columbus of the threat. After a brief skirmish, Claiborne's men retreated back into West Tennessee. Lowe responded by requesting extra men in the area west of the Tennessee River so as to protect the "many good and loyal citizens in this vicinity."[5] Between May 19 and 24, Gen. Isaac F. Quinby, commanding at Columbus, led a reconnaissance of some 2,500 men, including former Purchase Confederate deserters acting as spies, from Columbus down the Mississippi River to ascertain rebel strength at Fort Pillow, Tennessee. After arriving near the fort, Quinby was forced to withdraw his force back to Columbus after reports confirmed that a large guerrilla force was moving on Columbus and Mayfield.[6]

By mid-summer 1862, guerrillas had through recruitment steadily increased their presence in the Purchase. Purchase men flocked to Tennessee to join irregular outfits. Two Fulton County men, Capt. Henry A. Tyler and Capt. Gideon Binford, led a group of their neighbors to join the "renegade Tennesseans and runaway Kentuckians" at Col. W. W. Faulkner's headquarters at Dyersburg, Tennessee. Faulkner organized a regiment of Kentucky cavalry that eventually became part of the 12th Kentucky Cavalry, known popularly as Faulkner's Regiment. On August 8, he launched an unsuccessful expedition into Kentucky, hoping to recruit more men and capture cotton. Discovered by a small Union force outside Dyersburg, several of the Confederates were killed and many were captured. Three of the latter were Fielding Bland of Ballard County, and Henry Torpley and W. S. Bennett of Hickman County. From his headquarters at Trenton, Tennessee, Union Gen. Grenville M. Dodge of the Central Division of the Mississippi noted that Faulkner's men were "well armed and fought desperately." To stifle recruitment from the Purchase and West Tennessee, Dodge suggested burning out the entire area since local residents "paid no attention to the oath" and "feed and guide the rebels." He added with disgust that two slaves led the Federals to guerrillas as "no white man had the pluck to do it."[7]

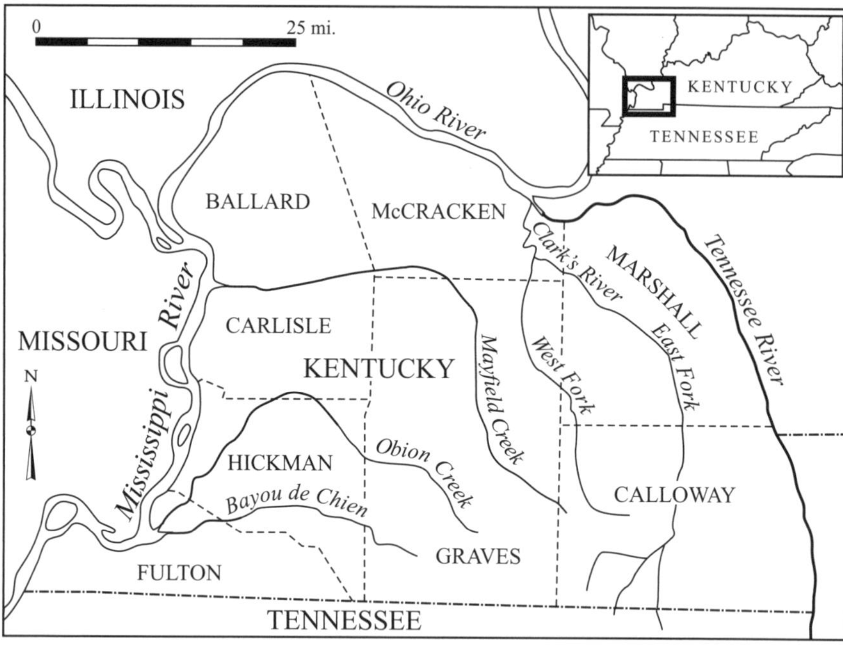

The counties and waterways of the Jackson Purchase during the Civil War.

Faulkner, in particular, kept the Union authorities on their toes in the summer of 1862. In August, Dodge and the 54th Illinois Infantry and the 2d Illinois Cavalry fought a desperate skirmish with Faulkner's men, which turned into hand-to-hand combat after the Kentuckians ran out of ammunition. Faulkner lost thirty-seven men in the skirmish, including sixteen who drowned in the Obion River while trying to reinforce the regiment. Of the Confederates, Dodge reported, "they lost everything. We got their horses, arms, and baggage. Some got away naked." Dodge did not celebrate the victory as he realized "several companies of cavalry from Kentucky are trying to push through South. This was the first that crossed the line."[8]

In October, Faulkner and his men—three hundred strong—attempted to recapture the former Confederate stronghold, Island Number 10, located in the Mississippi River near the Kentucky Bend. Using citizens from Hickman and Fulton counties as guides, Faulkner advanced on the island by moonlight, arriving at four in the morning. The plan was to drive the Northern troops from the island and take the town of Hickman, the hometown of many of his men. Faulkner's men advanced within a hundred yards of the camp when a Federal sentinel fired upon the advancing column. The rear forces of the Confederates fired into their own front, leading to the impression that Union forces were advancing from behind. In the ensuing confusion, Faulkner and his men, believing themselves to have been ambushed, withdrew. The 2d Illinois Cavalry gave chase and captured twelve men as well as Colonel Faulkner, Capt. R. M. Meriwether, Capt. H. B. Blakemore, and Adj. L. H. Johnson.[9]

The attempt to recapture Island Number 10 was part of Faulkner's and other guerrillas' attempts to intercept illicit goods moving up and down the Mississippi River. Throughout the war, illegal trade along the Purchase's waterways was a constant thorn in the side of the Federal army. As historian E. Merton Coulter has pointed out, one of the Union Army's primary problems with Kentucky during the war was allowing legitimate commerce while attempting simultaneously to crush trade with the Confederacy.[10] Though Lincoln was most concerned with the cotton trade in the Purchase, liquor, livestock, and produce were traded in abundance, most troublesomely with guerrillas. The rivers surrounding the Purchase became the theater of war as Federal gunboats plied the waters in search of both guerrillas and illegal trade between the Confederacy and Kentucky and Tennessee. Lt. Cdr. LeRoy Fitch of the U.S. Navy shut down river traffic between Paducah and the Illinois and Indiana shore in October. He also confiscated all rivercraft in an attempt to squash the practice and forbade any vessel from stopping on the Kentucky side of the rivers. Still, the trade did not stop. Commanders at Columbus and Paducah reported in the late summer of 1862 that they had confiscated large amounts of cotton, corn, whiskey, and salt headed South.[11]

By fall 1862, insurgent attacks in West Tennessee and Kentucky had infuriated General Grant. He responded with a series of orders designed to punish "persons acting as guerillas" and their supporters within the community. To curtail the destruction of Federal army supplies and property, and to reimburse the government, Grant authorized the seizure of "a sufficient amount of personal property from persons in the immediate neighborhood sympathizing with the rebellion." Grant further ordered that captured guerrillas also were to be denied treatment as prisoners of war.[12]

In September 1862, General Quinby reported prophetically from Columbus his belief that the insurgents in west Kentucky, Tennessee, and Missouri were impossible to defeat with regular Union infantry. The guerrillas, he complained, had kept themselves apprised of his movements through "pony express," neighborhood networks, and clandestine tactics such as leaving letters and identifying marks on trees and bushes. Most disturbing was their practice of blending back into the populace as "peaceful farmers and citizens" until the danger of attack by Union forces passed. A local man, William P. Denny of Wadesboro, Calloway County, confirmed these claims, noting that several "boys from here" joined guerrilla groups. He added that several walked about the town of Murray in full daylight without fear of recourse.[13]

As 1862 drew to a close, a hardened and fearless Confederate commander plotted a raid into West Tennessee and Kentucky. From December 19, 1862, through January 1863, Gen. Nathan Bedford Forrest led an audacious raid, the first of many to come, into West Tennessee to destroy Union supply lines. His main objective was the Mobile & Ohio Railroad, which ran from Columbus to Jackson, Tennessee. The railroad supplied Grant as he confronted Vicksburg. In late December, Forrest captured the towns of Jackson and Humboldt, destroying tracks, trestles, rolling stock, and burning stores and munitions. On Christmas Eve, Forrest captured Union City. Later that night he dispatched approximately forty men to Moscow, Fulton County, to destroy the railroad bridge over Bayou de Chien. The small Union force guarding the bridge believed the guerrillas to be a much larger force and abandoned the works without a fight.[14]

Following Forrest's raid on Moscow, Gen. Thomas Davies, commander of the Union garrison at Columbus, wrote to Gen. Henry Halleck that he felt Paducah was secure and that Columbus was "out of all danger." He did request additional troops, however, after learning from a "reliable source" that Forrest's men intended to take New Madrid and Island Number 10. The main area in danger was the tiny town of Hickman, which Davies ordered evacuated of its 150-man garrison. In addition to destroying six hundred rounds of ammunition on Island Number 10, Davies and his men heaved two sixty-four-pounder navy guns into the Mississippi River to prevent them from falling into rebel hands. In the end, Forrest's destruction along the Mobile & Ohio Railroad left it useless to the Union Army for a prolonged period of time. In addition to knapsacks and blankets, wagons, horses, and artillery, Forrest also captured ten thousand stands of small arms and one million rounds of ammunition. He likewise killed or captured over two thousand Union troops and recruited large numbers of West Tennessee and Kentucky men to his ranks. Most importantly, Forrest ascertained that the Purchase area was protected by three insufficient garrisons located at Paducah, Columbus, and Fort Heiman.[15]

As 1863 dawned, Grant's forces in the Mississippi Valley numbered approximately 132,000. Gen. Stephen Hurlbut's Sixteenth Corps, consisting of close to 65,000 men, protected West Tennessee and the Purchase. At

Columbus, Hungarian-born Gen. Alexander Asboth commanded. As a garrison commander, he turned out to be prone to exaggeration when it came to insurgent activity in the area. Soon after taking command, he fired off a frantic telegram to Gen. C. S. Hamilton, commander of the West Tennessee District, warning that close to four thousand guerrillas were marching on Island Number 10. Asboth begged for more cavalry to reinforce Hickman and Clinton as well as an additional gunboat. Hamilton denied Asboth's request, replying that no more than three hundred guerrillas were known to be in the area. He admonished the Hungarian, "your dispositions are reproved." Hurlbut, commanding at Memphis, took Asboth more seriously, however, and sent additional troops to Hickman and Columbus, claiming that the "amount of rascality" in the district "is beyond all estimate."[16]

Throughout February, Asboth attempted to quell the guerrillas in his district. Like Grant before him, he held the civilian population culpable for insurgent activity. He issued General Order Number 11, which affected citizens specifically living along the lines of the Mobile & Ohio Railroad. He condemned the "lawless band of guerillas" who plagued the Union garrisons and railroads and stated that they owed their existence to the large numbers of "disloyal" civilians of the Purchase. He thus would insure that civilians would "be held responsible, with their persons and property" for the acts of the guerrillas whom they "cherish." He further ordered that any family living near the scene of a guerrilla attack would be arrested and held hostage.[17]

In March Asboth fired off another panicky telegram, insisting that Paducah and Columbus were the targets of guerrillas in the area. He reported that "I have hardly anything herewith to check an invasion of the six counties between Columbus and Tennessee." He proposed instead the creation of more garrisons at Mayfield and Murray in addition to those already active at Clinton and Benton, so as to make a "chain of communication to control properly this portion of Kentucky."[18] In mid-June 1863, however, Grant ordered Hurlbut to strip his district of manpower and redirect the forces toward Mississippi and the Vicksburg campaign. Grant notably exempted the forces stationed at Paducah and Columbus. The removal of garrisons in West Tennessee, Mayfield, Benton, Murray, and Fort Heiman allowed local partisans like Jacob Biffle, Jeffery Forrest, J. F. Newsom, and James R. Chalmers to roam at will. Biffle, who made sport of destroying telegraph wires between Columbus and Jackson, Tennessee, was especially vexing to Hurlbut, who labeled the Tennessean a "damned Rebel."[19]

Predictably, no one was more worried at Columbus than Asboth. He protested to General Halleck that in "the whole country between the Tennessee and Mississippi River . . . secessionism prevails and guerillas are constantly organizing." Of the ten thousand troops who previously guarded the area between Paducah and Corinth, he complained, only four thousand remained. After pleading with a flippant Halleck not to pull troops out of Hickman and Columbus, "Old Brains" informed Asboth, "I think you have no forces against you but guerrillas. They will *only* devastate the country."[20]

Guerrillas in the area also responded to local elections. In the summer of 1863, Purchase citizens went to the polls to elect a new congressman. To quell rebel sympathy, on July 14 Hurlbut issued Special Order Number 159, which barred all Confederate sympathizers in the Purchase from running for office, serving as electors, and voting. On July 29, Asboth attached additional measures to Hurlbut's orders and prohibited anyone heard "uttering disloyal language and sentiments" from running for office. He likewise ordered all county judges to appoint only Union men to the positions of clerk and judge. They in turn removed all pro-Southern candidates from poll books. Asboth also ordered that all candidates and electors take the oath of allegiance. In addition, the Democratic candidate, Lawrence Trimble, was arrested two weeks prior to the election and held until the day after.[21]

The crackdown on political activity by the Federals and the arrest of Trimble led to another increase in guerrilla activity. On July 16, two days after the issuing of Order Number 159, three bands of insurgents attacked and occupied the town of Hickman and plundered the stores of the Union men in town. The guerrillas also carried a list of loyal men whom they intended to capture and murder. Upon hearing of the list, many Union men fled to Columbus out of fear.[22] The day after the raid, five of the men forced to flee wrote to Asboth requesting protection. The petitioners—H. S. Campbell, Montraville Wilson, George C. Hallet, W. K. Lyle, and I. M. Gest—stated that "we are now here as refugees . . . finding it unsafe to return. With our families still there, our feelings and apprehension may well be imagined." J. C. Bonner, captain of the gunboat *New Era,* visited the town after the "outrages" and believed he could confidently vouch that loyal citizens deserved protection. He reported that many former rebel sympathizers in Hickman were "now ready to protect the town from all assaults that may be made by guerillas . . . the Southern sympathizers themselves have asked for protection of the United States."[23]

The pleas from Hickman's citizens convinced Union officials to enact sweeping measures. In August, the new commander at Columbus, Gen. J. A. Smith, wrote General Hurlbut for permission to raise a group of Home Guards in the Purchase. Smith had received a petition from the Union men in the area, vouched for by Judge Rufus K. Williams, insisting their neighborhood was "infested at times with small rebel or guerilla bands" who avoided capture. Smith noted the men promised to "apprehend these guerillas . . . and bring them to me at this post, or kill, destroy or drive them from their country." On September 14, Hurlbut issued General Order Number 129, which encouraged post commanders in Kentucky and Tennessee to promote the formation of "Home Guards," and to be organized under state militia laws to "repress all robbery, violence, and irregular warfare" within their respective districts. General Smith and his recruiting agent, Col. George C. Hallet, placed posters across the area asking, "Who will refuse this opportunity of manifesting his patriotism and his manhood in defense of his home, his wife, and his children?" Many did; in Fulton County, Eliza Howard noted that "General Hurlbut's orders has stirred up the people very much here . . . they are running." Hallet confessed that enlistment numbers were poor, but at least 150 men from across the Purchase answered the call and joined the Kentucky State Home Guards.[24]

Insurgents in the area responded accordingly. They robbed several stores in Murray and Mayfield and harassed several loyal citizens.[25] In early November guerrillas went to Mayfield, where they "robbed every store, broke up the railroad, and destroyed the rolling stock."[26] Col. Stephen Hicks called out all soldiers and citizens to stand fast in case of another attack; Hicks seemed pleased to report that several citizens answered his call. The guerrillas also captured Congressman Lucien Anderson and several other local loyalists. Newspapers reported the use of bloodhounds by the Confederates to hunt down Union men in the vicinity. Anderson was little more than a pariah in many parts of the Purchase, and the guerrillas hoped to use him as an exchange for Col. Trusten Polk of Missouri, who was being held prisoner at Johnson's Island. Luckily for Anderson, the guerrillas released him unharmed.[27]

Despite the attacks, local men were still reluctant to join the Home Guards. In November, Col. George Hallet traveled to Hickman to recruit local men. Hallet appealed to their patriotism, even their manhood, but to no avail. The only solution, he informed Gen. Jeremiah Boyle, was to conscript men to serve in a militia to destroy the "bandits." To justify his desperate measure, Hallet pleaded with his supervisor:

> Believe me General, the discourse upon which the body politic is now suffering, requires a desperate remedy. Without this, all attempts to clear out this part of Kentucky will be pointless. When before in the history of

> civilized warfare, has an enemy, other than a barbarous and savage one, been found so lost to every sense of humanity, as to fire upon steamboats and passenger trains in upon which peaceable women and children, not to say men, are being transported[?] Shall things remain so?[28]

What Hallet did not know was that the Federal army and local Unionist leaders in the Purchase were devising a new method to combat guerrillas and lackluster Home Guard recruitment in the area. In January 1864, Paducah became the first area in Kentucky in which the Union Army recruited black soldiers. In November 1863, following his capture by guerrillas, Congressman Anderson wrote a letter to President Lincoln requesting that the first black troops come from his district. In early 1864, Union Adj. Gen. Lorenzo Thomas came to Paducah to raise a colored artillery regiment. Thomas appointed Lt. Col. Richard Cunningham of the 2d Illinois Artillery to take charge of recruitment. From January to March 1864, he recruited African American soldiers into the 8th Kentucky Heavy Artillery, Colored. In theory, the army was allowed to enlist only ex-slaves who fled to the Purchase from Tennessee and other seceded states; slaves from Kentucky could enlist if their owners were members of the Confederate Army or had been convicted of aiding and abetting the army or guerrillas. At recruiting stations in Paducah and Columbus, however, Kentucky slaves were accepted routinely. As early as February 1863, "contraband" slaves from the Purchase had been used to repair fortifications, prompting civil authorities in the area to capture and "return them to their owners *or them that claimed to own them.*" In early 1863, the Western Sanitary Commission established a soldiers' home at Columbus and also employed several escaped slaves as workers. In late February, the chaplain of the 1st Kansas Infantry, stationed at Columbus, complained to the president of the Sanitary Commission that "the slave hunters have come down on us to day backed up with the Sheriff. They marched into our office . . . & asked permission to search the house for their fugitives." The African American employees hid themselves, the chaplain warned, with "fire arms." He cautioned "there may be scenes in the home."[29]

After official recruitment began, a barrage of protests followed, including a nine-page letter to President Lincoln from Governor Bramlette, who charged Cunningham with stealing slaves. Several farmers in the Purchase complained that Cunningham led small groups of soldiers to farms at night to recruit their slaves. As an inducement, he offered each slave a $300 bounty, plus freedom for himself and his family. The population of Paducah and Columbus exploded when soldiers' families followed them to camp. The army removed many of the contraband families to Island Number 10 to appease local slaveholders' fears.[30]

In response to the recruitment of black soldiers, guerrillas launched a new round of attacks in the area. In January, Colonel Hallet of the newly formed 40th Kentucky Militia reported that a group of "scoundrels . . . residing in the extensive bottom stretching down along the Mississippi" carried off approximately $800 worth of dry goods at Hickman. At the end of February a band attempted an attack on the Paducah Railroad, but were caught at Dukedom, on the Tennessee–Kentucky border. A raid on the town of Mayfield, however, did succeed. On February 29, insurgents entered the town, looted three stores belonging to Union men, and killed J. B. Happy, a wealthy farmer and "good Union man." They likewise took as prisoner a local preacher, "Parson" William Dugger, whom they put "in heavy bonds." The murder of Happy and the capture of Dugger were not random acts of violence; both men had recently been appointed by the provost marshall to collect bonds for the benefit of Mayfield Unionists robbed by guerrillas the previous fall. The money for the bonds would come from "disloyal" citizens. For their efforts, Happy and Dugger both received $50 per month to be paid from the fund they collected. Under the circumstances, the men were no doubt seen as traitors to their community, out to take advantage of their neighbors for their own benefit.[31]

In February 1864, meanwhile, the Treasury Department finally removed all trade restrictions from Kentucky and Missouri, prompting Gen. H. T. Reid at Cairo to worry about goods leaving Paducah, Hickman, and Cairo and making their way illegally to Tennessee and to insurgents. Congressman Lucian Anderson also worried and warned Lincoln of the dangers of opening unrestricted trade: "Permit me to say if this is done, down will go all the hopes of the Union men, especially in my district. This unrestricted trade in my district is what the rebels want; and if trade is thus opened, the rebels will be supplied with every thing they desire, which will go into the houses of rebels in their Army. I protest against it so far as the first District is concerned, and ask you candidly to take the matter into serious consideration before acting." On March 11, guerrillas raided Clinton and captured forty horses and robbed two stores. The following day brought additional raids in the area, including one on Mayfield, which left several citizens fleeing toward Paducah and the protection of the Union Army. Col. William H. Lawrence despaired over the situation, stating, "it now becomes a military necessity, in my opinion, to prevent the large shipment of goods to these defenseless towns."[32]

The commander at Cairo, Gen. Mason Brayman, agreed. He felt that free trade in the area contributed to much of the problem, stating that those engaged were "pernicious beyond measure; corrupting those in service, and furnishing needed supplies to enemies." Brayman claimed possession of intercepted correspondence that proved Paducah traders who had taken the oath and were issued permits by Union authorities were conducting business across the Purchase with rebel traders with permits issued by Forrest.[33]

Unlike Asboth, Brayman felt that the additional outposts across the Purchase actually aided the guerrillas instead of impeding them. He characterized the small outposts like the one at Hickman as dens for "smugglers and contraband dealers" and suppliers of guerrillas. He further charged that guerrillas benefited from the "loose trade regulations and supplies at small garrisons." As a result, he pulled forces out of the tiny garrison at Hickman. With little manpower and few guns, Brayman justified the abandonment of the town as a necessity so as to protect the rivers and important military points.[34]

The raids on Clinton and Mayfield that March were only precursors to a larger, much more organized raid. This time, the Confederates avoided the small garrisons and made a bold move on the town of Paducah itself, the symbol of Union occupation in the Purchase. On March 25, Forrest himself led close to two thousand men into Paducah, including members of the 3rd Kentucky and 7th Kentucky Mounted Infantry. The 3rd and the 7th were made up of men from the Purchase and led by Paducah son Col. A. P. Thompson. Like the other Purchase men, he was eager to return home. Forrest placed Thompson in command to give him the honor of "capturing his home town."[35]

On March 24, a flurry of messages between Union commanders went out warning that Forrest was advancing on the Purchase and "conscripting everybody." Col. Stephen G. Hicks at Paducah found the prospect of a raid by Forrest daunting, but he seemed equally concerned with the insurgents across the Purchase who would join the "Wizard of the Saddle's" ranks. On the same day that Forrest's men attacked Union City, Hicks reported that thirty-five bushwhackers had met the railroad train in Mayfield, killed one black man, and fired several shots at a local Unionist. At the small village of Fancy Farm, Graves County, guerrillas shot the postmaster, robbed a number of stores owned by loyal men, sacked the Catholic church, and captured five prisoners. The Federal commander noted that "no Union man can go out" because "the interior is full of guerrillas."[36]

Jennie Fyfe, a young nurse from Lansing, Michigan, who had recently arrived in Paducah to serve at the U.S. Army Hospital, found the town abuzz with rumors of impending attacks. The streets, she noted, were full of soldiers, not civilians. The army stood ready to fire the commissary stores should Forrest and his men attack since they "did not wish to hold Paducah, but plunder it." Even secessionists in the town were trying to prevent guerrilla attacks, Fyfe noted, out of fear for their own property. Secessionists and Unionists alike did not have long to wait for Forrest's next move.[37]

Anticipating an attack, Hicks took his 650-strong force to Fort Anderson, located in a supply depot. Situated on the western end of town, the fort was around 400 feet long, ran 160 feet toward the Ohio River, and was surrounded on four sides by deep ditches filled with water. Several of the men who retired to Fort Anderson were members of the U.S. 8th Colored Heavy Artillery, who would now get their first taste of battle as Forrest entered Paducah. The Confederates also faced Union gunboats *Peosta* and *Paw Paw* on the Ohio River, which arrived an hour before the rebels entered town. Hicks ordered the evacuation of the town's women and children to the fort and across the river to Illinois. Townspeople hurried to gather up family members and valuables and headed toward the river. As Union troops assisted them into boats, Forrest's men hid along the riverbank and fired at the gunboats, secure in the knowledge that Federal troops would not return fire and put women and children in danger. Of his journey across the Ohio to the Illinois shore, Paducah native Louis F. Kolb recalled clinging "fast to the bottom of the boat" as shots whizzed all around them.[38]

The majority of Forrest's men retired to the center of town in late afternoon to rob and pillage, while his sharpshooters positioned themselves in houses along the riverfront to fire at the gunboats and the fort. They also reportedly forced five nurses at the local hospital to stand in front of their lines, preventing fire from Union forces. For the next several hours, Federal troops at Fort Anderson fired on Forrest's men nonetheless as the gunboats pounded the town.[39]

Forrest sent a flag of truce to the fort demanding surrender and promising "no quarter" should he have to attack. Several newspapers later reported that Confederate Kentucky troops in particular were outraged at the presence of African American troops in the fort. One correspondent wrote that the troops in Forrest's command were overheard swearing to "kill every damned nigger" inside the fort. Jennie Fyfe and her fellow nurses at the hospital, meanwhile, desperately tried to protect the sick black troops in the hospital, noting that if the "rascals" get hold of them, "they will show them no mercy."[40]

While his men continued pillaging, Forrest sent the flag of truce twice more; both times, Colonel Hicks refused. Orders went out to the 3rd Kentucky and 7th Kentucky to charge the fort. According to Henry George, the Kentuckians had no knowledge of the deep ditches around the fort until they were within a short distance of their objective. By then it was too late. Shots from within the fort and shells from the gunboats decimated the attackers. Thompson himself, "within sight of the place of his birth," died when a shell blew his body to bits.[41]

As evening fell and Union authorities took stock of the damage, they determined to punish the townspeople, believing that they had welcomed Forrest into their town. The gunboats opened fire on the houses that held Forrest's sharpshooters while the town itself was "shelled and made a ruin over their heads." Colonel Hicks ordered the burning of all houses within musket range, an act for which Major General Hurlbut later lauded as "well deserved." The *New York Times* admonished those who found fault with the shelling of Paducah, noting "their sympathies might well be expended on Charleston."[42]

Forrest's raid convinced Union authorities as well as Purchase citizens that previous attempts to quell guerrilla activity were useless. In the aftermath, however, the Union high command laid the blame directly at the feet of the disloyal people of western Kentucky. In particular they blamed the constant supply of illegally traded goods in the Purchase with furnishing Forrest's troops. "That large force could not have remained so long, and probably would not have come at all" without the provisions provided by illicit trade, they concluded. Purchase citizens invited Forrest and his men into western Kentucky, they stated, to disrupt elections and to instill "insurrectionary control." With summer fast approaching, the people of the Purchase paraded their rebel sympathies and determined to "kill, plunder, and expel from their homes all loyal men."[43]

As predicted, insurgent activity continued throughout the summer. Though the majority of the Kentucky soldiers returned to Tennessee and Mississippi with Forrest, some remained behind both to visit family and wreak havoc. Throughout April and May, bands of former Confederates scoured the countryside. Henry Ford of Graves County, for example, reported a bay horse, ten bushels of wheat, and a "fine lot of corn" stolen from his home. Ford had served as commissary sergeant for the 15th Kentucky (US) for twelve months and was accused of being a member of a Unionist guerrilla unit and spy for the Federals. Using psychological intimidation, the guerrillas also took several articles of his clothing and suspended them from trees in his yard. Ford believed it was "emblematic of the treatment that I would receive if caught." Later that summer, Ford fled his home out of fear. John Greathouse of Hickman also fled his home for Cairo after "evil and disposed persons" in his community accused him of aiding Federal soldiers and robbed him of two ferry boats and a skiff.[44] In Ballard County, Confederate guerrillas scoured the countryside in search of mounts, leading Michael Blackburn, a local farmer, to hide his horses in a swampy area along the Mississippi River. In their quest for the horses, raiders ransacked Blackburn's home, "shot two of his dogs, threatened to kill his entire family, and took as a hostage Blackburn's youngest son."[45]

In May, guerrillas murdered three Unionists in Marshall County. They likewise led an attack on one of their favorite targets, the town of Mayfield, home of the leading Unionists in the area, Congressman Lucian Anderson and Judge R. K. Williams. They captured ten soldiers guarding the town. An enraged commander of the town reported that "the anti-unionism is so strong in this district that large bodies of guerrillas, led by men of respectable families, assemble in the best settled parts." He worried that insurgents would discourage the few Unionists in the area and proposed the arrest of ten influential rebel sympathizers in the neighborhood to be held as hostages for the safe return of the soldiers.[46]

By the summer of 1864, the small Unionist minority, led by Anderson and Williams, begged Lincoln himself to send an able commander to combat the guerrilla menace. Determined to take a hard line with the people of the Purchase, Lincoln sent Gen. Eleazor A. Paine to Paducah in July 1864. Determined to punish the people for Forrest's audacious attack, he would employ draconian measures, including the execution of several suspected guerrillas.

Paine, however, was not new to the Jackson Purchase in 1864. He in fact was placed in command following Grant's occupation of Paducah in 1861, but was later removed for treating civilians too harshly. Local Confederate R. C. Woolfolk reported that Paine threatened to shoot him if he did not remove a Confederate flag from his home. Others noted Paine for his remarkable expletives: "God-damn you, I will dig a hole, shoot you in the damn head, and put you in it" had been one of his favorite warnings back in 1861.[47]

After his removal from Paducah in 1861, Paine commanded divisions at the battles of New Madrid, Island Number 10, and the siege of Corinth.

From 1862 until 1864, he established headquarters at Gallatin, Tennessee, to guard the railroads in western Tennessee and police the civilian population of the town. In Gallatin, Paine was rumored to have executed several suspected spies without trial, adding to the already ruthless reputation he had gained in Paducah in 1861. He likewise reportedly killed returning rebel soldiers who had taken the oath of allegiance. In April 1864, Paine went under orders to Tullahoma to guard the railroad bridges over the Duck and Elk rivers.[48]

Under Special Order Number 83, Paine took charge of the entire Purchase as well as the post at Cairo. Gen. Henry Prince at Columbus and Gen. Solomon Meredith at Cairo were to report to him.[49] Ironically, Paine arrived in Paducah on July 19, the same day President Lincoln issued General Order Number 233 suspending the writ of habeas corpus and establishing martial law in Kentucky.[50]

After settling in at his headquarters, Paine outlined his "plan of salvation." To prevent illicit trade and trafficking to guerrillas, Paine forbade any rebellious citizen from circulating any amount of money—"not a dollar"—and required his approval and signature for all money transactions. He seized the bank deposits of all suspected secessionists for government use and placed an ad valorem tax of twenty-five cents on all tobacco, cotton, and other merchandise sold in the district. The tax would go to the coffers of the provost marshal, Maj. Henry Bartling, to compensate Union refugees. All Union widows in the district would receive $5,000 to be paid from a $100,000 fine levied on Purchase secessionists. To the businessmen who protested, Paine added, "I will teach you that having encouraged this rebellion, having comforted and aided your country's enemies, you must, aye, shall reap a traitor's reward."[51]

Paine was also incensed with the dearth of Union volunteers in the Union Army from the area. He informed the men in his area that they "must fight" for the Union. He accused them of cowardice and racism: "You are all of you able-bodied men, but think yourselves too good to fight, afraid of Federal bullets or something else. And when I come to get your niggers to make soldiers of them you set up such a howl."[52] Instead of forcing them to "fight," however, Paine forced the citizens of Mayfield to construct a fort around their much-maligned city. Under the direction of Col. W. W. McChesney, townspeople had to perform hard labor unless they paid exorbitant fines, ranging from $5 to $400, depending on individual wealth.[53]

Paine later banished citizens from the Purchase to Canada and reportedly executed over forty people, many accused of guerrilla activities. After ordering African American troops to execute a suspected insurgent by the name of Kesterson in July 1864, Paine then appointed P. B. Jacobs, a reported Southern sympathizer, to ride out to every guerrilla commander in the area and read a proclamation: "I have this day shot Captain Kesterson, taken prisoner in guerrilla warfare, and shall shoot in like manner all prisoners so taken, and if I am credibly informed of retaliation being practiced on Union men living in my district I will walk out five of the most prominent citizens of Paducah . . . make them 'kneel down' and 'shoot them. I will do it, so help me God.'" Paine, meanwhile, held Jacobs's father and brother hostage for ten days until his return. Jacobs came back, carrying with him the proclamation and the signatures of all the rebel leaders on the back.[54]

After receiving complaints from Governor Bramlette, citizens, and other Union commanders, Lincoln removed Paine from command. Though he commanded the area for only two months, his tenure would forever determine how the Jackson Purchase saw the war. Federal occupation became a defining feature of the war in the Purchase. The harder the guerrillas pressed Federal authorities, the more strident the Union authority became. Though the insurgents did not play a decisive role in the outcome of the war in the region, the efforts to stop them most certainly influenced public perception of the Federal government and Union cause in the decades following the war. For the people of the Purchase, the Union Army would always be an occupier, a tyrannical force that believed all citizens to be disloyal. As such, the area would embrace the Lost Cause ideology that enveloped the state in the decades following the war. Guerrillas became heroes, Home Guards and Unionists were vilified or forgotten, and the Confederate "cause" became righteous. Thus for the citizens, guerrillas, and Federal authorities alike, the Jackson Purchase would always be "Kentucky's South Carolina."

Notes

1. United States War Department, *The War of the Rebellion: A Compilation of the Official Records of the Union and Confederate Armies*, 128 vols. (Washington, D.C.: U. S. Government Printing Office, 1880–1901), ser. 3, vol. 4, 688–90 (hereafter cited as *OR*); ibid., vol. 39, pt. 2, 260–61; "Report of J. A. Geneva to Secretary of War Edwin M. Stanton," War Department, Bureau of Military Justice, Washington, D.C., Dec. 1, 1864, RG153, MM1609, Folder 4, National Archives and Records Administration, Washington, D. C.

2. For more on the history of the Jackson Purchase, see Patricia Hoskins, "'The Old First Is with the South': The Civil War, Reconstruction, and Memory in the

Jackson Purchase Region of Kentucky" (Ph.D. diss., Auburn Univ., 2009). See also John E. L. Robertson, "Paducah," *The Kentucky Encyclopedia* (Lexington: The Univ. Press of Kentucky, 1992), 705–6. For more on the secession crisis in the Jackson Purchase, see Berry F. Craig, "The Jackson Purchase Considers Secession: The 1861 Mayfield Convention," *Register of the Kentucky Historical Society* 99 (2001): 339–61 (hereafter cited as *Register*).

3. Benjamin Franklin Cooling, *Fort Donelson's Legacy* (Knoxville: Univ. of Tennessee Press, 1997), 164–67; Benjamin Franklin Cooling, *Forts Henry and Donelson: The Key to the Confederate Heartland* (Knoxville: Univ. of Tennessee Press, 1987), 44–62.

4. *OR*, vol.17, pt. 2, 7; vol. 16, pt. 2, 20; Hunter B. Whitesell, "Military Operations in the Jackson Purchase Areas of Kentucky, 1862–1865," *Register of the Kentucky Historical Society* 63 (Apr. 1965): 147. The district also included the region of Tennessee between the Mississippi and Tennessee rivers, as well as the northern half of the state of Mississippi. Though reorganized several times more throughout the war, the Purchase remained separated from other military districts of Kentucky until the fall of 1864.

5. *OR*, vol. 10, pt. 1, 880–84.

6. Ibid, 897–98.

7. Ibid., vol. 17, pt. 1, 29–30; Henry George, *History of the 3d, 7th, 8th, and 12th Kentucky, CSA* (Louisville, Ky.: C. T. Dearing Print, 1911), 68; John Y. Simon, ed., *Papers of Ulysses S. Grant* (Carbondale: Southern Illinois Univ. Press, 1967), 5:314. Henry A. Tyler, a lawyer, was in his early twenties at the outbreak of war. After the war, Tyler returned to Hickman, Fulton County, and continued a successful law practice. In 1870 his estate was valued at $30,000. By 1900, he and his sons had opened a manufacturing company in Hickman. *Eighth and Ninth Census of the United States, 1860 and 1870, Fulton County, Kentucky,* http://www.ancestry.com.

8. *OR*, vol. 17, pt. 1, 32–33.

9. Ibid., 460–61.

10. Simon, ed., *Papers*, 267, 426; *OR*, vol. 13, 552–55; see also E. Merton Coulter, "Commercial Intercourse with the Confederacy in the Mississippi Valley," *Mississippi Valley Historical Review* (Mar. 1919): 377–95, and David G. Surdam, *Northern Naval Superiority and the Economics of the American Civil War* (Columbia: Univ. of South Carolina Press, 2001). Most vexing to Grant during the early part of the war was the movement of cotton along the Mississippi and Tennessee rivers. Grant reacted by forbidding trade between Illinois and Kentucky, then later required permits for any vessel traveling west of Louisville on the Ohio River. Hoping to pacify Unionist planters in the border states as well as the South, and realizing that most of the North and indeed the world needed the cotton the South provided, President Lincoln relaxed trade restrictions along the Mississippi River in summer 1862. By the fall, over $3 million worth of cotton had been traded northward.

11. United States Naval War Records Office, *Official Records of the Union and Confederate Navies in the War of the Rebellion* (Washington, D.C.: Government Printing Office, 1894–1922), vol. 23, 435 (hereafter cited as *ORN*); Amy Hill Shevitz, *Jewish Communities on the Ohio River: A History* (Lexington: Univ. of Press of Kentucky, 2007), 99–105.

12. *OR*, vol. 17, pt. 2, 69.

13. Ibid., pt. 1, 145–48; Barbara Denny George, *The 1860–1862 Journal of William Peter Denny* (Melber, Ky.: Simmons Historical Publications, 1995), 26–27.

14. *OR*, vol. 17, pt. 1, 592–97.

15. Ibid., pt. 2, 498–500; *ORN*, vol. 23, 652–53. See also Cooling, *Fort Donelson's Legacy*, 164–67; Gen. Thomas Jordan and J. P. Pryor, *Campaigns of General N. B. Forrest and Forrest's Cavalry* (New York: De Capo Press, 1996); Brian Steel Wills, *A Battle from the Start: The Life of Nathan Bedford Forrest* (New York: Harper Collins, 1992), 154–56.

16. *OR*, vol. 24, pt. 3, 30–34, 73–74.

17. Ibid., 74.

18. Ibid., vol. 23, pt. 2, 99–101, 150–51; vol. 24, pt. 3, 20–21, 99–102. Before its abandonment in March 1863, Fort Heiman was briefly transferred to the Department of the Cumberland.

19. *OR*, vol. 24, pt. 3, 415.

20. Ibid., 249, 413–15.

21. Ibid., vol. 23, pt. 2, 570–72.

22. *ORN*, vol. 25, 309–10.

23. *OR*, vol. 23, 825–27. Of the list of Unionists found in the petition, only two are listed in the 1860 census. H. S. Campbell was born in Ohio and worked for a livery stable in 1860. At the time of the raid in 1863, he was serving as revenue officer of Hickman. Montraville Wilson was a master brick mason in 1860, and in 1863 he was serving as enrolling officer for the Union Army in Fulton County.

24. *OR*, vol. 30, pt. 3, 66–67; David Nelson Current, *Lincoln's Loyalists: Union Soldiers from the Confederacy* (Boston: Northeastern Univ. Press, 1992), 57; Eliza Howard to William Allen Howard, Nov. 24, 1863, Howard Collection, Manuscripts Department, Lilly Library, Indiana University, Bloomington, Ind.; Adjutant General's Roster of the Civil War, Fortieth Kentucky Militia, Fulton, Graves, and Calloway Counties, Kentucky Department of Military Affairs, Military Records and Research Bureau, Frankfort, Ky.

25. *OR*, vol. 30, pt. 2, 645–48; Special Orders Number 217, Issued by Maj. Gen. Stephen Hurlbut, Memphis, Tenn., Sept. 10, 1863, RG 393, National Archives, Department of Kentucky 1862–69, Records of the Provost Marshall, Miscellaneous Records, E2238.

26. *OR*, vol. 31, 839; *ORN*, vol. 25, 490–91, 530.

27. *ORN*, ser. 2, vol. 6, 552,709; ibid., ser. 2, vol. 25, 529; *New York Times*, Nov. 8, 1863. Trusten Polk was the former governor and senator of Missouri. He was expelled from the Senate when he joined the Confederate Congress. He likewise served in the Missouri State Guard under Sterling Price's command. In 1863, Jefferson Davis appointed him judge of the Trans-Mississippi Department and ordered him to Little Rock. Upon learning that Federal authorities captured his family, he set out to find them. He was captured sometime in September 1863. See Lawrence O. Christensen et al., eds., *Dictionary of Missouri Biography* (Columbia: Univ. of Missouri Press, 1999), 619, and David C. Aamodt, "Conviction of Duty: The Life of Senator Trusten Polk" (master's thesis, Central Missouri State Univ., 1994).

28. Col. George Hallet to Gen. John Boyle, Nov. 4, 1863, Adjutant General's Roster of the Civil War, Fortieth Kentucky Militia, Fulton County, Kentucky.

29. *OR,* ser. 4, vol. 4, 138; Ira Berlin, Steven F. Miller, Joseph P. Reidy, and Leslie S. Rowland, eds., *Freedom: A Documentary History of Emancipation: 1861–1867,* ser. I, vol. II, *The Wartime Genesis of Free Labor: The Upper South* (London: Cambridge Univ. Press, 1993), 630–40.

30. *OR,* ser. 3, vol. 4, 178–79, 436–38; John E. L. Robertson, *Paducah: Frontier to Atomic Age* (Mount Pleasant, S.C.: Arcadia Publishing, 2012), 40–53; "Paducah Letter," *Louisville Journal,* Jan. 26, 1864; John David Smith, "The Recruitment of Negro Soldiers in Kentucky, 1863–1865," *Register of the Kentucky Historical Society* 72 (1974): 364–90; Michael T. Meier, "Lorenzo Thomas and the Recruitment of Blacks in the Mississippi Valley, 1863–65," in *Black Soldiers in Blue: African American Troops in the Civil War,* ed. John David Smith (Chapel Hill: Univ. of North Carolina Press, 2002), 249–76; Marion B. Lucas, *A History of Blacks in Kentucky* (Frankfort: Kentucky Historical Society Press, 2003), 160. See also Victor B. Howard, *Black Liberation in Kentucky: Emancipation and Freedom, 1862–1884 (Lexington: Univ. Press of Kentucky, 1983).*

31. Col. George Hallet to Gen. D. W. Lindsey, Jan. 12, 1864, Kentucky Department of Military Affairs, Military Records and Research Bureau, Frankfort, Ky., Adjutant General's Roster of the Civil War, Fortieth Kentucky Militia, Fulton County, Ky.; *OR,* vol. 32, pt.1, 417, 485; Col. Stephen Hicks, Special Orders Number 29, Feb. 5, 1864, RG 393, Department of Kentucky 1862–69, Records of the Provost Marshall, Miscellaneous Records, E2238, National Archives and Records Administration, Washington, D.C., http://www.ancestry.com. J. B. Happy was forty-three in 1860 and owned an estate valued at $16,000. "Parson" Dugger was William Dugger, a local preacher in his late fifties with an estate valued at $8,300.

32. *OR,* vol. 32, pt. 2, 427; vol. 32, pt. 1, 493–94.

33. Frank Moore, ed., *Rebellion Record: A Diary of American Events, 1864* (New York: Von Nostrand, 1865), vol. 8, doc. 1, 1–8.

34. *OR,* vol. 32, pt. 1, 504; Moore, *Rebellion Record,* doc. 1, 1–8.

35. George, *History of the 3rd, 7th, 8th, and 12th Kentucky, CSA,* 73; John Allen Wyeth, *That Devil Forrest: Life of General Nathan Bedford Forrest* (New York: Harper and Row Publishers, 1959), 326–27. The other brigades were commanded by Col. Robert M. McCulloch, Col. Tyree Bell, and Col. R. V. Richardson. See also Robert Selph Henry, *"First with the Most" Forrest* (Indianapolis: Bobbs-Merrill, 1944), 235–36; Thomas Jordan and J. P. Pryor, *The Campaigns of Lieutenant General N. B. Forrest and of Forrest's Cavalry* (Cambridge, Mass.: Da Capo Press, 1996), 403–4; John Watson Morton, *The Artillery of Nathan Bedford Forrest's Cavalry* (Nashville: Publishing House of the M. E. Church, South, 1909), 106–7; Wills, *Battle from the Start,* 169–72. According to the 1860 census, Thompson was thirty years old, with an estate valued at $23,000. He and his wife lived in downtown Paducah and were the owners of seven slaves. *Eighth Census of the United States, 1860, McCracken County, Kentucky,* http://www.ancestry.com.

36. *OR,* vol. 32, pt. 1, 541, 628; pt. 2, 126–31.

37. Jennie Fyfe to Nell Fyfe, Mar. 30, 1864, Fyfe Family Papers, Special Collections, Bentley Historical Library, University of Michigan, Ann Arbor, Mich.

38. *Paducah News-Democrat,* Mar. 25, 1927; *OR,* vol. 32, pt. 1, 540–49.

39. *OR,* vol. 32, pt. 1, 540.

40. Ibid., 549; Jennie Fyfe to Nell Fyfe, Mar. 30, 1864, Fyfe Family Papers; Moore, ed., *The Rebellion Record,* 499–510.

41. *OR,* vol. 32, pt. 1, 549. Jordan and Pryor, *Campaigns,* 408–12, state that the charge on Fort Anderson was advanced by Col. A. P. Thompson and not ordered by Forrest. *New York Times,* Apr. 1, 1864; Jennie Fyfe to Nell Fyfe, Mar. 30, 1864, Fyfe Family Papers.

42. *New York Times,* Apr. 1, 1864.

43. *OR,* vol. 32, pt. 1, 512–15; Moore, ed., *Rebellion Record,* 1–8, 515–18.

44. "Account of Damages by Rebel Guerrillas on Henry Ford of Graves County, Kentucky, July 24, 1864," Sworn Affidavit of John Greathouse, Sept. 1864, Letters Received, Department of Kentucky, 1862–69, E2173, Box 1, Records of the U.S. Army Continental Command, 1821–1920, RG393, National Archives and Records, Washington, D.C. Ford was a modest farmer living in Graves County during the war. In 1860, John Greathouse was listed as a middling farmer in Hickman. It is possible that he operated a ferry during the war as Hickman was on the Mississippi and many residents of that town were known to engage in trade along the river during the war. *Eighth Census for the United States, 1860, Hickman and Graves County, Kentucky,* http://www.ancestry.com.

45. Donna C. Browning, *A History of Carlise County, KY, 1820–1900* (Milburn, Ky.: Self-published, 1976), 10. Michael Blackburn moved to Ballard County between 1860 and 1870. In 1870, he was a middling farmer with an estate valued at $945. His sons, Levander "Lee" and John Calhoun, were still living at home. *Ninth Census of the United States, 1870, Ballard County, Kentucky,* http://www.ancestry.com.

46. *OR,* vol. 39, pt. 1, 24–26.

47. Willis Danforth, "How I Came to Be in the Army and General E. A. Paine's Plan of Federal Salvation," in Military Order of the Loyal Legion of the United States, Wisconsin Commandery, *War Papers Read before the Commandery of the State of Wisconsin, Loyal Legion of the United States* (Milwaukee: Burdick, Armitage, & Allen, 1891), 1:324–38; Lewis Collins, *History of Kentucky* (Lexington, Ky.: Henry Clay Press, 1968), 140; Thomas W. Durham and Jeffery L. Patrick, eds., *Three Years with Wallace's Zouaves: The Civil War Memoirs of Thomas Wise Durham* (Macon, Ga.: Mercer Univ. Press, 2003), 59–61.

48. Walter T. Durham, *Rebellion Revisited: A History of Sumner County, Tennessee from 1861–1870* (Gallatin, Tenn.: Sumner County Museum Association, 1982); *OR,* vol. 32, pt. 2, 532. The diary of Alice Williamson, a young woman living in Gallatin during Paine's reign over the town, details the supposed atrocities committed by the general. See Alice Williamson Diary, Special Collections Library, Duke University, online archival collection, http://scriptorium.lib.duke.edu/williamson/.

49. "Explanations of Brigadier General E. A. Paine, recently in command of the Western District of Kentucky required by the report of Brigadier General Joseph Holt, Judge Advocate General of the United States, Washington, D.C.," in Records of the Office of Judge Advocate General (Army) Court Martial Case Files, 1809–94 RG153, MM1609, Folder 3, National Archives and Records Administration, Washington, D.C.

50. *OR,* vol. 39, pt. 2, 181–82.

51. Danforth, "How I Came to Be in the Army," 333–38.

52. "Explanations of Brigadier General E. A. Paine."

53. Ibid.

54. Danforth, "How I Came to Be in the Army," 324–38. The "Jacobs" man whom Paine sent out with the proclamation was one of the sons of E. P. Jacob, a neighbor of L. S. Trimble, the Peace Democrat who was imprisoned during the August 1863 state elections. Jacob's other neighbor was J. C. Noble, the vehement and vocal rebel newspaper publisher. Jacob had three sons listed in the 1860 census—Charles, Richard, and Fredrick—all of whom were in their early twenties or late teens. *Eighth Census of the United States, 1860, for McCracken County, Kentucky,* http://www.ancestry.com.

Our Friends, the Enemy

Federal Occupation and the Unionist Regiments of Middle and West Tennessee

Derek W. Frisby

Col. John Rogers of the 1st West Tennessee Infantry (US) wrote to Tennessee's military governor, Andrew Johnson, in August 1862, stressing the importance of recruiting more Unionists for West Tennessee counterguerrilla operations. "Cavelry from other states is almost inefectual [*sic*] for that purpose," Rogers argued, and as proof, he related the story of his unit's recent successes in tracking down and arresting guerrillas in an area where previous Federal expeditions had been "baffled" for months. West Tennessee Unionists had succeeded where these "strangers" had failed because they were well acquainted with the terrain and its inhabitants, and this special knowledge allowed them to obtain intelligence that had otherwise eluded Federal units. Colonel Rogers told Johnson, "My own experience here Governor satisfies me that the *Rebels* in Tennessee can only be quelled by Tennesseans."[1]

Rogers's letter alludes to the complex relationship between Southern Unionists and Federal soldiers while conducting counterinsurgency operations throughout the western portions of Tennessee during the American Civil War. Federal armies occupied much of Middle and West Tennessee for nearly the entire war, but they found their authority in that region constantly challenged by guerrillas and by regular incursions of Confederate cavalry. To assist in countering these threats and restoring political authority, they reluctantly enlisted Southern Unionists. Many people, both in the North and South, believed that nurturing Southern Unionism would aid the Federal government, not only in achieving the military objectives of the war, but also the political objectives of reconstruction as well. Instead of creating an atmosphere of cooperation and peace, however, joint operations between

Southern Unionists and Federal troops, unfortunately, produced an explosive air of suspicion and animosity that persisted well beyond the war's end. The strained relationship between Tennessee Unionists and Federal troops was personified best by the response of French Republicans upon the arrival in Paris of their vengeful enemies following Napoleon's 1814 defeat—"nos amis, nos ennemis [Our friends, our enemies]."[2]

For almost a year, Tennessee Unionists anxiously awaited their liberation by Federal forces advancing into the Upper South. A secessionist "reign of terror" had muted their Unionist voices and prevented any significant action against their oppressors. Then in February 1862, Union Gen. Ulysses S. Grant's attacks on Fort Donelson and Fort Henry renewed hope that stability and order would soon be restored. President Abraham Lincoln had indeed predicated the nation's military and political restoration strategies upon reviving the strong Unionist elements of Southern society that he believed had been subjugated by secessionist fraud, intimidation, and violence.

Initial encounters with Southern civilians led Federal authorities to believe that a latent Unionism would reassert itself behind the army's advance to restore the nation. Several gunboats headed up the Tennessee River in February 1862 and encountered a "gratifying sense of loyalty" among the residents. "Men, women, and children several times gathered in crowds of hundreds," one Federal Navy lieutenant said, and "shouted their welcome and hailed their national flag with an enthusiasm there was no mistaking." "If we dared express ourselves freely you would hear such a shout greeting your coming as you ever heard," one Unionist exclaimed. He intimated to the Federal sailors, "We know there are many Unionists among us, but a reign of terror makes us afraid of our shadows. . . . Bring us a small organized force with arms and ammunition for us, and we can maintain our position and put down rebellion in our midst."[3]

Less than six months later, the Union Army had occupied all of western Tennessee. A St. Louis newspaper correspondent advancing with Union troops in West Tennessee reported: "A strong Union sentiment prevails around us." As for the intermittent guerrilla activity, the region was now under martial law and the officers in charge knew, according to this reporter, "how, and when, to turn the screws so as to make loyalty set well on the unruly." Another Unionist offered a similar remedy, saying, "A little bone and nerve liniment freely administered to some rampant individuals and West Tennessee is fully redeemed." Gen. Henry Halleck, the region's commander, concurred, saying, "The enemy is all but driven out of West Tennessee. . . . The regeneration of the state cannot be far off."[4]

But Halleck's slow advance toward Corinth and Memphis in the spring of 1862 forced the Federals to relocate along the railroads traversing western Tennessee as the rivers fell to their summer levels, making it nearly impossible to transport supplies inland via waterways. Much of this railroad network ran through the fervently secessionist southwestern counties of West Tennessee. Therefore, the Federal troops abandoned the predominantly Unionist counties and moved their area of operations into the very belly of the beast. This strategic relocation would have serious repercussions in the Federals' attitudes toward Southern civilians and their ability to exert their control over the region.

Federal authorities hoped that by respecting Southern civilians' rights and property, they could bolster Southern Unionists, and together they could move quickly to quell the rebellion. At the war's outbreak, senior Federal officers considered the destruction of civilian property to be "impolitic and unjust," serving only to transform apathetic or otherwise peaceful citizens into "bitter and implacable enemies." Using this "conciliatory" approach, Union military forces took great pains to avoid inflicting damage upon civilians, and they even curtailed foraging in an effort to foster Unionism among the Southern populace.[5]

But the scope and brutality of the internecine warfare during the Federal occupation of Missouri had soured Federal officers, such as General Halleck, on a purely conciliatory approach. So, as he prepared to invade western Tennessee, Halleck adopted a "pragmatic" occupation policy that abandoned attempts to exploit the Confederacy's internal divisions with the hope of eliminating the inherent distractions of unconventional warfare that accompanied such efforts. The pragmatic policy then sought to concentrate on military objectives rather than civilian pacification and essentially take the Southern citizenry out of the equation for victory all together.

The first test of this "pragmatic" doctrine came as the Union Army pushed into West Tennessee. To limit interaction with local Southerners and better protect their extended rail supply lines, Federal troops cloistered themselves in numerous, widely dispersed garrison towns along western Tennessee's railroads. Therefore, the Federal occupation took on what historian Stephen V. Ash calls a "distinctive geography," depriving Federal troops of their ability to protect the Unionists, who often lived in Tennessee's poorer rural areas beyond the rail lines. Federal authority emanated only a short distance from the garrison towns into the "no-man's-land" and Confederate frontier, areas where guerrillas, bushwhackers, and Confederate cavalry frequently operated with impunity. They subsequently reduced patrolling to lessen their vulnerability to guerrilla attack and to stem the indiscriminate confiscation and looting that seemed to inspire the soldiers whenever they left camp.[6]

The strain of occupation duty in the openly hostile territory of "no-man's-land" Tennessee quickly took its toll on the Federal troops and their attitude concerning Southern Unionism. Attacks by guerrillas and Confederate cavalry seemed to materialize out of thin air, increasingly frustrating Federal garrison troops who were unable to leave their towns in order to engage their enemies. False alarms created constant anxiety and the tedium of garrison duty mentally fatigued the Federal soldiers, who were already physically exhausted from the change of climate, camp sickness, and the general hard, monotonous labor associated with military service. When troops did leave the garrison town's confines, they released their pent-up frustrations on Southern civilians by confiscating or destroying civilian property with little, if any, regard for the citizens' professed loyalties. Moreover, to relieve themselves of the responsibilities associated with administering civil government, Federal commanders restored many former local officials to power. Many of these officials had supported secession, and this policy alienated and politically emasculated Unionist leaders within their own communities.

The contradictions between Federal occupation policies and practices impeded the growth of Tennessee Unionism. The *Memphis Bulletin* complained about the Federal soldiers' debauchery and that their impunity toward Southerners had led them to assume an "unbridled license" to ravage the city. "It is no excuse to say 'they are all secesh,' 'they must be crushed,' 'they have brought this war on themselves.' If this were true, which it is not," argued the *Bulletin,* "It is no matter to be decided by the private judgment of a common soldier." "We are in a deplorable situation," claimed Pitser Miller, a Bolivar, Tennessee, Unionist writing to Andrew Johnson. He estimated that when Federal forces arrived in June, some 80 percent of the population supported the Union, but the secessionist minority was "more active and got the ballance [*sic*] very quiet." Union officers had given orders prohibiting pillaging, but "the men plundered every thing [*sic*] they could lay their hands on whether they had any use for it or not. . . . [with] no distinction Scarcely made between Union and Secesh," leaving them without the means to make a living or defend themselves. According to Samuel Tipton, a West Tennessean who was serving in the Federal army, "The progress of Unionism [in West Tennessee] is not so rapid as could be wished." He explained that it was "checked in part by the appointments made and by the want of discipline in the army." Tipton believed that the Federal practice of installing local governments with former secessionists who had only recently taken the oath of allegiance rather than known Union men and the high number of Federal troops infected with the "disease or distemper" of pillaging "will more than counteract the good effects" of Federal occupation and deter any "would be friends." Once West Tennesseans were assured of their "rights and property being protected," Tipton argued, a strong Unionism would reassert itself among the general population. "At present," said Tipton, "[Unionists] have no such assurance and feel as though all the falsehoods which have been told to them of our coming here to rob and devastate their property was coming true." He therefore pleaded with Johnson "to throw the shadow of your protecting wing over our now troubled and bewildered fellow citizens."[7]

Without protection or patronage from Federal authorities, Unionists had little incentive to declare their allegiance openly and assist in suppressing the rebellion. One Southern Unionist found "little favor arising from his Union professions," describing his situation as "being placed between two fires—and flanked beside." If Unionists professed their willingness to aid Federal troops, then they risked retaliation from Confederate guerrillas when the Federals returned to their garrisons or moved farther south. If, on the other hand, they appeared at all unfriendly toward the Federals, then they were suspected of being rebels and subject to property confiscation or destruction. Additionally, marauding bands of rebel cavalry and guerrillas scoured the countryside, conscripting any available male for service and taking any supplies they required from local residents. Thus, the crescendo of Tennessee Unionism fell suddenly silent as Unionists searched for a strategy to protect their property and families. This silence, along with the stepped-up guerrilla activity, convinced the Federals that virtually all Southerners were virulent secessionists and guerrilla supporters.[8]

With all the instability, Tennessee Unionists sought refuge by hiding in the secret backcountry camps or by fleeing to towns just across the northern Tennessee border. "Such oppression and tyriny [*sic*] the world has never known. . . . they have left the Country In smoking ruins," said one West Tennessee Unionist, who also opined that the net effect of such efforts would only strengthen Unionist sentiment among the populace. Despite this constant harassment, there were hundreds—perhaps thousands—of loyal West Tennesseans "hiding about their farms, in the swamps, &c to keep out of the way" of bushwhackers and small squads of rebels lurking behind the lines. According to another loyal citizen, these fugitives stood "ready at a moments [*sic*] warning to take up arms and defend their homes from these ruthless Outlaws." If "clothed with the Proper authority," then they would "bring the guilty to Justice so that Peace and quietude may again be restored in this now distracted land."[9]

As early as June 1861, Tennessee Unionists had begun organizing to protect themselves against an increasing number of guerrilla attacks, but they met with unexpected resistance from Federal authorities. Some joined Federal regiments from other states, but the majority preferred to serve in paramilitary units that remained closer to their homes in order to protect their families. Representatives from one such group, located in the woods of Carroll County, came to the Federal commander of Paducah, Kentucky, seeking assistance, but were turned away. The Unionists returned to their camp "heartbroken" over this rebuff. Emerson Etheridge, West Tennessee's Ninth District congressman, now a leader among the Unionist refugees in Paducah, claimed that a full Unionist brigade could be raised from his home county alone. He complained loudly about the Federal authorities' unwillingness to utilize local Unionists in restoring law and order to the region. Etheridge and several other West Tennessee Unionists begged the governor to capitalize on the growing dissatisfaction with the Confederacy and call up the militia or authorize the formation of Home Guards to protect loyal citizens. "Until the rebels are made to suffer in the guts, they will be insolent," Etheridge told Governor Johnson, "*Now* is the time for action. A countercurrent has set in—and a little energy will produce the best results."[10]

Despite their constant pleading, Tennessee Unionists still lacked the approval of Governor Johnson to organize armed resistance nearly six months after the Union first occupied the region. The governor's office frequently appeared preoccupied with liberating Johnson's home in East Tennessee rather than dealing with the already occupied western districts of the state. Without any official direction on how to utilize these local volunteers, the Federal army refused to employ Unionists in any capacity other than as scouts and guides. Though often ridiculed for their irregular appearance, Unionists quickly won the praise of their Federal counterparts for their uncanny ability to move about the country and find the enemy. One commander remarked that his contingent of Unionist scouts would leave the camp at daybreak in small groups, but by mid-afternoon, all would intuitively locate the column, even while on the march, and reassemble in full strength. He joked that should his regiment ever get into a fight, he hoped it would occur around noon so they could have the Unionists' full services. West Tennessee Unionist Fielding Hurst, after his repeated requests to Johnson and local Federal commanders were ignored, traveled to Nashville in person to demand his commission to muster a Unionist regiment. Johnson, already under pressure from President Abraham Lincoln to restore civil authority to the occupied areas, finally authorized the formation of Tennessee Unionist regiments. The most prominent of these units were the 5th Tennessee Cavalry from Middle Tennessee, formed under William B. Stokes; West Tennessee's 6th Tennessee Cavalry, led by Fielding Hurst; the 7th Tennessee Cavalry, commanded by Isaac Hawkins; and the 14th Tennessee Cavalry, headed by William Bradford. Federal authorities believed that these newly formed Unionist regiments could assist Gen. William T. Sherman's reinvigorated Federal counterinsurgency operations during the fall of 1862 as the region prepared to hold civil elections in December, the first such popular canvass since secession.[11]

The efforts to reconstitute Tennessee's civil government received increased momentum when Lincoln issued the preliminary Emancipation Proclamation. Lincoln's political tact toward emancipation stunned Southern Unionists, for a small yet significant percentage of them owned slaves. Though these slaveholding Unionists professed to be fighting for the "Union as it was" or "the old Government," many felt somewhat betrayed by Lincoln's emancipation course. Tennessee's "only road of escape" from the proclamation, in the Unionists' estimation, was to restore civil government, at least in the portions of the state under Federal control. Once this was accomplished, Tennessee might be exempted from the president's emancipation edict. It might also end the state's military occupation, which was becoming a drain on the Federal manpower available for frontline service, and at least in the estimation of several Unionists, hampering the restoration of order and hindering the further return of Unionist sentiments among the citizenry. Lincoln exempted Tennessee from his Emancipation Proclamation on January 1, 1863, in the hopes of sustaining Unionism in the state. "Your proclamation of the 1st excepting Tennessee has disappointed and disarmed many who were complaining and denouncing it as unjust and unwise," Johnson explained to Lincoln, "I think the exception in favor of Tennessee will be worth much to us." Just what the value of Tennessee Unionism would be remained to be determined as the New Year began.[12]

Another impetus for the restoration of civilian government was the Federal army's transition from a "pragmatic" to a "hard-war" strategy. Concentrating on the destruction of the Confederacy's supporting infrastructure in the fall of 1862, Federal soldiers initiated "hard war" and stepped up their confiscation and destruction of Tennesseans' property, again with little regard for their loyalties or higher headquarters' pleas to cease such activities. A Michigan soldier noted the inevitable results: "What few Union men there may have been [in the South] have of course been obliged to seem secesh and help the rebel cause with property or in some other way which of course marks them as rebels themselves in our books, unless they can do some corresponding service for us." Even when local Unionists provided Federal troops with goods or services, junior officers were under orders to give receipts, but few receipts were actually dispensed. Those fortunate enough to have receipts found redeeming them later difficult because they had to prove that their loyalty had never wavered during the war, and as a Federal soldier remarked, "that is a pretty hard thing for any of them to do in this country." Unionists reasoned that the only solution to the excesses of the Federal occupation troops and the scourge of the guerrillas was to end martial law by reconstituting civil authority. "The great evils we suffer from this war arise from the fact that we are deprived of constitutional guarantees," exclaimed the Unionist *Memphis Bulletin.* The paper's editors further declared that through restoring the machinery of civil government, Tennessee held the key to its own salvation, and "while we have not one particle of cruelty in our nature [toward Northern authorities], we yet think that the patience of Uncle Sam may be exhausted [with Southerners]."[13]

Exemplifying this impatience was Gen. William T. Sherman. Once a proponent of the "conciliatory approach," Sherman was growing increasingly weary of attempting to differentiate between Unionists and secessionists. "It is about time the North understood the truth," he told his brother John, "That the entire South, man, woman, and child are against us, armed and determined." Like any professional soldier, Sherman deplored war, but if necessary, he said, "let the means be adequate," among them "confiscation and colonization." "My full belief is that we must colonize the Country *de novo,*" he argued, "and [the North] should remove five millions of our people at once south of the Ohio River taking the farms and plantations of Rebels." It was simply unreasonable to "expect to overrun Such a Country or subdue such a people in two or five years." More realistically, he estimated that such an effort was "the task of half a century."[14]

Sherman begged politicians to understand these grim realities in letter after letter throughout the summer and into the early fall of 1862. Many politicians and government officials had proceeded on the assumption that those not actively engaged in the war were their allies in the restoration process. But to commanders in the field, this belief had complicated the conduct of military affairs, created civil disorder in areas captured by Union armies, and jeopardized soldiers' lives. "Whilst the whole South is in deep intense earnest we of the north still try reconciliation," Sherman grumbled, and such a policy only undermined his work in Memphis. "I am putting the screws to [Southerners]," he continued, "but [I] find more trouble in combating the North whose merchants and traders think they have a right to make money out of the present state of things." In Sherman's view, "The Government of the United States may now safely proceed on the proper Rule that all in the South are Enemies of the North. 'Tis idle to talk of Union men here. . . . Changing the opinions of the People of the South[,] that is impossible," Sherman lectured, "they must be killed or dispossessed. We have finished the first page of this war in vainly seeking a union sentiment in the South . . . and are about Entering on a Second period." This new phase of the conflict that Sherman would later personify sought to radicalize Union war aims and occupation policy, essentially erasing the distinctions made between secessionist and Unionist Southerners.[15]

Given the precarious nature of the Federal position in the latter part of 1862, Sherman's glum assessment was understandable; guerrillas and Confederate raiders undermined the military and political situation. Tenuous supply lines reduced combat power and left the Western Theater in a stalemate. Yet, as a seemingly counterintuitive solution to his political-military Gordian knot, he implemented draconian policies of "collective responsibility" (punishing the citizens for the sins of a few guerrillas in their midst). Amazingly, this tactic bore fruit. Guerrilla attacks became less frequent and discipline in the Federal ranks seemed to be improving, albeit slowly. A Unionist spirit began to manifest itself. "Some of the rebels however told me while I was out in rebeldom that there were quite a number of them Unionists [in West Tennessee]," said Henry Eells after coming in from a patrol along the Mobile & Ohio Railroad near Bolivar. For nearly a year, Unionists had huddled together inside garrison towns seeking protection from Confederate cavalry, guerrillas, and secessionist neighbors. From their islands of safety and with the help of Union troops, Tennessee Unionists hoped to broaden their support, smite their enemies, and reclaim the state. Northerners venturing into the state found such Unionist enclaves heartening in the face of continued Confederate resistance. A Union officer from Jackson, Tennessee, reported to Gov. Andrew Johnson, "Every one [*sic*] is taking the oath of Allegiance and we are compelled to protect the Secessionists from the Union men for their animosity is so bitter." As Federal forces entered Dresden, Tennessee, citizens greeted them with a massive pro-Union demonstration and with cheers resonating from the houses. Later, at Huntingdon, one soldier saw the "Stars and Stripes . . . floating from a pole the first time I have seen it in that way since we left Memphis."

Even Sherman's trademark pessimism about Southern Unionism seemed to abate as December's elections approached. "We have roused also the Union element," he told Halleck, and "have shaken [the people's] faith in the secession authorities, so that we have really a substantial beginning of the conversion of the people to our cause." West Tennessee, according to Sherman, was "free of the enemy, save very small bands of guerrillas, whom the people will dispose of rather than feed and submit to." Sherman also informed Grant that Memphis Union clubs were presently organizing rallies and flag decorations for homes, and that he was "satisfied a change of opinion is rapidly growing here which I endeavor to foster and encourage."[16]

To the chagrin of Unionists and Federal authorities alike, the December 1862 elections in West Tennessee turned into a political and military debacle. Secessionists nominated candidates with the hope of using the elections to restore their leaders to power. A dispute over the authority to issue writs of election between General Grant and Governor Johnson resulted in two different dates being set for the contest, creating a great deal of confusion among county election officials. Additionally, a well-timed raid by Confederate Gen. Nathan Bedford Forrest into West Tennessee intimidated many potential Unionist voters from venturing out to the polls. Whenever and wherever the polls did open, they usually did so within sight of Confederate pickets or had their voter registers and ballot boxes confiscated or destroyed by rebel soldiers. Given these circumstances, the results should come as no surprise. In the final tally, just over 10 percent of West Tennesseans cast their ballots during the election. Though this result was not enough to convince Congress to seat the winner of the election, Alvin Hawkins (cousin of Isaac), back to Tennessee's Ninth District House seat, it was enough to convince Lincoln to exempt Tennessee from the final Emancipation Proclamation.

Forrest's raid also demonstrated his ability to strike deep into the heart of Federally occupied territory and exert Confederate authority, further undermining any groundswell of Unionism there. Forrest staged an elaborate ruse to exaggerate his numbers and tricked nearly all of Hawkins's 7th Tennessee Cavalry (US) into surrendering. Later, Forrest, though surrounded, managed to defeat the Federals at the battle of Parker's Crossroads. Fielding Hurst's Unionists attempted to engage Forrest as he attempted to slip back across the Tennessee River into Middle Tennessee, but they were flanked and forced to retreat, too. These inglorious defeats created a growing rift between Federal officers and West Tennessee Unionists. Federal commanders blamed Unionists for their reverses on the battlefield, charging them with insubordination, incompetence, and cowardice during the fighting.[17]

Displeased by these allegations, as well as with the Federal government's inability to pay them for almost a year's service, supply them with adequate equipment, or protect their families from guerrilla attacks, Colonel Hurst decided to seek victory over the guerrillas on his own terms. Grant received numerous reports of depredations being carried out by Hurst's regiment, and he threatened to disband them. Another Federal officer, Col. Isham Haynie from Illinois, claimed that deserters and "other bad men" made up the majority of Hurst's command, and that while avenging their private grievances, they were impossible to control. Hurst responded to these allegations by calling Haynie a "drunken little Irishman" and claimed that "the Ill treatment of Tennesseans Received at the hands of the authorities from southern Ill[inois]" had caused his regiment considerable embarrassment and impaired its success. He then asserted that Federal authorities had been inadequate for the task of eliminating guerrillas, saying that if Unionist regiments were given the proper equipment, then "we will do the fighting."[18]

West Tennessee Unionists grew increasingly frustrated over the indifference of Governor Johnson and Federal authorities to their plight. Samuel Tipton, a West Tennessean serving in the Union Army, warned that the impression one looting Federal soldier imparts to "our would-be friends through this country, will do more to counteract the good effects of half a dozen good union Regts." He remained convinced that West Tennesseans would exhibit their Unionism if assured that their rights and property would be protected. "As things are going here at present," he noted, "they have *no such* assurance and feel as though all the falsehoods which have been told to them of our coming here to rob and devastate their property was coming true." Hurst said that he himself had been "once Robed by the Rebels and three times by the damned [Illinois] troops who have more sympathy for a Rebel than they have for a loyal man in Tennessee." "My men feel that they have been badly treated," Hurst told Johnson, "No pay and but little thanks." Colonel Hawkins agreed and declared that rebel sympathizers often received more protection from guerrilla outrages than Unionists did, despite the Federals' "undisputed possession" of western Tennessee. Furthermore, when Federal forces left an area, Hawkins said guerrillas returned to their "hellish work of Desolation and Ruin. . . . [T]hey come from their hiding places and resume their *fiendish work* such as *plundering* the *families* of *union Soldiers chasing, Running down and catching union men with Blood hounds. . . .* The *aged Fathers* and *Mothers, little Brothers* and *sisters,* the *wives* and *children of the union soldiers will be reduced to beggary* and *compeled to flee the country for Bread.*" He warned Johnson that "unless Relief can be given to that country soon, there will be nothing left worth living for, tis even now a perfect Hell for the Loyal people there. . . . [S]omething must be speedily done or our country is ruined."[19]

As more and more Northern troops withdrew from Tennessee for Vicksburg and the Chattanooga campaigns, the increased need to patrol the rear areas throughout Middle and West Tennessee caused a temporary truce in the infighting between Federals and Unionists. From March to July 1863, several joint Federal-Unionist operations produced a number of high-profile defeats and captures of infamous guerrilla bands terrorizing western Tennessee. Encouraged by these victories, several towns formed Home Guards and reclaimed their communities from the guerrillas. Gen. Stephen Hurlbut, commander of the forces stationed throughout West Tennessee, said the region was in a "plastic state" ready to be "moulded into a shape fitting for an honorable return into the Union."[20]

But an escalating cycle of violence fueled by the increased acrimony between the West Tennessee–raised Confederate and Unionist units during these operations tempered this success. Relatives and former neighbors separated by their loyalties frequently skirmished and committed numerous atrocities against each other and their families. Federal commanders hypocritically chastised Hurst and his men for their part in these actions and subjected him to several court-martials for disobeying direct orders. They also levied fines against the regiment's payroll for damages inflicted upon civilians, although Hurst claimed Federal units, not Unionists, had perpetrated some of these incidents. In fact, several Federal regiments had acted in similar fashion and suffered similar embarrassments during the same period, but these incidents never seemed to attract the same attention or generate the same enmity among the senior Federal officers as those involving Southern Unionist regiments.[21]

Federal commanders gradually became convinced that the continued presence of Middle and West Tennessee Unionist units was militarily and politically counterproductive. In Middle Tennessee, one senior Federal officer remarked in August 1863 that the 5th Tennessee was "excessive trouble, and worrying and plundering through the country whenever they go out." Furthermore, he charged that the unit lacked discipline and that several instances of these Unionists "insulting unprotected females" had been reported. Another commander in January 1864 reported that the 5th Tennessee was "neither well-drilled, disciplined, or equipped" and recommended that the unit should be split up. Stokes's men were ridiculed as reckless and denied remounting and refitting unless they chose to "pitch in" and "help yourself to [enemy] horses." By the end of the war, the 5th Tennessee had sortied on many guerrilla-hunting expeditions with some success; however, Federal authorities refused to recognize their contributions. Around Nashville, Union Gen. Robert Milroy said the regiment was "utterly void of order and discipline. . . . The field officers have no conception of their obligations and duties; have no control over their subordinates or men." Many were absent without leave and, as a whole, were little more than "a rabble." Milroy suggested the "worthless" unit be sent out of Tennessee to prevent desertion and make them more effective to the government. The war ended before any orders to that effect could be issued.

West Tennessee Unionists continued to suffer insults at the hands of both Federal and Confederate forces. General Hurlbut at Memphis likewise complained in late 1863 that "Hawkins [7th Tennessee Cavalry] is a very inferior officer and should be gotten rid of," and that both the 6th and 7th Tennessee had "behaved badly." In early 1864, he attempted to recall them to Memphis, where he vowed "to make something of them or break them," but before they could comply with the recall order, Forrest attacked again, capturing Hawkins's regiment a second time at Union City and routing Hurst's force just outside of Memphis. The Confederates then attacked a third West Tennessee Unionist regiment, the 14th Tennessee Cavalry (US) still in the process of recruiting at Fort Pillow, Tennessee, just sixty miles above Memphis. The battle, known as the Fort Pillow Massacre, resulted in extraordinarily high casualties among the Unionists and the United States Colored Troop garrison stationed with them. Almost two-thirds of the 7th Tennessee Cavalry and a comparable percentage of the 14th Tennessee's survivors died in Confederate captivity, most at the infamous Andersonville prison camp, while the 6th Tennessee limped ignominiously back toward Memphis. Imprisoned after his second capitulation of the war, Hawkins was unable to defend himself against the charges of cowardice and incompetence leveled by his superiors and even by some of his own disgruntled officers who had later escaped; however, Hurst continued to condemn the treatment of West Tennessee Unionists at the hands of Federal authorities. Hurst claimed that since the inception of his regiment, "impediments and bearriers of evry [*sic*] conceivable Shape have been thrown in our way by those, who ought to have been our friends. . . . No favors have been Shown to us and no encouragement whatsoever has been extended towards us, all the Success we [have] had being attributable *alone* to the genuine patriotism and Self Sacrifice" of West Tennessee Unionists. He asked that his regiment be transferred to a department where they could be under a Tennessean, or "at least men who *believe* that there is some patriotism South of the Ohio River." He received his wish as the 6th Tennessee Cavalry was sent to sit out the remainder of the war in Nashville.[22]

After the Confederate surrender, Middle and West Tennessee Unionists returned home to enjoy the spoils of their victory, but instead found their victory spoiled. Wartime animosities spilled over into the postwar period. Stokes earned a spot in Congress, but Redeemers swept him out in the 1870 elections. The Confederate commander of West Tennessee requested as a term of his surrender that neither Hurst's or Hawkins's men be sent back to the region in any official capacity, saying, "the feeling that exists between the men of these commands and the citizens is such that private malice and private revenge might be the result" and hinder restoration of order there. Unionists veterans therefore found themselves "ostracized and proscribed socially . . . compelled to discard the blue they have worn with honor, to protect themselves from insult and violence" as the Redeemers quickly claimed Tennessee. Yet, both Hawkins and Hurst continued to lobby on behalf of Unionists in the postwar period. Hurst returned to his home in McNairy County (the northern part was known as the "Hurst Nation" for the Unionist solidarity displayed by all but a few of the Hursts in the area) and became a circuit court judge and commander of the local Grand Army of the Republic post, but many former Confederates in McNairy County still considered him a traitor and outlaw. After Hurst's death in 1882, his enemies often vandalized or desecrated his grave site. The demonization of Hurst and his Unionist regiment became cemented in local legend over the years as evidenced by the following poem, which appeared in the *Confederate Veteran:*

Despair for the children
who lie now in bed.
The widow, the aged
the soldier who bled.
For out of the "Nation"
comes a sickness and curse -
God save us all
From the demon called Hurst.

Like vandals of old
through our land they did ride
With Hunger and Death
always close by their side.
Came Terror, his herald -
but the wailing comes first . . .
We know he is coming,
That demon called Hurst.[23]

Meanwhile, Hawkins served three consecutive terms in Congress and later struggled to present the claims of West Tennessee Unionists before a skeptical and contentious Southern Claims Commission, which proclaimed that all Southerners had been secessionists unless they could prove beyond a doubt otherwise. As stated earlier, overcoming the prejudices of Northerners toward any Southerner was a task that proved especially difficult for West Tennesseans. Many on the Commission had served in the area during the war and as a result of their experience, had presumed it to be entirely secessionist. Not surprisingly, West Tennesseans, though their section had been under a more comprehensive and more extended Federal occupation, had their claims rejected at almost double the rate of East Tennessee Unionists.[24]

The performance of West Tennessee Unionist regiments during the war convinced many Federal leaders that Southern Unionists were of little military value and that their activities only exacerbated an escalating cycle of violence in the area. The early shift of Union operations to the railroad towns and counties of the region's southwest corner had left Unionists in the outlying pro-Union counties relatively defenseless, and the subsequent evolution of pragmatic and hard-war occupation policies to deal with the situation further undermined rather than nurtured West Tennessee Unionism. Additionally, the nature of the Federal occupation in West Tennessee fed the perception that all Southerners were cut from the same secessionist cloth, whatever their claims to the contrary, and that Southern Unionists could never be equal partners with Northerners in the nation's reconstruction. For their part, West Tennessee Unionists continued to feel betrayed and abandoned by Federal authorities. As a result of their suspicions and animosities, both sides squandered an opportunity to aid one another in restoring order to West Tennessee, and their failure profoundly affected the region and its inhabitants for decades.

Similar outcomes have become an all too common occurrence since the emergence of "total war." Conflicts that were once fought exclusively between armies began to engross entire societies, threatening civilians and soldiers alike, regardless of whether they were at the front, in the rear, or in areas removed from the fighting but beset by guerrillas. In the American historical experience, traditional military operations have been the exception; "the small, savage wars of peace," as Richard Kipling once termed insurgencies and occupations, have been the norm. The experiences of Federal forces and Unionists in Middle and West Tennessee once again remind us that while main force units determine the outcome of a war, it is the response to an insurgency that often determines the character of the peace.[25]

Notes

1. John A. Rogers to Andrew Johnson, Aug. 20, 1862, LeRoy Graf and Ralph Haskins, eds., *The Papers of Andrew Johnson,* 15 vols. (Knoxville: Univ. of Tennessee Press, 1967–99), V:626–27 (hereafter cited as *Johnson Papers;* if followed by the volume and page number, the reference refers to published letters, while references to documents not included in a published edition will be followed by "LC," the Library of Congress's microfilm publication of Johnson's papers). Union officials later arrested Rogers for abandoning a fort near Humboldt on Dec. 20, 1862, and relocating to the safest part of town against direct orders. This prompted Rogers to resign his commission.

2. E. Cobham Brewer. "Our Friends the Enemy," *Dictionary of Phrase and Fable* (Philadelphia: Henry Altemus, 1898); Bartleby.com, http://www.bartleby.com/81/6838.html.

3. Report of Lt. Seth L. Phelps, commanding U.S. gunboat *Conestoga,* Feb. 10, 1862, U.S. Government, *Official Records of the Union and Confederate Navies in the War of the Rebellion,* 27 vols. (Washington, D.C.: U.S. Government Printing Office, 1927), vol. 22, 571–74 (hereafter cited as *ORN*); Jay Slagle, *Ironclad Captain: Seth Ledyard Phelps and the U.S. Navy, 1841–1864* (Kent, Ohio: Kent State Univ. Press, 1996), 165.

4. *St. Louis Daily Democrat,* June 26, 1862; Henry Halleck to Johnson, June 22, 1862, *Johnson Papers,* V:494; Absalom H. Markland to Johnson, June 21, 1862, ibid., V:494–95.

5. Mark Grimsley, *Hard Hand of War: Northern Policy towards Southern Civilians, 1861–1865* (New York: Cambridge Univ. Press, 1995), 15–22, 48–51. Grimsley notes that the historical experience of the three wars most familiar to American officers—the War for American Independence, the Napoleonic Wars, and the Mexican War—had elements of a "hard-war" strategy, but such elements (i.e., guerrillas, foraging, rights of noncombatants) were ignored in favor of concentrating on achieving decisive victory on the battlefield.

6. Grimsley, *Hard Hand of War,* 23–119; Stephen V. Ash, *When the Yankees Came: Conflict and Chaos in the Occupied South* (Chapel Hill: Univ. of North Carolina Press, 1995), 76–107; Bruce Catton, *Grant Moves South, 1861–63* (New York: Little, Brown, and Company, 1960), 269–323.

7. *Memphis Bulletin,* July 25, 1862; Pitser Miller to Andrew Johnson, Mar. 7, 1863, *Johnson Papers,* VI:166–67; Samuel Tipton to Andrew Johnson, June 20, 1862, ibid., V:492–93.

8. Grimsley, *Hard Hand of War,* 96–170; Ash, *When the Yankees Came,* 76–131; Catton, *Grant Moves South,* 269–323.

9. Robert Norvell to Johnson, June 10, 1862, *Johnson Papers,* V:462–63; Henry Halleck to Johnson, June 8, 1862, ibid.,V:455; O. P. Weigart to Johnson, June 3, 1862, ibid., V:435–38; Richard Nelson Current, *Lincoln's Loyalists: Union Soldiers from the Confederacy* (New York: Oxford Univ. Press, 1992), 29–60; Nathan Moran, "Military Government and the Divided Loyalties: The Union Occupation of Northwest Tennessee, June 1862–August 1862," *West Tennessee Historical Society Papers* 48 (1994): 91–94.

10. Emerson Etheridge to Johnson, Dec. 19, 1861; Robert Link to Johnson, Dec. 19, 1861, *Johnson Papers,* V:65–68; and Jacob Perkins, *Trails, Rails, and War: The Life of General G. M. Dodge* (Indianapolis: The Bobbs-Merrill Co., 1929): 109–10.

11. Current, *Lincoln's Loyalists,* 29–60; Nathan Moran, "Military Government and the Divided Loyalties: The Union Occupation of Northwest Tennessee, June 1862–August 1862," *West Tennessee Historical Society Papers* 48 (1994): 91–94. As evidence of Johnson's belief that liberating East Tennessee should take precedence over other portions of the state, his Authorization to Raise Troops from the War Department, dated August 1, 1862, stated, "The troops . . . when organized are first to be employed in an expedition for the redemption of East Tennessee from rebel rule, unless such redemption shall have been sooner accomplished"; *Johnson Papers,* V:587. Current's treatment focuses on Johnson's efforts to recruit in East Tennessee and has little discussion of such activities in West Tennessee. For brief unit histories of Tennessee Unionist regiments, see Tennessee Civil War Centennial Commission, *Tennesseans in the Civil War,* pt. I (Knoxville: Univ. of Tennessee Press, 1964). Emerson Etheridge to Johnson, Dec. 19, 1861; Robert Link to Johnson, Dec. 19, 1861, *Johnson Papers,* V:65–68; and Perkins, *Trails, Rails, and War,* 109–10.

12. Alvin Hawkins, *House Report No. 46,* U.S. Congress, 37th Cong., 3rd sess.; Johnson to Lincoln, Jan. 11, 1863, *Johnson Papers,* VI:114. Grant to Johnson, July 25, 1862, ibid., V:567–68; John Tarkington and Fielding Hurst to Johnson, July 22, 1862, Dodd [Dodge] to Johnson, Aug. 12, 1862, and Johnson to John McClernand, Aug. 12, 1862, ibid., LC; *Memphis Bulletin,* Sept. 30, Oct. 11, 17, 25, and Nov. 2, 1862.

13. Grimsley, *Hard Hand of War,* 96–170; Samuel Henry Eells to Friends, Sept. 3, 1863, Samuel Henry Eells Collection, Manuscript Division, LC (hereafter cited as the Eells Collection, LC); Michael Fellman, *Inside War: Guerrilla Conflict in Missouri during the Civil War* (New York: Oxford Univ. Press, 1989), 48–49; *Memphis Bulletin,* Sept. 30, Oct. 11, 17, 25, and Nov. 2, 1862.

14. Sherman to John Sherman, Sept. 22, 1862, and Sherman to John Sherman, Aug. 13, 1862, Brooks D. Simpson and Jean V. Berlin, eds., *Sherman's Civil War: The*

Selected Correspondence of William T. Sherman, 1860–1865 (Chapel Hill: Univ. of North Carolina Press, 1999), 272–73, 301–2.

15. Sherman to Ellen, Aug. 10, 1862, Sherman to Salmon P. Chase, Aug. 11, 1862, and Sherman to Thomas Ewing Sr., Aug. 10, 1862, ibid., 263–64, 266–67, 269–72; and Sherman to Grant, Oct. 4,1862, United States War Department, *The War of the Rebellion: A Compilation of the Official Records of the Union and Confederate Armies,* 128 vols. (Washington, D.C.: U.S. Government Printing Office, 1880–91), vol. 17, pt. 2, 259–62 (hereafter cited as *OR,* and all references are to series 1 unless otherwise indicated).

16. Eells to Uncle and Aunt [George and Sarah Fletcher], Apr. 28, 1862, Eells Letters, LC; Adalbert Bly, Jan. 9, 1863 (part of letter dated Dec. 25, 1862), Adalbert Bly Letters, State Historical Society of Wisconsin, Madison, Wis.; Sherman to Grant, Nov. 8, 1862, and Sherman to Halleck, Nov. 17, 1862, *OR,* vol. 17, pt. 2, 322–34, 351–52; Sherman to Ellen, Oct. 1, 1862, Simpson and Berlin, eds., *Sherman's Civil War,* 309–11.

17. Thomas Jordon and J. P. Pryor, *The Campaigns of General Nathan Bedford Forrest and of Forrest's Cavalry* (New York: DaCapo Press, 1996), 200–203; Lonnie Maness, *An Untutored Genius: The Military Career of Nathan Bedford Forrest* (Oxford, Miss.: Guild Bindery Press, 1990), 85–91; Benjamin F. Cooling, *Fort Donelson's Legacy* (Knoxville: Univ. of Tennessee Press, 1997), 166–70; Grimsley, *Hard Hand of War,* 101; Alvin Hawkins, *House Report No. 46,* U.S. Congress, 37th Cong., 3rd sess.; Calvin Ezell to Johnson, Jan. 10, 1863, *Johnson Papers,* VI:112; Johnson to Lincoln, Jan. 11, 1863, ibid., VI:114; Grant to Johnson, Jan. 16, 1863, ibid., VI:121; Benjamin Nabors to Johnson, Feb. 5, 1863, ibid., VI:136–37; *OR,* vol. 17, pt. 1, 552–54, 560–67, 590–91.

18. Grant to commanding officer at Bethel, Tenn., Oct. 25, 1862; Col. William R. Morrison (Colonel Haynie's adjutant) to Maj. John A. Rawlins, Oct. 25, 1862, John Y. Simon, ed., *The Papers of Ulysses S. Grant,* vol. 6, *September 1, 1862–December 8, 1862* (Carbondale: Southern Illinois Univ. Press, 1977), 195–96; Brayman to Brig. Gen. Jeremiah Sullivan, Dec. 31, 1862, *OR,* vol. 17, pt. 1, 481–85; Hurst to Rawlins, Dec. 10, 1863, Regimental Letter Book, 6th Tennessee Cavalry.

19. Samuel Tipton to Johnson, June 20, 1862, *Johnson Papers,* V:492–3; Hawkins to Johnson, Aug. 9 and Oct. 1, 1863, ibid., VI:322–23 and 398–99. Hurst to Johnson, Mar. 11, 1863, Regimental Record Book, 6th Tennessee Cavalry; emphasis in original.

20. Hurlbut to Johnson, Sept. 15, 1863, *Johnson Papers,* V:368.

21. Gary Blankinship, "Fielding Hurst: Tennessee Tory: A Study of a West Tennessee Unionist of the American Civil War" (master's thesis, Memphis State Univ., 1977); and Gary Blankinship, "Fielding Hurst and the Hurst Nation," *West Tennessee Historical Society Papers* 34 (1980): 71–87; Kevin McCann, *"Hurst's Wurst": A History of the Sixth Tennessee (U.S.) Cavalry* (Ashland City, Tenn.: Kevin McCann, 1995). For a brief regimental history of the 6th Tennessee Cavalry (US), see Tennessee Civil War Centennial Commission, *Tennesseans in the Civil War,* I:333–36.

22. Stephen A. Hurlbut to A. J. Smith, Oct. 26, 1863, and Hurlbut to J. D. Stevenson, Nov. 7, 1863, *OR,* vol. 31, pt. 1, 747, and pt. 3, 82; Fielding Hurst to Andrew Johnson, Apr. 29, 1864, *Johnson Papers* (Misc. Collection), Ac. No. 124, Tennessee State Library and Archives, Nashville, Tenn. (hereafter cited as TSLA); Fielding Hurst to Alvin C. Gillem, June 29, 1864, Tennessee Adjutant General Records, TSLA.

23. Blankinship, "Fielding Hurst"; McCann, *"Hurst's Wurst";* Charles Lufkin, "West Tennessee Unionists in the Civil War: A Hawkins Family Letter," *Tennessee Historical Quarterly* 46 (1987): 33–42; W. Clay Crook, "Hurst!," *Confederate Veteran* (Spring 1992): 20–23.

24. From the author's study of more than nine hundred Southern Claims Commission cases from West Tennessee, approximately three-quarters were rejected, while only about 45 percent were denied from East Tennessee. Isaac Hawkins operated a law practice with his cousin, Alvin, who assisted him in arguing the cases before the Southern Claims Commission. Alvin later rose through the Republican Party ranks to become Tennessee's governor in 1880. For biographical information on the Hawkins family, see Lufkin, "West Tennessee Unionists in the Civil War," 33–42.

25. Stig Forster and Jorg Nagler, *On the Road to Total War: The American Civil War and the Wars of German Unification, 1861–1871* (Cambridge: Cambridge Univ. Press, 1997).

Franklin
The Thunder Drum of War

WILEY SWORD

An aged combat veteran, many years following the Civil War, thought about what he had seen during that conflict and focused on the Battle of Franklin. He said it was "The Thunder Drum of War": the most terrible personal combat experience that he and his comrades had endured during the war. Especially to the Confederate survivors, the ordeal at Franklin was such an utter horror that many said the terror they had faced there, together with the enormous futility of that battle, could never be fully explained or told. To them, it was a literal hell on earth that defied explanation or description.[1]

Ironically, for many years the Battle of Franklin was little known to the general public. If mentioned at all in many history books, it was often described in a few sentences and depicted as only a minor occurrence in a war overburdened with tragedy. Even the battlefield itself, overrun by 1940s-era wooden-frame houses, ramshackle warehouses, and the sprawl of urban civilization, reflected its undistinguished status.

Today, in the light of a better understanding of the realities of the Battle of Franklin and a more objective interpretation, we can consider that Franklin was one of the war's most terrible, if fascinating, events. Specifically, the Battle of Franklin endures as one of the greatest martial spectacles of the entire Civil War. For sheer drama, for military pageantry, for a bold demonstration of the essence of the Southern spirit, and perhaps even as an ultimate example of the valor of the American fighting man, the vicious encounter at Franklin on November 30, 1864, seems without parallel.

Indeed, beneath the long-obscured legacy of Franklin lies one of the Civil War's most compelling, if tragic, stories. A Union officer, sickened by the grisly carnage on the battlefield, made a particularly revealing and profound comment: "I feel like one who witnesses a bitter wrong, a monstrous injustice," said Capt. James Sexton in 1864. "Call it glorious to die a horrible death surrounded by an awful butchery, a scanty burial by enemy hands, and then total oblivion; name blotted out and forever forgotten—where is the glory?"[2]

That question will forever haunt the families of thousands of America's slain, for as a common query into the insanity of war, it might have been written by millions of soldiers in countless wars throughout history. Yet, it is particularly appropriate to the victims of one the war's most tragic events, the Battle of Franklin.

The 1864 invasion of Tennessee by the Southern army, which led to this bloodbath, was a bold attempt to change the course of the war. Its purpose was to destroy the will of the Northern populace in supporting an exceedingly costly and burdensome war. A continued "butcher's bill" of casualties and the enormous financial drain, it was hoped, would so dishearten the North as to result in a negotiated settlement. With the fate of cities such as Nashville and Cincinnati hanging in the balance, even President Abraham Lincoln became personally involved. Thus, from its inception, the 1864 Confederate invasion of Tennessee involved high military drama.[3]

Within the soul of the war-maimed and discredited Southern Gen. John Bell Hood burned a fiery purpose during the autumn of 1864. Driven and tormented by the loss of Atlanta in early September 1864 to Union Gen. William Tecumseh Sherman's relentless armies, Hood decided to place his future on an enormously risky venture. Rather than withdraw farther south after Atlanta, Hood sought to conduct a bold offensive. With President Jefferson Davis's approval, he began planning for an invasion of Tennessee, Kentucky, and perhaps beyond. Thus, when Sherman's columns marched south, ravaging Georgia during the "March to the Sea," Hood's Army of Tennessee turned north, in search of a redeeming victory. As such, the Tennessee campaign of 1864 involved a serious gamble for both sides.

Sherman, by abandoning conquered Southern territory in his rear, was gambling that veteran troops left behind under a good general might thwart the depleted but still powerful Confederate Army of Tennessee. Indeed, to stop Hood and his men, Sherman detached from his main army only two experienced combat units, the Fourth and Twenty-third Corps, a total of about 22,000 men. Other elements of this makeshift defensive army had to be improvised from various scattered rear echelon troops, even as several detached divisions of the Sixteenth Corps under Gen. Andrew J. Smith were hastened to Nashville from western Missouri. In mid-November 1864, their arrival and the formation of a respectable army seemed much in doubt.[4]

In charge of this crucial makeshift force for the Union was the outcast Virginian, Gen. George H. Thomas. Thomas had risen above suspicions about his Southern background to become one of the most competent generals of the Union Army. Yet, Thomas was known as a cautious, methodical general of deliberate movement. This raised grave concerns about his ability to hold off the invading Confederates until reinforcements reached Nashville and were organized into an effective army.

In order to buy time, Thomas had sent his veteran troops to southern Tennessee under the moderately experienced Gen. John M. Schofield, one of Hood's ex-classmates at West Point. Schofield had taken position at Pulaski, Tennessee, about fifteen miles north of the Alabama border, and was instructed by Thomas to delay Hood's advance, yet not fight a pitched battle unless it was unavoidable.[5]

With the advance of the Confederate Army northward from the vicinity of Florence, Alabama, on the raw and blustery morning of November 21, 1864, Schofield appropriately withdrew his 22,000 troops north to the village of Columbia, located on the banks of the Duck River. Then when Hood, with about thirty thousand men, advanced to Columbia about a week later, Schofield withdrew to the north bank across the rain-swollen stream. Yet the Union commander was anxious to delay Hood's further advance. Indeed, the key to Schofield's behavior for the next few days was his anticipation that General Thomas at Nashville would advance to Columbia with the Sixteenth Corps, then en route to Nashville from Missouri. Thus, Schofield determined to retreat from Columbia only when actually compelled to do so.[6]

Gen. John Bell Hood, on the other hand, was intent on striking rapidly for Nashville. Known as "Sam" to his close friends, Hood was a curious mixture, a man of physical gallantry and an aggressive fighter. In mid-July 1864, Hood had been suddenly ordered to replace Joseph Johnston as commander of the Tennessee army. However, while attempting aggressively to defend Atlanta, Georgia, Hood's headlong frontal assaults against prepared breastworks became both a costly failure and a personal disaster. Hood's loss of Atlanta in late August severely damaged his reputation and brought angry demands for his removal. Hood saw the need for his redemption with a major victory, and his answer was the invasion of Tennessee, an attempt to achieve the success he and the South so desperately needed.[7]

By November 28, with Hood confronting Schofield at Columbia, he was now only about forty miles south of Nashville. Since the Yankees continued to hold their position on the north bank of the Duck River, Hood saw that the obvious solution was to outflank Schofield. By fording the river east of town and racing ahead to Spring Hill, twelve miles in Schofield's rear, Hood hoped to cut off the Federal troops.[8]

Despite Schofield's anticipation of this very scheme, Hood's plan worked to perfection on November 29. With Forrest's cavalry clearing the way, Hood's troops were able to march over backwoods country roads to reach Spring Hill, ahead of all but a small detachment of Union infantry sent there to guard a wagon train. Yet, following the rebels' late-afternoon arrival, only about two hours of daylight remained in which to overwhelm Spring Hill's defenders and cut off Schofield's retreat from Columbia.[9]

Following an initial attack that pushed the outnumbered Union soldiers back to the outskirts of the town, the Confederates suddenly and inexplicably halted. Moreover, they failed to again advance that day. Although most of Schofield's main force was strung out in a long column of retreat from Columbia, along a road by which they must pass under the very muzzles of the rebel guns at Spring Hill, Hood and his generals did nothing.

Due to garbled communications and faulty leadership, the Confederate Army remained idle, even after dark as Schofield's bone-weary troops marched into and past Spring Hill on their way to Franklin. During the night the Union commanders pushed their men hurriedly onward, pressing hard to reach the safety of the north bank of the Harpeth River, another twelve miles distant at Franklin.[10]

This enormous lost Confederate opportunity at Spring Hill resulted in bitter, lifelong accusations among the rebel high command. General Hood had been in the saddle since 3 A.M. and was greatly fatigued. After leaving control of tactical operations that afternoon to Gen. B. F. "Frank" Cheatham, Hood went to the rear to rest, and went to bed early that evening. When awakened and told that some Yankees were seen on the march, Hood said it was all right, they had the enemy trapped and they would finish up their divided forces in the morning. Hood never dreamed that Schofield would attempt to unite his columns and march past the deployed Confederate forces at Spring Hill that night.[11]

When Hood arose on the morning of November 30 and discovered that the entire Federal army had moved past before daylight, he was described as being as "wrathy" as a rattlesnake. Angrily, Hood chastised his generals, especially Frank Cheatham and his subordinates, Gen. John C. Brown and Gen. Pat Cleburne. Each was blamed for a lack of aggressiveness in attacking the enemy. The extent of Hood's despair on the morning of November 30 was revealed by his instructions to Maj. Gen. Stephen D. Lee, left behind on November 29 with his corps at Columbia to deceive Schofield into thinking the Confederates were still there.[12]

When Lee arrived at Spring Hill early on the morning of November 30, he was told only to rest his troops. Hood did not expect Schofield's fleeing army to halt short of Nashville, and Lee was told to rest his men, then follow Hood's advance columns at his own leisure.[13]

Much to the Confederate commander's surprise, he learned later that morning that he had overestimated Schofield's ability to escape. Once on the road to Franklin, Hood saw the vast quantity of abandoned debris thrown away by the retreating Yankees in their hasty march. The enemy seemed demoralized and desperate to get away. Soon Forrest's cavalry, well in advance, sent word that the entire Union Army was observed within the village of Franklin, hastily preparing to cross the Harpeth River on two rickety, makeshift bridges.[14]

Hood's emotions must have been extreme. It appeared that Schofield's army had been brought to bay after all! Quickly, Hood sent his infantry columns forward at the double-quick. Then, from Winstead Hill, two miles south of Franklin, the Confederate commander ordered a massive frontal attack before the enemy could escape.[15]

Yet, Hood's tactical dispositions were a tip-off of the intense resentment and frustration smoldering within him because of the Spring Hill fiasco. By design, Cheatham's men were going to be his shock troops that day. Hood sought to purge their ranks of what he felt was a reluctance to fight unless protected behind breastworks.[16]

Cheatham's corps was assigned to assault the center of the Union line, where the extensive earthworks were the strongest. If not outright punishment for their behavior at Spring Hill, the assault at Franklin would be a severe lesson to Cheatham and his soldiers. There was an immediate uproar among Cheatham's commanders. Division commander General Cleburne exchanged angry words with Hood before the attack. Cleburne made it known that the pending assault over open terrain against strong, well-prepared, and fortified enemy lines was courting disaster. Hood, in turn, told Cleburne that there was concern about his troops' willingness to fight manfully on an open battlefield. Concealing his anger behind a stern expression, Cleburne rode away, determined to show his mettle. To his officers, who questioned the wisdom of a frontal attack across two miles of open ground, Cleburne replied, "If we are to die, let us die like men!"[17]

Despite a lack of artillery (most had been left behind with Stephen D. Lee's column, so that only two Confederate batteries were present to cover the assault) and the protestations of experienced commanders such as Forrest, who pointed out that the Confederate Army could easily outflank Schofield's troops and cut off their retreat to Nashville by using nearby Hollow Tree Gap, Hood remained adamant and insisted on a frontal assault—this despite missing a major segment of his army in Lee's corps.[18]

Thus, about 4 P.M. on November 30, 1864, the Confederate Army of Tennessee, about 23,000 strong, marched as if on parade toward the fortified earthworks surrounding Franklin.[19] The scene was awe-inspiring: long ranks of men in butternut and gray, stretching for nearly two miles across the open plain. Bands began playing "Dixie" and "The Bonnie Blue Flag." The steady tramp of marching feet made a sound like "the hollow rumble of distant thunder," thought an amazed participant. The weather was mild, Indian summer–like, and the Confederate lines appeared, noted an observer, as "a living wall of men and glistening steel." Waving above the closely aligned ranks were a multitude of red St. Andrew's cross battle flags. It was nearly sundown, and the soft autumn rays of the setting sun glinted off the polished gun barrels of thousands of Southern infantrymen as the gray ranks grimly surged forward.[20]

If one of the grandest spectacles of the war, surpassing in magnitude even Pickett's famous charge at Gettysburg, it quickly became one of the most terrible events in American history. Facing emplaced batteries—the poised rifles of twenty thousand Federal infantry in stout entrenchments—it was, as the Southern riflemen soon clearly saw, the very sacrilege of purposeful combat. Across that two-mile valley of entirely open ground moved Cheatham's and A. P. Stewart's men, terribly torn at every step by blasts of artillery and volleys of musketry. Closing to within several hundred yards, the ranks of Pat Cleburne's and John C. Brown's divisions sprinted toward the blazing Union breastworks. Here they found disaster in full measure. Placed in front of the Yankee earthworks, they discovered a nearly impenetrable tangle of thorny Osage orange shrubs, and beyond this a ditch nearly three-feet deep, just in front of an earthwork of piled rails covered with dirt. Thick head logs on the top of the parapet provided cover for defending riflemen to shoot without exposing their heads. Near the framework of the old Carter cotton gin were openings for artillery, each embrasure filled with the flaming muzzle of a Yankee cannon.[21]

This once-pastoral land became almost instantly a vast slaughter ground. Tangled by the thickets of Osage orange, ripped by shotgun-like blasts of canister, and exposed to withering volleys of rifle fire, the front line of attacking Confederates was smothered by the firestorm before even reaching the outer ditch. It seemed to one soldier that if he reached out his hand, it would be struck by dozens of whizzing bullets. To another terrified Southern rifleman, who had joked with his comrades about who would win the race to be the first within the Yankee lines, it now was a race in reverse—to

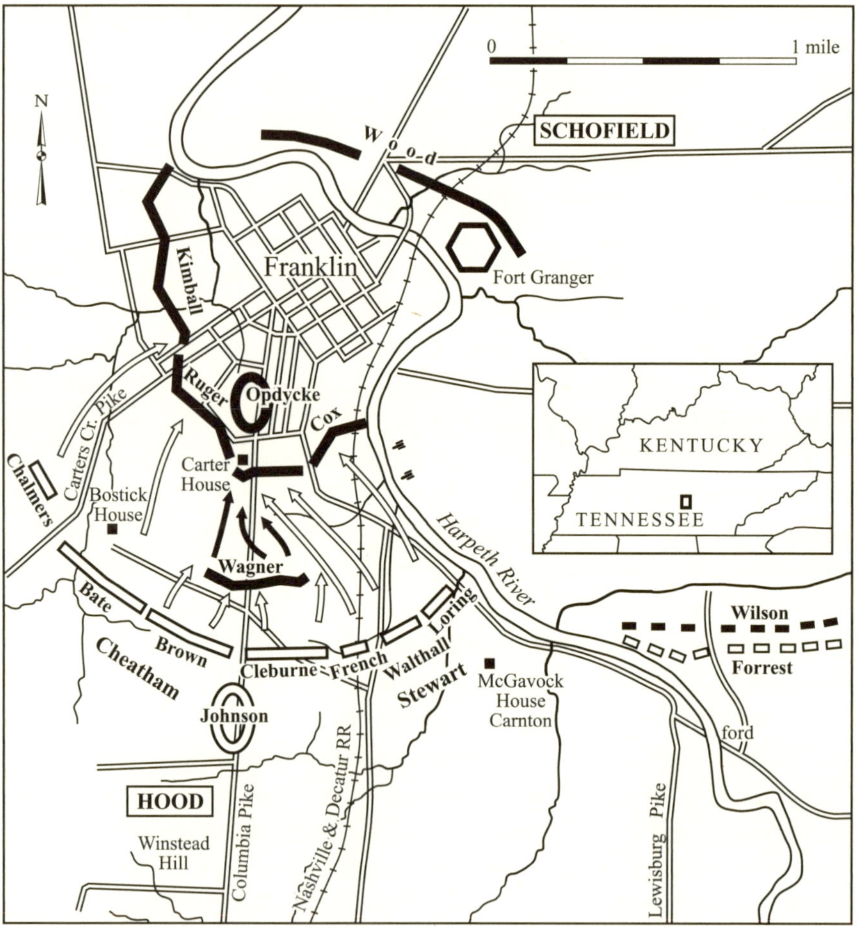

Battle of Franklin.

see who could escape the fastest. All over the ground, men lay writhing in agony and screaming at the top of their lungs. Yet their cries were lost amid the deafening gunfire. Billowing gun smoke quickly shrouded this awful scene in an eerie gray fog.[22]

Through this chaos and madness moved other yelling Confederates, members of trailing brigades who desperately sought to pass through the raging storm of death. Yet they, too, met with agonizing losses. Many of Hood's men had been led to believe that they were facing only the enemy's rear guard, and that once the gray ranks advanced, Schofield's demoralized troops would retreat. Instead, they confronted multiple emplaced batteries and the poised rifles of almost as many enemy soldiers as the 23,000 Southerners who participated in Hood's assault. "We were led out into a slaughter pen to be shot down like animals," later wrote a disgusted Confederate officer. "It was an attempt to make good by reckless daring the blunder [at Spring Hill] which incapacity had occasioned the preceding day," he added. Indeed, facing that terrible whirlwind of death at Franklin was later described by many veterans as their most excruciating personal ordeal—the very worst experience of their lifetime.[23]

Among those to fall in front of the Carter cotton gin was the brilliant Confederate commander, Pat Cleburne, shot through the heart while in the forefront of the attack. He required no man to go where he would not, and the gross outrage of his men in losing perhaps the South's finest combat general was later a terrible blow to the morale of the entire army.[24]

Yet, amazingly, despite the awful carnage in front of the Union breastworks, there was the sudden prospect of Confederate victory. Due to the incidental placement of two Federal brigades in an open cornfield, well in advance of the main earthworks, there was rampant confusion at the very center of the Union lines.

These unfortunate troops were those of Gen. George D. Wagner, who had been on rear guard duty during the retreat from Spring Hill. By mid-afternoon, Wagner had relieved himself of the day's frustrations by consuming the contents of his whiskey flask. If not drunk, Wagner was nearly so.[25]

His anger with Col. Emerson Opdycke, who commanded a third brigade in Wagner's division, was much of the problem. When retreating that afternoon from Winstead Hill, just south of Franklin, Wagner had told Opdycke to position his brigade in an open cotton field along with the division's other two brigades—both of which were about a half-mile in advance of the main works. Angrily, Opdycke refused to do so. His men had formed the rear ranks during the retreat from Spring Hill and had not even had time to make coffee or eat breakfast.[26]

Although Wagner threatened to arrest him, Opdycke ignored Wagner's orders and continued north with his brigade until they passed beyond the main line of entrenchments at the Carter House. Here he found an open space some two hundred yards north of the Carter dwelling, and in the early afternoon halted his men and allowed them to cook their long-overdue breakfasts.[27]

Yet, Opdycke's insubordination was to prove the saving grace of Schofield's army. When Cleburne's and Brown's divisions overran Wagner's two isolated brigades posted in the open cotton field, these wildly retreating Union soldiers prevented the main line from firing due to the fear of hitting their own men.[28]

With the Confederates close behind, a gathering stampede of Union fugitives swept along the Columbia Pike past and through the main earthwork fortifications at the Carter House. Panic seized the defenders at the main line as well, and they, too, began running away. Amid all this chaos, in the rear, behind the Carter House, stood Opdycke's brigade.

Due to the confusion, an Illinois major misconstrued a hasty attempt by Opdycke to shift some troops to the other side of the road. Thinking an advance was intended, the major suddenly shouted, "Forward to the works!" Opdycke was shocked, and at first attempted to halt this movement. Yet he soon realized it was hopeless to try and stop the men. Quickly, he also gave the order to advance.[29]

Like two ocean waves crashing together, the on-charging ranks of Federals and Confederates met in the yard of the Carter House. It soon became one of the most vicious hand- to-hand engagements of the war. For about twenty minutes, Cleburne's and Brown's men, many of whom were nearly exhausted from chasing Wagner's men for half a mile, fought Opdycke's soldiers with bayonets, clubbed muskets, swords, revolvers, rocks, and even bare hands.[30]

Finally, Opdycke's brigade, with the aid of several other units, was able to halt the Southern breakthrough. Both lines soon stabilized, with the Confederates holding tenaciously to the outer ditch at the main line, while the opposing Yankees clustered along a secondary line, only a few yards away at the edge of the Carter garden. For hours a deadly firefight continued here, but neither side was able to advance.

Due to an offset angle in the main line of earthworks, where the Carter cotton gin protruded beyond the main line at the Columbia Pike, the Union soldiers defending the gin house were able to fire into the flank and rear of the rebels huddled in the outer ditch near the Carter House. This deadly enfilade fire killed so many Confederates that the ditches were soon piled with dead and wounded, lying one on top of the other. To protect themselves, the survivors literally crawled behind and hid under the bodies. There was no escape. To attempt to retreat across that deadly open ground was certain death. Yet, to remain in the ditches was to be shot into from the exposed flank.[31]

Many times Hood's men valiantly attempted to cross over the parapets to attack and clear out the opposing lines. They were always hurled back. Thousands of dead and dying littered the ground between the two barricaded lines. Screams of agony and cries for help went unheeded. The 175th Ohio Infantry, a new unit, continued firing into the ditch despite shouts from some trapped gray soldiers to cease firing—they wanted to surrender. Yet the boys from the 175th were so nervous, noted a nearby soldier, that they kept firing. "So much the better," he later mused, "all they kill we won't have to fight or feed anymore."[32]

The outer three-foot-deep ditch remained a seething cauldron of hell. There was no way to escape safely. The trapped gray soldiers just lay there suffering. Many sustained repeated wounds and their blood ran into pools. Some men even began chewing on their fingers amid the intense terror, their intense pain, and to keep from crying out like wild animals. One soldier later remembered he was raving with thirst, yet when he attempted to drink from the water in the ditch, it tasted of blood and he spat it out. This incredible ordeal continued minute by agonizing minute for several hours until, at last, darkness came and some of the trapped men were able to crawl away from that hideous ditch.[33]

Amazing as it seems today, despite the awful butchery, Hood would not accept his inevitable defeat. Desperately he sent some of Lee's newly arrived troops to make a frontal night assault against those same strong, impenetrable Union lines. They, too, were slaughtered like so many sheep during a fearful firefight that lit up the night as if it were daylight. In all, by mid-evening Hood's grand frontal assault at Franklin had become a horrid disaster.[34]

Yet, the brooding Hood continued to plan stubbornly on another fight. Incredibly, that night he issued orders for another massed assault, which would begin at 9 A.M. the following morning. Mercifully, Hood's second assault never occurred. After five hours of vicious fighting, Schofield's troops withdrew at about 2 A.M. and were discovered marching to Nashville during the night. Schofield had decided not to risk further combat once his wagons had been safely moved across the Harpeth River. The Union retreat from Franklin belied the results; however, it had been one of the most stunning defeats ever endured by a Southern army. Essentially, the Army of Tennessee was a wreck. About seven thousand casualties had been taken in two hours of daylight and three of darkness.[35]

Sixty-five commanders of divisions, brigades, or regiments numbered among the casualties. Thirteen of twenty-eight Southern general officers exposed in the fighting were killed, wounded, or missing. Among the irreplaceable slain was Pat Cleburne, together with five other Confederate generals: John Adams, John C. Carter, States Rights Gist, Hiram Granbury, and Otho F. Strahl.[36]

The aftermath of Franklin was predictable. The surviving Confederates were allowed to wander the corpse-strewn battlefield and were appalled by what they saw. With so many bodies literally piled one on top of another in the outer ditches, the utter futility and brutal waste of life were fully apparent. The terrible fusillade of bullets had been so intense that it furrowed the open ground along the breastworks, giving it the appearance of a plowed farmer's field. Southern morale was soon at a nadir. Why, oh why, had they been allowed to wander over that terrible battlefield, a soldier asked. Thereafter many men were so demoralized that their spirit to endure further was broken. The repeated disasters under Hood—from Atlanta to Franklin—had taken their full toll. The men now understood they were not being led to victory, but only repeatedly into a vast slaughter pen. "The terrible specter of Franklin stalked among us," wrote a Mississippi private. The Army of Tennessee seemed to be a hollow shell—intact in form only.[37]

The subsequent disaster at Nashville two weeks later only accentuated what had occurred at Franklin. With the full-scale attack by Gen. Thomas's forces on December 15 and 16, the most decisive defeat of the entire war was completed. The Confederate Army of Tennessee gave way to a spreading panic on the second day at Nashville. At this point, the gaunt gray soldiers seemed concerned only with their own survival. The psyche that had led to this ultimate disaster was not the fear of fighting, which this valiant army had done for so long and so well. Rather, it was the fear of wasting their lives—of being sacrificed on the battlefield for too long for no sensible purpose. Hood's soldiers had suffered so often that further ordeal just did not make sense. Since Franklin, the Army of Tennessee had been a disaster waiting to happen. Hood had lost in little more than a month's campaign about twenty thousand men from an army of perhaps 38,000; nearly a two-thirds loss ratio.[38]

In mid-January 1865, only about fourteen thousand men remained of

Hood's once-mighty army. Ultimately, the consequences of these disasters led directly to the South's final defeat. A Mississippi sergeant of Sears's Brigade perhaps best summed up the awful tragedy when he wrote: "My heart is full of tears. [Hood's campaign] is the most disastrous of any we have yet sustained. When I reflect on all the woes and misery, on the thousands of slain and maimed heroes who have poured out their blood as water, I feel a wild spirit of resentment. The real sentiment of this army is for peace on almost any terms."[39]

Today, after the elapse of nearly 150 years, we consider the grim carnage at Franklin and wonder what the grizzled veterans who sacrificed so much at Franklin would say if they could be here today. What would they want us to most remember and hold in our thoughts? Would they agree that Gettysburg, Antietam, or other famous Eastern battles should receive the vast majority of our attention? Would they condone nearly every schoolboy knowing of Pickett's Charge, but never having heard of Hood's bloodier assault at Franklin?

Having long studied their stories, I have a keen perspective of what the veterans of Franklin might hold precious for future generations. It is that they performed their full duty and met one of life's severest challenges with valor, honor, and dignity. In facing that terrible hell-on-earth in that god-forsaken ditch at Franklin, they had a fierce pride in knowing they had met extreme adversity—the greatest test of life—and prevailed in a personal sense. Those Southern soldiers who charged the Union entrenchments at Franklin knew above all else that our destiny extends only as far as our inner values. Thus, today we have their enduring testimony that it is mankind's indomitable spirit that counts the most. It is their investment in us, and this is both their legacy and our promise for a better tomorrow.

Notes

1. W. S. Thurston, *History One Hundred Eleventh Regiment O.V.I.* (Toledo, Ohio: Anderson and Bateman, 1894), 87; Daniel C. Govan, letter, Dec. 4, 1864, Southern Historical Society Collection, University of North Carolina Library, Chapel Hill, N.C. (hereafter cited as SHC).

2. Capt. James A. Sexton, "The Observations and Experiences of a Captain of Infantry at the Battle of Franklin, November 30, 1864," *Military Essays* (MOLLUS, Illinois Commandery) (Chicago: Cozzens & Beaton Co., 1907), 4:483.

3. For the general background of the Tennessee campaign, see Wiley Sword,

Embrace an Angry Wind: The Confederacy's Last Hurrah, Spring Hill, Franklin and Nashville (New York: HarperCollins Publishers, 1992), 1ff.

4. William T. Sherman, *Memoirs of General William T. Sherman,* 2 vols. (New York: Appleton and Company, 1875), 2:158–59; United States War Department, *War of the Rebellion: Official Records of the Union and Confederate Armies* (Washington, D.C.: Government Printing Office, 1880–1901), ser. 1, vol. 39, pt. 1, 588ff, 858ff (hereafter cited as *OR*).

5. *OR,* vol. 45, pt. 1, 895, 1034.

6. Ibid., 650, 657, 669, 670, 687, 730, 731, 752, 955, 956, 1106.

7. Thomas Lawrence Connelly, *Autumn of Glory: The Army of Tennessee, 1862–1865* (Baton Rouge: Louisiana State Univ. Press, 1971), 468ff.

8. *OR,* vol. 45, pt. 1, 657.

9. Ibid., 1085, 1087, 1090.

10. Sword, *Embrace an Angry Wind,* 152ff.

11. *OR,* vol. 45, pt. 1, 713, 770, 764; Benjamin F. Cheatham, "The Lost Opportunity at Spring Hill," *Southern Historical Society Papers* 9 (1881): 542–41; Frank H. Smith, *History of Maury County, Tennessee,* bk. 1 (Columbia, Tenn.: n.p., 1969), 238–39.

12. J. P. Young, "Hood's Failure at Spring Hill," *Confederate Veteran* 16 (March 1908): 32; *OR,* vol. 45, pt. 1, 657.

13. Letter of Gen. S. D. Lee, Dec. 6, 1864, James Thomas Harrison Papers, SHC, Chapel Hill, N.C.

14. R. R. Hancock, *Hancock's Diary: Or a History of the Second Tennessee Confederate Cavalry* (Nashville: Brandon Print Co., 1887), 520; *OR,* vol. 45, pt. 1, 239,653; Bromfield L. Ridley, *Battles and Sketches of the Army of Tennessee* (Mexico: Missouri Print & Pub. Co., 1906), 409.

15. S. A. Cunningham, "Disastrous Campaign in Tennessee," *Confederate Veteran* 12 (1904): 12–339; S. D. Lee letter, Dec. 6, 1864, SHC.

16. John Bell Hood, *Advance and Retreat: Personal Experiences in the United States and Confederate States Armies* (1880; repr., Lincoln: Univ. of Nebraska Press, 1996), 290; *OR,* vol. 45, pt. 1, 731; Irving A. Buck and Thomas Robson Hay, *Cleburne and His Command* (Jackson, Tenn.: McCowat-Mercer Press, 1959), 290.

17. Howell Purdue and Elizabeth Purdue, *Pat Cleburne: Confederate General* (Hillsboro, Tex.: Hill Jr. College Press, 1973), 420; Buck and Hay, *Cleburne and His Command,* 290.

18. John Allan Wyeth, *Life of Nathan Bedford Forrest* (New York: Harper & Bros., 1899), 544.

19. Levi T. Scofield, "The Retreat from Pulaski to Nashville," *Sketches of War History* (MOLLUS, Ohio Commandery) (Cincinnati: Military Order of the Loyal Legion of the United States, 1888), 133; I. G. Bennett and William M. Haigh, *A History of the Thirty-Sixth Regiment Illinois Volunteers* (Aurora, Ill.: Knickerbocker & Hodder, 1876), 650.

20. Bennett and Haigh, *A History of the Thirty-Sixth Illinois,* 650; Sword, *Embrace an Angry Wind,* 187.

21. Ridley, *Battles and Sketches of the Army of Tennessee,* 418; Smith, *History of*

Maury County, Tennessee, 202; N. A. Pinney, *A History of the One Hundred Fourth Regiment Ohio Volunteer Infantry* (Akron, Ohio: Werner & Lohmann, 1886), 60.

22. George W. Gordon, *Memoir of Franklin* (n.d.), Carter House Archives, Franklin, Tenn; *OR,* vol. 45, pt. 1, 232; David R. Logsdon, ed., *Eyewitnesses at the Battle of Franklin* (Nashville: Kettle Mills Press, 1991), 25, 26, quoting Joseph N. Thompson in *Williamson County Historical Journal,* 1984, 15.

23. James D. Porter, "Spring Hill and the Battle of Franklin," *Confederate Veteran,* 12:346; Gustavius W. Dyer and John Trotwood Moore, comp., *The Tennessee Civil War Veterans Questionnaires,* vol. 5 (1831; Easley, S.C.: Southern Historical Press, 1985); W. J. Worsham, *Old Nineteenth Tennessee regiment, C.S.A.* (Knoxville, Tenn.: Press of Paragon Print. Co., 1902), 379.

24. Sword, *Embrace an Angry Wind,* 223–24.

25. Marshall P. Thatcher, *A Hundred Battles in the West—St. Louis to Atlanta, 1861–1865, The Second Michigan Cavalry* (Detroit: Marshall P. Thatcher, 1884), 208, 249.

26. W. H. Newlin et al., *A History of the 73rd Regiment of Illinois Infantry Volunteers* (Springfield, Ill.: Regimental Reunion Association of Survivors of the 73d Illinois Infantry Volunteers, 1890), 451; Edward Whitesides, letter, Oct. 27, 1890, Shellenberger Papers, Library of Congress.

27. Ibid.; Newlin et al., *A History of the 73rd Regiment,* 402, 433, 459.

28. Shellenberger Papers, *Battle of Franklin,* Cleveland, Ohio, 1899, 35; Erastus Winters, *In the 50th Ohio Serving Uncle Sam* (Cincinnati: East Walnut Hills, n.d.), 120; David S. Stanley, *Personal Memoirs of Major General David Sloane Stanley, U.S.A.* (Cambridge, Mass.: Harvard Univ. Press, 1917), 207.

29. Newlin et al., *A History of the 73rd Regiment,* 433–61.

30. Ibid.; Scofield, "The Retreat from Pulaski to Nashville," 134.

31. Virgil S. Murphey (17th Alabama Infantry), diary, 1864, Southern Historical Collection, University of North Carolina, Chapel Hill, 6–7; Gordon, *Memoir of Franklin; OR,* vol. 45, pt. 1, 421–22; Jacob D. Cox, *The Battle of Franklin,* Tennessee, Nov. 30, 1864 (1897; Dayton, Ohio: Morningside, 1983), 47ff.

32. Isaac Miller (Co. E, 93rd Ohio Volunteer Infantry), letter, Dec. 2, 1864, Wiley Sword Collection, Suwanee, Ga.

33. Newlin et al., *A History of the 73rd Regiment,* 449, 479; *Confederate Veteran,* 2:186, 282; 21:345; W. D. Mintz Memoir, Carter House Archives.

34. Newlin et al., *A History of the 73rd Regiment,* 478–79; *Confederate Veteran,* 10:501.

35. *OR,* vol. 45, pt. 1, 658, 694, 721; Ridley, *Battles and Sketches of the Army of Tennessee,* 411.

36. *OR,* vol. 45, pt. 1, 684, 686; Sword, *Embrace an Angry Wind,* 269–70.

37. Newlin et al., *A History of the 73rd Regiment,* 479.

38. Sword, *Embrace an Angry Wind,* 377, 425; *OR,* vol. 45, pt. 1, 40, 46–49, 344, 356, 715, 716; ibid., vol. 45, pt. 2, 345, 370, 650.

39. Sword, *Embrace an Angry Wind,* 426; William P. H. Chambers diary, Feb. 1865, Mississippi Department of Archives and History, Jackson, Miss.

Part II

Leaders

Reconsidering Felix Zollicoffer

The Influence of Weather and Terrain in the Rise and Fall of a Military Commander in Appalachia

Brian D. McKnight

When historians debate the notable commanders of the Civil War, certain names stand tall and others shrink in comparison. Within the Appalachian region, most of the commanders in both armies fall into the latter category. It would be easy to study these men if they were Lees, Jacksons, and Grants, but in the intermountain region, they were Marshalls, Echols, and Joneses. For each army, Appalachia was a backwater with geographical features that aided in its defense, so soldiers fewer in number and often lesser trained could be quickly put into safe service there. With these green troops on the ground, the terrain naturally constrained and slowed movement, which could be used to each army's advantage. The first regional commander to comprehend these elemental strengths was Confederate Gen. Felix K. Zollicoffer. By the time of his death in early 1862, Zollicoffer had acquitted himself very well in thwarting Abraham Lincoln's wishes to mount a Union invasion of East Tennessee, and he had done so by understanding how weather and terrain could be manipulated to his advantage.

Felix Zollicoffer's Civil War career actually began months before the first shots were fired. In February 1861, he arrived in Washington, D.C., as part of Tennessee's delegation to the Virginia-called peace conference.[1] During the preceding weeks, Kentucky Sen. John J. Crittenden had crafted a set of proposals that he hoped would make up an effective compromise. However, by the time the Peace Conference opened on February 4, Crittenden's proposals were dying on the vine.[2] As a member of the Tennessee delegation, Zollicoffer arrived three days later, joined the Committee on Credentials, and participated little, if any, in the debates.[3] By the time he returned to Tennessee, the promise of the Peace Commission had faded as it had adopted a nearly identical agenda to that of Crittenden.[4]

Once home, Zollicoffer began aligning himself with Southern secessionists. On May 9, almost a month before Tennessee seceded from the Union, he accepted a commission as brigadier general in the Provisional Army of Tennessee and two months later received a regular commission in the Confederate Army. During his two months' service as a state militia officer, he had various responsibilities, from inspecting factories that could be used to make the materiels of war to training and encamping newly arrived recruits. He soon commanded Camp Trousdale, near the Tennessee–Kentucky line north of Nashville, where thousands of men were turned into soldiers.[5]

Like the soldiers at Camp Trousdale, Zollicoffer, too, was learning. Having no prior military service, he found himself immersed in the work of preparing for war with no previous experience. By far, his greatest asset was the fact that he was a Tennessean who understood Tennesseans—a quality Tennessee politicians recognized as very important. For that, he was given one of the first Confederate commands in the state and would be sent to East Tennessee, where his men were desperately needed.

Zollicoffer's assignment to the mountains of East Tennessee was necessitated by a call for help from Landon Carter Haynes, a resident of Carter County. On July 6, 1861, he wrote Confederate Secretary of War Leroy P. Walker, informing him of rumors about Union arms being smuggled from Kentucky into East Tennessee, destined for the hands of those loyal to Lincoln. Haynes was also concerned with the permissiveness within the Confederate state of Tennessee. He warned Walker that United States Congressman Thomas A. R. Nelson had reportedly urged a large crowd in Haynes's home county to resist the Confederate cause despite Tennessee's official status as part of the Confederacy and promised any Union man the support and protection of the United States.[6] Although Haynes suggested the names of a few people he felt could properly manage the situation, the Confederate leadership chose Felix Zollicoffer.

Responding to the apparent crisis, Zollicoffer's command filtered into East Tennessee during July and was sent to guard Cumberland Gap. By August 6, a fast-working Zollicoffer, with four thousand men, was responding to various threats to his command. He wrote to Gen. Samuel Cooper that his local informants had reported "that different bodies of men in the counties of Southeastern Kentucky, estimated to amount in the aggregate to several thousand, are under military organization, and are threatening

Felix Zollicoffer. (Library of Congress)

to force a passage through the mountains into East Tennessee."[7] Although he greatly overestimated the number of organized Union men in southeastern Kentucky, he certainly understood that Camp Dick Robinson had been built on the road between London and Lexington as a depot for both troops and supplies. With such a large camp present on the main north-south thoroughfare and an ever-present threat of a Union invasion of East Tennessee, Zollicoffer knew he had to provide the strongest possible defenses for the Gap.

These military successes came with the support of the region's friendly terrain. With steep sides and a narrow pass, the topography of the Cumberland Gap suggests that it would be easily defended. Nineteenth-century commanders drew comparisons to the climactic battle of the Persian War and saw some level of historical determinism in this Appalachian Thermopylae. The confidence and historical awareness of the Civil War soldier occupying the Gap was so complete that there was little question as to their fate. James Henry Rogers, a Confederate soldier, wrote that the Gap was the "Thermopylae of the state . . . well fortified by nature . . . with a little labor can be made almost impregnable."[8] Another Southerner channeled the story of Thermopylae when he wrote that the "gap is one of the strongest fortified places I ever saw . . . ten thousand men could hold it successfully against one hundred thousand."[9] With such statements, Cumberland Gap was doing its job—encouraging a sense of security and complacency.

With all possible invasion routes plugged, it became important for Zollicoffer to build static defenses at pinch-points like the main pass. In addition to the earthworks and log works that sprang up on the mountainsides overlooking the all-important road, the area was quickly deforested to provide for soldiers' cabins, firewood, and clear visibility. With firing lanes cleared, the few field guns that Tennessee had at its disposal were likely moved to the Gap during September, but Zollicoffer needed more. He asked for ten twelve-pounders by the end of September, but these could not be supplied.[10] By November 2, well after Zollicoffer's men had fought in the region's initial battles, the Union Army was beginning to move slowly toward the Gap, and Zollicoffer had received only three cannon and two Parrott guns. He reminded Secretary of War Judah Benjamin that he desperately needed the guns, and that only one of the three possible routes of advancement from Kentucky was properly fortified.[11] Although the all-important Cumberland Gap was well defended, western passes at Jacksboro and Jamestown, both convenient approaches to Knoxville, were still relatively open. If the enemy made it to Knoxville, railroads could be used to the east, south, and west, making deeper penetration into Confederate territory much easier.[12] Without adequate artillery to break an enemy advance, a frustrated Zollicoffer had to rely on the steady erosion of the road conditions that came with autumn weather to slow whatever forward movement the enemy might decide to make.[13]

Depending on the deterioration of the roads to help with fall defense was a good plan for a commander in Civil War–era Appalachia. William F. Patterson, captain and engineer for Union Gen. George W. Morgan, described the conditions of the mountain roads leading south from Barbourville to the area of the Gap. He relayed a story about a large rock that had either fallen or been pushed down a hill into the road. The stone was so large and the spot so narrow that it prevented the passage of anything larger than the individual soldier. The men were forced to break off a side of the rock before they could get wagons by in a single file and continue on their journey.[14] With such examples unencumbered by weather, the complications that came with fall and spring rains are not surprising. Patterson struggled with roads whose rills and runnels turned into full-fledged streambeds every time heavy rains came. He told of having to dump trees and brush into these deep chasms and run them over with wagons in order to make the road passable again.[15]

Indeed, the bad roads were legendary. A year after Zollicoffer's realization, Morgan described the eighty miles of road connecting Crab Orchard, Kentucky, with Cumberland Ford as "nearly impassible."[16] He noted that "At many places the narrow roads, walled in by the mountains, had become torrents" so bad that "sometimes the horses were obliged to swim" through the deep, soupy mess.[17] Archibald Means confirmed Morgan's sentiment when he used the same language to describe the road conditions: "After leaving Crab Orchard," he "found the roads in an almost impassable condition."[18] Connecting the weather with problems of supply is as simple as Morgan's statement that the roads were so bad that short trains of no more than twelve wagons could make only "three to four miles a day."[19] Twelve wagons at a time making only four miles a day is no way to supply an army dependably, particularly a geographically isolated one, and Zollicoffer seemed to see that eventuality.

On top of those handicaps was the problem of securing the road, even if it were passable. Sitting squarely in the middle of one of the most geographically challenging regions of the war, opposing armies quickly learned that guerrillas, even pickets, could make a difference in their daily operations. With narrow mountain passes, which often held the only usable road, there was a great degree of predictability to the different armies' movements, which could be exploited by a handful of riflemen or interrupted by a team of men with axes. Zollicoffer seemed to understand that holding the road would put him into position to control it by both regular and, if necessary, irregular means.

Historians have traditionally blamed Lincoln's timid generals for the Union's missed opportunities in East Tennessee, but that is only part of the explanation. Felix Zollicoffer, whose brief wartime career has often been the butt of jokes, displayed all the traits of a professional soldier in those pivotal first months of the Civil War. Through his work of securing the routes into East Tennessee, he effectively delayed a Union invasion by making it an increasingly dangerous proposition to any general who might try it. By not only defending the passes, but also moving along the roads into Kentucky and placing advance forces, he forced a potential invader to move his army into long, narrow traps that might be sprung by ambush at any moment on poor and path-like mountain roads. Ultimately, both sides came to the uneasy determination that without a planned offensive movement through the Gap, there was little benefit in holding it. William

McCart said the same thing when he wrote of leaving the area, "believing it was a place that was of no profit to either side for them to try to hold."[20] It was true: the Cumberland Gap was the strongest position that George Morgan had "ever seen, except Gibraltar."[21] It did appear to be "the best natural fortified place to be in, in the world."[22] But at the same time, it was a place where "100,000 can't whip out 20,000 but it is one of the easiest places in the world to starve out a set of men."[23] Like so many other elements of the Appalachian Civil War, those things that initially appear to be strengths sometimes become profound weaknesses with the passage of time and the change in circumstances.

Far from the mountains, out of the weather, and working from his desk, Abraham Lincoln was also thinking about the Cumberland Gap. Not surprisingly, by late September, he was already thinking further ahead than his generals. He wrote Indiana Gov. Oliver P. Morton of his hope that "Zollicoffer has left Cumberland Gap (though I fear he has not). He suspected that if Zollicoffer had abandoned the Gap, he did so out of the fear that the mass of men at Camp Dick Robinson, "re-inforced from Cincinnati," was planning to move against him rather than Zollicoffer's own preparations to move into Kentucky.

For one of the few times during the war, Lincoln's estimation was completely wrong. Instead of slinking away from the Gap, Zollicoffer had quickly realized that the area's geography was as much a determining factor as enemy infantrymen. With hollows funneling all traffic along creek and riverbeds, there were surprisingly few routes into Tennessee that needed to be covered and they often required only token resistance. Understanding this, Zollicoffer reinforced the Gap and then the valley towns leading to the Gap from Kentucky. With a long line of defensive positions that took advantage of the local terrain, a Union invasion became treacherous. He also seemed to understand that every day he delayed a possible Union advance, the more distant a possibility it became.

Unlike many of Lincoln's generals, Zollicoffer understood that offensive movement also provides significant defensive strength. As soon as his initial preparations at Cumberland Gap had been completed, Zollicoffer began preparing to take the initiative and move into Kentucky. Understanding the limitations of the terrain, the newspaperman-turned-Confederate general used his common sense to surmise that he could protect the Gap by moving troops far forward of it and garrisoning the towns along the way. As an invading force moved closer, it would meet stronger and stron-

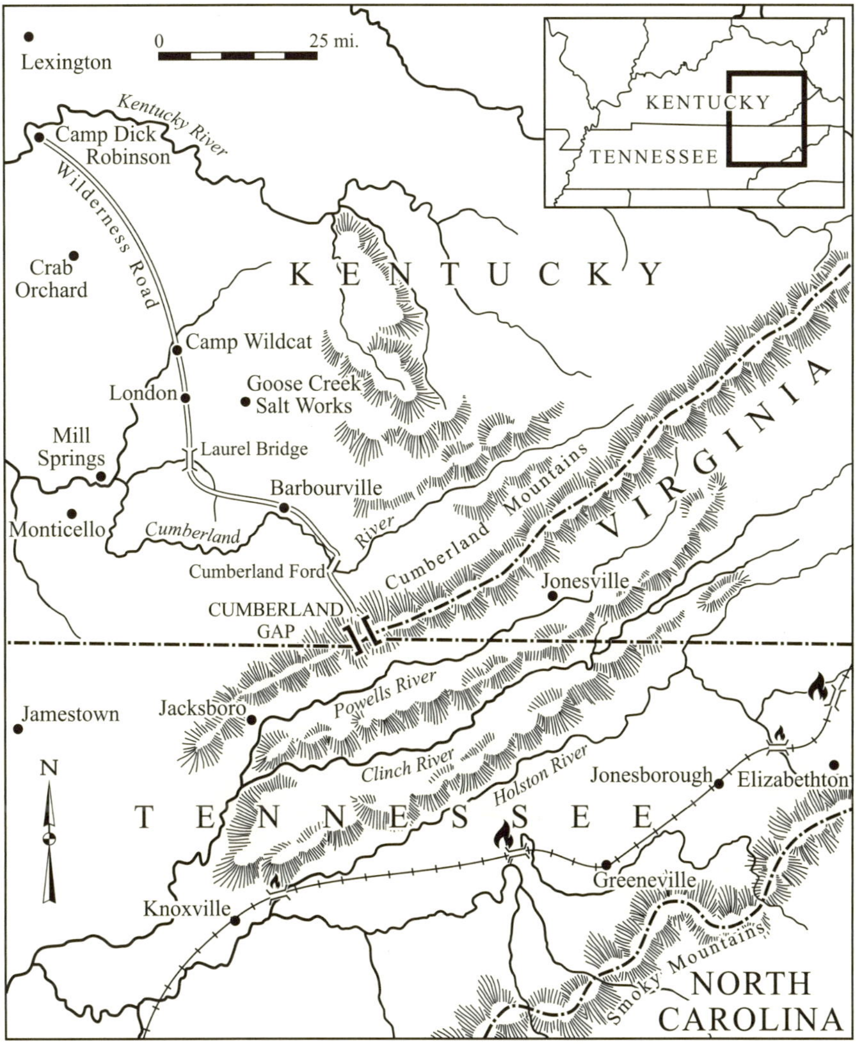

Transportation Routes North and South. Note the successful and unsuccessful attempts to fire the bridges on the East Tennessee & Virginia Railroad.

ger resistance and give the Confederates ample time to prepare for what might otherwise have been a surprise attack.[24]

Surprisingly, Zollicoffer, whom history has remembered as a bumbler whose final mistake resulted in his own death, sprang into effective action. During the coming weeks, he stuck to a comprehensive plan to defend not only the Gap itself, but forward positions through which an enemy would have to advance and various lesser gaps along the Cumberland range that might allow the Federals to get into his rear or bypass his position completely. In his August 6 letter to Gen. Samuel Cooper, he illustrated the importance of controlling these avenues of travel by informing Richmond of the recent arrest of the Unionist Congressman Nelson and his transfer under guard to Abingdon, Virginia.[25] If Nelson were using the route to get to Washington, Zollicoffer reasoned that others would seek to do the same and be able to provide the Union Army with a thick file of accurate regional intelligence.

As for the topographical details, Zollicoffer sent Cooper a copy of his best map of the area with a thorough description of his intentions. Noting the important Union military concentrations in the region, the major gaps through the mountain range, and a general description of the terrain facing him, Zollicoffer announced his plan for a network of cavalry scouts between advance posts and his infantry posts that could carry information quickly. He envisioned having constant patrols in and around some of the more vulnerable advance positions and along the roads and bridle paths that could both cut Union lines of communication out of East Tennessee while guarding against a possible Federal approach. Since most of the roads led to Cumberland Gap, Zollicoffer surmised that his reserve force could be quickly mobilized in the direction of most invaders.[26] The detail of Zollicoffer's work was thorough enough that by September 9, G. S. Dowis of Whitley County, Kentucky, wrote that Southern soldiers had "blockaded every pass between Tenn and Ky."[27]

On September 19, 1861, Zollicoffer's men initiated the war's first engagement on Kentucky soil. Feeling strongly that "an onward movement towards those who threaten invasion" was his best course of action, he ordered his men out of Camp Buckner at Cumberland Ford and put them on the road to Barbourville.[28] As of August 29, Zollicoffer had learned of one thousand Union soldiers at Barbourville, but they had departed, leaving behind a Home Guard made up of only 150 local men possessing "very valiant hearts but timid legs." As the Confederates got closer to the town, more Home Guards slipped away, leaving only about thirty-five men to stand up for Barbourville by the time Col. Joel Battle arrived and attacked the town.[29] Early on September 19, Battle's eight hundred Confederates emerged from a dense fog and fell upon the small local militia.[30] Although the Unionists were outnumbered twenty-three to one, they fought bravely, firing several shots each and broke for the hills only when Confederate cavalry crossed the creek and appeared ready to approach them from the rear. Ultimately, the victory at Barbourville brought no tangible results to Zollicoffer's cause other than destroying Camp Andy Johnson, inflicting a dozen casualties on the local Home Guards, and taking twenty-five stands of arms, but it officially initiated the Civil War in Kentucky.[31]

With much progress made in planning and implementing a defense of Cumberland Gap and a small but meaningful skirmish at Barbourville won, Zollicoffer began looking deeper into Kentucky for his next opportunity. A week after his men took Barbourville, he outlined his next plan. Looking to the most obvious target, Zollicoffer began planning to send men to take Laurel Bridge, on the road to Camp Dick Robinson, but only as a diversion masking his grander plan. His real interest lay in the Clay County's Goose Creek Salt Works. Owned by the Garrard family, it was one of the most productive saltworks in Kentucky and could help supply the Confederacy with its main mineral of food preservation. Theorizing that if he sent men to take the bridge from the estimated one hundred to five hundred Home Guardsmen defending it, his salt expedition would be disguised. Zollicoffer guessed that the whole affair would take five or six days to complete and result in dozens of wagonloads of precious salt.[32] By October 3, Col. James Rains had pulled off his commander's audacious plan to steal Kentucky salt. Although an original order from Zollicoffer had fallen into the hands of Union Col. Theophilus T. Garrard, one of the owners of the works, he had learned of it too late to prevent the raid. Garrard wrote that he could not doubt the authenticity of the order "because they carried out the instructions to the letter."[33]

That expedition went off without a hitch. Zollicoffer reported that the Confederates pushed between six hundred and fifteen hundred Unionists back toward Laurel Bridge, where they captured "8,000 cartridges, 25,000 caps, 3 kegs of powder, 6 barrels of salt, 2 wagons and teams, . . . 3 other horses, 25 pairs of shoes, and several guns." In his report, Zollicoffer returned to one of his objectives when he noted that a good number of the Unionist force at Laurel Bridge had apparently come from Camp Dick Robinson. The group tasked with raiding the saltworks used the attack on Laurel Bridge as a cover for their own movement. They left the works with a wagon train hauling all the salt there—two hundred barrels—and returned to camp without incident.[34]

Another of the ways that Zollicoffer separated himself from many of his contemporaries was through his concern for Kentuckians and his understanding of their complex loyalties. When he sent men to Goose Creek to take the salt, he ordered the officer in command of the expedition to submit a receipt for what he took.[35] The receipt could then be submitted to the Confederate government for reimbursement in Southern currency at the going rate of forty cents per bushel. Zollicoffer hoped that such behavior would help ingratiate local citizens with the Southern army, but paying Kentuckians in what many of them considered a foreign currency was tantamount to outright theft. Either oblivious to the reality of his men's behavior or hoping to conceal the depredations from his superiors, Zollicoffer wrote Gen. Albert Sidney Johnston: "I am carefully respecting the rights of the citizens, and am making some favorable impression on their sentiments I hope."[36] The reality was much worse. Zollicoffer could not even enjoy his successes because of reports of his soldiers' bad behavior toward citizens. In his official report, he wrote: "I regret to have to report that I learn that some of our soldiers committed discreditable trespasses on the property of private citizens on the route." He promised to investigate the allegations and punish the men responsible in the hopes that it might "thwart progress I was making in conciliating masses of ignorant people here who were hostile because they were told we would have no respect for their personal or property rights."[37] In reality, most Kentuckians east of the Jackson Purchase looked upon the Confederate cause with suspicion, if not outright hostility. One Kentuckian writing an influential friend in Frankfort around the time of the fight at Barbourville felt confident that "The mountaineers will whip Zollicoffer as soon as they get ammunition. By all means send them *lead, lead, lead!*"[38]

Within only a few weeks, the aggressive Zollicoffer was again moving northward toward the Laurel Bridge for the second time in a month. To capture and hold the bridge and the Wilderness Road that it carried meant that another of the impediments separating Zollicoffer from the Kentucky heartland had been removed. After gathering intelligence that suggested 4,500 Union soldiers had moved in a southerly direction out of Camp Dick Robinson, Zollicoffer wrote Col. W. W. Mackall, assistant adjutant general to Albert Sidney Johnston. He feared that the Union contingent was heading south with the intent of attacking the recently successful Confederates and asked if he could seize the initiative and "meet them halfway."[39] Having performed flawlessly up to that point, Zollicoffer had earned the confidence of Johnston, and Mackall replied, "Exercise your own discretion in attacking the enemy."[40]

Zollicoffer's plan was simple: Move north up the Wilderness Road and attack the Unionists where he found them, then wheel southwest to Albany, Kentucky, where eight hundred Union soldiers were encamped and dispatch them. The morning after he received permission to attack the Union, he ordered a cavalry company to London, Kentucky, within fifteen miles of where he would eventually find the enemy. Returning the following day, the cavalrymen reported that 3,300 Union soldiers had taken positions at the junction of the Wilderness Road and the Richmond Road, just south of the Rockcastle River, at a location called Camp Wildcat.[41]

It was at this point that Zollicoffer's luck began to run out. Despite the poor hand he had been dealt in terms of manpower and geography, Zollicoffer had done more with less than most people could imagine. He had mitigated his weaknesses by being aggressive and had moved quickly as a way to keep his enemy on the defense. However, his personal alacrity became a hostage to circumstances. Primarily, his supplies were slow in arriving. He confided to Albert Sidney Johnston that he "would move forward and attack them instantly but for unexpected deficiency in subsistence stores." Ten days earlier, he had ordered his commissary to gather thirty days' rations for five thousand men, but little had been done. He lamented the fact that he did not have enough for five days and would not be able to go on the offensive without at least ten days' worth.[42] It took more than a week for Zollicoffer's supply train to arrive at Camp Buckner with enough provisions to outfit the invasion.[43]

Finally, on October 16, Zollicoffer ordered his command onto the road toward the Rockcastle Hills. As his force moved northward, Unionists watched intently. Col. T. T. Garrard, on October 17, reported that the Confederates were "9 miles beyond London" with an overestimated six thousand men. Garrard pleaded with his superior, Gen. George H. Thomas, warning him, "I must have aid here to-morrow" and that since the enemy camp was at least twenty-five miles distant, "Your artillery can reach here before the enemy does."[44] By the next day, Garrard was still waiting for a reply from Thomas when he wrote a second note confirming his intelligence that "Zollicoffer is coming on with a large force and six pieces of artillery." Meanwhile, Col. John Coburn met with Garrard and was ordered to bring his regiment forward in preparation for a likely battle with the Confederates. Coburn frustrated Garrard by claiming that he could not do so without being ordered by Thomas, and Garrard pleaded with his superior to have this done. Fearing the consequences of facing a heretofore larger and more effective enemy force, Garrard informed Thomas that he was making preparations to abandon Camp Wildcat if reinforcements did not soon arrive. Frustrated by Thomas's silence, Garrard vented: "I have no idea of having my men butchered up here, where they have a force of six or seven to one, with artillery.

I would like to hear from you immediately."[45] By October 19, Garrard was beside himself. He reported the latest information to Thomas and frantically reminded him that "I have not heard one word from you since I wrote on the morning of the 17th instant."[46] Whether Thomas had grown tired of a subordinate commander who raised too many unnecessary alarms, was preoccupied with Gen. William Tecumseh Sherman's visit to Camp Dick Robinson, or expected that Garrard would quiet down once the reinforcements who were en route finally arrived, he certainly had a problem on his hands. To solve this problem, Thomas chose Polish-born Gen. Albin Schoepf, whose Austrian military training and experience made him a valuable commander. Having been a commissioned officer in the Union Army only since September 30, Thomas immediately tested Schoepf's mettle.

Although Garrard may have doubted Thomas's interest in assisting him, the general was hard at work hurrying men to Garrard's location. Certainly, Garrard had reason to worry. As commander of the 7th Kentucky, his men were the only infantry at the location and there was less than a full regiment fit for duty. In hopes of getting enough men onto the field to staunch the expected Confederate assault, Thomas dispatched the 14th and 17th Ohio, 33rd Indiana, and a battery from the 1st Ohio Artillery, and Schoepf rode at the front of the column, leading them toward their destination.[47]

In the meantime, Zollicoffer's force was moving north along the Wilderness Road en route to Wildcat. Harboring no illusions of catching the Unionists by surprise, Zollicoffer was convinced that he would face a much larger force than his initial scouts had confirmed. Only ten miles away from Camp Wildcat on the morning of October 20, Zollicoffer learned that the Union situation had not appreciably changed over the previous days. With this knowledge, Zollicoffer's confidence soared while unseen Union reinforcements closed in on his destination.[48]

Arriving on the night of October 20 was Schoepf, who, without any knowledge of the situation, met with and deferred to his colonels, who had organized the existing defenses. Just as it had done for Zollicoffer previously, the terrain gave Schoepf the advantage. Zollicoffer's approach was uphill as he expected, but he did not fully appreciate the funnel shape of the narrow draw that would suck him in between two steep and high ridges running along each side. Perceptively, as Zollicoffer led his men to the field as dawn broke on October 21, he sent one regiment to occupy Begley Hollow Heights on the left side of his approach. He expected the road to be blocked as it had been along his earlier route, but the combination of the narrow passage and the felled trees made the advance torturously slow.

Fearing what might lie around the next corner, Zollicoffer ordered his old friend, Col. James Rains, up the main road to probe the defenses and examine the path ahead.[49]

Schoepf's deference to his colonels from the night before apparently continued on the morning of the battle. The best decision of the battle was the recognition of Round Hill's importance. It was a high, steep-sided knoll to the right of Zollicoffer's line of approach that was occupied by a small contingent of Home Guards. One would expect that a well-trained military man like Schoepf would see the advantage of this high ground, but numerous reports placed the responsibility for recognizing Round Hill's strategic potential in the hands of the same group who had guided his decision making the night before. With the importance of Round Hill realized, Schoepf ordered men into position, thereby completing the funnel that would draw in Zollicoffer's Confederates.

Round Hill would spell doom for both Zollicoffer's attempt to take Camp Wildcat and his growing reputation as a military commander. As he struggled to find a safe way up the grade and through the natural gauntlet created by the steep hills on each side of the road, he began to question his decision. Although he continued to press forward into the teeth of a strong Union defense, Zollicoffer revealed his doubts to both Cooper and Mackall a few days later when he wrote that after reconnoitering the approach shortly before the battle commenced, "I became satisfied that it could not be carried otherwise than by immense exposure, if at all."[50] Certainly, Round Hill was formidable. Tall and steep, the Unionists had discovered its importance barely ahead of the Confederates.

Rather than backing away from this fight, Zollicoffer continued to push his men closer to the well-positioned Yankees. By the time the battle began, the 33rd Indiana held Round Hill and watched as Zollicoffer's regiments advanced up the road and toward their position. Rather than attacking the main camp along the road, the Confederate 11th Tennessee wheeled off the road and began marching broadside toward the widest part of Round Hill while the 7th and 29th Tennessee approached through the woods, intending to hit the Union left flank. After an hour of midday fighting, the 11th Tennessee withdrew back down the road from whence they came, leaving the 17th Tennessee to attempt a flanking movement around the Home Guards holding down the 33rd's left. A combination of the terrain on the north side of Round Hill and the arrival of the 17th Ohio spelled doom for the Confederates, who withdrew back toward their camp and shifted their strategic focus westward to the South Rim of Begley Hollow Heights.[51]

In the early afternoon, Zollicoffer tried to salvage the day with a coordinated attack on both Round Hill and the South Rim. As it stood, both Union and Confederate regiments were divided between the two locations with five hundred yards and the Wilderness Road separating them. Additionally, the regiments of both armies were largely fragmented with parts of the 33rd Indiana holding both the Union far left and far right and members of the 29th and the 17th Tennessee fighting on both sides of the road. For this final assault, Zollicoffer ordered the 29th and the 17th Tennessee to resume their attack on Round Hill and sent other elements of the 29th and 17th Tennessee to scale the South Rim in the hopes they could reach the 7th Kentucky (US) firmly entrenched along the ridgeline. Zollicoffer's full plan would never be initiated as he held the 11th and 20th Tennessee and the 15th Mississippi in reserve awaiting word of Confederate success on the mountain. If and when the word came, these three regiments were to drive up the Wilderness Road, where they expected to split the Union forces and meet token resistance.[52]

By the time the sun began to set on October 21, the Battle of Wildcat Mountain was over. Neither Zollicoffer nor Schoepf had performed well. Zollicoffer entered the battle confident that he was facing only a single regiment, and when he found reinforcements, he did not adjust his plan accordingly. Although Schoepf was the Union commander on the field, he behaved like a field officer awaiting the decisions of others rather than making them himself. Perhaps Schoepf did the right thing? After all, he understood the power of his geographic position and let the battle come to him without making any of the mistakes often made in haste. With those things in mind, the most credit falls to the battlefield's terrain, which helped the Federal army win the decisive victory. By the end of the day, 3,200 Confederates had been on the field with 2,000 participating in the fighting—62.5 percent—while the Union Army committed only 45 percent of its 3,550 men to the fight. Perhaps the formidable terrain illustrated the futility of the fight as casualties were remarkably light with the Confederates reporting a loss of eleven killed and forty-two wounded and the Union suffering four killed and eighteen wounded.[53]

Originally, Zollicoffer had planned to follow up his victory at Camp Wildcat with a movement on Monticello and Somerset, but after his defeat, he withdrew to lick his wounds. In order to do this, though, Zollicoffer had to put time, distance, and impediments between his men and Schoepf's emboldened Unionists. Schoepf's men inadvertently helped Zollicoffer by sleeping on their arms in expectation of a renewed attack the next morning.

By the time the Unionists learned of Zollicoffer's retreat, he had a five-hour head start. In the coming days, there were many questions asked as to why Schoepf did not pursue the Confederates and follow up his initial victory with a complete defeat of the enemy, but T. T. Garrard helped answer the question by explaining what the Union commanders knew and when they knew it. He advised: "We have a great many here who know precisely how to manage affairs when the enemy is out of hearing, but would be as much at a loss to do so in a fight as I would be."[54] After retreating eighteen miles on October 22, Zollicoffer camped his men between London and Barbourville on the Laurel River. The next day, they withdrew another twelve miles and returned to their old camp at Cumberland Ford. Although it was normally a very strong position behind the only river crossing for miles, Zollicoffer feared that he might be trapped as "The road over the Log Mountains will soon become almost impassable between here and the Cumberland Gap." On October 30, Zollicoffer and his men, having used the expectation of coming bad weather and resulting bad roads as part of their defensive strategy, returned to a strengthened encampment at the Gap.[55]

Zollicoffer would remain at Cumberland Gap for only a few days before resuming his intent to move on central Kentucky. By November 5, he received intelligence that there were no Federal forces south of Monticello and that the time was right for another invasion of Kentucky.[56] As his route to Barbourville was approaching impassibility by that time, Zollicoffer saw a western approach through Jacksboro and toward the Cumberland Plateau as his best opportunity to get back into Kentucky. On November 7, Zollicoffer moved west to Jacksboro, where he ordered the northbound roads blockaded. With the prospect of Cumberland Gap being made very strong within only a few days and his work at Jacksboro proceeding efficiently, Zollicoffer planned to move to Jamestown from where he would turn north toward Monticello.[57]

At the same time that Zollicoffer was planning an invasion of Kentucky, Unionist Tennesseans in Kentucky were hoping to invade their home state. Samuel P. Carter, a native of East Tennessee and career naval officer, had been transitioned into the army and promised a soldier's commission as a brigadier general at the outset of the war in the hopes that he could use his regional connections to that part of the state for the Union. November 16 brought Carter welcome news from his younger brother, William. As a partner in the work of the Union, William had just coordinated and helped carry out a series of bridge-burnings along the routes of the East Tennessee & Virginia Railroad and the East Tennessee & Georgia Railroad. With local citizens excited to the point of action and knowing that the destruction of these vital east-west links would result in a firm response by the Confederate Army, Samuel Carter urged General Thomas to "urge the commanding general to give us some additional force and let us advance into East Tennessee; now is the time."[58]

For Zollicoffer, the war was about to change with the appointment of George B. Crittenden as general and commander of the District of East Tennessee. Crittenden, whose military background included a West Point education, two different stints in the United States Army, two years in the Army of the Republic of Texas, and some time as a prisoner of war in Mexico as a result of the Mier Expedition, had largely remained a military man through the influence of his famous father. Promoted to major general and given command of the Department of East Tennessee on November 9, the professionally trained and experienced Crittenden was expected to serve as an upgrade over Zollicoffer.[59] This change of command, however, proved troublesome for the curious reason that Zollicoffer was never informed of the move. As late as November 28, three full weeks after Crittenden's ascendance, Zollicoffer wrote to Gen. Albert Sidney Johnston's headquarters: "I am not yet aware that Major-General Crittenden has assumed command in this district."[60] Finally, on December 10, Zollicoffer informed Johnston's headquarters of what it should have already known: "Major-General Crittenden has assumed command, and is, I think, now at Knoxville."[61]

By November 27, most of Zollicoffer's force lay on the south bank of the Cumberland River across from Mill Springs. He was certain that there were no Union forces on his side of the river and was sending out men to examine ferries and roads for possible later use. He reported confidently that the land was bounteous, providing "an abundance of beef, pork, and corn, at low prices," and that "The better classes of citizens sympathize with us" in this part of Kentucky.[62] Knowing that there were eight hundred Union men north of the river at Waitsborough, Zollicoffer ordered two regiments across to the northern bank, but the swollen river prevented his order from being carried out. Finding only two small boats available locally, Zollicoffer realized that he would have to build his own. On November 30, he wrote that he was "preparing to provide the means of crossing the river" by using "The lumber and the saw-mill here," but that would take time.[63] Two days later, he wrote Mackall again and noted for a second time his intention to build "transports to enable me to cross, but I fear there will be several days' delay."[64] On December 9, he again wrote Mackall, this time reporting that "Five regiments, seven cavalry companies, and four pieces of artillery are now across," leaving him with twice that force remaining on the south bank, but that night, fate intervened.[65]

On the night of December 9, Zollicoffer received two long-overdue messages from Mackall dated December 4. Mackall referenced Zollicoffer's message of November 27, but may have meant November 28 in which Zollicoffer inferred that he would keep his force south of the Cumberland.[66] The December 4 message from Johnston's headquarters approved Zollicoffer's plan and made his guarding the road to Somerset and Monticello his strategic priority.[67] Arriving with this correspondence, dated the same day, was a copy of Special Orders Number 127, which gave to Gen. William Hardee command of all territory north of the Cumberland River.[68] To this news, Zollicoffer responded, "I infer from yours that I should not have crossed the river, but it is now too late. My means of recrossing is so limited, I could hardly accomplish it in face of the enemy."[69] Zollicoffer was not only astride the Cumberland River with a growing Union force moving in his direction, he was also in two different commands.

Seeing trouble brewing on the south bank of the Cumberland River, Federal authorities ordered General Schoepf out of London, Kentucky, to keep Zollicoffer from crossing. Schoepf, who had repulsed Zollicoffer three weeks earlier at Wildcat Mountain, moved west with two regiments and a single battery of guns. Schoepf was lucky to arrive in time to begin digging entrenchments. By December 2, his camp was being shelled from the south bank of the river and reinforcements were desperately needed. Thomas ordered more troops to Schoepf's aid, but Gen. Don Carlos Buell withheld one of those regiments and "expressly forbade Thomas to send additional reinforcements to Somerset without his approval." Buell's reservations were based on his dissatisfaction with the Lincoln administration's involvement in military affairs. Both Lincoln and Buell agreed that East Tennessee should be liberated, but that was the extent of their cooperation. Buell believed that Lincoln's idea of invading the region through the eastern mountains was dangerous and, if poorly done, might result in the destruction of his army. Buell remained convinced that Zollicoffer's advance was a sideshow and that the real victory in Tennessee would come at Nashville.[70] To be sure, Buell's foot-dragging made Zollicoffer's crossing of the Cumberland easy, but Zollicoffer's command decisions are worthy of consideration.

The real question for Zollicoffer is whether or not he ever intended to remain on the south bank. He argued that he did not receive any correspondence from Johnston's headquarters from December 4 until late on December 9. Taking him at his word suggests that he originally intended to stay south of the river, but decided to cross after having second thoughts. However, historian Kenneth Hafendorfer identifies a pattern of behavior that suggests that Zollicoffer may have been in the habit of writing his superiors with conservative plans while acting much more boldly, understanding that if he was successful, few complaints would be lodged. It apparently began on November 4, when Zollicoffer wrote Johnston's headquarters suggesting that he be given permission to move the bulk of his force to near Jamestown, Tennessee, where his and Gen. Simon Bolivar Buckner's forces could mutually support each other, if necessary. Although he stated that he would not act until he received a response from Johnston, the next day he wrote confirming that he had already put the plan into motion.[71] Later in the month, Zollicoffer ordered two regiments to cross the Cumberland without specific authority to do so in the hopes that his men would drive off the Federals at Waitsborough. Hafendorfer sees this as Zollicoffer "pushing beyond his implied intentions."[72] Finally, Zollicoffer wrote to Johnston on December 2 stating his intention to move a significant part of his force to the north bank of the river. By this time, what began at Cumberland Gap as Zollicoffer wanting to move closer to Jamestown was becoming a full-scale military invasion of the Kentucky heartland.[73]

To be sure, by December 10, Zollicoffer knew he had made a mistake. He wrote to Johnston outlining his current state of affairs with the byline of Beech Grove, a site that was on the north bank of the Cumberland. Zollicoffer had been pushing to go on the offensive for months and had won much praise and some success in doing so. Now it appeared that his individual wishes no longer fit into a growing and clarifying Confederate military strategy. As only a man like Zollicoffer could do, he suggested that the best way to fix this mistake was for his command to be expanded on the very ground that Johnston wished him not to occupy. He explained the situation regarding his position in glowing terms, even claiming it to be "a much stronger natural position for defense than that on the south bank," even though he was now nearly surrounded by a broad river prone to flooding. He also freely noted that he had no idea how many Federals he might be facing or their specific locations, but he felt confident that if Buckner could provide a feint from the direction of Columbia, "it would probably save me from concentration in front until I could be strengthened." Finally, and perhaps strategically, he noted that Crittenden had assumed command.[74]

Now present on the Cumberland River, Crittenden was able to supervise Zollicoffer's activities and to put a stop to his independent operations. Apparently, he could no longer be trusted to operate freely within the broader military organization. Indeed, he had shown himself to be more interested in martial glory than strategic accomplishment. Perhaps he had learned these things from men like fellow Nashvillian, Gen. Gideon Pillow, who commanded volunteer forces in Mexico and suffered from the same types of weaknesses. Maybe his career in the newspaper business had taught him that the end trumps the means when it comes to public perception. Whatever the reason, Zollicoffer's heretofore glorious military career came to a crashing halt on the north bank of the Cumberland River.

While Zollicoffer's independence ended then and there, he remained part of the Confederate presence facing Union troops under the command of generals George Thomas and Albin Schoepf. More than a month passed before noticeable movement was seen. At midnight on January 19, 1862, the battle of Mill Springs began with a Confederate attack upon Thomas's not yet consolidated force. Crittenden's preemptive action was the perfect response to his grim situation. With half of his army across a now-swollen river and facing an enemy force growing and massing, he believed that striking the first blow was a logical course of action in such desperate times. The attack moved forward with Zollicoffer at the front commanding as if his military career depended upon it. A lull ensued after the initial attack, and in the dark Zollicoffer met his fate while scouting what he soon realized was the front line of battle.[75]

The conditions surrounding his death have for 150 years plagued Zollicoffer's otherwise strong legacy. As a result, historians sometimes debate over whether or not Zollicoffer was a capable commander and often come to the consensus that he was not. In reality, as historian Thomas Connelly rightly noted, "Zollicoffer was actually a capable strategist," his Civil War career began well and shone brightly until he pushed his luck against an entrenched and superior force at Camp Wildcat.[76] Afterward, he spent his remaining months trying to regain the offensive and shake off what he likely considered the thankless job of defensive warfare. With his ambition and ego apparently driving his actions, he went on the offensive once more, but under a cloud of skepticism. Perhaps Zollicoffer's battlefield death during one of the most pronounced military failures of the war provided him with the necessary historical camouflage and may have saved his pride from a worse fate than if he had lived.

In addition to the conjecture about Zollicoffer, one can make more certain determinations. From his first experience at Cumberland Gap, the weather and terrain were major factors in his decision making. Initially, he saw them as willing assistants in his efforts to defend against a Union invasion of East

Tennessee. When he advanced on Camp Wildcat, he clearly saw an opportunity to attack a much smaller force, but he did not recognize the power of the terrain on that field. As a result, the newly reinforced Union presence there turned the geography on Zollicoffer and cost him his glowing reputation as a strategist. Finally, when he decided to recapture the success he had enjoyed at Cumberland Gap, Cumberland Ford, and Barbourville, by returning to the offensive on the Cumberland River, he overreached again with the help of the terrain and weather. Whether it was the muddy roads that minimized the Union threat or the rising rivers that locked Zollicoffer on the wrong side of the Cumberland on more than one occasion, the unique nature of Appalachia's terrain combined with the cold and rainy seasons to present all Civil War commanders with a formidable challenge. Zollicoffer was the first to see these difficulties up close and initially saw them as advantages, but as situations changed and the region's war progressed, those factors turned on him.

Notes

1. Raymond E. Myers, *The Zollie Tree* (Louisville, Ky.: Filson Club Press, 1964), 44.

2. Albert D. Kirwan, *John J. Crittenden: The Struggle for the Union* (Lexington: Univ. of Kentucky Press, 1962), 406–8.

3. L. E. Chittenden, *A Report of the Debates and Proceedings in the Secret Sessions of the Conference Convention* (New York: D. Appleton and Co., 1864), 26.

4. Kirwan, *Crittenden,* 409–10.

5. Myers, *The Zollie Tree,* 45.

6. Landon C. Haynes to Hon. L. P. Walker, July 6, 1861, United States War Department, *The War of the Rebellion: A Compilation of the Official Records of the Union and Confederate Armies* (Washington, D.C.: Government Printing Office, 1880–1901), ser. 1, vol. 4, 364–65 (hereafter cited as *OR;* unless otherwise indicated, all citations are to series 1).

7. Felix K. Zollicoffer to Adj. Gen. S. Cooper, Aug. 6, 1861, ibid., 381–83.

8. James Henry Rogers Diary, Mar. 15, 1862, James Henry Rogers Papers, Robert W. Woodruff Library, Special Collections, Emory University, Atlanta, Ga.

9. William Chunn to his wife, Sept. 14, 1862, William Augustus Chunn Letters, Robert W. Woodruff Library, Special Collections, Emory University, Atlanta, Ga.

10. F. K. Zollicoffer to Secretary of War, Sept. 29, 1861, *OR,* vol. 4, 432.

11. F. K. Zollicoffer to Hon. J. P. Benjamin, Nov. 2, 1861, ibid., 501–2.

12. F. K. Zollicoffer to Lt. Col. Mackall, Nov. 2, 1861, ibid., 502.

13. F. K. Zollicoffer to Col. John P. Murray, Oct. 28, 1861, ibid., 483; F. K. Zollicoffer to Lt. Col. Mackall, Oct. 29, 1861, ibid., 487; and F. K. Zollicoffer to Col. W. B. Wood, Oct. 29, 1861, ibid., 488.

14. Untitled and undated wartime reminiscences of William F. Patterson, William Franklin Patterson Papers, Library of Congress, Manuscript Division, Washington, D.C.

15. Untitled and undated wartime reminiscences of William F. Patterson, ibid.

16. George W. Morgan to Col. James B. Fry, June 22, 1862, American Civil War Collection, Abraham Lincoln Library and Museum, Special Collections, Lincoln Memorial University, Harrogate, Tenn.

17. Ibid.

18. Archibald Means to Mr. John Means, May 4, 1862, Means Family Papers, Margaret I. King Library, Special Collections and Archives, University of Kentucky, Lexington, Ky.

19. George W. Morgan to Col. James B. Fry, June 22, 1862, American Civil War Collection, Lincoln Memorial University.

20. William E. McCart Reminiscences (typescript), Park Archives, Cumberland Gap National Historical Park, Middlesboro, Ky.

21. George W. Morgan to Col. James B. Fry, June 22, 1862, American Civil War Collection, Lincoln Memorial University.

22. McCart Reminiscences.

23. Ibid.

24. Abraham Lincoln to Oliver P. Morton, Sept. 29, 1861, in *Abraham Lincoln: Speeches and Writings, 1859–1865,* ed. Don E. Fehrenbacher (New York: Library of America, 1989), 271.

25. F. K. Zollicoffer to Adj. Gen. S. Cooper, *OR,* vol. 4, 381–82.

26. Ibid., 382–83.

27. G. S. Dowis to Mr. Sam Steele, Sept. 9, 1861, Steele Family Papers, private collection of Samuel Robert Steele, Green Bay, Wis.

28. F. K. Zollicoffer to Lt. Col. Mackall, Sept. 24, 1861, *OR,* vol. 4, 424–25; and F. K. Zollicoffer to Gen. A. S. Johnston, Sept. 19, 1861, ibid., 199.

29. F. K. Zollicoffer to General Cooper, Aug. 29, 1861, ibid., 397; and Eastham Tarrant, *The Wild Riders of the First Kentucky Cavalry: A History of the Regiment in the Great War of the Rebellion* (Lexington, Ky.: Henry Clay Press, 1969), 36.

30. F. K. Zollicoffer to Lt. Col. Mackall, Sept. 24, 1861, *OR,* vol. 4, 424–25; and F. K. Zollicoffer to Gen. A. S. Johnston, Sept. 19, 1861, ibid., 199.

31. F. K. Zollicoffer to Gen. A. S. Johnston, Sept. 19, 1861, ibid., 199; and Thomas L. Connelly, *Army of the Heartland: The Army of Tennessee, 1861–1862* (Baton Rouge: Louisiana State Univ. Press, 1967), 87–88.

32. F. K. Zollicoffer to Lt. Col. Mackall, Sept. 26, 1861, *OR,* vol. 4, 429; Larry J. Daniel, *Days of Glory: The Army of the Cumberland, 1861–1865* (Baton Rouge: Louisiana State Univ. Press, 2004), 22–23; Myers, *The Zollie Tree,* 53–54; Brian D. McKnight, *Contested Borderland: The Civil War in Appalachian Kentucky and Virginia* (Lexington: Univ. Press of Kentucky, 2006), 38–39; and Connelly, *Army of the Heartland,* 88.

33. T. T. Garrard to Gen. George H. Thomas, Oct. 3, 1861, *OR,* vol. 4, 291–92.

34. F. K. Zollicoffer to Lt. Col. Mackall, Sept. 30, 1861, ibid., 202.

35. Ibid.

36. F. K. Zollicoffer to Lt. Col. Mackall, Sept. 26, 1861, ibid., 429.

37. F. K. Zollicoffer to Lt. Col. Mackall, Sept. 30, 1861, ibid., 202.

38. John F. Fisk to Hon. R. Buckner, Sept. 22, 1861, ibid., 268.

39. F. K. Zollicoffer to W. W. Mackall, Oct. 3, 1861, ibid., 435.

40. W. W. Mackall to General Zollicoffer, ibid.

41. Kenneth A. Hafendorfer, *The Battle of Wild Cat Mountain* (Louisville, Ky.: KH Press, 2003), 71–72.

42. F. K. Zollicoffer to Lt. Col. Mackall, Oct. 6, 1861, *OR*, vol. 4, 439; and Hafendorfer, *Battle of Wild Cat Mountain*, 73.

43. Hafendorfer, *Battle of Wild Cat Mountain*, 78.

44. T. T. Garrard to Gen. George H. Thomas, Oct. 17, 1861, *OR*, vol. 4, 309; and Daniel, *Days of Glory*, 23–24.

45. T. T. Garrard to Gen. George H. Thomas, Oct. 18, 1861, *OR*, vol. 4, 310.

46. T. T. Garrard to Gen. George H. Thomas, Oct. 19, 1861, ibid., 311–12.

47. Tarrant, *Wild Riders of the First Kentucky Cavalry*, 41.

48. Hafendorfer, *Battle of Wild Cat Mountain*, 115.

49. Ibid., 152–54.

50. F. K. Zollicoffer to Adjutant General Cooper, Oct. 26, 1861, *OR*, vol. 4, 210.

51. Hafendorfer, *Battle of Wild Cat Mountain*, 217–22.

52. Ibid., 224–31.

53. Ibid., 239.

54. T. T. Garrard to Gen. George H. Thomas, Oct. 25, 1861, *OR*, vol. 4, 319.

55. Hafendorfer, *Battle of Wild Cat Mountain*, 261–69; F. K. Zollicoffer to Lt. Col. Mackall, Oct. 29, 1861, *OR*, vol. 4, 487; and F. K. Zollicoffer to Col. W. B. Wood, Oct. 30, 1861, ibid., 490.

56. Geo. R. McClellan to General Zollicoffer, Nov. 5, 1861, *OR*, vol. 4, 521–22.

57. F. K. Zollicoffer to Gen. S. Cooper, Nov. 8, 1861, ibid., 530–31.

58. McKnight, *Contested Borderland*, 125; Noel C. Fisher, *War at Every Door: Partisan Politics and Guerrilla Violence in East Tennessee, 1860–1869*, Civil War America Series (Chapel Hill: Univ. of North Carolina Press, 1997), 51–52; and S. P. Carter to Brig. Gen. George H. Thomas, Nov. 16, 1861, *OR*, vol. 4, 359–60.

59. Jon L. Wakelyn, *Biographical Dictionary of the Confederacy* (Westport, Conn.: Greenwood Press, 1977), 153–54.

60. F. K. Zollicoffer to Lt. Col. Mackall, Nov. 28, 1861, *OR*, vol. 7, 715.

61. F. K. Zollicoffer to Lt. Col. Mackall, Dec. 10, 1861, ibid., 753.

62. F. K. Zollicoffer to Gen. S. Cooper, Nov. 27, 1861, ibid., 706–7.

63. Kenneth A. Hafendorfer, *Mill Springs: Campaign and Battle of Mill Springs, Kentucky* (Louisville, Ky.: KH Press, 2001), 69; and F. K. Zollicoffer to Lt. Col. Mackall, Nov. 30, 1861, *OR*, vol. 7, 725.

64. F. K. Zollicoffer to Lt. Col. Mackall, Dec. 2, 1861, *OR*, vol. 7, 10.

65. F. K. Zollicoffer to Lt. Col. Mackall, Dec. 9, 1861, ibid., 10–11.

66. F. K. Zollicoffer to Lt. Col. Mackall, Nov. 28, 1861, ibid., 715.

67. F. K. Zollicoffer to Lt. Col. Mackall, Dec. 4, 1861, ibid., 734.

68. Special Orders No. 127, Dec. 4, 1861, ibid.

69. F. K. Zollicoffer to Lt. Col. Mackall, Dec. 10, 1861, ibid., 753; and C. David Dalton, "Zollicoffer, Crittenden, and the Mill Springs Campaign: Some Persistent Questions," *Filson Club History Quarterly* 60, no. 4 (Oct. 1986): 465–66.

70. Daniel, *Days of Glory*, 46–47; and Brian Steel Wills, *George Henry Thomas: As True as Steel* (Lawrence: Univ. of Kansas Press, 2012), 132–33.

71. Hafendorfer, *Mill Springs*, 55–56.

72. Ibid., 69.

73. Ibid., 81.

74. F. K. Zollicoffer to Lt. Col. Mackall, Dec. 10, 1861, *OR*, vol. 7, 753.

75. Daniel, *Days of Glory*, 52.

76. Connelly, *Army of the Heartland*, 87.

Don Carlos Buell

Misunderstood Commander of the West

Stephen D. Engle

In his review of Stephen W. Sears works *George B. McClellan: The Young Napoleon* and *The Civil War Papers of George B. McClellan,* Russell Weigley posed the rhetorical question: "What are we to make of Major-General George B. McClellan?"[1] After all, he was, as Gen. Ulysses S. Grant observed, "one of the mysteries of the war."[2] In the 150 years since the Civil War, many contemporaries and historians alike have sought to uncover what made McClellan the commander he was and was not, and why he was seemingly incapable of bringing about complete victory on the battlefield. Upon his death in 1885, the New York *Evening Post* concluded that "Probably no soldier who did so little fighting has ever had his qualities as a commander so minutely, and may we add, so fiercely discussed." "How are we to understand the collapse of so much promise," wrote Weigley.[3] The fascination with and the attempt to define the very man who helped give shape to the Civil War and the Union Army has produced several theories driven by questions seeking to solve the mystery behind the man and the commander: "did the war actually ruin his ability to command," "did he ruin himself by delusions," "did the war claim his leadership and move on," or "was he unable to use the army he created[?]" The difficulty, as T. Harry Williams contended more than thirty years ago, was that studying George B. McClellan was "like studying several men or soldiers in one."[4]

One of those McClellan-like men to whom Williams referred was Don Carlos Buell, whose career in the Western Theater of the Civil War mirrored McClellan's career in the East, and who, like McClellan, contemporaries regarded as one of the least understood generals among the Union high command. In his *Story of the Civil War,* John Codman Ropes argued triumphantly that Buell was "a thorough soldier; not even McClellan surpassed him in intimate knowledge of the various duties of officers and men, or in strength of conviction that prolonged and unremitting attention to their duties was the only means by which the volunteer regiments could ever acquire the solidity of an army." Buell, he contended, "was a strict—in fact, almost too strict—disciplinarian; but he was a great deal more than this: he sought to imbue his troops with the same principles of military duty which he held himself; his ideal of the soldier's character was of the highest, and the services which he rendered in this regard to the troops of his department . . . cannot be overestimated." According to Ropes, "in military sagacity, in clear and unprejudiced vision, in decision of character, he [Buell] had few equals among the generals on either side."[5]

A reviewer for *The Literary Era* applauded Ropes's portrayal of Buell, and described the commander as "one of the least understood among the eminent generals of the war." The reviewer further allowed that it was "one of the interesting questions of the Civil War why this fine soldier and able commander should not have exercised the influence upon events which his character and ability naturally suggest." "He seems, unfortunately," the reviewer noted, "for his country as well as for himself—never to have commanded the full trust to which his merits entitled him. If instead of McClellan, Buell had been called to Washington, if instead of Halleck Mr. Lincoln had chosen him for a military advisor, it is not a violent presumption that the history of events would now furnish much more satisfying reading." "It is perhaps an unprofitable speculation," he observed, "but it is not improbable that had Gen. Buell been given full opportunity, the country might have been saved a great deal of humiliation and loss, and the war brought earlier to a close; but whether this would actually have been for the benefit of mankind is another question."[6]

Modern scholars have been less charitable toward Buell, often comparing him to McClellan and characterizing him as a general who was temperamentally unable to seek complete victory. They acknowledge the similarity between his operations in the West and McClellan's operations in the East in 1862, which led to their downfall. Buell and McClellan drew upon essentially the same military philosophy to justify their actions, both commanded armies during a changing political environment, and both were better at creating armies than using them successfully. Both emphasized preparation more than movement, and both evaded combat because they feared defeat. Buell maintained that his objective was "not to fight

Don Carlos Buell.
(Library of Congress)

great battles, and storm impregnable fortifications, but by demonstrations and maneuvering to prevent the enemy from concentrating his scattered forces." War had a "higher object than that of mere bloodshed," Buell believed. "If precaution and the observance of rule diminish the number of battles," he maintained, "and sometimes miss the accidental success which folly or recklessness might have gained, it is nevertheless true that in the end they usually triumph."[7]

Buell asserted that carefully concentrating a well-organized force against an outnumbered enemy constituted solid tactics, and he strove to develop within his volunteer army an efficient and effective fighting force. His conception of war, however, eventually frustrated not only his soldiers, who would lose respect for him, but also political and military superiors who grew tired of his maddeningly slow campaigns and his refusal to accommodate the changing nature of war. When President Abraham Lincoln referred to McClellan as a general who "has got the slows," he might just as well have been speaking of Buell, for the president grew frustrated by the summer of 1862 over the commander's tedious march to Chattanooga.[8] So frustrated was Lincoln that at one point he remarked to Halleck that a "McClellan in the army was lamentable, but a combination of McClellan and Buell was deplorable."[9]

Not uncommon for military commanders, especially in the Civil War, Buell fought two wars—one against the Confederates on the front line, and one with politicians and soldiers in the rear. Some of his own soldiers even criticized him in letters home, to governors, or to journalists. A political conservative, Buell, like McClellan, would have been a better general had he been more tactful with politicians and accepted the changing nature of the war, even while he disagreed with it. The Civil War was as much a political contest as it was a military contest, driven by political and public opinion that affected military strategy. Successful commanders secured the favor of political leaders or at least cultivated neutrality that insulated them from criticism. Buell had difficulty adjusting to the political demands of war because he detached himself from political leaders and the rank-and-file soldiers and strove to maintain a purely militaristic and professional demeanor within his command. He purposely separated himself from the sources of his army's strength to avoid political problems and failed to realize that cultivating cooperation among these constituents might prove helpful. Consequently, he had little patience for the political posturing of Northern governors, who attempted to supervise the welfare of their soldiers. Not a particularly stellar cadet at West Point, Buell, nonetheless, embraced the science of war more than the art of war, and yet he still observed that war was not solely governed by science and rules, nor was it merely a matter of knowing what risks to take. Warfare also demanded a blending of science and common sense with the less tangible quality of art, and the degree to which commanders could combine these elements determined their chance for success. Yet, Buell lacked the command instincts that proved necessary in waging a political war with volunteer armies.[10]

Buell's initial foray into command came in the autumn of 1861, when McClellan tapped him to command the Department of the Ohio and to strengthen its army. Buell was adept at creating a national army out of a state-oriented volunteer culture in the midst of an already intensifying war with political leaders and a critical public watching his every move. Having served in the Seminole and Mexican wars, he had significant experience in commanding soldiers and had seen considerable combat. His leadership abilities reflected an aptitude for command, but he had spent the last thirteen years in the adjutant general's office, which made him overly systematic and stifled his imaginative flare for command. William B. Shanks, a correspondent for the New York *Herald,* noted the significance of these years as a military bureaucrat, remarking that they had "smothered the fire in his heart, the impulsive in his nature, and . . . taught [him] not to feel." He was "too cool" in danger; there was no "originality of his conceptions."[11] Upon his arrival in Louisville in mid-November, Buell assumed an overwhelming responsibility. McClellan had sponsored Buell, one of his most trusted subordinates, because he believed that Buell would be one of "the great men of the war."[12] Like McClellan, Buell was respected for his high degree of professionalism, and Northerners believed that much could be expected from the new commander. The fact that he loathed abolitionists and wanted to protect Southerners' constitutional rights so as not to widen further the gulf between the North and South made him all the more attractive as a commander in Lincoln's critical border state—Kentucky. His opportunity to be one of the war's great men was magnified in the region because the fate of the Bluegrass State, and perhaps of the war in the West, hinged on his ability and judgment to maintain the Union's upper hand in the region. Generals Robert Anderson and William T. Sherman, Buell's predecessors in the Department of Ohio, had buckled under pressure. According to the correspondent of the Chicago *Tribune,* "Anderson was a gentleman of no mind. Sherman is possessed of neither mind nor manner. We are thankful now that we have a man who combines both."[13] When Assistant Secretary of War Thomas A. Scott arrived in Louisville in early February 1862, he was greatly impressed with Buell. "In General Buell we have a very superior officer—calm, prudent and with great power to control—with fair facilities he will show good results."[14]

The war beyond the Appalachian Mountains presented both Union and Confederate leaders with significant military complications because of the divided population, geographical diversity, and vast resources. Gen. Albert Sidney Johnston's seventy thousand Confederates defended a five-hundred-mile line stretching from the Appalachian Mountains to the Ozarks and occupied one-third of Kentucky. That the Union line stretched from eastern Kentucky to southwest Missouri and contained about ninety thousand fragmented troops distressed Buell, especially since Sherman left him with no strategic plan. Worse yet was that 23,000 of the nearly 30,000 troops in his department had been organized into two divisions to operate on a three-hundred-mile front in the upper South. Moreover, forty regiments were in recruiting districts scattered throughout Kentucky—a state where loyalties were bitterly divided. Buell could now appreciate Sherman's demands for more troops even though he boasted to McClellan that he was willing to try with considerably less.[15]

In the fall of 1861, there was no reason to doubt that Buell was equal to the task of organizing this fragmented conglomeration into a coherent army that could be used to both occupy the state and to maneuver offensively. He concluded that "the first thing to be done was to organize, arm, equip, and mobilize this heterogeneous mass."[16] Although this was a "difficult and tedious" task, he managed in a relatively short time to make the "mass" into an army.[17] Buell possessed a strong professional and disciplinary pride and was meticulous in the reorganization. Although making soldiers out of civilians revealed perhaps Buell's greatest strength, his determination to detach the men from their state governors indicated the difficulty of reconciling his own view of the war with its undeniably political nature. State governors took an active role in raising, equipping, and supporting volunteers, and they naturally wanted to retain significant authority and influence over them, especially when it came to procuring supplies. Governors had proven early in the war that commanders and soldiers alike came to lean on them for assistance. Certainly not atypical of Civil War generals, Buell took a very narrow view of political authority. The president alone could dictate matters of military protocol, Buell believed, and governors had no place in the chain of command. To limit further the governors' attachment to their soldiers, Buell made his headquarters the sole source for military information. With great assurance he wrote to McClellan in his first few weeks that while he was annoyed by the "officiousness of Governors," he would "be able to correct" these political-military problems "entirely." He failed to realize the potentially explosive nature of his decisive actions with state leaders.[18]

Buell displayed considerable confidence as commander of the Army of the Ohio, even if he lacked confidence in his volunteer soldiers. That confidence extended to his attitude about the enemy, particularly early in his command. Buell was a methodical commander and was painfully conscientious in undertaking his initial moves in the Western Theater, allowing the

Confederates to make some forays into his Department. Regarding Confederate Gen. Felix Zollicoffer's invasion of Kentucky in the winter of 1861–62, he wrote to McClellan: "I do not mean to be diverted more than is absolutely necessary from what I regard as of the first importance—the organization of my forces, now little better than a mob. I could fritter the whole of it away in a month by pursuing these roving bugbears."[19]

More than any other campaign, Lincoln's desire for Buell to move into East Tennessee tested the commander's twenty-year military philosophy. Given East Tennesseans' Unionist proclivities, the president wanted Buell to move into the region and protect the citizens and the area's resources. Lincoln and McClellan both had explained to Buell the rationale for undertaking such an operation, but Buell balked at the enterprise and instead suggested capturing Nashville. Whether or not it made political sense was irrelevant to Buell. In his mind, East Tennessee afforded little military advantage, and he argued that the military risks outweighed the political gains involved, especially in winter. Nashville could be reached by water and rail, he maintained, and occupying the Tennessee capital gave the army certain advantages, since it would enable his army to move south and remain close to a main railroad with his supply base at Louisville. Most importantly, maintaining this supply line would allow him to rely on the Union for resources and not have to live off the countryside. In addition to these movements, Buell suggested sending two flotilla columns up the Tennessee and Cumberland rivers. He was confident this plan would clear the Confederates from Kentucky and Tennessee. Moreover, Buell viewed the East Tennessee campaign to be a military risk since the practical and logistical problems of such a movement suggested that his army might have to fight for certain strategic positions such as the Cumberland Gap rather than maneuvering for its capture. He did not want, and in fact refused, to bypass Middle or West Tennessee to move to East Tennessee because of the problems of supplying an army away from the railroad in Confederate territory. Buell's emphasis on good communications reflected his desire to make his occupation of East Tennessee permanent.[20]

Buell's Nashville scenario impressed McClellan, and it did make better military sense. But political pressure was mounting in Washington as Congress had come into session, formed a Joint Committee on the Conduct of the War, and debated the merits of Lincoln's limited war aims. Perhaps against his better military judgment, even McClellan acquiesced to these political considerations, and urged his subordinate to comply with moving into East Tennessee. Besides, when he called on Henry W. Halleck, commander of the Department of Missouri, to move into Tennessee to support Buell, Halleck refused. Instead, when Lincoln asked Halleck his opinion of Buell's plan, Halleck replied that Buell's flotilla plan was "madness." Soldiers could not be removed from Missouri, Halleck argued, without losing the state. The civil-military chaos in Missouri justified Halleck's refusal, but the two commanders extended their reasons for delay in cooperating for over a month. The longer the war stood still militarily, the more it advanced politically, and throughout January 1862, the Union high command made little progress in moving the war.[21]

While Halleck and Buell debated, Ulysses S. Grant finally secured Halleck's permission to send a reconnaissance up the Tennessee River from Cairo, and on February 6, Union Navy Flag Officer Andrew H. Foote took Fort Henry and opened the war in the West. Emboldened by his success, Grant casually informed Halleck that he would next take nearby Fort Donelson. Grant's news inspired Halleck to call on Buell for support, but Buell remained focused on Nashville and refused. He tried to persuade Buell by offering him command of the Cumberland column and Grant's future services, but Buell forfeited the opportunity to assist Halleck, and Halleck never forgot it. On February 16, Grant captured Fort Donelson on the Cumberland River, which afforded Halleck the opportunity to proclaim himself the genius of Grant's success. The following day, Halleck wired McClellan: "Make Buell, Grant, and Pope major-generals of volunteers and give me command in the West, I ask this in return for Donelson and Henry."[22] Though it took a few weeks for Lincoln to decide, Halleck would ultimately get the command of the West. Grant's operations had been even more successful than he could have imagined, as his Donelson victory removed Johnston's western army from the region, and allowed Buell without firing a shot to move deeper into Tennessee and accept the surrender of Nashville on February 27.[23]

Buell's occupation of the Tennessee capital was a significant turning point in the Western Theater, as it highlighted the two-dimensional war the Union Army was waging—occupation and restoration of the civilian populace to the Union and defeat of the Confederate Army. With Nashville in Union hands, it was Lincoln's desire to institute a conciliatory policy intended to repatriate Southerners in the region. Yet, there was much fighting to be done to defeat Johnston's Confederate Army. Buell's army was caught between managing these two goals. Some of this was because in mid-March Lincoln appointed Tennessee's Unionist Sen. Andrew Johnson military governor of the state, and he had arrived in Nashville demanding that the city be protected. Johnson's situation was pressing and the politics of war in Buell's department changed his course. If Buell marched south without considering Johnson's wishes, he might risk losing a region and a city already in Union control. On the other hand, if he delayed forming a junction with Grant, he would leave Grant at risk on the Tennessee River.[24]

Johnson's appointment as military governor coincided with Lincoln's decision to relieve McClellan as general-in-chief, and left him in command of what was to be known as the Department of the Potomac. With McClellan now a subordinate, Buell also became a subordinate—to Halleck, whom Lincoln appointed as supreme commander of the Department of the Mississippi, which included Buell's command. Certainly Buell's close relationship to McClellan had done little to enhance his position in the eyes of politicians at that point, but he preferred it to taking orders from Halleck, who now dealt with the president directly. Nonetheless, these changes came about at a time when the Confederates were planning to reclaim Tennessee, and neither Halleck nor Buell was aware of the counteroffensive about to begin in the West.[25]

Of all the areas in the Confederacy that Halleck had his sights on that spring, none was more vital than where the Memphis & Charleston Railroad joined with the Mobile & Ohio Railroad at Corinth, Mississippi. Subjugating the Southern populace required that Union armies seize resources that could weaken the Confederate war effort and convince them to come back to the Union. Halleck ordered Buell to march his army to Savannah, Tennessee, for the campaign against Corinth, and Buell obliged. But he decided first to make arrangements to secure the wide geographical area still under his responsibility. Perhaps if Buell had been aware of Grant's vulnerable position or that Johnston intended to concentrate at Corinth he would have rushed to Savannah, but since neither Grant nor Halleck expected a battle before Buell arrived, why hurry? After all, Halleck had only ordered Buell to Savannah "as rapidly as possible." "As rapidly as possible" might have implied "haste," but to Buell it essentially meant whenever he was ready for his army to march in full—again exercising his own judgment. His decision to build a permanent frame bridge across the Duck River reflected his rigid belief in logistics over movement in the overall success of a campaign. He advised Grant and Halleck of his progress toward Pittsburg Landing, and neither commander said his rate of marching was too slow. Nonetheless, his delay at Duck River was still a factor in his late arrival at Shiloh.[26]

However careless Grant was in his approach to Pittsburg Landing, when the Battle of Shiloh opened on the morning of April 6, 1862, he stayed the course in part because he knew Buell was coming. Once Buell arrived, he had retreated to defendable ground, and was more determined to counterattack. The addition of Buell's men on the second day of the battle, April 7, added to Union victory—although contemporaries and scholars debate the degree to which his arrival influenced the outcome. Moreover, some soldiers had begun to question Buell's judgment regarding the conduct not so much of his battlefield presence, but of the campaign in getting to Pittsburg Landing. Criticism of Buell's slowness had begun to trickle down through the ranks during and after the march to Shiloh. Pvt. Edgar Kellog, of the 24th Ohio, commented: "Why we advanced so slowly, I do not know—and I could not—at the time—see any reason for it."[27]

After Shiloh, Halleck moved south to capture the Confederate stronghold at Corinth, Mississippi. He supervised Buell's operations closely, limiting his independence and bothering Buell. The relationship between Halleck and Buell illuminated the difficulties of sustaining productive command relationships, and it was another indication of Buell's unwillingness to conform to someone else's ideas.[28] Buell's role in the capture of Corinth placed him in a somewhat similar position to the one he had after capturing Bowling Green and Nashville. Although Halleck captured Corinth without a fight, the Confederate Army escaped. Buell was again associated with slow movement and the failure to meet and defeat the enemy. Ohio officer John Beatty perceptively characterized the failure to capture the Confederates at Corinth as a significant missed opportunity in the war, arguing that the enemy "still lives, is organized and ready to do battle on some other field."[29]

By the summer of 1862, the culmination of a series of political and military factors directly affected Buell's reputation as commander of a large western army. He had increasingly put himself at odds with not only state leaders west of the Appalachians, and journalists who followed his army, but also Lincoln, Stanton, and Halleck. He had difficulty adapting to the strategy of an expansive war that included prohibiting the return of fugitive slaves to their masters, and the acceptance that his soldiers were becoming more politicized about the nature and conduct of Union war aims. He failed to accept the political realities that the war was fundamentally changing from a limited war for limited goals to a conflict that was moving toward employing all avenues that might lead to victory and had little room for conservative generals resistant to confiscation and emancipation.[30]

Under Halleck's orders, Buell departed Corinth in June and moved east to Chattanooga for two reasons: political pressure to seize East Tennessee and a presumed lack of Confederate operations in the region. Buell was to seize key points on the Memphis & Charleston Railroad, repair the railroad from Corinth to Chattanooga as the army advanced east, and occupy the region along the way. He was uncomfortable with Halleck's plan because placing his army on the Memphis & Charleston Railroad, which ran south of the Tennessee River for eighty miles, forced him into a barren countryside infested with Confederate cavalry. The inhospitable military realities of protecting more than three hundred miles of supply lines against such foes as John Hunt Morgan and Nathan Bedford Forrest were troublesome to Buell. His initial reluctance to obey Halleck's orders aroused a bitter debate between the two commanders—an extension of the earlier argument regarding Grant's move on forts Henry and Donelson, and perhaps Buell's slow progress in moving toward Corinth. Buell was not enthusiastic about the prospects of the Chattanooga campaign, and instead he determined to move on Chattanooga along the Nashville & Decatur Railroad to Murfreesboro, and then proceed east to the Tennessee River and south to Chattanooga. This would march him toward his supplies and back into Middle Tennessee and in the end, he believed, accomplish something more strategically valuable to the Union in the West.[31]

Buell's overland campaign was a series of unfortunate circumstances both politically and militarily, and it began as onerously as it ended. While the repair crews worked tirelessly on the railroad, quartermasters labored arduously to move supplies from the main depot to the army now stretched out across enemy territory. A drought had drained the Tennessee River so much so that only a few light freight boats could be used in forwarding supplies to Florence and they were forced to halt at Eastport, Mississippi. To compound his efforts, Confederate raiding parties routinely destroyed the exposed line of track and delayed his march. Worse yet was that Andrew Johnson complained to Halleck, Stanton, and Lincoln that Buell's advance toward Chattanooga was too slow and that it had left Nashville almost defenseless. Many soldiers similarly became disheartened over Buell's maddeningly slow progress and the daily grind of laboring on the railroad instead of campaigning. Pvt. Samuel T. Smith of the 15th Indiana wrote: "we have nothing to do but drill about hours in the [sun] except work on the railroad."[32] For Buell, the problem of advancing to Chattanooga manifested itself sooner than expected.

Whatever logistical problems the army endured that summer, many soldiers and politicians considered Buell himself the chief cause of the tediously slow campaign. He lacked enthusiasm for the advance partly because he had little faith in Halleck's plan and partly because he was concerned about supplies and the vulnerability of his army in hostile territory. He explained his rationale for resisting the campaign, but political leaders were interested more in results than explanations. Whatever diligence Buell displayed in coping with the logistical problems was overshadowed by his lack of accomplishing the administration's objective. So slow was his progress that in mid-July, Halleck informed Buell that his time was about up. "The President telegraphs that your progress is not satisfactory," he wired, "and that you should move more rapidly. . . . so rapid as to remove all cause of complaint, whether well founded or not."[33] Buell replied by providing Halleck with an overview of the realities of his campaign and regretted that it was "necessary to explain the circumstances which must make my progress seem so slow," and that "the dissatisfaction of the President pains me exceedingly."[34] Buell nonetheless reasoned that the object was not only to reach his goal, but also to be in a situation to fight and occupy the city upon arrival without living off East Tennesseans. He devoted significant amounts of time and men to repair the railroad, which for security reasons required thoroughly scouting his advance and protecting his rear. Buell regarded the railroad as crucial to his success, especially since he realized that it would be impossible to hold Chattanooga once there without holding the railroad that could be used to transport supplies to his army. Despite these problems, he told Halleck that he expected to accomplish the operation "without unnecessary delay and in such a manner as neither to jeopardize my army nor its honor nor trifle with the lives of loyal citizens betrayed to the [vengeance] of the enemy by a promised protection and hurried abandonment."[35]

Buell's circumstances could easily be explained, and he repeatedly made his position known to the War Department. The railroad was crucial to the overall success of his campaign, and the ability to reach Chattanooga to a great degree was attributable to Buell's ability to protect the railroad. It is conceivable, however, that Buell's conception of war also played a factor in the conduct of his campaign just as it had in previous movements. His movements mirrored his belief in a limited strategy for limited goals, and consequently his operations during the Chattanooga campaign helped to support that belief—whether by design or not. His operations played into the strength of the Confederate cavalry and the weakness of his own, and demonstrated the complications of relying on the railroad for supplies, especially in offensive operations.[36] Buell's Chattanooga experience highlighted the administration's intolerance over painfully cautious and slow campaigns and their commanders. Had Middle Tennessee or North Alabama abounded with forage, Buell was still unwilling to carry out a "live off the land" campaign. His decision not to "live off the country" was rooted more so in his belief that it led to pillaging and troublesome complications rather than the absence of agricultural resources. Union supply depots could supply Union soldiers, he maintained. Buell strove for good discipline over military success, which meant that his army could move only as fast as repair crews could rebuild bridges and re-lay rails. John Beatty recalled that Buell "was inaugurating the dancing-master policy: By your leave, my dear sir, we will have a fight; that is, if you are sufficiently fortified. No hurry; take your own time."[37]

Buell's conciliatory attitude also reflected his limited view toward war. Not only did Buell issue and enforce orders against foraging, but he also put his men on half rations. To the soldiers it appeared that he was less concerned with their welfare than he was with the comfort and welfare of the enemy. In his Order 13a, which essentially outlined his rules for the conduct of his army in occupied territory, Buell stipulated that the army's purpose was not to invade the rights of "our fellow-countryman," but rather to "maintain the integrity of the Union" and to protect Southerners' private property and constitutional rights.[38] If the army did not antagonize civilians by pillaging or forceful requisitions, it would not suffer the rage of the Confederate countryside. In fact, he believed that a benevolent policy would entice Southerners away from the Confederacy. To some degree his policies had a positive effect. Mary Jane Chadick, resident of Huntsville, Alabama, declared that Buell's policies had made a favorable impression upon the citizens, but to the "great dissatisfaction of his soldiers."[39]

McClellan made Buell aware of the nature of the conflict when he appointed him to command in Kentucky and sent the commander precise written instructions explaining Lincoln's policies for Northern armies. "You will please constantly bear in mind the issue for which we are fighting," he emphasized to Buell. "That issue is the preservation of the Union and the authority of the General Government over all portions of our territory," he outlined, and "we shall most readily suppress this rebellion and restore the authority of the Government by religiously respecting the constitutional rights of all."[40] By the summer of 1862, however, Lincoln, Congress, and many Northerners had moved beyond this attitude. In July, the 37th Congress passed legislation that instituted a more severe war policy. The most significant for Buell was the Confiscation Act, which punished traitors by confiscating their property, thereby broadening the Union's mission and the use of its armies in winning the war. These laws brought about a significant hardening attitude in the army and no doubt among civilians, and expectedly enflamed the Southern citizenry.[41]

Buell had the misfortune of being in the midst of an extensive overland campaign in hostile territory when Congress established this policy. He and a few subordinates believed there was some evidence that his policies had merit. Buell's Chief of Staff James B. Fry and Col. Marc Mundy, among others not particularly fond of Buell, considered Buell's conciliatory policy somewhat effective in winning Confederate sympathizers back to the Union, yet even they understood that his rigid determination to stay the course undermined his reputation in his army and in Washington. However noble his intentions may have been in following the administration's earlier desires to repatriate Southern civilians peacefully, keeping his army on limited rations, while ordering payments made to citizens for the damages incurred by Union troops, eroded the goodwill he maintained in the early tenure of his command. Even when he needed horses, Buell gave stern instructions. "In taking horses," he recommended, "it must be done in such a way that orderly persons shall not be deprived of what may be necessary for their ordinary work." When Buell's army needed slaves to construct fortifications in the vicinity of Huntsville, he ensured that in impressing slaves, "care should be taken to equalize the number in all instances, leaving a sufficient number to do the ordinary business of the farm house."[42]

The timing of Buell's actions, combined with the exhaustive nature of his campaign and the growing impatience and frustration among soldiers, created intense animosity toward him among his soldiers. Colonel Mundy later testified before the Buell Commission that his policies and disciplinary measures "no doubt sowed the seeds of insubordination." Henry Seys, of the 15th Ohio, wrote to his wife in mid-July that "Buell treats these miserable traitors most graciously . . . [whereas] [they] should be most soundly thrashed."[43] Reuben D. Mussey, also under Buell's command, concluded that "the commanding general was either a traitor or an embecile [*sic*]." He demanded an end to his "rose water policy." "We have stood [guard] over Rebel property long enough . . . ," he wrote. "[Buell] has endeavored to make his corps a mere police for the better protection of the Rebels."[44] Buell was neither a traitor nor an imbecile, but his rigid policies sowed the seeds of insubordination and demoralization. Northern reporters angry at Buell for prohibiting them from camp wrote scathing articles aimed at discrediting not only his policies but the commander himself. Some clamored for his removal. This criticism spread among officers and soldiers, who criticized Buell in letters to their governors. Several Midwestern governors, including Oliver P. Morton, Richard Yates, and David Tod, joined Andrew Johnson in condemning the commander. These governors wrote Lincoln protesting Buell's treacherous policies, complaining that he was losing the confidence of his soldiers and contributing to a lack of volunteering. Given the importance of the upcoming elections, these chief executives alerted Lincoln to the political ramifications of keeping Buell in command—ramifications that loomed larger for Lincoln's political strategy for winning the war than Buell's conciliatory strategy for winning the peace.[45]

Unfortunately for Buell, his beliefs more than his actions undermined his leadership. T. Harry Williams characterized him as a "McClellan without charm or glamour," and suggested that was the reason he was so unpopular.[46] As the war evolved, so did political and military attitudes, yet he cared nothing for popularity or the approval of others. Both McClellan and Sherman, for example, were harder on pillagers than was Buell because both commanders recognized more than Buell that the political implications of military operations dictated military policies, especially in occupied regions. Yet, Buell was reluctant to modify policies even when it became evident that they adversely affected morale in the ranks. He was emotionally distant, seldom in public, and therefore was perhaps unaware that his soldiers viewed his policies as outdated. They saw Buell only when he made his hasty, "sour-mouthed inspections." "The good he took for granted," wrote historian Shelby Foote, "it was the less-good he was looking for, and he seldom failed to find it."[47] Consequently, his rigid demeanor seemed to invite rather than diffuse criticism. Some subordinates considered him a "direct, martial-spirited man," while others viewed him as aloof and cold and associated that demeanor with a number of negative qualities ranging from military ineptness to collusion with the enemy. The dissatisfaction of the soldiers added to the impracticality, both politically and militarily, of his superiors to support him.[48]

Buell's self-imposed principles and fixed rules seldom allowed compromise. He believed that the respect and confidence of his troops was a critical factor to commanding an army, yet he squandered the early support. Knowledge of war was of no use to Buell if he failed to maintain the soldiers' confidence. Northerners blamed Buell for his army's failure to catch Confederate Gen. Braxton Bragg at Chattanooga. He alone received the condemnation for the abortive campaign. In mid-August 1862, Bragg's movement north into Kentucky brought about the demise of Buell's tenure as a commander in the West. The maneuvering between Buell and Bragg ended at Perryville, where on October 8 the two armies clashed amid the hills surrounding the town. What began with scattered skirmishing soon gave way to full-scale intense fighting. By 2 P.M., the Confederates struck a surprise attack into the Union flank, commanded by Alexander McCook's men, and fighting escalated. Philip Sheridan organized a Union counterattack late in the afternoon, drove the Confederates back through Perryville, and waited for Buell to come to his defense with the rest of the army. Yet, the hilly terrain and atmospheric conditions created an "acoustic shadow" that muffled the battle sounds. These conditions deprived Buell of the knowledge that a portion of his army was hotly engaged, and he lost the opportunity to bring his entire army against Bragg and pull off a decisive victory. Consequently, he allowed Bragg to escape from the battlefield. Early dispatches appeared to hand Buell the victory. Anson Stager wired Stanton two days following the battle that Buell had fought a great battle and had "completely used up the rebel force," arguing that "there is no mistaking the victory this time."[49]

Despite not losing the battle, Buell had failed to pursue Bragg. Lincoln grew further frustrated by Buell's poor performance at the battle of Perryville and his failure to pursue Bragg after the battle disgusted Midwestern politicians, who pressured the president to remove him. Illinois Republican Horace White wired Lincoln that military operations of late and the commands of McClellan and Buell would ruin the state's November election. "*If* we are beaten in this State two weeks hence," he wrote, "it will be because McClellan & Buell *won't fight. . . .*" Lincoln relieved Buell on October 30, 1862, and the command of the Army of the Ohio fell to Gen. William S. Rosecrans.[50] The news elated many Northerners, including the editor for the *Christian Advocate and Journal,* who remarked that "the most cheering item of news this week is the announcement that the dilatory Buell, who has been an incubus on our western army for the past year, has been relieved of his command, or, rather, that his command has been relieved of him. . . ."[51]

The changing nature and conduct of the war in 1861–62 highlighted and undermined Buell's significance in the West. Those first months when he replaced Sherman, Buell showed that he was an effective organizer and administrator. He was given an extraordinary command under chaotic circumstances, and he quickly won the confidence and respect of his men and superiors. As the war in the West progressed, however, civilian and political attitudes changed and so began the slow erosion of Buell's usefulness. The commander was either unable or simply refused to change with it. Had he been more flexible in his military philosophy and sensitive to the political aspects of the Civil War, it would have served him well and perhaps prevented him from carrying the seeds of his own demise. Buell's failure to change reflected his strict adherence to a static military philosophy. He fully understood that preserving the Union was Lincoln's primary objective and that war was the means of reaching it. He believed that limited means could achieve this goal. Moreover, he understood that war was shaped by policy, and that the two could never be considered separately, but he never managed to reconcile his military beliefs with those of the administration, and, thus, never calibrated the conduct of his military operations to political necessity. He emphasized using limited military means to achieve political ends, and as the Union's aims changed, he became dispensable to Lincoln's evolving national strategy for winning the conflict at all costs.[52]

Shortly after his dismissal, the War Department established a commission to investigate Buell's tenure in the West and to "report an opinion in the case." It convened for nearly six months between November 27, 1862, and adjourned May 6, 1863, summoned seventy-two witnesses, and amassed a report totaling more than seven hundred pages. It summarized Buell's march to Chattanooga, the invasion of Kentucky, the pursuit of Bragg, and his conciliatory policy. Although the commission was neither a court-martial nor a court of inquiry and had no legal authority, many Northerners interpreted the secret investigative sessions as a move to convict Buell for the mismanagement of his operations.[53]

Perhaps most important about the commission itself was not so much its condemnation of Buell for his shortcomings as a commander, but rather that it represented the ideological debate between limited and total war aims. The testimony by the defense and the prosecution essentially reflected the dissimilar philosophical views of war. Buell served as his own counsel and, thus, his defense represented the philosophy of limited war, emphasizing preparation, movement, and maneuver over combat. The prosecution represented warfare of momentum, which concentrated on the ends instead of the means in achieving military objectives. Throughout the proceedings Buell defended his conception of limited war. He argued that the commission had erroneously criticized his Chattanooga and Kentucky campaigns for being "too slow," when in fact he contended that his occupation of East Tennessee was to be permanent, thereby justifying his methodical movements. He contested the commission's opinion that he could have acted differently, arguing that his decisions were based on the circumstances at the time.[54]

After months of debate, the commission acquitted Buell of wrongdoing, but the war had moved beyond his usefulness as a commander. For over a year after the commission adjourned, Buell was kept waiting without orders and then discharged from his volunteer commission. In May 1864, Buell resigned his regular commission, ending his military career. His mark on the Army of the Ohio remained shrouded by the mystery of its commander whose conservative temperament and military philosophy rendered him out of touch with the Union's new aims. He refused to see confiscation and emancipation as preconditions for reconstruction and failed to calibrate his conduct with the administration's desires. His insistence on conciliation after the Lincoln administration abandoned it was only partially the cause of his dismissal. The fact was that he refused to embrace the kind of war necessary to win. In the end, Lincoln moved beyond the commanders who built and managed armies and instead embraced those who used them effectively to bring him success.[55]

Notes

1. Review of Stephen W. Sears, *George B. McClellan: The Young Napoleon* (New York: Ticknor and Fields, 1988), by Russell Weigley in *Civil War History* 35 (Dec. 1989): 329–32; Wilmer L. Jones, ed., *Generals in Blue and Gray: Lincoln's Generals* (Westport, Conn.: Praeger, 2004), 1:89–101, appropriately entitles his biographical entry for Buell "The McClellan of the West."

2. John Russell Young, *Around the War with General Grant* (New York: Subscription Book Department, 1879), 2:210–16; Warren W. Hassler Jr., *General George B. McClellan: Shield of the Union* (Baton Rouge: Louisiana State Univ. Press, 1957), xv; Leslie J. Rowland, *George B. McClellan and Civil War History: In the Shadow of Grant and Sherman* (Kent, Ohio: Kent State Univ. Press, 1998), 166; see also Ethan S. Rafuse, *McClellan's War: The Failure of Moderation in the Struggle for the Union* (Bloomington: Indiana Univ. Press, 2005), 384.

3. *New York Evening Post,* Oct. 30, 1885, as quoted in Sears, *McClellan,* 401; Review of Sears, *McClellan,* in *Civil War History,* 329–32.

4. T. Harry Williams, *McClellan, Sherman, and Grant* (New Brunswick, N.J.: Rutgers Univ. Press, 1962), 12, although it is sorely outdated. For the best overview on the literature related to McClellan's command, see Joseph L. Harsh, "On the McClellan-Go-Round," *Civil War History* 19 (June 1973): 101–18.

5. John Codman Ropes, *The Story of the Civil War: A Concise Account of the War in the United States of American between 1861 and 1865* (New York: Putnam's Sons, 1933), 1:199.

6. J. H. C., review of John C. Ropes, *The Story of the Civil War* (New York: Putnam's Sons, 1933), vol. 1, in *The Literary Era* 1 (Dec. 1894): 287–88; also cited in "n.t.," *United Service: A Quarterly Review of Military and Naval Affairs* (Mar. 1895): 280.

7. McClellan and Buell corresponded at length over the nature and conduct of their respective commands that fall, and especially Buell's command in Kentucky; see U. S. Department, *War of Rebellion: A Compilation of the Official Records of the Union and Confederate Armies,* (Washington, D.C.: Government Printing Office,

1880–1901), ser. 1, vol. 7, 487–88 (hereafter cited as *OR*); T. Harry Williams, "The Military Leadership of North and South," in *Why the North Won the Civil War,* ed. David H. Donald (Baton Rouge: Louisiana State Univ. Press, 1960), 42–49; Stephen D. Engle, *Don Carlos Buell: Most Promising of All* (Chapel Hill: Univ. of North Carolina Press, 1999), 88, 119; see also Maurice comte de Saxe, *Reveries or Memoirs upon the Art of War* (1757; repr., Westport, Conn.: Greenwood Press, 1971); Henri Antoine Jomini, *Summary of the Art of War,* G. H. Mendell and W. P. Craighill, trans. (Philadelphia, Pa.: Lippincott, 1863); Mark Peine, "The Buell Military Commission" (master's thesis, Univ. of North Dakota, 1977), 41–43; Stephen W. Sears, ed., *The Civil War Papers of George B. McClellan: Selected Correspondence, 1860–1865* (New York: Da Capo Press, 1992), 131–46; see also Buell to McClellan, Nov. 16, 1861, and other letters in the George B. McClellan Papers, Library of Congress, Washington, D.C.; Jones, ed., *Generals in Blue and Gray,* 1:89–101.

8. T. Harry Williams, *Lincoln and His Generals* (New York: Alfred A. Knopf, 1952), 177; see also Herman Hattaway and Archer Jones, *How the North Won: A Military History of the Civil War* (Champaign: Univ. of Illinois Press, 1982), 266.

9. John Niven, ed., *Salmon P. Chase Papers* (Kent, Ohio: Kent State Univ. Press, 1993), 1:35–60; David Donald, ed., *Inside Lincoln's Cabinet: The Civil War Diaries of Salmon P. Chase* (New York: Longmans, Green, 1954), 20, 103, 107–8; John Niven, *Salmon P. Chase: A Biography* (New York: Oxford Univ. Press, 1995), 294.

10. Stephen D. Engle, "Don Carlos Buell: Military Philosophy and Command Problems in the West," *Civil War History* 41 (June 1995): 89–115; Rodney E. Dillon Jr., "Don Carlos Buell and the Union Leadership," *Lincoln Herald* 82 (1980): 363–73; Engle, *Buell,* 85–98; see also James Chumney Jr., "Don Carlos Buell: Gentleman General" (Ph.D. diss., Rice Univ., 1964), 2–21, 188–202 passim, an excellent work that provides another viewpoint of Buell.

11. William B. Shanks, *Personal Recollections of Distinguished Generals* (New York: Harper and Brothers, 1866), 252; Gerald J. Prokopowicz, *All for the Regiment: The Army of the Ohio, 1861–1862* (Chapel Hill: Univ. of North Carolina Press, 2001), 35–49.

12. Williams, *Lincoln and His Generals,* 47; James Guthrie to Joshua F. Speed, Nov. 22, 1861, Joshua F. Bullitt to Joshua F. Speed, Nov. 22, 1861, Abraham Lincoln Papers, American Memory Online, Library of Congress, Washington, D.C. (hereafter cited as LP, LC), described the enthusiasm with which Kentuckians would receive Buell's appointment to the Department of the Ohio.

13. *Chicago Tribune,* Nov. 9, 1861; *Cincinnati Daily Commercial,* Nov. 9, 1861; John F. Marszalek, *Sherman: A Soldier's Passion for Order* (New York: Free Press, 1993), 160–61; Lloyd Lewis, *Sherman, Fighting Prophet* (New York: Harcourt, Brace, 1932), 197–98; Engle, *Buell,* 86.

14. Scott wrote several letters to Stanton that February regarding Buell's command. See Scott to Stanton, Feb. 1, 2, 4, 6, 7, 1862, Edwin M. Stanton Papers, Library of Congress, Washington, D.C.; on Scott, see Samuel R. Kamm, "The Civil War Career of Thomas A. Scott" (Ph.D. diss., Univ. of Pennsylvania, 1940), 93; Stanton's impressions of Buell were initially favorable, but waned during the summer of 1862. See Benjamin P. Thomas and Harold M. Hyman, *Stanton: The Life and Times of Lincoln's Secretary of War* (New York: Knopf, 1962).

15. *OR,* ser. 1, vol. 16, 23–24; Charles Roland, *Albert Sidney Johnston: Soldier of Three Republics* (Austin: Univ. of Texas Press, 1964), 260–70; Earl J. Hess, *The Civil War in the West: Victory and Defeat from the Appalachians to the Mississippi* (Chapel Hill: Univ. of North Carolina Press, 2012),4–26; Freeman Cleaves, *Rock of Chickamauga: The Life of General George H. Thomas* (Norman: Univ. of Oklahoma Press, 1948), 87–93; Brian Steel Wills, *George Henry Thomas: As True as Steel* (Lawrence: Univ. Press of Kansas, 2012), 116–44; Engle, *Buell,* 88–100.

16. *OR,* ser. 1, vol. 16, 23–24. Buell gave this lengthy testimony before the Military Commission; Engle, "Military Philosophy and Command Problems in the West," 89–115; Prokopowicz, *All for the Regiment,* 35–49.

17. *OR,* ser. 1, vol. 16, 24.

18. *OR,* ser. 1, vol. 7, 482–83, 511–12; Prokopowicz, *All for the Regiment,* 46–54; Larry J. Daniel, *Days of Glory: The Army of the Cumberland, 1861–1865* (Baton Rouge: Louisiana State Univ. Press, 2004), 33–56; Jones, ed., *Generals in Blue and Gray: Lincoln's Generals,* 1:89–102; Engle, *Buell,* 89–98. On the relations between commanders and governors, see William B. Hesseltine, *Lincoln and the War Governors* (New York: Alfred A. Knopf, 1948), 249–72; see also Geoffrey Perret, *Lincoln's War: The Untold Story of America's Greatest President as Commander in Chief* (New York: Random House, 2004), 113–14, 121, 133–34; see also Mark Wilson, *The Business of the Civil War: Military Mobilization and the State, 1861–1865* (Baltimore, Md.: Johns Hopkins Univ. Press, 2006), which analyzes the transition from a state-generated procurement mobilization to a national procurement operation.

19. *OR,* ser. 1, vol. 7, 482–83, 509–13; Prokopowicz, *All for the Regiment,* 35–59; Daniel, *Days of Glory,* 33–56; Engle, *Buell,* 121–22.

20. *OR,* ser. 1, vol. 7, 482–83, 530–68; Lincoln to Buell, Jan. 6, 7, 13, 1862, Buell to Lincoln, Jan. 5, 1862, LP, LC; Roy P. Basler, ed., *The Collected Works of Abraham Lincoln* (New Brunswick, N.J.: Rutgers Univ. Press, 1953), 5:86, 90, 92; Engle, *Buell,* 99–113; Daniel, *Days of Glory,* 57–81; Hess, *The Civil War in the West,* 25–26.

21. *OR,* ser. 1, vol. 7, 532–33; John F. Marszalek, *Commander of All Lincoln's Armies: A Life of General Henry W. Halleck* (Cambridge, Mass.: Harvard Univ. Press, 2004), 109–21; Stephen Ambrose, *Halleck: Lincoln's Chief of Staff* (Baton Rouge: Louisiana State Univ. Press, 1962), 20. Buell and Halleck shared no affinity for one another and both were pressed by the demands of their respective departments.

22. *OR,* ser. 1, vol. 7, 628; Benjamin F. Cooling, *Forts Henry and Donelson: The Key to the Confederate Heartland* (Knoxville: Univ. of Tennessee Press, 1987), 81–101, 122–231; Stephen D. Engle, *Struggle for the Heartland: The Campaigns from Fort Henry to Corinth* (Lincoln: Univ. of Nebraska Press, 2001), 27–84; Hess, *The Civil War in the West,* 34–35.

23. Marszalek, *Commander of All Lincoln's Armies,* 117–21; Engle, *Buell,* 190–211; Roland, *Johnston,* 291–99; John M. McKee, *The Great Panic: Being Connected with Two Weeks of the War in Tennessee* (Nashville, Tenn.: Johnson and Whiting, 1862), 29–30; Walter T. Durham, *Nashville: The Occupied City* (Nashville: Tennessee Historical Society, 1985), 1–45; see also Stephen V. Ash, *When the Yankees Came: Conflict and Chaos in the Occupied South, 1861–1865* (Chapel Hill: Univ. of North Carolina Press, 1995); Stephen V. Ash, *Middle Tennessee Society Transformed, 1860–1870* (Baton Rouge: Louisiana State Univ. Press, 1988).

24. *OR*, ser. 1, vol. 7, 487–88; LeRoy P. Graf and Ralph W. Haskins, eds., *The Papers of Andrew Johnson* (Knoxville: Univ. of Tennessee Press, 1979), 5:62,69, 109, 112, 177–95; Marszalek, *Commander of All Lincoln's Armies*, 119–24; Hans L. Trefousse, *Andrew Johnson: A Biography* (New York: Norton, 1989), 192–96; Engle, *Buell*, 200–219.

25. Basler, ed., *Collected Works of Abraham Lincoln*, 5:155; Sears, *McClellan*, 155–67.

26. Larry J. Daniel, *Shiloh: The Battle That Changed the Civil War* (New York: Simon and Schuster, 1997), 63–115; Brooks D. Simpson, *Ulysses S. Grant: Triumph over Adversity, 1822–1865* (Boston, Mass.: Houghton, Mifflin, 2000), 120–31; Marszalek, *Commander of All Lincoln's Armies*, 120–26; Engle, *Buell*, 209–27; Timothy B. Smith, *Corinth 1862: Siege, Battle, Occupation* (Lawrence: Univ. Press of Kansas, 2012), 6–32; see also Donald A. Clark, "Buell's Advance to Pittsburg Landing: A Fresh Look at an Old Controversy," *Tennessee Historical Quarterly* 68 (Winter 2009): 355–90.

27. Edgar Kellog Papers, "Recollections of Civil War Service," Apr. 6, 1862, Civil War Miscellaneous Collection, United States Army Military History Institute, Carlisle, Pa.; Simpson, *Grant*, 120–31; Daniel, *Shiloh*, 63–115; Prokopowicz, *All for the Regiment*, 83–112.

28. Smith, *Corinth 1862*, 33–82; Engle, *Buell*, 240–55; Marszalek, *Commander of All Lincoln's Armies*, 120–31.

29. John Beatty, *The Citizen-Soldier: or, Memoirs of a Volunteer* (Cincinnati, Ohio: Wilstach, Baldwin, 1879), 146; Smith, *Corinth 1862*, 83–116; Engle, *Buell*, 24–55.

30. *OR*, ser. 1, vol. 16, pt. 2, 15; Engle, "Military Philosophy and Command Problems," 89–115; Marszalek, *Commander of All Lincoln's Armies*, 120–31; Prokopowicz, *All for the Regiment*, 113–36; Engle, *Buell*, 254–60.

31. George A. Bruce, "General Buell's Campaign against Chattanooga," in *Campaigns in Kentucky and Tennessee, Including the Battle of Chickamauga, 1862–1864, Papers of the Military Historical Society of Massachusetts* (Boston: Military Historical Society of Massachusetts, 1910), 7:110–15; Hattaway and Jones, *How the North Won*, 214–17; James B. Fry, *Operations of the Army under Buell* (New York: D. Van Nostrand, 1884), 17–29; Don Carlos Buell, *Statement of Major General Buell in Review of the Evidence before the Military Commission Appointed by the War Department in November, 1862. Campaign in Kentucky, Tennessee, Northern Mississippi, and North Alabama in 1861 and 1862* (Cincinnati, Ohio: n.p., 1863), 14–15; Prokopowicz, *All for the Regiment*, 237–53; Daniel, *Days of Glory*, 91–106; Engle, *Buell*, 257–71.

32. Harry Virgil Smith, ed., *The Life and Letters of Pvt. Samuel Thomas Smith Fifteenth Indiana Regiment Volunteers* (Bloomington, Ind.: Monroe Historical Society, 1976), 35; Graf and Haskins, eds., *Papers of Andrew Johnson*, 5:485–86; Andrew Johnson to Lincoln, July 10, 1862, LP, LC; Bruce, "Buell's Campaign against Chattanooga," 110–15; Engle, *Buell*, 257–71; Trefousse, *Johnson*, 156–60; Daniel, *Days of Glory*, 91–106; Prokopowicz, *All for the Regiment*, 237–53.

33. *OR*, ser. 1, vol. 16, pt. 2, 15, 75, 104; ibid., ser. 1, vol. 10, pt. 2, 232–33, 244, 254, 267–68, 280–81; B. H. Robertson, "Memoranda on the Civil War," *Century Illustrated Magazine* 37 (Nov. 1888): 149–51; Engle, *Buell*, 257–85; Kenneth P. Williams, *Lincoln Finds a General* (New York: MacMillan, 1952), 4:25–51, provides an excellent analysis of Buell's Chattanooga campaign.

34. *OR*, ser. 1, vol. 16, pt. 2, 122–23.

35. *OR,* ser. 1, vol. 10, pt. 2, 628; ibid., ser. 1, vol. 16, pt. 2, 122–23; Hattaway and Jones, *How the North Won,* 215; Engle, "Military Philosophy and Command Problems in the West," 106–8; Williams, *Lincoln Finds a General,* 4:25–51.

36. Engle, "Military Philosophy and Command Problems in the West," 108; Daniel, *Days of Glory,* 107–82. Even William T. Sherman, a general who used railroads efficiently, recognized that "railroads [were] the weakest things in war . . . since a single man with a match [could] destroy and cut off communications"; Rachel Sherman Thorndike, ed., *The Sherman Letters: Correspondence between General and Senator Sherman from 1837 to 1891* (New York: Charles Scribner's Sons, 1894), 136; Robert G. Angevine, *The Railroad and the State: War, Politics, and Technology in Nineteenth-Century America* (Stanford, Calif.: Stanford Univ. Press, 2004), 145; Hattaway and Jones, *How the North Won,* 250; Chumney, "Gentleman General," 104; Peine, "Buell Commission," 30; Williams, *Lincoln Finds a General,* 25–51.

37. Beatty, *Citizen-Soldier,* 152; Mark Grimsley, *The Hard Hand of War: Union Military Policy toward Southern Civilians, 1861–1865* (New York: Cambridge Univ. Press, 1995), 85, also provides an excellent analysis of Buell's conciliatory policy; Engle, *Buell,* 268; Prokopowicz, *All for the Regiment,* 113–46.

38. *OR,* ser. 1, vol. 7, 669–70; Grimsley, *Hard Hand of War,* 78–85; Engle, *Buell,* 184–86; Daniel, *Days of Glory,* 107–82.

39. Mary Jane Chadick Diary, July 27, 1862, Special Collections Department, William R. Perkins Library, Duke University, Durham, N.C.; see also Nancy M. Rohr, ed., *Incidents of the War: The Civil War Journal of Mary Jane Chadick* (Huntsville, Ala,: Silver Threads Publishing, 2005), 81; Williams, *Lincoln Finds a General,* 30–45; Engle, "Military Philosophy and Command Problems in the West," 108–9.

40. Sears, *Papers of McClellan,* 125–26; *OR,* ser. 1, vol. 4, 342; Engle, *Buell,* 79–98; Mark Grimsley, "Conciliation and Its Failure, 1861–1862," *Civil War History* 39 (Dec. 1993): 317–36; *OR,* ser. 1, vol. 4, 355–56.

41. Basler, *Collected Works of Lincoln,* 5:328–31, 241; Grimsley, *Hard Hand of War,* 68–71, 78–85.

42. *OR,* ser. 1, vol. 16, 8–9; ibid., ser. 1, vol. 16, pt. 2: 53–54, 155–56, 290–92; Peine, "Buell Military Commission," 46–47; Engle, "Military Philosophy and Command Problems in the West," 109–11; Stephen D. Engle, "Generalship on Trial: Don Carlos Buell's Campaign to Chattanooga," in *Civil War Generals in Defeat,* ed. Steve E. Woodworth (Lawrence: Univ. Press of Kansas, 1999), 95–117; Andrew Johnson to Lincoln, July 10, 1862, LP, LC.

43. Henry Seys to "My Very Dear Wife," July 12, 1862, Schoff Civil War Collection, William L. Clements Library, University of Michigan, Ann Arbor; Engle, "Military Philosophy and Command Problems in the West," 111.

44. Reuben D. Mussey to William H. Smith, July 6, 1862, William Henry Smith Papers, Ohio Historical Society, Columbus, Ohio; Engle, "Military Philosophy and Command Problems in the West," 111.

45. *Cincinnati Gazette,* July 24, Aug. 4, 18, 1862; *Indianapolis Daily Journal,* July 16, 18, 1862; *New York Tribune,* Aug. 8, 1862; *Cincinnati Daily Commercial,* July 12, 17, 24, 1862; Chumney, "Gentleman General," 144–45; *OR,* ser. 1, vol. 16, 637–42; Trefousse, *Johnson,* 156–63; Oliver P. Morton to Lincoln, Oct. 7, 1862, LP, LC; Stephen Engle, "'It

is Time for the States to Speak to the Federal Government': The Altoona Conference and Emancipation," *Civil War History* 58 (Dec. 2012): 416–50; Alexander K. McClure, *Abraham Lincoln and Men of War-Times* (Philadelphia, Pa.: Times Publishing Company, 1892), 383–89; William D. Foulke, *Life of Oliver P. Morton* (Indianapolis, Minn.: The Bowen-Merrill Company, 1899), 1:183–99; Gov. David Tod to Stanton, Oct. 3, 1862, Telegraphic Dispatches, ser. 144, Ohio State Archives, Columbus, Ohio; Alexander Varian to sister, Oct. 5, Varian to Nettie, Nov. 8, 1862, Alexander Varian Papers, Western Reserve Historical Society, Case Western University, Cleveland, Ohio.

46. Williams, *Lincoln and His Generals,* 48.

47. Shelby Foote, *The Civil War: A Narrative* (New York: Random House, 1958), 1:145, 563–64.

48. Lew Wallace, *Lew Wallace: An Autobiography* (New York: Harper and Brothers, 1906), 1:644–45; Frederick D. Williams, ed., *The Wild Life of the Army: The Civil War Letters of James A. Garfield* (East Lansing: Michigan State Univ. Press, 1964), 49.

49. Anson Stager to Edwin M. Stanton, Oct. 10, 1862, LP, LC; Kenneth W. Noe, *Perryville: This Grand Havoc of Battle* (Lexington: Univ. Press of Kentucky, 2001), 124–343 passim, for Buell's role at Perryville; Earl Hess, *Banners to the Breeze: The Kentucky Campaign Corinth, and Stones River* (Lincoln: Univ. of Nebraska Press, 2000), 30–92; Wills, *George Henry Thomas,*154–61; Stephen D. Engle, "Success, Failure, and the Guillotine: Don Carlos Buell and the Campaign for the Bluegrass State," *The Register of the Kentucky Historical Society* 96 (Autumn 1998): 315–49.

50. Horace White to Lincoln, Oct. 22, 1862, LP, LC; see also Buell to Lincoln, Sept. 10, Oliver P. Morton and Richard Yates to Lincoln, Oct. 25, 1862, Samuel Shellabarger to Lincoln, Oct. 22, 1862, LP, LC; Basler, *Collected Works,* 5:409; Gov. James F. Robinson argued against the removal of Buell in late September after the death of Nelson informing Lincoln that "the removal of Genl Buell at this time will operate most disastrously upon the Union Cause in Ky . . . his Removal will prove serious to our prospects in Ky the army will be dispirited & dissatisfied. . . ." Robinson to Lincoln, Sept. 29, 1862, LP, LC; Joseph Holt wrote Lincoln that he was satisfied that "the heart of Ky will be rejoiced at your recent displacement of Genl Buel, whose gross incapacity & inaction have given up the whole state to the ravages of the rebels. . . ." Holt to Lincoln, Oct. 28, 1862, LP, LC; see also James W. White to Lincoln, Nov. 10, 1862, LP, LC; White was a Republican judge in New York City.

51. "Progress of the War," *Christian Advocate and Journal,* Oct. 30, 1862, 349; *Saturday Evening Post,* Nov. 1, 1862.

52. Engle, *Buell,* 321–44 passim; Engle, "Military Philosophy and Command Problems in the West,"112–15.

53. Francis F. McKinney, "The Trial of General Buell," *Michigan Alumnus Quarterly Review* 64 (Mar. 1958): 163–68; Peine, "Buell Military Commission," 20–43 passim; *OR,* ser. 1, vol. 16, 3–908 passim; much of this volume is devoted to the Buell Military Commission; Engle, "Military Philosophy and Command Problems in the West," 112–15; McClure, *Lincoln and Men of War-Times,* 383–89.

54. *Washington Capital,* n.d., newspaper clipping found in Don Carlos Buell Papers, in possession of the author and the Filson Club Historical Society, Louisville, Ky., as quoted in Chumney, "Gentleman General," 11–17; Buell to Almon F. Rock-

well, July 10, 1864, Almon F. Rockwell Papers, Library of Congress, Washington, D.C.; Engle, *Buell,* 321–63; *Providence Daily Journal,* Aug. 13, 1864.

55. *Washington Capital,* n.d., newspaper clipping found in Buell papers, FHS; Chumney, "Gentleman General," 11–17; Engle, *Buell,* 337–54.

Braxton Bragg and the Stones River Campaign

Earl J. Hess

Gen. Braxton Bragg has long been something of a whipping boy among Confederate generals. His first biographer, Don C. Seitz, apologized that "It is not a grateful task to write the biography of a much hated man, whose military efforts led to defeat."[1]

Bragg's reputation with his contemporaries was problematic to say the least, and modern historians have continued to view him with a jaundiced eye. That is unfortunate, for the man's impact on the Civil War in the Western Theater was enormous, and that impact was not entirely negative. The Stones River campaign offers a good opportunity to present a more balanced assessment of Bragg's generalship, one that recognizes he was at least attempting a coherent and proper strategy and that he adopted a good tactical plan to achieve it. I do not intend to paint Bragg or his career in any unwarranted light, but I do argue that Bragg conducted the Stones River campaign with more success than is generally accorded to him.

Historians have been almost universally critical of Bragg's conduct in the fierce battle of Stones River, or Murfreesboro as the Confederates called it. While Seitz commented only that Bragg inflicted more damage to the Federals than his own army sustained, Grady McWhiney more deeply analyzed the general's handling of the Army of Tennessee on December 31, 1862, and January 2, 1863. McWhiney also provided one of the few relatively even-handed treatments of Bragg at Stones River, although he laced it with considerable criticism of the general as well.[2]

McWhiney argued that the position Bragg selected for his troops outside Murfreesboro was not the best ground for thirty thousand men to hold. It was largely level, cut up with patches of cedar forest and limestone outcroppings, and his army's line was bisected by Stones River itself. Yet McWhiney admitted that Bragg had legitimate reasons for holding Murfreesboro, which lay only thirty miles southeast of the Federal stronghold of Nashville. It allowed Bragg to gather food from the surrounding area and establish a Confederate presence in Middle Tennessee following the failure of his Kentucky invasion the previous summer. Because of these reasons, Bragg chose as good a position as was available to him. But McWhiney believed Bragg committed "a serious tactical error" in not fortifying his line.[3]

McWhiney also faulted Bragg for adopting a complicated attack plan against the Federal army commanded by William S. Rosecrans after the Yankees advanced from Nashville and closed in on his position outside Murfreesboro. McWhiney believed that the right wheel, requiring most divisions of Bragg's army to swing across the countryside for up to three miles while maintaining close contact with each other in an extended line, was impossible to conduct. McWhiney also severely criticized Bragg for misusing his only unengaged division, that commanded by John C. Breckinridge, on the afternoon of December 31. Instead of using Breckinridge's troops to reinforce William J. Hardee, who was in charge of the most extended part of the wheeling movement, he insisted that Breckinridge's men be shifted from the far Confederate right to hit the Union center, leaving it up to another corps commander, Leonidas Polk, to determine how to use Breckinridge's men for that purpose. Polk unwisely threw the brigades into piecemeal attacks, which succeeded no better in pushing the Federals back than his own troops had done earlier in the day. McWhiney also argued that even if Jefferson Davis had not insisted on detaching Carter L. Stevenson's division from the Army of Tennessee to Mississippi just before the campaign started, Bragg would not have used that division in the right way and at the right time to insure rebel victory at Stones River on December 31.[4]

McWhiney assessed Bragg's conduct of the attack on December 31 in a way that would resonate among other historians. "Bragg's tactical plan lacked that subtlety and flexibility so necessary for success; it had within itself all the elements of failure." Even if successful, it would push the Federals back into a more compact defensive position while forcing his own army to extend in a less compact formation, and with too few troops to make that more extended position tenable.[5]

But McWhiney censured Bragg even more for ordering Breckinridge's division into a frontal attack against Union troops who had crossed Stones River and taken possession of some high ground that could dominate the

Braxton Bragg. (Library of Congress)

area east of the stream on January 2. This famous assault, which was bluntly repulsed by a combination of massed Union artillery fire and an equally massive Union infantry attack, resulted in heavy casualties.[6]

After achieving an impressive tactical success on December 31 and suffering a sound tactical defeat on January 2, Bragg felt compelled to retreat from Murfreesboro on the night of January 3–4. His decision was based on the exhaustion of his men, a report that Rosecrans's army was larger than the Confederates had thought, and another report that the Federals were receiving reinforcements.[7]

After McWhiney, the next major study to look at Bragg was Thomas L. Connelly's *Autumn of Glory,* the second part of a two-volume history of the Army of Tennessee. Connelly's treatment of Bragg at Stones River is thoroughly negative, more so than McWhiney's. He faulted Bragg for wanting to hold Murfreesboro because supplies had already been gleaned from the area and the position could be easily outflanked by a system of good roads extending from the Nashville area.[8]

Connelly spared no invective when criticizing Bragg's attack plan. It asked too much of his troops and he did not provide for a ready reserve to aid Hardee when the latter commander needed it. In detailing the conduct of the right wheel attack on December 31, Connelly focused extensively on the problems rather than the accomplishments, and he virtually ignored the effect of this attack on the Federal army. He also criticized Bragg for not having a contingency plan in case the assault of December 31 failed to force Rosecrans to retreat. Connelly wrote of Bragg's "inability to adjust to a new situation," and referred to "Bragg's apparently confused state" after the vicious fighting of December 31.[9]

Connelly also condemned Bragg for Breckinridge's attack on January 2. It was a hasty decision, pushed through against Breckinridge's protest. Connelly is more forgiving with Bragg's decision to retreat from Murfreesboro, laying out the reasons that could have driven any commander to that decision.[10]

Subsequent historians followed the line of both McWhiney and Connelly in assessing Bragg's handling of the Stones River campaign. James Lee McDonough, in his general history of the battle, echoed virtually all the major criticisms offered by the previous historians. "With the exception of the devastating opening flank attack on the morning of December 31," McDonough concluded, "Bragg fought the battle of Stones River badly."[11]

Peter Cozzens authored the book that has stood as the standard history of Stones River for the past twenty years, and he also largely followed the lead established by McWhiney and Connelly. On all major points of interpretation and analysis, Cozzens believes these previous historians were right. A recent biography of Bragg by Samuel J. Martin does take a more sympathetic view of the general during the Civil War at large. Martin, however, fails to analyze Bragg's performance at Stones River other than to accept Bragg's version of controversial events without question. The most recent study of the battle, by Larry Daniel, offers the most tempered treatment of Bragg at Stones River. Daniel does criticize his selection of a line of defense on December 28 and characterizes his decision to strike the Round Forest on December 31 with Breckinridge's men as "disastrous," although Daniel recognizes that Bragg had few other good options.[12]

Except for Martin, historians have crafted a consistent view of Bragg at Stones River, one that emphasizes mistakes, oversights, and setting impossible goals for his men. It is a picture of failure because, in the end, Bragg retreated from the field, and Stones River became one more episode in which the general contributed to Confederate defeat in the Civil War.

But there is opportunity in the Stones River story to craft a more favorable view of Bragg, highlighting legitimate aims and careful efforts to achieve those goals. It is a story of clear vision and partial success, with failure largely coming about through circumstances beyond his control. This interpretation is based on four avenues of approach: (1) breaking away from the old assumption that Bragg was a miserable failure in everything that he touched; (2) looking at the effect of Bragg's actions on his Federal opponents; (3) looking at the views of Bragg's own men more carefully; and (4) comparing Stones River to other campaigns in the Civil War. In the end, I do not argue that Bragg was a western version of Robert E. Lee, but that he does not deserve to be classed among the lowest level of failed generals.

Let us start with Bragg's choice of Murfreesboro. Taking up a position close to Nashville made strategic sense. Lee also tried to keep Federal forces as far from Richmond as feasible; he pushed the theater of operations from the capital some sixty miles north in the summer of 1862 and more or less maintained it along the line of the Rappahannock and Rapidan rivers (except to invade Maryland and Pennsylvania) for nearly two years. In essence, Bragg was doing something similar when he concentrated the Army of Tennessee at Murfreesboro.[13]

"I hope thus to force him to fight or fall back," Bragg wrote of his opponent. He meant to act aggressively if the Federals came out of the city, sending cavalry to cut Union supply lines. In general orders issued to his troops, Bragg envisioned the next confrontation as "the great struggle which must soon settle the question of supremacy in Middle Tennessee." The great Union defeat at Fredericksburg on December 13, 1862, seemed to support Bragg's strategy. George W. Brent, his assistant adjutant general, noted in his journal that this defeat ought to teach Northerners "how idle & foolish their efforts [are] to subdue us." In short, if Bragg could defeat or severely punish Rosecrans only thirty miles outside Nashville in a similar way that Lee punished Ambrose Burnside at Fredericksburg, Confederate forces in both theaters might exhaust Northern will to continue fighting.[14]

Bragg was aware that Murfreesboro offered a poor defensive position and that supplies were scarce in its vicinity. "Our position not very secure. Supplies short," Brent noted as early as November 28. "If enemy were to press us vigorously, disaster would befall us." But the strategic opportunities at Murfreesboro seemed bright enough to risk these problems, justifying a view of Bragg as a more daring commander than is generally acceded.[15]

Ironically, the prevailing mood among Rosecrans's men seemed to play into Bragg's strategy. Rosecrans rejuvenated the Army of the Ohio after replacing Don Carlos Buell on October 27, 1862. He concentrated the troops at Nashville, reestablished adequate supply lines to the city, and infused a greater spirit of confidence among the men. Temporarily renamed the Fourteenth Corps (not until after the battle of Stones River was the field force designated the Army of the Cumberland), it now consisted of at least as many troops as Bragg had in his army and quite possibly many more, according to recent research. The Federals were full of confidence in "old Rosy." "You may expect to hear that the rebels are soundly whipped down here," Col. Hans Christian Heg of the 15th Wisconsin told his Gumild, "I do not think there will be another such affair as at Fredericksburg." Brigade commander Edward Needles Kirk assured his wife that "we are all anxious to get as far South as the Tennessee River before winter sets in."[16]

Self-confidence is an important component of an army's make up, but it can go too far. The confidence in Rosecrans created an unrealistic view of the fighting power of their enemy; many Federals believed that Bragg's troops could never stand up to Rosecrans's men. The army's chief of staff, Lt. Col. Julius P. Garesche, reflected and probably reinforced an overwhelming confidence in the future at army headquarters. "Rosecrans has never yet lost a battle," he informed his wife Marquitta. "He has now a magnificent Army. It is not now, that he would allow himself to be beaten by an Army like that of Bragg." Garesche went even further when he told his wife, "I don't think they will dare accept battle from him." The chief of staff worried more that Bragg would play out a Fabian strategy, luring Rosecrans deep into the heart of the Confederacy to extend Union supply lines to a dangerous degree, than that the rebels would stand and fight at Murfreesboro. When headquarters learned by Christmas Day that Bragg had sent off Stevenson's division to Mississippi, Garesche was convinced there would be no fight when Rosecrans left the next day to advance on Murfreesboro. "All of our principal officers have finished by sharing my opinion, that we will have no battle."[17]

Garesche can be forgiven for his ultra-optimistic view that Bragg and his veterans would not stand and fight, for he had never served in the field since the war began. But, according to Garesche, all of Rosecrans's commanders agreed with his view. The strange opinion that the Confederates would take flight gave Bragg an opportunity to offer battle with a slight emotional edge, often important in military operations.[18]

The Washington authorities put enormous pressure on Rosecrans to move quickly. General-in-Chief Henry W. Halleck assured him in early December that much depended on his success. Abraham Lincoln was very anxious that Middle Tennessee be cleared of rebel troops to show the English

Parliament that the Federals were winning the war, else he feared its members might succumb to the demands of textile manufacturers for Confederate recognition in order to regain access to Southern cotton. Since Parliament was scheduled to resume its deliberations in January 1863, Lincoln felt that December was a critical month. "It may be, and perhaps is, the very turning point in our foreign relations," Halleck told Rosecrans. From hindsight we can see that this fear was overblown, but hindsight did not help the contemporaries of December 1862. If Bragg could have hurled Rosecrans back to Nashville in defeat, it might have had a critical effect on American public opinion and perhaps the actions of the English government.[19]

Rosecrans advanced from Nashville on December 26, sixteen days past the arbitrary deadline Lincoln had set. The idea that Bragg would run rather than fight continued to hold sway among the Union generals. When Rosecrans heard unsubstantiated reports that the Confederates were evacuating Murfreesboro on the evening of December 29, he readily believed them and ordered wing commander Thomas L. Crittenden to cross the river and advance into town. Crittenden's subordinates, Thomas J. Wood and John M. Palmer, knew better, and twice asked Crittenden to postpone the order before the wing commander did so. Before that, however, one of Wood's brigades crossed Stones River in the gathering darkness, ran into a heated fight with defending Confederates, and retreated to the Federal side.[20]

During Rosecrans's advance toward Murfreesboro, Bragg's thinking was to offer battle "a short distance" from town. He established his line on December 28 and the two armies concentrated and confronted each other by December 30. "Gen Bragg determined to await no longer the tardy movements of the enemy & resolved to attack him," Brent wrote. Philip Sheridan, one of Rosecrans's best division commanders, later criticized the army commander for assuming that Bragg "would continue passive, remain entirely on the defensive." Bragg was one step ahead of his opponent.[21]

Historians have criticized Bragg's selection of ground because it offered no defensive advantage to the Confederates, but the Federals were positioned on the same ground and had no defensive advantage either. In that case, Bragg's move to seize the tactical offensive was a brilliant way to turn this problem into an advantage.

The fighting on December 31 was a Confederate tactical success, despite the problems involved in wheeling several divisions over cluttered terrain for as much as three miles. The Confederates took the Federals by surprise, they outflanked their right, a brigade of cavalry supported the rebel infantry advance, and the Unionists were on the defensive all day. Historians, especially Connelly, have emphasized the problems associated with that massive right wheel, but even a simple, straight forward advance often was conducted with many problems. To expect any army to pursue such a movement as Bragg's on December 31 in a clean way is expecting far too much. What impresses me is how well the Army of Tennessee managed to do it. The units were unable to maintain a continuous line; the action devolved into coherent movements by individual brigades only loosely coordinating their endeavors with those to right and left. Losses were heavy, but the sum result was to drive two-thirds of Rosecrans's army back to the Nashville Pike and the railroad, inflicting equally heavy casualties on the Federals, and coming close to crushing the Fourteenth Corps. The scholarly literature often fails to appreciate fully the Confederate tactical achievement on December 31.

Bragg accurately reflected that achievement when he sent a telegram on January 1 announcing the success to Richmond. It inspired great jubilation and hope nationwide when made public. His soldiers uniformly viewed the results of December 31 as a magnificent victory. "It is enough to say that we gave the miserable abolition invaders one of the worst whipings [*sic*] they have ever had," exulted John Kennedy Street of the 9th Texas.[22]

The Federals admitted they had been outgeneraled and had come dangerously close to disaster. Many of them were emotionally traumatized, and hoped merely for night to fall so they could retire out of reach of the Rebels. A great many Yankees also came away from the fighting of December 31 with deep admiration for their enemy's ability. Regimental commander Benjamin Scribner referred to "the snap and vim" of Bragg's assault, while John Brandon Guthrie of the 1st Kentucky (US) told his aunt: "it is wonderful to me the bravery with which his men fight. I believe that if we had half the Discipline in our Army that he has in his we could whip him anytime." Willis Jones of the 84th Illinois assured his family right after the battle, "when you here folks sa that the rebbles wont fite[,] tel them to cum an try them[,] I tel you tha fite like Tigers."[23]

Confederate prisoners told George Gresham Sinclair of the 89th Illinois that they fought so well because they were desperate. If they lost the fight, "they would have to retreat to the devil only knows where and if they gained the day that Nashville was theirs and nothing could ever get them out of Kentucky again."[24]

Of course, historians' criticism of Bragg for not having a reserve handy to send to Hardee at the critical moment is justified, but tempered by the fact that he had no troops to spare for this task (having to retain Breckinridge's division east of the river to hold the Confederate right). It is also tempered by the fact that it often was difficult for any commander to know when and where to deploy reserves until hindsight allowed them clearer vision. Actually, Bragg's attempt to crush the Union center on the afternoon of December 31 made sense at the time; if the Union right was being steadily driven back and the center was holding firm around the area of the Round Forest and the Nashville Pike, then collapsing the center could have forced the entire Federal army to abandon the field.

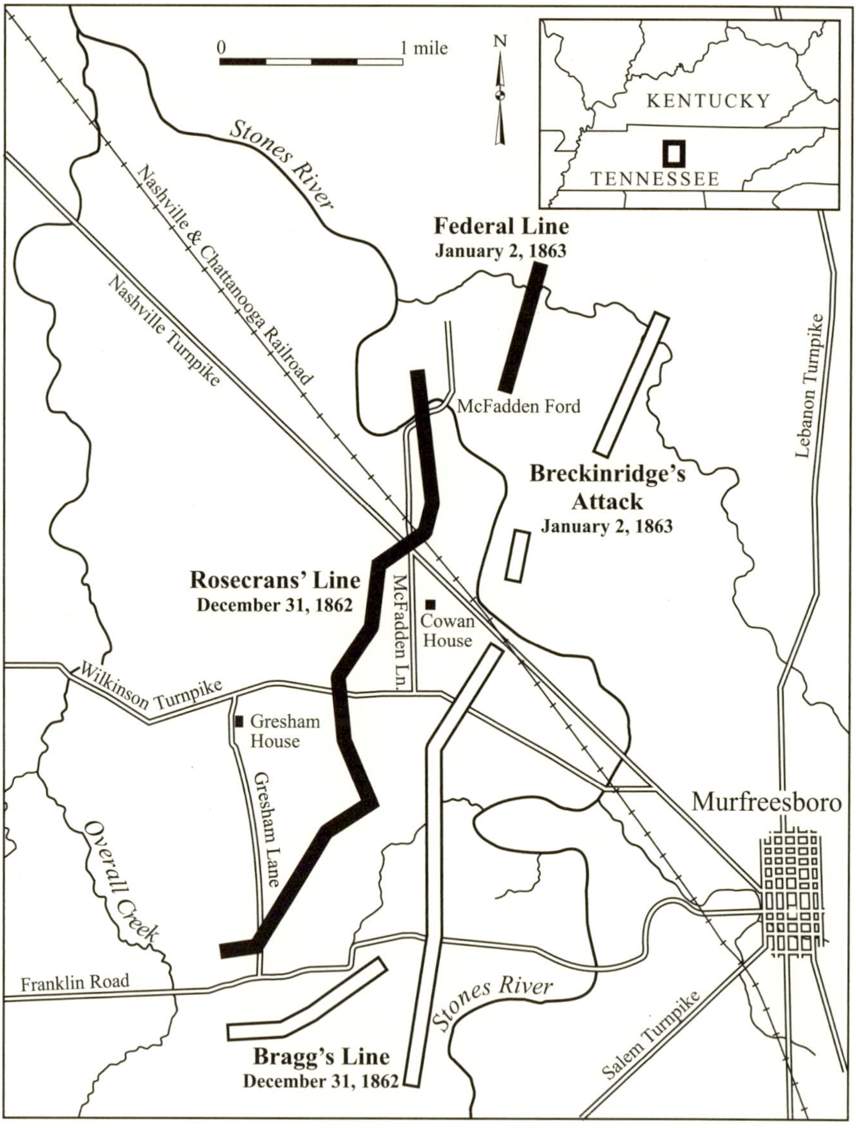

Battle of Stones River.

It is less easy to justify Bragg's decision to attack the Federal left on January 2. Such an assault made much more sense on December 31 as a support to Polk's and Hardee's attacks west of the river than it did two days later.

Bragg's decision to retreat from Murfreesboro on the night of January 3 muddled public perception of his conduct in the Stones River campaign. Among his own soldiers, Bragg's decision created divergent opinions. Confederate cavalrymen who were involved in the supporting operations on Hardee's flank during the advance on December 31 bitterly denounced their general for retreating.[25]

Most of Bragg's foot soldiers reacted to the fall back from Murfreesboro in one of three ways. Some of them joined the cavalrymen in condemning their commander for retreating. Charles George of the 5th Georgia argued that Bragg "was the only one the Yanks whipped[,] his men were all right and expected to be let at the yanks any moment but [he] insisted we had to *skedaddle*." An Arkansas captain moaned that Bragg "had the independence of the Confederacy and a glorious peace in his grasp, but . . . by bad management, he has opened his hands and let the prize fly."[26]

Other Confederates were puzzled by the decision to retreat, or they tempered their frustration over it with an understanding of why Bragg had given up the field. Brigade leader James Patton Anderson found it difficult to understand why the army retreated after its success on December 31, but admitted that the troops were exhausted and suffering from exposure. Anderson also argued that the retreat severely lowered his men's morale and their faith in Bragg. "It may be strategic," wrote the chaplain of the 8th Texas Cavalry for a hometown newspaper. "It may be a needful change of base—time will decide the wisdom of our withdrawal from the battle-field after holding it three days."[27]

But there were many Confederates who fully supported Bragg's decision to retire. John Kennedy Street told his family that "all were sadisfied [*sic*] that Bragg knew what he was doing and were willing to do his bidding sadisfied [*sic*] that all would work out right in the end." These men who supported Bragg's decision cited the arrival of Union reinforcements, an advantage Bragg could not counter, as the primary reason for pulling away. "We had everything to lose and nothing to gain by risking another battle immediately," wrote Arkansas surgeon W. L. Gammage. A member of Vaughan's Tennessee brigade wrote in the *Memphis Daily Appeal* that "it would have been the policy only of a suicidal general to have done otherwise than to retire when General Bragg did." A soldier in Stanford's Mississippi Battery further stated, "Like a good General he wants to save his men. If the 'Army of Tennessee' were annihilated, we have no new troops to fill its place." C. Irvine Walker, a member of Arthur M. Manigault's brigade staff, grew tired of newspaper criticism of his commanding general. "I tell you, if Genl. Bragg had not fought the battle as he did, surprising the enemy by the desperate charges of our men, he would have been compelled to leave the field, if not beaten, at any rate ten times worse off than we were."[28]

Bragg's retreat created fear among some observers that he might continue falling back if Rosecrans pursued him. Bragg tried to reassure everyone from the president to his own troops that he intended to hold as much of Tennessee as possible. He also meant to take the tactical offensive again if Rosecrans continued to move against him, and assured everyone that only overwhelming numbers had caused his retreat from the battlefield. "I have saved my Army, in good condition," he told Davis, "and shall be able to meet the Vandals again when they advance." John Kennedy Street heard Bragg give a speech to the troops stationed at Winchester in which the general "had no idea of abandoning Tenn but would defend the state against the invader to the last extremity." Bragg also told them that "he did not feel disposed to sacrifice his men to no purpose."[29]

Some of Bragg's higher ranking officers began to complain about his leadership after the retreat, and Bragg, stung by virulent newspaper criticism, decided to force a showdown with his subordinates. Against the advice of his own staff, he issued a circular letter on January 11 requesting the generals to state whether they had lost confidence in him and to affirm that they had supported his decision to retire from the battlefield. Most of those who replied admitted that retreat was the best option, but many of them openly stated that the army had lost confidence in its commander. Bragg engaged in a fierce struggle with division leader Breckinridge, blaming him for poor performances on both December 31 and January 2. He also censured division commander Benjamin F. Cheatham for being visibly intoxicated during the battle of the first day.[30]

On the surface, Bragg essentially won the struggle for command against his subordinates. He subdued their criticisms, continued to hold Davis's support, and refused to resign. Joseph E. Johnston played an important role in supporting Bragg during this controversy. Appointed commander of two departments in the West in late 1862, Johnston was sent to Tullahoma to investigate the furor and recommend to Davis what should be done. The visit went off very well as far as Bragg was concerned, for Johnston issued a glowing assessment of his performance at Stones River. As he explained to Louis T. Wigfall, Bragg "had done more execution in proportion to numbers than any other in this war. That, you will surely admit, gave him a claim to retain his command. . . . I did not say that Bragg was a great general—that was no part of the question—but that his recent operations had been highly creditable & of course he could not decently be relieved then."[31]

Indeed, other Confederate officers echoed Johnston's assessment. Dabney H. Maury at Mobile concluded that Bragg's "partial success in Tennessee," viewed within the context of more strident Confederate victories in Mississippi and Virginia that winter, "have contributed to restore confidence" among many Southerners.[32]

Within the Fourteenth Corps, which was renamed the Army of the Cumberland soon after the battle, soldier morale was very high. The rank and file fell in love with Rosecrans because their commander had shown himself to the troops in the hottest fighting, encouraged them in their crisis, and eventually won the engagement through sheer determination. Fred Knefler of the 79th Indiana thought Rosecrans was "as brave and gallant as Julius Caesar," while Hans Christian Heg thought his commander would become "the great man in this war yet. I think he is the best, bravest and biggest general we have got." Some of Rosecrans's generals faulted his personality, his apparent favoring of Catholics, his sometimes overly excitable nature, but only Phillip Sheridan faulted him for allowing Bragg to seize the tactical initiative and dictate the flow of events on December 31, and even that criticism appeared in Sheridan's postwar memoirs rather than soon after the battle.[33]

Not long after the engagement, Thomas L. Crittenden accompanied Rosecrans in a ride through Crittenden's camps. Rosecrans responded to the cheers of the men by telling them, "'All right, boys, all right; Bragg's a good dog, but Hold Fast's a better.'" Crittenden wrote after the war that this "well expressed my feeling as to the kind of victory we had won." In short, Crittenden thought that all the Federals had accomplished was survival, with a small, incremental gain of Middle Tennessee territory as a bonus.[34]

Crittenden did not necessarily speak for the rank and file. The soldiers overwhelmingly classified Stones River as a great victory because they repelled the Confederate onslaught, saved the army, and compelled the enemy to give up the field. They believed that Bragg's men suffered enormously and left Murfreesboro demoralized. There were some who admitted to doubt about what had been accomplished, but they were in a minority.[35]

Doubts were far more serious and widespread among Rosecrans's officers than among the men, testifying to the effect of Bragg's strike on December 31 and its near success in crippling the Federal army. The higher ranking officers had a wider perspective on the scale of damage the enemy inflicted, and more responsibility to bear for failure on the field. "The results of the battle were not what we had hoped," admitted Crittenden, "and yet there was a general feeling of elation." On the tactical level, Crittenden sarcastically wrote that the "battle was fought according to the plan of General Bragg. Indeed, our uniform experience was—at Perryville, at Stone's River, at Chickamauga—that whenever we went to attack Bragg we were attacked by him, and so our plan had to be extemporized."[36]

Sheridan also saw little gain in the outcome of the Stones River campaign. He admitted that to have lost it and fallen back to Nashville would have been strategically disastrous, but the outcome was "a costly victory, which was not decisive enough in its character to greatly affect the general course of the war."[37]

Confederate assessment of the battle's outcome tended to be quite positive. Bragg himself proclaimed in a message to his troops that their accomplishments had been "unparalleled." He listed the losses inflicted on Rosecrans (including thousands of casualties, thirty guns, seven thousand small arms, and eight hundred wagons), and boasted of a moral victory over the Federals. "In retiring to a stronger position without molestation from a superior force, you have left him a barren field in which to bury his hosts of slain and to rally and recuperate his shattered ranks." Moreover, "we shall yet teach him a severe lesson for the rashness of penetrating a country so hostile to his cause." Joseph E. Johnston also issued congratulatory orders proclaiming Stones River "an exploit unparalleled in modern battles."[38]

Most Confederate soldiers and their officers agreed that the Army of Tennessee had been successful on December 31, even if the retreat reduced the strategic benefits and public perception of their achievement. James Patton Anderson told his wife in one letter that the cost of the victory was not worth the results, but in the next letter argued that Rosecrans's command was so worsted on the battlefield that it could not possibly continue advancing for a long time to come.[39]

A theme in soldier commentary on Stones River recognized that Bragg had taught Rosecrans a lesson about invading rebel territory, and perhaps it was prompted by Bragg's own message to his troops. A. T. Gay of the 31st Tennessee argued that another such "victory" by the Federals "will soon force them to recognize us as an independent nation." Hannibal Paine of the 26th Tennessee put it bluntly when he wrote: "All of the soil that Rosencrans gains now is going to cost him blood."[40]

The policy of wearing down the enemy through bloody fighting, even if giving up the field, struck the right note with many Confederate soldiers. In fact, Surgeon W. L. Gammage argued that it was "our true policy," for "time wears out a Federal army whilst it always strengthens ours." Soldiers assumed their commander would continue to draw Rosecrans farther south to extend the Union line of supply.[41]

Many Confederates hoped to exhaust Union willpower to continue fighting as well. Alfred Tyler Fielder prayed that the enemy would "learn from this that they cannot conquer us and go home and let us enjoy our rights as they wish to enjoy theirs." C. Irvine Walker cited the rise of Copperhead sentiment, the increasing financial burden of prosecuting the war, and the imminent collapse of Northern currency as factors in his hope that Lincoln's war effort would fail. Then Northerners would "come cringing to our feet, begging for the peace we have so long offered them." Dunbar Affleck of the 8th Texas Cavalry thought neither side would win the military struggle, for "the Yankeys cant [*sic*] whip us and we can never whip them, and I see no prospect of peace unless the Yankees themselves throw down their arms, and refuse to fight any longer."[42]

The Confederates could not know that morale among Rosecrans's troops actually was very high after Stones River, but the same was not true of Rosecrans and his higher ranking subordinates. The Federal commander boasted of his intention "to push them to the wall" on January 6, but by January 11 he informed Washington of reports that Bragg was receiving reinforcements. A widespread belief circulated around Murfreesboro that the Confederates would take the offensive. As a result, Rosecrans stayed where he was, extending the stay for six months of comparative idleness. Rosecrans's men assumed that he would restart the campaign throughout January and February; not until March were there signs that winter quarters at Murfreesboro would be their home indefinitely. The Confederates interpreted this long delay as a lack of willpower on Rosecrans's part to resume the offensive they had bluntly stopped at Murfreesboro.[43]

The Confederates may have been right. When Rosecrans requested the views of his subordinates on the next stage in the struggle for Middle Tennessee, division commander Thomas J. Wood replied on April 6 that the army needed to have an overwhelming numerical superiority over Bragg. To engage in another fight where the opponents were of equal strength, as at Stones River, "was simply a prize fight," Wood contended, "yielding the victor little more than the ground he stands on, and by no means compensating for the expenditure of human life necessary to obtain the results." Wood indicated that a strong feeling of doubt and hesitancy had infiltrated the high command. To approach the Army of Tennessee with insufficient force, Wood continued, was to "expose ourselves to defeat."[44]

Bragg deserves more credit for his handling of the Army of Tennessee than historians have usually given him. He had a coherent and viable strategy—to hold a forward position and punish the enemy as much as possible, striking for a moral victory as much as a military one. He seized the tactical initiative, held it for the length of a bloody day of fighting during which his army drove the Federals back as much as three miles, inflicted stunning losses on them, and shattered the complacent notion that the conquest of Middle Tennessee would be easy. So far, this description could easily be applied to Lee's operations in Virginia as well.

Historians have criticized Bragg for adopting an attack plan on December 31 that forced the Federals back into a more compact defensive position, but the same could be said for Stonewall Jackson's attack at Chancellorsville on May 2, 1863. Historians uniformly praise Lee for the success of that flank attack, but in reality it merely blunted the Federal right flank before stalling in the darkness of the Wilderness. Moreover, Lee's army remained disunited after the attack stalled, and only fierce attacks by the Confederates on the morning of May 3 pushed the Federals back and reunited the Army of Northern Virginia, representing the true turning point of Lee's great victory at Chancellorsville.[45]

I would argue that Bragg's attack on the Union right wing on December 31 was more successful than Jackson's attack on the Federal right on May 2, for Hardee and Polk conducted that difficult advance while maintaining general connection with other parts of the army. Of course, Bragg's course of action after December 31 left him open to legitimate criticism—the attack of January 2 was an awful failure, but the decision to disengage and retire was at least partially justified. Lee did not retire from the field at Chancellorsville and outlasted his stunned opponent, according Lee not only the battlefield victory but almost legendary status as a tough, tenacious fighter.

Also, Bragg's almost insane desire to root out dissidents among his officers after the battle caused untold trouble for him. Virtually no other high-level Civil War commander acted in this way, and it heavily colored contemporary opinion of his generalship. He was severely criticized for retreating from Murfreesboro, but Joseph E. Johnston retreated nearly a hundred miles in more than two months, under nearly continuous contact with the

Federals, while he commanded the Army of Tennessee during the Atlanta campaign of 1864. The rank and file, as well as the officer corps, almost uniformly trusted and loved Johnston, rather than criticized him for this abdication of territory without fighting a major battle.[46]

Contemporary criticism of Bragg tended to be inspired by his contentious personality, his inability to get along with his subordinates. St. John R. Liddell, one of Bragg's brigade commanders, penned a telling commentary on the general's personality flaws. "Bragg's manner made him malignant enemies and indifferent, callous friends."[47] An important reason for Lee's and Johnston's esteem among their contemporaries was that both men tended to keep themselves above personal squabbles, conducting themselves with a dignity that inspired respect.

An assessment of Bragg's generalship on the field should not be clouded or influenced by the personality troubles he generated off the field. His conduct of the Stones River campaign came close to the strategy adopted by Lee in Virginia, an apparently winning strategy, at least for a time, in keeping the Army of the Potomac far from Richmond and straining Northern willpower to continue the war. Bragg failed to accomplish that fully at Murfreesboro, but he at least attempted and partially succeeded in doing so.

Notes

1. Don C. Seitz, "Foreword," in *Braxton Bragg: General of the Confederacy* (Columbia, S.C.: The State Company, 1924), n.p.

2. Ibid., 250.

3. Grady McWhiney, *Braxton Bragg and Confederate Defeat*, vol. 1, *Field Command* (New York: Columbia Univ. Press, 1969), 347–48.

4. Ibid., 352, 359–60, 363.

5. Ibid., 363–65.

6. Ibid., 367, 369–70.

7. Ibid., 374.

8. Thomas Lawrence Connelly, *Autumn of Glory: The Army of Tennessee, 1862–1865* (Baton Rouge: Louisiana State Univ. Press, 1971), 14–15, 23–24, 47, 49.

9. Ibid., 52–58, 61–62.

10. Ibid., 62–64, 66–67.

11. James Lee McDonough, *Stones River—Bloody Winter in Tennessee* (Knoxville: Univ. of Tennessee Press, 1980), 73, 146, 148–51, 221–23.

12. Peter Cozzens, *No Better Place to Die: The Battle of Stones River* (Urbana: Univ. of Illinois Press, 1990), 30, 60, 150; Samuel J. Martin, *General Braxton Bragg, C.S.A.* (Jefferson, N.C.: McFarland, 2011), 220–43; Larry J. Daniel, *Battle of Stones River:*

The Forgotten Conflict between the Confederate Army of Tennessee and the Union Army of the Cumberland (Baton Rouge: Louisiana State Univ. Press, 2012), 46–49, 162.

13. Francis Augustin O'Reilly, *The Fredericksburg Campaign: Winter War on the Rappahannock* (Baton Rouge: Louisiana State Univ. Press, 2003), 11, 33–35; Stephen W. Sears, *Chancellorsville* (Boston: Houghton Mifflin, 1996), 110–14; Gordon C. Rhea, *The Battle of the Wilderness, May 5–6, 1864* (Baton Rouge: Louisiana State Univ. Press, 1994), 8–10.

14. General Orders No. 151, Headquarters, Department No. 2, Nov. 20, 1862: Bragg to Cooper, Nov. 22, 1862, United States War Department, *The War of the Rebellion: A Compilation of the Official Records of the Union and Confederate Armies,* ser. 1, vol. 20, pt. 2, 411–12, 416 (hereafter cited as *OR;* all citations are to series 1); George W. Brent journal, Dec. 21, 1862, Braxton Bragg Papers, Folder 22, Western Reserve Historical Society.

15. George W. Brent journal, Nov. 28 and Dec. 2, 1862, Braxton Bragg Papers.

16. Theodore G. Blegen, ed., *The Civil War Letters of Colonel Hans Christian Heg* (Northfield, Minn.: Norwegian-American Historical Association, 1936), 158–59, 180; Kirk to his wife, Dec. 8, 1862, Edward Needles Kirk Correspondence, Historical Society of Pennsylvania.

17. [Louis Garesche], *Biography of Lieut. Col. Julius P. Garesche, Assistant Adjutant-General, U.S. Army* (Philadelphia: J. B. Lippincott, 1887), 415, 425, 428, 430. Interestingly, none of the previous historians who have written about Stones River mention this sense of overwhelming confidence at Rosecrans's headquarters. See McDonough, *Stones River,* 64–79, Cozzens, *No Better Place to Die,* 44–47, and Daniel, *Stones River,* 28–32, for examples.

18. [Garesche], *Biography of Lieut. Col. Julius P. Garesche,* 38–39, 348, 363, 394.

19. Halleck to Rosecrans, Dec. 5, 1862, *OR,* vol. 20, pt. 2, 123–24.

20. [Garesche], *Biography of Lieut. Col. Julius P. Garesche,* 432–33; Crittenden to Goddard, Jan. 15, 1863, Wood to Starling, Jan. 6, 1863, *OR,* vol. 20, pt. 1, 448, 459, 463; John McAuley Palmer to Trumbull, Jan. 11, 1863, Lyman Trumbull Collection, Abraham Lincoln Presidential Library; Gilbert C. Kniffin, "The Battle of Stones River," in *Battles and Leaders of the Civil War,* ed. Robert Underwood Johnson and Clarence Clough Buel (New York: Thomas Yoseloff, 1956), 3:613–14; Larry J. Daniel, *Days of Glory: The Army of the Cumberland, 1861–1865* (Baton Rouge: Louisiana State Univ. Press, 2004), 203–4; Cozzens, *No Better Place to Die,* 65–67. For additional sources dealing with Federal musings as to whether Bragg would run or fight, see William Wallace to his wife, Jan. 9, 1863, in *Belmont Chronicle,* Jan. 29, 1863; [Ebenezer Hannaford], "In the Ranks at Stone River," *Harper's New Monthly Magazine* Nov. 1863, 812; George F. Gill diary, Dec. 29, 1862, Filson Historical Society; G. L. S. to William Wheatcroft, Jan. 11, 1863, Civil War Letters, Indiana Soldiers, Abraham Lincoln Presidential Library; McCook to Garesche, Dec. 29, 1862, *OR,* vol. 20, pt. 2, 267.

21. George W. Brent journal, Dec. 27–28, 1862, Braxton Bragg Papers; P. H. Sheridan, *Personal Memoirs* (Wilmington, N.C.: Broadfoot, 1992), 1:244.

22. Connelly, *Autumn of Glory,* 47, 49; McDonough, *Stones River,* 75; Bragg to [not stated], Jan. 1, 1863, *OR,* vol. 52, pt. 2, 402; Johnston to Bragg, Jan. 1, 2, 1863: Seddon to Kirby Smith, Jan. 4, 1863, *OR,* vol. 20, pt. 2, 475, 476, 484; Street to Ninnie, Jan. 3, 1863, John Kennedy Street Papers, Southern Historical Collection, University of

North Carolina; Henry Watson to his father and mother, Jan. 22, 1863, 10th Texas Cavalry Regimental File, Stones River National Battlefield; William Lee White and Charles Denny Runion, eds., *Great Things Are Expected of Us: The Letters of Colonel C. Irvine Walker, 10th South Carolina Infantry, C.S.A.* (Knoxville: Univ. of Tennessee Press, 2009), 45.

23. Lydia Minturn Post, ed., *Soldier's Letters, from Camp, Battle-Field and Prison* (New York: Bunce and Huntington, 1865), 181–82; B. F. Scribner, *How Soldiers Were Made: Or The War as I Saw It under Buell, Rosecrans, Thomas, Grant, and Sherman* (Chicago: Donohue and Henneberry, 1887), 85; Guthrie to his aunt, Jan. 10, [1863], John Brandon Guthrie Papers, Rare Books, Manuscript, and Special Collections, Duke University; Fisher to his mother, Jan. 7, 1863, Horace Newton Fisher Papers, Massachusetts Historical Society; Jones to his wife and children, Jan. 5, 1863, Willis Jones Papers, Pearce Civil War Collection, Navarro College; George H. Berry to his wife, Jan. 12, 1863, 89th Illinois Regimental File, Stones River National Battlefield; William Roberts Stuckey to his wife, Jan. 20, 1863, 42d Indiana Regimental File, Stones River National Battlefield; Bartholomew to Frank, Jan. 5, 1863, Arza Bartholomew Letters, George G. Christman Collection, Archives of Michigan.

24. George Gresham Sinclair to Frank, Jan. 6, 1863, 89th Illinois Regimental File, Stones River National Battlefield.

25. Robert W. Williams Jr., and Ralph A. Wooster, eds., "With Terry's Texas Rangers: The Civil War Letters of Dunbar Affleck," *Civil War History* 9, no. 3 (Sept. 1963): 313; Jesse Burke Heard, ed., *Terry Ranger Writes Home: Letters of Pvt. Benjamin F. Burke Written While in Terry's Texas Rangers, 1861–1864* (n.p., 1965), page numbers not given, but letter to father and mother dated Jan. 16, 1863, www.terrystexasrangers.org; Pauline S. Goldman, ed., "Letters from Three Members of Terry's Texas Rangers, 1861–1865" (master's thesis, Univ. of Texas, 1930), n.p., but Robert Edward Hill to his sister, Jan. 12, 1863, www.terrystexasrangers.org.

26. McDonall diary, Jan. 4, 1863, Augustus O. McDonall Papers, Special and Area Studies Collections, University of Florida; Charles George to Mary, Jan. 24, 1864, George Family Papers, Special Collections and Archives, Auburn University; Kenneth A. Hafendorfer, ed., *Civil War Journal of William L. Trask: Confederate Sailor and Soldier* (Louisville, Ky.: KH Press, 2003), 97; Irving A. Buck, *Cleburne and His Command* (New York: Neale, 1908), 84; Howard M. Ingham, "Captain Valentine Merriwether M'Gehee," *Publications of the Arkansas Historical Association* 4 (1917): 144.

27. Anderson to Et, Jan. 8, 1862 [1863], James Patton Anderson Papers, Special and Area Studies Collections, University of Florida; Thomas W. Cutrer, ed., *Our Trust Is in the God of Battles: The Civil War Letters of Robert Franklin Bunting, Chaplain, Terry's Texas Rangers, C.S.A.* (Knoxville: Univ. of Tennessee Press, 2006), 115; Trimmier to his wife, Jan. 12, 1863, Theodore Gillard Trimmier Papers, Tennessee State Library and Archives.

28. Street to Ninnie, Jan. 3, 1863, and Jan. [n.d.], 1863, John Kennedy Street Papers, Southern Historical Collection, University of North Carolina; Bell to his wife, Jan. 11, 1862 [1863], Alfred W. Bell Papers, Rare Books, Manuscript, and Special Collections, Duke University; Ambrose Doss to his wife, Jan. 8, 1863, 19th Alabama Regimental File, Stones River National Battlefield; D. H. Rogers to H. M. Lea, Jan. 20, 1863, Lea Family Civil War Letters, Mississippi Department of Archives and

History; L. W. Hunter to his sister, Jan. 24, 1863, Horn Collection, Special Collections, Mississippi State University; W. L. Gammage to John H. Bonner, June [n.d.], 1863, Civil War Miscellany, Dolph Briscoe Center for American History, University of Texas, Austin; "C" to editors, Jan. 20, 1863, *Memphis Daily Appeal,* Jan. 29, 1863; Leigh to editors, Jan. 12, 1863, *Memphis Daily Appeal,* Jan. 22, 1863; H. J. H. Rugely, ed., *Batchelor-Turner Letters, 1861–1864* (Austin, Tex.: Steck, 1961), n.p., but B. F. Batchelor to his father, Jan. 25, 1863, www.terrystexasrangers.org; White and Runion, eds., *Great Things,* 40, 47.

29. Lynda L. Crist et al., eds., *The Papers of Jefferson Davis* (Baton Rouge: Louisiana State Univ. Press, 1997), 9:30, 33; William A. Brown memoirs, 86, Stanford's Mississippi Battery Regimental File, Stones River National Battlefield; McWhiney, *Braxton Bragg,* 374; Bragg to Ewell, Jan. 8, 1863, *OR,* vol. 52, pt. 2, 404; Street to Ninnie, Jan. [n.d.], 1863, John Kennedy Street Papers, Southern Historical Collection, University of North Carolina.

30. Connelly, *Autumn of Glory,* 73–76, 81–82, 84; George W. Brent journal, Jan. 12, 1863, Braxton Bragg Papers.

31. Connelly, *Autumn of Glory,* 77–79, 80–81, 90–92; Joseph E. Johnston to [Wigfall], Apr. 1, 1864, Louis Trezevant Wigfall Family Papers, Library of Congress.

32. Dabney H. Maury to Samuel Cooper, Jan. 14, 1863, Confederate Military Leaders Collection, Museum of the Confederacy.

33. John Beatty, *Memoirs of a Volunteer, 1861–1863* (New York: W. W. Norton, 1946), 156; Fred Knefler to Wallace, Mar. 28, 1863, Lew Wallace Papers, Indiana Historical Society; Blegen, ed., *Civil War Letters,* 171; Milo S. Hascall, "Personal Recollections and Experiences Concerning the Battle of Stones River," *Military Essays and Recollections: Papers Read before the Commandery of the State of Illinois, Military Order of the Loyal Legion of the United States* (Chicago: Cozzens and Beaton, 1907), 4:149, 151–54; John McAuley Palmer to Trumbull, Jan. 11, 1863, Lyman Trumbull Collection, Abraham Lincoln Presidential Library; Palmer to his wife, Jan. 21, 1863, John McAuley Palmer Collection, Abraham Lincoln Presidential Library; Sheridan, *Personal Memoirs,* 1:244.

34. Thomas L. Crittenden, "The Union Left at Stone's River," in *Battles and Leaders of the Civil War,* ed. Robert Underwood Johnson and Clarence Clough Buel (New York: Thomas Yoseloff, 1956), 3:634.

35. Landrum to Obed, Jan. 7, 1863, George W. Landrum Papers, Ohio Historical Society; William Roberts Stuckey to his wife, Jan. 20, 1863, 42d Indiana Regimental File, Stones River National Battlefield; Bartholomew to Frank, Jan. 5, 1863, Arza Bartholomew Letters, George G. Christman Collection, Archives of Michigan.

36. Crittenden, "Union Left," 633–34.

37. Sheridan, *Personal Memoirs,* 1:239, 243; Thomas B. Van Horne, *History of the Army of the Cumberland, Its Organization, Campaigns, and Battles* (Cincinnati: Robert Clarke, 1875), 1:252–53.

38. General Orders No. 4, Headquarters, Johnston's Command, Jan. 28, 1863: "Bragg to Soldiers of the Army of Tennessee," Jan. 8, 1863, *OR,* vol. 20, pt. 1, 675.

39. "G" to editor, Jan. 12, 1863, *Memphis Daily Appeal,* Jan. 30, 1863; A. B. Flint to John Clark, Feb. 24, 1863, Herbert Earle Buchanan Family Papers, Special Collec-

tions, University of Arkansas, Fayetteville; M. H. S. to editor, Jan. 13, 1863, *Selma Morning Reporter,* Jan. 27, 1863; Anderson to Et, Jan. 8, 11, 1862 [1863], James Patton Anderson Papers, Special and Area Studies Collections, University of Florida.

40. A. T. Gay to his father, Mar. 14, 1863, 31st Tennessee Regimental File, Stones Rivers National Battlefield; Hannibal Paine to his sister, Jan. 10, 1863, Colville and Paine Family Letters, Special Collections, University of Tennessee, Chattanooga.

41. W. L. Gammage to John H. Bonner, June [n.d.], 1863, Civil War Miscellany, Dolph Briscoe Center for American History; Crittenden to Bettie, Jan. 20, 1863, John Crittenden Collection, Special Collections and Archives, Auburn University.

42. Ann York Franklin, comp., *The Civil War Diaries of Capt. Alfred Tyler Fielder, 12th Tennessee Regiment Infantry, Company B, 1861–65* (Louisville, Ky.: Ann York Franklin, 1996), 98–99; White and Runion, eds., *Great Things,* 47; Rugely, ed., *Batchelor-Turner Letters,* n.p., www.terrystexasrangers.org; Williams and Wooster, eds., "With Terry's Texas Rangers," 314.

43. Rosecrans to Wright, Jan. 6, 1863, Rosecrans to Stanton, Jan. 11, 1863, *OR,* vol. 20, pt. 2, 303, 317; Peterson to his folks, Jan. 10, 1863, Elisha A. Peterson Papers, Rare Books, Manuscript, and Special Collections, Duke University; Culbertson to his wife, Jan. 7, 1863, William Culbertson Papers, Rare Books, Manuscript, and Special Collections, Duke University; Fisher to John Ward, Jan. 10, 1863, Horace Newton Fisher Papers, Massachusetts Historical Society; Jacques Martin to his mother and brother, Jan. 9, 11, 1863, 6th Ohio Regimental File, Stones River National Battlefield; Samuel A. McClelland to his cousin, Jan. 25, 1863, 78th Pennsylvania Regimental File, Stones River National Battlefield; Hurd to his brother, Feb. 10, 1863, Benjamin Hurd Letters, W. S. Hoole Special Collections Library, University of Alabama; Robert Mitchell to Munn, Feb. 22, 1863, Briggs-Mitchell Family Papers, Chicago History Museum; Amos E. Wood to Robert, Feb. 18, 1863, Robert H. Caldwell Papers, Rutherford B. Hayes Presidential Center; McGregor to Wiley, Feb. 9, 1863, William McGregor Papers, Pearce Civil War Collection, Navarro College; John E. Lane to Ellen Crist, Feb. 9, 1863, Crist Manuscripts. Lilly Library, Indiana University; R. Lockwood Tower, ed., *A Carolinian Goes to War: The Civil War Narrative of Arthur Middleton Manigault, Brigadier General, C.S.A.* (Columbia: Univ. of South Carolina Press, 1983), 58; Walter Gibson Peter to his sister, May 12, 1863, Peter Family Papers, Special Collections, University of Virginia.

44. Wood to Garfield, Apr. 6, 1863, *OR,* vol. 23, pt. 2, 213.

45. Sears, *Chancellorsville,* 272–300.

46. Albert Castel, *Decision in the West: The Atlanta Campaign of 1864* (Lawrence: Univ. Press of Kansas, 1992), 191–95, 208, 258–60, 283–85, 333–34, 337–38, 363–65. For a good summary of newspaper attacks on Bragg, and Bragg's attacks on his generals after the battle, see Daniel, *Stones River,* 204–10.

47. Nathaniel C. Hughes, ed., *Liddell's Record: St. John Richardson Liddell* (Dayton, Ohio: Morningside, 1985), 116–17.

Mutual Antagonists

Braxton Bragg, Frank Cheatham, and the Army of Tennessee

Christopher Losson

An army specifically and the military in general represent unique subcultures in American society with institutional goals that derive from national interests. Yet as an institution, an army is subject to the entire varied features attendant to any other such entity, including an individual family. As a hierarchical body there is an army commander, subject to civilian control. In the Confederacy this meant that President Jefferson Davis had considerable authority over military matters, exercised through a secretary of war and with the advice and consent of the Confederate Congress. In turn, individual army commanders led a body that included high-ranking subordinates, such as corps, division, and brigade leaders and that extended down to the rank and file. Any institution is subject to pressures and stress related to its nature, the personnel involved, and its relative success or failure. In a crisis, pressure ratchets up. The Confederate Army of Tennessee, the main fighting force in the Western Theater, had more than its share of crises. The commander of the army for much of the war, Braxton Bragg, proved to be a controversial and polarizing leader. One of Bragg's primary tormentors was Benjamin Franklin Cheatham, habitually referred to as "Frank" by his family, friends, and soldiers. Cheatham, in command of a division, eventually came to loath Bragg, a hostility that was fully reciprocated. The rancor undeniably contributed to tension within the officer corps of the army. It also undermined efficiency and the potential success of the force on and off the battlefield. Bragg and Cheatham both behaved badly toward one another even though both undoubtedly shared the goal of winning independence for the Confederacy. An examination of the relationship between the two men reveals that their mutual antipathy resulted from very human emotions and responses. Their friction derived from poor initial impressions, Bragg's health, mutual frustration, slights (both real and perceived), infighting among the high command, and unwillingness to shoulder blame for individual or collective failures.

It should be noted at the outset that this was not a contest between equals. Bragg bore far more responsibility and exercised more power than Cheatham. To characterize this as a one-sided contest is inaccurate, however, since Cheatham possessed allies within and outside the army that helped thwart Bragg's efforts against him. The two men arrived at their Civil War destinations from somewhat different routes. Bragg was born in 1817 in North Carolina, graduated fifth in the West Point class of 1837, and served in the Seminole Wars, where health problems first appeared that would plague him for the remainder of his life. Bragg served with distinction in the Mexican War, winning two brevet promotions and managing his battery adroitly at Buena Vista. That he was a formidable disciplinarian may explain why two attempts on his life were made by soldiers under his command in Mexico; in each case a shell exploded in his tent, but Bragg avoided injury. Bragg continued in the army, where he acquired a reputation for quarreling with superiors and subordinates alike, until he resigned in 1856 to manage a Louisiana sugar plantation. This was occasioned by Bragg's marriage earlier to Eliza (Elise) Brooks Ellis, a wealthy Louisiana resident whose fortune allowed Bragg to purchase the plantation.[1]

When Louisiana seceded in January 1861, Bragg was placed in command of the state's forces. Two months later, Jefferson Davis appointed Bragg a brigadier general in Confederate service. Sent to Pensacola, Bragg labored energetically to drill and train the volunteers assembled there. His efforts won the approval of Davis, who promoted Bragg to major general in September and shortly thereafter assigned him command of Alabama and western Florida. Following the disastrous collapse of the Confederate line in Kentucky and evacuation of Nashville in early 1862, Bragg was ordered with his troops to join Albert Sidney Johnston's force at Corinth, Mississippi. During the Battle of Shiloh on April 6, Bragg served as chief of staff and commanded the Second Corps, which was heavily engaged against Federal forces in the center of the battlefield. Later in the day he directed piecemeal attacks against the Hornets' Nest. By late afternoon, Johnston was dead and successor P. G. T. Beauregard suspended operations for the day, a move Bragg believed cost the Confederates a victory. The next day a reinforced Federal army under Ulysses S. Grant counterattacked and

Benjamin Franklin Cheatham. (Library of Congress)

compelled Beauregard to initiate a withdrawal to Corinth. Beauregard and Davis had clashed previously over military affairs, and when Davis heard that Beauregard had taken an unauthorized leave of absence for health reasons, he promptly made a change in command. Beauregard's replacement was Bragg, who was on far friendlier terms with Davis, and Bragg secured promotion to full general on April 12, 1862. He thus became the fifth ranking officer in Confederate service. Bragg also now commanded the entire army, where one of his subordinate officers was Frank Cheatham.[2]

Benjamin Franklin Cheatham was born in 1820 on a plantation near Nashville. He was descended on his maternal side from James Robertson, the founder of Nashville and a key figure in early Tennessee history. He was educated successively by a tutor, a Princeton graduate at a school in Nashville, and at a college in Kentucky. He apparently never completed his formal education, probably due to family financial difficulties, and worked in Philadelphia for a time in a dry goods store. Upon returning to Nashville he joined the Nashville Blues, a local militia company. War with Mexico afforded the Blues an opportunity for actual military service, and they became part of the 1st Tennessee Regiment. Cheatham was a captain in the regiment, which was attached to Gen. Zachary Taylor's army in northern Mexico. He distinguished himself during the attack on Monterrey in September 1846 and participated in the siege of Veracruz. When Gen. Winfield Scott decided to release volunteers near the end of their twelve-month enlistment, Cheatham returned to Nashville along with fellow survivors of the Blues. During the fall of 1847 he energetically recruited a new regiment that would serve for the duration of the war. The 3rd Tennessee Regiment, with Cheatham as its colonel, arrived in Mexico in mid-November. It saw little action, but did arrive in Mexico City in mid-January 1848, when a deadly measles outbreak swept through the regiment. Against this sad backdrop, the remaining members of the regiment returned home.[3]

Cheatham participated in the California Gold Rush and upon his return to Tennessee he farmed, narrowly lost a bid to become Nashville's mayor, and served briefly as proprietor of the Nashville Race Track. Upon Tennessee's secession he was appointed a brigadier general in the Provisional Army of Tennessee by Gov. Isham Harris. Cheatham set about helping to organize and train the thousands of recruits flocking to the colors. He was stationed for several weeks at Camp Brown, in Union City in West Tennessee. When the Confederate government accepted the Provisional Army's transfer into Confederate service, Cheatham was appointed a brigadier general, to date from July 9, 1861. He was part of a Confederate force that entered Kentucky that September, shattering Kentucky's tenuous neutrality. He and his men moved to Columbus, on the Mississippi River, and made plans to repel any Federal invasion down that waterway. This occurred on November 7, 1861, when a Union force led by Ulysses S. Grant landed near Belmont, on the Missouri shore opposite Columbus. Cheatham steamed across the Mississippi with reinforcements and helped lead a counterattack that drove the Federals back to their transports.[4]

When Federal army and naval units moved along the Cumberland and Tennessee rivers in early 1862, the Confederate position at Columbus became untenable. They fell back to Corinth as much of Middle Tennessee came under Union control. Despite the reversal, Cheatham's own fortunes rose when he won promotion to major general, largely due to the influence and prodding of Tennessee Sen. Gustavus A. Henry. The appointment was made on March 14, but was backdated four days to the same date that Henry dispatched a letter to Jefferson Davis, urging Cheatham's promotion.[5] He was assigned command of two brigades and two artillery batteries. At Shiloh his brigade went into action under the command of Gen. Leonidas Polk, a West Point classmate of Jefferson Davis who had eschewed a military career for an ecclesiastical one. When the war began, Davis asked Polk to don a uniform again and Polk left behind his post as Episcopal bishop of Louisiana to serve the Confederacy. Early during the engagement, Cheatham's two brigades were dispatched to different areas on the battlefield. Cheatham accompanied his 2d Brigade to the far right, where they took part in assaults against the Hornets' Nest. After it was finally subdued, Cheatham began collecting a variety of intermingled units toward the Tennessee River when Beauregard halted further operations. Cheatham took portions of his division three miles to the rear and they moved forward the next day and collided with Federal forces. They fought for several hours before being driven back; ultimately they disengaged and joined the remainder of the army in its retreat to Corinth.[6]

Beauregard's removal and Bragg's ascent inevitably altered relations between Bragg and Cheatham. Prior to Beauregard's dismissal, Bragg held superior rank over Cheatham, but since he was not Cheatham's corps commander, they did not necessarily have many dealings. That necessarily changed after Bragg's promotion. He naturally wished to put his own stamp on the army, and Bragg provided two vital qualities the army needed: discipline and organization. In the weeks after Shiloh, he worked assiduously to shape the army into a trained, well-ordered fighting force. As part of this process, Bragg sought to replace officers he deemed unworthy and install men he felt were better suited for command.[7] This is analogous to any situation in which a new executive (for example, a collegiate or professional football coach) seeks to appoint individuals they feel best meet the needs of the organization. What complicated matters in a Civil War army was that the individuals already appointed to their positions and approved by Congress were not as easy to remove as, say, a previous coaching staff.

Bragg's efforts focused on Polk's Corps to some extent because his initial impressions upon seeing the troops who came from Columbus were quite negative. Bragg described them as "a mob" and decried their lack of discipline. He obviously compared them unfavorably to the troops he had trained in Florida and brought to Corinth. Leonidas Polk also aroused Bragg's enmity, in large measure because Bragg firmly believed that Polk lacked the qualities required of a corps commander. Bragg perhaps reasonably surmised that a man who had never actually utilized his West Point education in military service was a novice, albeit a high-ranking one. He once characterized Polk as "an old woman, utterly worthless." This was not an opinion shared by Jefferson Davis, with the result that Bragg's machinations against Polk ran into opposition in Richmond.[8] If securing Polk's removal proved problematic, Bragg evidently felt more secure in seeking replacements lower in the officer corps. After arguing that only William J. Hardee was a suitable major general, Bragg alleged that the army possessed a number of "dead-weight" officers who were "only encumbrances and would be better out of the way." When War Department officials queried Bragg about these officers, he specifically named three major generals: Cheatham, George Crittenden, and John McCown, and three brigadiers: William H. Carroll, James M. Hawes, and James H. Trapier.[9]

Bragg did not specify what his objections to these officers were or why he wanted them replaced. Some of them had a reputation for imbibing alcohol frequently. Both Carroll and Crittenden were charged with drunkenness and arrested by Hardee, acting on Bragg's orders. Carroll was also charged with incompetence and neglect of his regiment. Both left the army, as did Hawes and Trapier. The two men who remained were Cheatham and McCown. Assuming that alcohol was at least a partial reason for Bragg's desire to remove these six particular officers, his campaign was relatively successful.[10] Evidence proves that Cheatham did drink to excess on occasion and if Bragg viewed him as a habitual drinker, it is logical that he would want him removed from divisional command. But Cheatham was not as easily reassigned or relegated elsewhere as the four whose removal Bragg won. He had the protection of Polk, for one thing. Although they were certainly dissimilar in many ways (for instance, Cheatham did not formally join a religious denomination until after the war), both men bonded together, perhaps because each possessed qualities that the other admired. Both must have become aware very early of Bragg's antipathy, an issue that would naturally draw them together. And Cheatham had powerful allies among Tennessee's politicians, including Governor Harris, Senator Henry, and Congressman Henry S. Foote. To remove him would potentially inspire angry protests to Davis and the War Department.[11]

Another factor was a growing appreciation of Cheatham by his men, who were conscious of his solicitude on their behalf and his willingness to share battlefield risks with them. The Tennessee connection undoubtedly contributed to the bond between Cheatham and the men in his division. Cheatham was approachable, so much so that occasionally soldiers asked things of him that they "hesitated to ask . . . of their regimental commanders." His somewhat unpolished demeanor, his penchant for cursing, a good horse, and the occasional bottle all served to humanize Cheatham to his

Braxton Bragg. (Library of Congress)

men. As their tenure together lengthened, the tie connecting Cheatham and his soldiers likewise deepened. "Why, old Frank is one of the boys," some of Cheatham's men told a woman who had known him in antebellum Nashville, adding that they would "go anywhere old Frank orders us, even were it in the cannon's mouth." As the war continued, this meant that any of Bragg's efforts against Cheatham would trigger massive discontent among many of the officers and men in his division.[12]

From Bragg's perspective, failure to oust Polk, Cheatham, and McCown meant that he was compelled to work with subordinates he found objectionable. He was by no means the only Civil War army leader on either side who faced this obstacle, but his reluctance to put much trust in these officers was a logical by-product. In an ideal world, everyone involved in this scenario would have realized that their fortunes were harnessed together, would have sought to bury the collective hatchet, and begun cooperating. That never happened. Instead, things worsened. During the summer and fall of 1862, Bragg initiated a boldly conceived invasion of Kentucky. The army transferred from its base in Tupelo and took varying paths through Alabama before coalescing in Chattanooga. From there it moved over the Cumberland Plateau and into Kentucky. The army progressed steadily as Bragg sought a rendezvous with a smaller army already in Kentucky under the command of Gen. Edmund Kirby Smith. Bragg subdued a Federal garrison on the Green River at Munfordville in mid-September, and then took a portion of his army to Frankfort, where an inauguration of Richard Hawes as Confederate governor of Kentucky took place. Polk and Cheatham were at Bardstown, and reports of a growing concentration of Federal troops near there convinced Polk to convene a meeting of his top officers. They assented in his decision to ignore Bragg's order to move to Frankfort and Polk instead retreated east to Harrodsburg.[13]

In similar fashion, when Polk and a portion of the Army of the Mississippi were at Perryville with orders to attack an allegedly inferior force, Polk grew uneasy. He again convened a council of war, and Cheatham and other officers supported his intention to take a "defensive-offensive" stance until the size of the enemy's force could be ascertained. Polk did not inform his commander of this plan, and only when Bragg arrived around 10 A.M. on October 8 did Polk explain his refusal to obey orders.[14] Clearly frustrated, Bragg waited out a number of troop movements, including a shift of Cheatham's division from the left to the right of the Confederate line. Cheatham's three available brigades launched the attack around 2 P.M., and the fighting that ensued near Perryville was indescribably savage. Many of Cheatham's veterans later believed Perryville was their most severe battle during the entire war, and with good reason. His division bore the brunt of the fighting and suffered ghastly casualties. Before they were finally checked, they drove the Federal line back twelve hundred yards, compressed three Union lines into one, and shattered much of Alexander McCook's corps. They had won a decided tactical victory, but when McCook's captured papers were inspected at Bragg's headquarters, it was revealed that the Federals possessed well over three times as many men as the Confederates. Bragg gathered with his top officers early the next morning and informed them of the situation. They agreed that an immediate withdrawal was in order. Leaving behind their dead and many of their wounded comrades, Cheatham's survivors accompanied the remainder of the army to Harrodsburg, where both Bragg and Buell declined to renew the fight. Confederate officers from Kentucky were furious at Bragg's decision to abandon the campaign, but he squelched their objections and began an arduous movement through the mountains back into Tennessee.[15]

The dispiriting retreat from Kentucky aroused criticism of Bragg from within and outside the army. In his defense, drought conditions in central Kentucky had impeded efforts to forage effectively. Winter was coming on and much of Buell's army had not been engaged at Perryville. Confederate reversals in Maryland and Mississippi dampened hopes of success elsewhere and no reinforcements were coming to join Bragg. Rumors surfaced of a Union column coming down from Ohio. And Bragg was not alone in lamenting the lack of direct support from Kentuckians. Although the Confederates had been greeted warmly in portions of the Bluegrass State, few Kentucky males flocked to enlist. Yet little of this mattered to Bragg's critics. Jefferson Davis summoned Bragg for a visit to Richmond to discuss the campaign. Bragg denounced a number of his chief subordinates, especially Polk. Polk and Kirby Smith then made their way to Richmond, where they loudly complained about Bragg and urged that he be replaced. Davis, in the unenviable position of hearing several personal friends bitterly rail against one other, opted to retain Bragg in command.[16]

Sustained by the president, Bragg had secured Davis's permission to shift his army into Middle Tennessee. Before doing so, he reorganized his force and renamed it the Army of Tennessee. Bragg concentrated his force in the Stones River valley, near Murfreesboro, some thirty miles southeast of Nashville. Don Carlos Buell's dilatory pursuit of Bragg's army during the retreat from Kentucky had earned him the enmity of officials in Washington, including Abraham Lincoln, and he was replaced by William Rosecrans. Not content to allow Bragg to encamp so close to Nashville, Rosecrans brought a large army out of the capital in late December to challenge the Confederates. After some initial sparring, a major battle erupted on the last day of the year. Polk commanded the left wing of the army and placed Cheatham in charge of units from his own division and those belonging to fellow division commander Jones Withers. Bragg's plan called for attacks to be made against the Union right in succession, with Confederate brigades wheeling from left to right as they advanced. Things went awry almost from the outset as the lead brigade failed to wheel properly. Cheatham and Withers were both late in sending units forward, with the result that casualties mounted. By dint of hard fighting the rebels drove the Federals back, but their momentum was blunted by stout resistance in a four-acre area called the Round Forest.[17]

Cheatham's subpar performance was evidently influenced by a drinking spree; one source related that he fell off his horse while doffing his hat in an effort to encourage his troops. A Federal soldier captured at a house being used as a hospital saw both Hardee and Cheatham and judged the latter to be intoxicated. A soldier in one of Cheatham's Tennessee regiments added a brief two-word addition at the end of his diary entry: "Cheatham drunk."[18] These assessments conflict with other accounts by soldiers who saw Cheatham wielding his sword and personally leading attacks during the battle, and it is nearly impossible to reconcile the opposing viewpoints.[19] It is doubtful if Cheatham could have behaved in such a manner if he were staggeringly drunk, yet evidence certainly suggests that he was inebriated to some extent early in the day. If word reached Bragg during the battle of Cheatham's intoxication, he did not take action or remove him from command. New Year's Day passed relatively quietly, but the next day Bragg sent John C. Breckinridge's division forward against Federals ensconced on a ridge on the eastern side of Stones River. After some initial success, massed Union artillery tore huge holes in Breckinridge's ranks, and his men broke and streamed down the hill. Alarmed by the repulse, Bragg transferred a number of divisions to the eastern side of the river. As rain and sleet fell during the night, Cheatham and Withers were worried that their divisions would be isolated on the western bank of the steadily rising river. The two met, conferred, and drafted a letter to Bragg asserting that only three reliable brigades remained. They encouraged a withdrawal. The note went to Polk, who endorsed the advice. Although Bragg rejected the recommendation when awakened, he reversed himself during the day when he became convinced that Rosecrans had a larger force than first anticipated. As at Shiloh and Perryville, the Confederate Army had seized an initial advantage only to wind up retreating. Bragg got his army moving southward, first to Shelbyville and then to Tullahoma.[20]

In the aftermath of the withdrawal, the already strained relationship between Bragg and several of his subordinates deteriorated. Pressure built from the outside as Tennessee politicians, civilians, and newspapers criticized Bragg. The *Chattanooga Daily Rebel* falsely claimed that the retreat had been made against the advice of his subordinates, a charge that stung Bragg. He read the offending article to his staff members and then drafted a circular letter to his corps and divisional commanders. Bragg originally asked his subordinates to tell whether they had advised him to retreat. For corroboration, he enclosed copies of the note sent by Cheatham and Withers, along with Polk's endorsement. Bragg then added that Edmund Kirby Smith had been summoned to Richmond and believed that Smith would be appointed to supersede him in command. Perhaps to win support, Bragg then promised to "retire without a regret" if he had "lost the good opinion of my

Generals upon whom I have ever relied as upon a foundation of rock." If intended to shore up his support within the high command, Bragg's circular backfired dramatically. William J. Hardee, John C. Breckinridge, and Patrick Cleburne, of Hardee's Corps, all asserted that Bragg no longer held the trust of the army and should resign. Even Bragg's own staff had come to that conclusion in an earlier meeting.[21]

Polk was absent when the circular was first delivered, and Cheatham and Withers decided to wait for his return before replying. Cheatham did acknowledge that he was one of the first to recommend a withdrawal, but did not respond to Bragg's offer to resign. After Polk read the circular, he asked Bragg for clarification: Were there two questions in the circular? He certainly thought so, but "this indication seems not to have been so clear to the mind of General Cheatham and such other of my subordinate officers as responded." Bragg by now fully realized his error in asking his subordinates for their opinion regarding his fitness for command. He hastened to tell Polk that he was interested in just the decision to retreat from Murfreesboro, and Polk maintained that his endorsement to the note by Cheatham and Withers had been "deliberately considered" and he would give the same advice in similar circumstances.[22]

Cheatham and Polk were not so naive that they did not understand that there were indeed two questions in Bragg's circular. They obviously shared the same reservations as the officers who urged Bragg to resign, and their refusal to be candid with him was contemptible. Officers in Hardee's Corps heard of the evasive response by Polk and justifiably felt betrayed. John McCown bitterly wrote that Cheatham "said one thing behind Genl. Bragg's back and wrote him a totally different thing." Polk had a habit of stirring things up and then dodging responsibility, which he certainly exhibited in this instance. For men such as Cheatham and Polk, who had early on earned Bragg's scorn, failure to add their criticism smacks of cowardice. The best possible explanation for their uncharacteristic reluctance to blast Bragg was knowledge that word of Cheatham's intemperance on December 31 had reached Bragg. By refusing to add their voices to the chorus condemning Bragg, perhaps this could be glossed over. If this was their intent, it exploded in their faces as badly as Bragg's ill-advised query in his circular.[23]

Bragg first wrote Jefferson Davis in mid-January, explaining the reasons for the retreat from Murfreesboro and predicting that pressure would be brought on Davis to remove him from command. He lamented that he was attacked "as no man ever was, probably, except yourself," and complained that he was the victim of false rumors and reports by "newsmongers."[24]

Bragg then turned on his foes within the army. When Bragg wrote his official report of the battle, he pointedly omitted Cheatham's name off the long list of officers he commended for their parts in the engagement. This unleashed a furor in Polk's corps, and Cheatham's Tennesseans in particular felt that their considerable sacrifices had been deliberately snubbed by Bragg. They rallied around Cheatham. One of Polk's confidants wrote that the "Tennesseans could stand him pitching into McCown, but not Cheatham." The turmoil spread to Richmond, where Cheatham supporters in the Tennessee delegation railed against Bragg's report. An irate Cheatham met with Gov. Isham Harris and threatened to resign. Joseph E. Johnston conveyed this news to President Davis, but added that Harris was confident that he could "bring [Cheatham] to his senses." From Bragg's perspective, he may have supposed that he was letting Cheatham off lightly; after all, a major general drunk as a battle began was reason enough for immediate removal. To commend Cheatham would be construed as overlooking his delinquency; on the other hand, his refusal to do so generated enormous hostility in Cheatham's division. After all, some of them had seen Cheatham in action that day and were inspired by him. More significantly, snubbing Cheatham meant that the bravery exhibited by his soldiers was likewise ignored. Had Bragg praised Cheatham's regimental or brigade commanders without mentioning him specifically, perhaps some of this rancor could have been avoided, but Bragg probably was in no mood for this conciliatory gesture when he penned his report.[25]

Receipt of Polk's official report on the battle compelled Bragg to write Richmond and report on Cheatham's inebriation the first day at Murfreesboro. On April 9, 1863, Bragg wrote a response to Polk's report, which was dated March 21. Polk's account lauded both Cheatham and Withers for "their cordial support and co-operation" during the battle. Bragg objected to this praise of Cheatham, especially since Polk had conceded learning of Cheatham's intoxication. Polk assured Bragg that he had verbally admonished Cheatham, but Bragg insisted on a written censure. If that was ever written, no evidence of it has surfaced. Bragg had agreed to overlook Cheatham's intemperance only in light "of his previous distinguished services" and felt, probably correctly, that he was quite magnanimous in not bringing Cheatham up on charges. Why Bragg did not do so is something of a mystery, since he certainly felt evidence existed to prove his allegations. After all, he had wanted to get rid of Cheatham at the beginning of his command tenure. He may have been unwilling to risk the backlash that would inevitably arise in Cheatham's division had he attempted to oust the popular Tennessean. But Polk's report might inspire questions as to why Bragg did not similarly praise Cheatham in his own official report, and Bragg thereupon wrote Richmond to justify his omission. From the Confederate government's viewpoint, this was another flash point from an army where perpetual discord seemed to prevail. Secretary of War James Seddon regarded Bragg's letter as "very unfortunate" and recommended that "a court of inquiry should I suppose be ordered" when he forwarded the letter to Jefferson Davis. No evidence exists to suggest that such a court was ever convened to investigate the allegations against Cheatham, and he remained in charge of his division.[26]

Bragg next sought to open up the Kentucky campaign. He specifically objected to Polk's report, which failed to discuss Polk's meetings at Bardstown and Perryville. On both occasions Polk had won support from his junior officers to disobey Bragg's orders. Bragg sent out another circular to his officers, asked them about their role in the councils, and hinted that Polk would be held liable for his disobedience. Officers such as Cheatham were placed in an uncomfortable position since if Polk was convicted of disobedience, they, too, were culpable. Polk and Hardee did not respond, Cheatham curtly refused to answer the circular, and other officers hedged in their responses. It was the second time that a Bragg message had backed many of his officers into a corner, and the matter dragged on through April and May 1863 without a clear resolution.[27]

The Army of Tennessee's stay along the Duck River line at Tullahoma ended abruptly when William Rosecrans initiated a movement in June 1863 designed to deliver East Tennessee from Confederate control. By brilliant maneuvering, Rosecrans compelled Bragg to evacuate Tullahoma and move to Chattanooga. Persistent Federal threats convinced Bragg that Chattanooga could not be held and he retreated farther south, into northern Georgia. Mountainous terrain near Chattanooga presented challenges for both commanders, but Bragg had difficulty discerning where the enemy might appear. He did make two abortive attempts to strike isolated elements of the large Federal army on both September 11 and 13, but both efforts were botched. Justifiably frustrated by his army's inability to fall on portions of the enemy's host, Bragg retreated to Lafayette. Rosecrans finally deduced that the Confederates had not withdrawn farther south and united his army along the banks of Chickamauga Creek. A ferocious two-day battle began on September 19 as Bragg sought to strike the Union left flank. Bragg was unaware that Rosecrans had lengthened his line during the night, so when the rebels surged forward early in the morning, they ran headlong into Federal infantry. The ensuing fighting involved Cheatham's division, the largest in Bragg's army, which clashed with elements of six Federal divisions. Many of his regiments suffered heavily and one of his brigadiers, Preston Smith, was killed during a night attack when he rode into a detachment from a Pennsylvania regiment. The day's fighting consisted of piecemeal assaults that failed to crush the Union left, and one of Cheatham's men lamented in his diary that "Our men have suffered awful today and gained nothing."[28]

Fighting the next day took a decisive turn. Pressure on the Union left resulted in Rosecrans shifting troops from other parts of his line, and a Federal divisional commander pulled his units out of position, leaving a gaping hole in the line. Soon afterwards men from James Longstreet's Corps of the Army of Northern Virginia poured into the quarter-mile-wide opening, splintering the line and compelling Rosecrans to flee toward Chattanooga, along with much of his army. Only George Thomas's stout resistance along Snodgrass Hill prevented the rout from being complete, and after dark he quietly disengaged and made for Chattanooga as well. Chickamauga was the one great victory achieved by the Army of Tennessee, and when night fell on September 20, they were in the unfamiliar position of controlling the battlefield. Bragg was initially unconvinced, apparently upset that his original plan to overlap the Union left had gone awry. On September 22 Cheatham moved with his troops to Missionary Ridge, overlooking Chattanooga, and as his men ascended the rise, Federal defenders made little resistance and bolted. Cheatham surveyed the scene atop the summit and reported to his superiors that the only Yankee troops he saw had fled into the city.[29]

Victory at Chickamauga should have resulted in improved harmony within the officer ranks and strategy sessions on how to follow up the triumph. The exact opposite occurred. Bragg first attacked Thomas Hindman, who was blamed for not snaring Federals in one of the pre-Chickamauga efforts to smite isolated Union corps. The next target was Polk, whom Bragg blamed for not attacking at daybreak on September 20. Both were suspended and ordered to report to Atlanta. Polk immediately fired off several letters to President Davis and implored him to replace Bragg. He also wrote Robert E. Lee. In Polk's absence, James Longstreet became a leader in the anti-Bragg faction and orchestrated a circular that suggested that Bragg's ill health was grounds for his removal. Cheatham did not sign the circular, but twelve other officers did so. He did rally to Polk's defense, arguing that he had seen Polk at one of his batteries at sunrise on the second day of the battle. As the days and weeks elapsed, no plan emerged from headquarters on how to exploit the Chickamauga success. One of Cheatham's soldiers bitterly noted that Chickamauga was "the only good thing we have had during the war and through Bragg's imbecility we have thrown it away."[30]

Jefferson Davis decided that his personal intervention might calm the troubles swirling through the Army of Tennessee. He met with Polk en route to the army and heard him label Bragg an incompetent. Polk implored Davis to remove Bragg. On the night of October 9, Davis met with Bragg and his four corps commanders. Longstreet, Hill, and Simon Bolivar Buckner represented their own corps, while Cheatham sat in as temporary commander of Polk's corps. Davis asked the generals to state their views with regard to Bragg, perhaps assuming that they would be reluctant to criticize Bragg openly in such a forum. This proved untrue, and one by one the four generals recommended that Bragg be relieved from command. This must have been exceedingly awkward for everyone concerned, but Bragg had an ace in the hole. Even before the conclave, Davis had assured Bragg that he would be retained. Davis did gain Bragg's agreement to drop the charges against Polk when it was decided that Polk would transfer elsewhere. One general overheard Davis say that the fury against Bragg was "wholly wrong and . . . would eventually be the cause of disaster to that army." The officer urged Bragg to mend fences with his subordinates, but despaired of ever getting the antagonists to cooperate.[31]

Turmoil in the upper echelons became common knowledge among the rank and file and generated extensive comment. Many of Cheatham's veterans assailed Bragg and wanted him removed. An undeterred Bragg added more targets, among them generals D. H. Hill and John C. Breckinridge. Nathan Bedford Forrest left after a heated row with Bragg. Leonidas Polk had unwaveringly supported Cheatham in his dealings with Bragg, and with the bishop gone, Frank Cheatham decided he had had enough of serving under Braxton Bragg. On October 31, 1863, he made a formal request to be relieved from duty with the Army of Tennessee and asked that he be allowed to report to the secretary of war in Richmond. He thereupon took a leave of absence from the army. One of Cheatham's soldiers had noted darkly in his diary that "Should Bragg cause Cheatham to be removed half the Tennesseans will go home or [seek] some other arm of service." He also lamented the absence of Polk, who was "beloved by his troops and was the idol of our Div[ision]."[32]

Where Cheatham went after submitting his resignation is unknown, but it may have been to Atlanta, where he could commiserate with Polk and visit his sister, Martha. Richmond authorities rejected Cheatham's request. Adjutant and Inspector-General Samuel Cooper could not think of another command to which Cheatham could be assigned "consistent with his rank." Secretary of War James Seddon disapproved Cheatham's request and noted that he was opposed to "relieving any valuable and experienced offer in command because of personal dissatisfaction." He appealed to Cheatham's patriotism and urged him to give his "full support to any commanding general placed over [him]." Cheatham, unable to secure a position away from Bragg, returned to the army in late November, just as the Federals were prepared to drive the Confederates away from Chattanooga.[33] When Cheatham returned, he discovered that Bragg had thoroughly reorganized it. His division, comprised of almost all Tennessee units, was broken up. His new command was considerably smaller than his old division. He retained only six of his twenty-three Tennessee regiments, and those were under Marcus Wright, a Bragg loyalist. James Longstreet sought to mollify Cheatham by telling him that President Davis had suggested the change, since heavy casualties in a battle could cause enormous distress in one locale. Other army insiders recognized a different rationale for the reorganization. One opined that Breckinridge's and Cheatham's divisions were deliberately broken up to "break up cliques for political purposes" and to "keep down the anti-Bragg men."[34]

Cheatham arrived back with the army just in time to witness a massive Federal assault on November 24 against Confederates on the face of Lookout Mountain overlooking Chattanooga. A dense fog shrouded enemy movements and gave rebel defenders little time to react when Federals suddenly appeared. Although men under Edward C. Walthall tried valiantly to fend off their foes, his brigade lost an astonishing 972 men, of which 853 were listed as missing when Walthall made his report. Cheatham arrived during the night, just in time to see Confederates withdraw from the top of the mountain. Cheatham assumed command and Bragg ordered him to begin transferring troops from Lookout Mountain to Missionary Ridge. The next day Union efforts were beaten back on the right side of the Confederate line, but then soldiers from the Army of the Cumberland began clambering up the ridge. One breakthrough occurred but a few yards to Cheatham's left, and he urgently shifted troops to check the onrushing Yankees. These efforts succeeded and Walthall's depleted brigade, along with two of Cheatham's other brigades, held their ground until nightfall, when they began withdrawing down the ridge.[35]

Lookout Mountain and Missionary Ridge were unmitigated disasters, and Bragg at last wrote Richmond and asked to be relieved. The request was approved the following day and Hardee was placed in temporary command. While Bragg recognized that the battles around Chattanooga reflected badly on him, he was determined to share the blame. He fired off a letter to Davis lamenting the delinquencies of several of his commanders. Among his targets was Breckinridge, whom he accused of drunkenness for five days spanning the battles, and Cheatham. He claimed that Hardee would "assure you that Cheatham is equally dangerous," although this probably refers to his intemperance at Murfreesboro. Cheatham was undoubtedly one of the men whom Bragg referred to when he wrote that he could "bear to be sacrificed myself, but not to see my country and my friends ruined by the vices of a few profligate men who happen to have an undue popularity."[36] Although Cheatham had undeniably fought gallantly on Missionary Ridge, Bragg's report in the *Official Records* pointedly omits any mention of him. Even after he left the army, Bragg railed against Cheatham to several officers. His enmity remained intact well into the postwar era. In an 1873 letter, Bragg scathingly wrote that "In France or Germany, either [Cheatham or Breckinridge] would have been shot in six hours. With us they pass for heroes." He lambasted Cheatham and other critics as "imbeciles, traitors, rogues, and intriguing politicians."[37]

Jefferson Davis summoned Bragg to Richmond and appointed him as a military advisor. Cheatham almost assuredly doubted the wisdom of that move, but at least he no longer had Bragg to contend with as army commander. When Joseph E. Johnston took charge, he reorganized the army, and one of his acts was to restore Cheatham's Tennessee division. Doing so brought tremendous satisfaction to both Cheatham and his men and inspired in many of them a lifelong devotion to "Old Joe."[38] Yet Bragg could still criticize Cheatham and other members of the anti-Bragg bloc. In January 1864, much of the army's high command convened at the request of General Hardee to discuss a growing manpower shortage. At the meeting, Patrick Cleburne read a paper proposing that the army enroll slaves, a move that would not only augment numbers but would win support from Europe and reverberate politically in the North. As an inducement, Cleburne offered a guarantee that their service for the Confederacy would result in emancipation for themselves and their families. Many of the assembled officers were shocked at the proposal, which struck at the very heart of Southern society. A number of them gathered information and requested the opinion of men such as Cheatham, who had not attended the meeting. Cheatham received such a note from W. H. T. Walker on January 9 and testily declined to answer. That was enough to convict Cheatham in the eyes of the emancipation proposal's opponents, and his name was freely linked with Cleburne's supporters. When Bragg heard of the paper, he recognized that it could erode the influence of many of his longtime enemies. "It will kill them," he exulted to one officer. The proposal was suppressed at the insistence of President Davis, but it revealed tellingly the split among the Army of Tennessee's high command. Most of Cleburne's supporters were members of the anti-Bragg faction, while its vociferous critics had tended to support him. Even in Bragg's absence, the distrust generated by contradictory opinions between Bragg partisans and detractors influenced army politics and relationships.[39]

Too often overlooked in the debate over Bragg's abilities is the fact that he did have men who supported him, felt aggrieved when he was removed, and expressed their appreciation of him after the war. Generals such as Patton Anderson, William B. Bate, A. P. Stewart, W. H. T. Walker, Jones Withers, Marcus J. Wright, and others never joined in the maneuvering to oust Bragg. With high-ranking officers split over Bragg's fitness for command, two camps emerged. One, of which Cheatham was a prominent member, regarded Bragg with hostility and sought to undermine him. The other bloc felt that Bragg was being pilloried by a group of malcontents. This fundamental split inevitably created tension and dissension within the officer corps, and men who should have been more interested in fighting the Federals spent much of their time antagonizing one another. It is impossible to quantify to what extent this influenced events on the battlefield, but certainly it made for a tense atmosphere at the army's highest levels.

What of Bragg and Cheatham? Even Bragg's critics conceded that he was wholeheartedly devoted to the cause and worked tirelessly as commander. In fact, his staff worried in the summer of 1863 that his health was giving way. He had been entrusted by Jefferson Davis with command of the army after Beauregard's removal and felt duty bound to do all he could to justify Davis's faith. But most historians agree that Bragg was not the best choice for the position. He was probably better suited to be a subordinate or in an administrative post rather than the commander of a large army. For one thing, his chronic and serious health problems, which included boils, migraine headaches, dyspepsia, and other ailments, impaired his ability to lead. They naturally soured his disposition and made him cranky. His sense of duty was extremely rigid. He evidently subscribed to his wife's belief that soldiers from Louisiana and Mississippi could be relied upon and shared her distrust of Tennesseans. He was capable of forming strategic plans, but any deviation or problem that arose threw him. He could not adjust to events on the battlefield with alacrity. And Bragg had a habit of shifting blame for disappointments onto others. On several occasions he drove subordinates to the wall, assailed them for their failures and shortcomings, and took pains to humiliate them. Bragg was a proud man, but he often forgot that his subordinates were equally proud men who took umbrage when he rudely treated them.[40]

But from Bragg's perspective, his hands were often tied. He could not clean house early in his tenure as he desired. Worse yet, he had one corps commander, Polk, whom he clearly deemed an incompetent meddler. This may be likened somewhat to a new principal who would love to remove certain teachers from the classroom, but who cannot do so because those teachers are protected by tenure and perhaps a powerful union. Bragg had to make do with what he had, but had he gotten his way, the army would have been much different at its upper echelons. One unanswerable question is what kind of relationship Bragg would have maintained with different subordinates had he secured the removal of all his antagonists. He perhaps would have found other men more congenial and cooperative; alternately, he may have quarreled with them if things went wrong. If Bragg never held out an olive branch, neither did his foes in the army. Polk in particular intrigued against Bragg almost nonstop, but evaded responsibility for his actions whenever possible. If Bragg never acknowledged his own shortcomings, neither did men such as Cheatham and Polk. There is something very human in this: Who wants to look in the mirror and enumerate one's failings? It's easier to deflect onto others one's errors and failed decisions. Perhaps the reason that Robert E. Lee is so extolled for taking blame for Pickett's Charge is that such actions are rare. Braxton Bragg was certainly not the only Civil War general who was prone to blame others and minimize his own failures. Nor is this a phenomenon limited to the nineteenth century, but one alive and well in modern society.

Frank Cheatham was a hard fighter and extremely popular with many of his Tennesseans. He threw his energies into the war every bit as much as Braxton Bragg, albeit at a level where he had fewer headaches and responsibilities. On several battlefields he personally led attacks that inspired his men. But some historians believe firmly that he was unfit for command owing to his penchant for alcohol. One wrote that Cheatham "probably would have made an adequate brigadier" when sober.[41] Perhaps he should have been lower in the chain of command, but his friendship with Isham Harris helped him win a brigadier general's rank when the Provisional Army of Tennessee was accepted into Confederate service. In some senses

Cheatham may have grown into his military role better had he initially been appointed a colonel of a Tennessee regiment. Barring that, he may have benefited from a longer stay as a brigade commander. A strong division or corps commander may have recognized Cheatham's strengths and worked to shore up his weaknesses. As a brigade commander, he would have had fewer regiments to oversee than at the divisional level. It is not Cheatham's fault that his services at Belmont in November 1861 earned him promotion to major general before Shiloh, or that Gustavus Henry successfully pleaded his case with Jefferson Davis. If Cheatham had doubts about securing this rank, he never expressed them openly. And it is mere speculation to wonder how Cheatham would have fared with a different corps commander such as William J. Hardee, a much better soldier than Polk and one who was less likely initially to conspire against Bragg.

Cheatham's relationship with Bragg was strained from the start. If he was aware of Bragg's efforts to remove him early in his tenure, Cheatham would have had to have been a saint to disregard this obvious denigration of his talents. Frank Cheatham was not a saint. In Polk he found a willing partner in condemnation of Bragg, and in fact it is hard to think of a worse mentor for Cheatham than Polk. It is reasonable to believe that a man who had risen to the bishopric of a statewide diocese would have leadership abilities. But Polk never seemed to grasp that he was a subordinate, that his 1827 graduation from West Point was in the distant past, or that his knowledge of military affairs was badly outdated. After all, Jefferson Davis, his old classmate, had expressly urged Polk to enter the army and conferred a high rank when Polk acquiesced. Like Cheatham, Polk would have benefited from starting far lower in the Confederate chain of command than he did. Some may claim that the Confederacy would have been better off had Polk never donned a uniform. But as with Cheatham, one doubts that Polk ever second-guessed his high-ranking initial appointment. Whatever dissimilarities that existed between Cheatham and Polk were subsumed under their mutual antipathy and disregard for Braxton Bragg. As the months rolled by during the war, a larger body of officers coalesced against Bragg. The anti-Bragg faction consisted particularly of officers from Kentucky and Tennessee, and the attitude of these men spilled over into the rank and file. Even Cheatham's sister Martha expressed her wish that Bragg be relieved: "I wish you could get rid of Bragg—ev[e]ry body seems to hate him so," she wrote in 1863.[42]

Cheatham, Polk, and other Bragg critics evidently never gave much thought to their commander's serious health concerns, although Longstreet's petition to remove Bragg cited his health as a reason for the proposed change.

Apparently they never attempted to put themselves in his shoes and understand the demands placed upon him. They never praised his administrative and organizational efforts or offered their support. Instead they sniped incessantly at Bragg, minimized their own inadequacies, and produced a near-mutiny after Murfreesboro. Intrigue against Bragg stole time away from their main priority, which was defeating the Federals and securing Southern independence. In essence, the relationship between Bragg and Cheatham came down to a phrase one might hear in a schoolyard: "I don't like you," to which another would reply, "I don't like you either." It is perhaps more accurate to infer that the phrase should be "I hate you," a sentiment fully reciprocated by the other. Trust is a vital commodity in an army, just as it is in any institution, and it was almost entirely lacking in the relationship between Bragg and a sizable number of his subordinates.

Bragg disliked Cheatham because of a host of factors: his alleged drinking, his rough nature, his alliance with Polk, his membership in the anti-Bragg bloc, and his perceived support for Cleburne's emancipation proposal. That he was a Tennessean added to Bragg's suspicions. Once Cheatham openly urged Bragg's removal in the post-Chickamauga meeting with Jefferson Davis, Bragg thoroughly understood where things stood. Braxton Bragg was no saint either, and his decision to break up Cheatham's all-Tennessee division revealed his desire to punish one of his most unremitting foes. Cheatham disliked Bragg for his own reasons: Bragg was dour and distant, antagonistic, inflexible, quick to cast blame, and vindictive. His alliance with Polk and then other Bragg critics was a natural extension of Cheatham's disregard for his commander. It was an ugly relationship between two proud men who acted in very human ways, but one that hampered the efficiency and cohesion of the Army of Tennessee. The rank and file of that army certainly deserved better than the rancorous infighting that characterized most of Bragg's tenure. It is hard not to conclude that each of the principal antagonists in this drama—Bragg, Polk, and Cheatham—were all in some measure unfit for the great responsibilities they bore, in large part because each had won high rank early in the war. As a result, none had gone through a seasoning process and all were thrust into positions without benefit of natural trial and error, which may have aided them immeasurably.[43] Instead, all of these men struggled to adapt to their responsibilities and instead of shoring one another up, opted to bicker incessantly. The Army of Tennessee confronted a large number of obstacles during its existence; regrettably, the ill will and disharmony of many of its top generals were self-inflicted wounds.

Notes

1. Judith Lee Hallock, "Braxton Bragg," in *Encyclopedia of the Confederacy,* 4 vols., ed. Richard N. Current (New York: Simon and Schuster, 1993), 1:203–6; Ezra J. Warner, *Generals in Gray: Lives of the Confederate Commanders* (Baton Rouge: Louisiana State Univ. Press, 1959), 30–31; Jack D. Welsh, *Medical Histories of Confederate Generals* (Kent, Ohio: Kent State Univ. Press, 1995), 23–24.

2. Grady McWhiney, *Braxton Bragg and Confederate Defeat,* vol. 1, *Field Command* (New York: Columbia Univ. Press, 1969), provides the fullest treatment of Bragg's life and career through the spring of 1863. See Hallock, "Braxton Bragg," 203–6; Warner, *Generals in Gray,* 30–31; and Lawrence L. Hewitt, "Braxton Bragg," in *The Confederate General,* 6 vols., ed. William C. Davis (n.p.: National Historical Society, 1991), 1:113–15 for biographical sketches.

3. Christopher Losson, *Tennessee's Forgotten Warriors: Frank Cheatham and His Confederate Division* (Knoxville: Univ. of Tennessee Press, 1989), 4–19.

4. Ibid., 20–39.

5. G. A. Henry to Jefferson Davis, Mar. 10, 1862, in National Archives, RG 109; Cheatham's appointment as major general, in Benjamin Franklin Cheatham Papers, Tennessee State Library and Archives (hereafter cited as TSLA).

6. Losson, *Tennessee's Forgotten Warriors,* 41–51; United States War Department, *Official Records of the War of the Rebellion: A Compilation of the Official Records of the Union and Confederate Armies,* 128 vols. (Washington, D.C.: Government Printing Office, 1880–1901), vol. 10, pt. 1, 410–11, 438–42, 452–55(hereafter cited as *OR*).

7. McWhiney, *Braxton Bragg,* 264–66.

8. Ibid., 275–76; Thomas Lawrence Connelly, *Autumn of Glory: The Army of Tennessee, 1862–1865* (Baton Rouge, Louisiana State Univ. Press, 1971), 223; Richard Taylor, *Destruction and Reconstruction: Personal Experiences of the Late War* (New York: D. Appleton and Co.), 100; *OR,* vol. 10, pt. 1, 11–12, 17; ibid., vol. 10, pt. 2, 658, 663.

9. *OR,* vol. 17, pt. 2, 627–28, 673.

10. *OR,* vol. 10, pt. 2, 379; ibid., vol. 17, pt. 2, 627–28, 673; Warner, *Generals in Gray,* 44–45, 65–66, 128–29, 199–200, 310.

11. Losson, *Tennessee's Forgotten Warriors,* 53, 55–59.

12. Ibid., 56–59; Mrs. Irby Morgan, *How It Was: Four Years among the Rebels* (Nashville: Printed for the author. Methodist Episcopal Church, South, 1892); "Gen. Benjamin Franklin Cheatham," *Confederate Veteran* (Jan. 1894): 1.

13. Thomas Lawrence Connelly, *Army of the Heartland: The Army of Tennessee, 1861–1862* (Baton Rouge: Louisiana State Univ. Press, 1967), 197–201, 205–40, 245–52.

14. *OR,* vol. 16, pt. 1, 897, 1110, 1120; Connelly, *Army of the Heartland,* 259–61.

15. Losson, *Tennessee's Forgotten Warriors,* 63–74. The fullest and most detailed account of Perryville is found in Kenneth W. Noe, *Perryville: This Grand Havoc of Battle* (Lexington: Univ. Press of Kentucky, 2001).

16. *OR,* vol. 16, pt. 1, 1093; Connelly, *Autumn of Glory,* 270, 273–80.

17. *OR,* vol. 20, pt. 1, 706–22; ibid., pt. 2, 411–12, 417–18, 423–24; Cheatham's Murfreesboro Report, in Cheatham Papers, TSLA.

18. John Johnston to John Trotwood Moore (Tennessee State Archivist), June 9, 1927, Gideon Johnson Pillow Collection, TSLA; L. G. Bennett and W[ilia]m M. Haigh, *History of the Thirty-Sixth Regiment Illinois Volunteers* (Aurora, Ill.: Knickerbocker and Hodder, 1876), 348; William J. Rogers diary, Dec. 31, 1862, in Roy Black Papers, Southern Historical Collection, University of North Carolina.

19. Sam R. Watkins, "*Co. Aytch," Maury Grays, First Tennessee Regiment; or, A Side Show of the Big Show* (1900; repr., Dayton, Ohio: Press of Morningside Bookshop, 1982), 66–68; *Nashville Daily American*, Sept. 7, 1886.

20. Cheatham and Jones M. Withers to Bragg, Jan. 3, 1863, Leonidas Polk to Bragg, Jan. 3, 1863, both in Cheatham Papers, TSLA. Bragg inserted his reply at the bottom of Polk's note. Although the original note asserted that only three brigades remained reliable, Cheatham and Jones later corrected the wording to read "divisions" on Mar. 2, 1863. See *OR*, vol. 20, pt. 1,702. Accounts of Stones River (or Murfreesboro) can be seen in relevant sections of Connelly's *Autumn of Glory* and McWhiney's *Braxton Bragg*. Book-length treatments of the battle include works by Alexander F. Stevenson, *The Battle of Stone's River* (Boston: James R. Osgood and Co., 1884); James Lee McDonough, *Stones River—Bloody Winter in Tennessee* (Knoxville: Univ. of Tennessee Press, 1980); Peter Cozzens, *No Better Place to Die: The Battle of Stones River* (Urbana: Univ. of Illinois Press, 1990); and Larry J. Daniel, *Battle of Stones River: The Forgotten Conflict between the Confederate Army of Tennessee and the Union Army of the Cumberland* (Baton Rouge: Louisiana State Univ. Press, 2012).

21. *Chattanooga Daily Rebel*, Jan. 6, 1863; Bragg to Cheatham, Jan. 11, 1863, Cheatham Papers, TSLA; Patrick Cleburne to Bragg, Jan. 13, 1863, Braxton Bragg Papers, Duke University; *OR*, vol. 20, pt. 1, 682–84; Losson, *Tennessee's Forgotten Warriors*, 93–94.

22. Polk to Bragg, Jan. 30, 1863, Frederick M. Dearborn Collection of Military and Political Americana, The Houghton Library, Harvard University; *OR*, vol. 20, pt. 1, 701 (Bragg to Polk, Jan. 30, 1863) and 702 (Polk to Bragg, Jan. 31, 1863).

23. Losson, *Tennessee's Forgotten Warriors*, 94; Gideon Pillow to Maj. [Wm. Clare], Mar. 9, 1863, William P. Palmer Collection, Western Reserve Historical Society.

24. Bragg to Jefferson Davis, Jan. 17, 1863, Harry L. and Mary K. Dalton Collection, Duke University.

25. Draft of General Bragg's Official Report of the Battle of Murfreesboro, Feb. 23, 1863, Palmer Collection, Western Reserve; W. D. Gale to Leonidas Polk, Mar. 27, 1863, Leonidas Polk Collection, Archives of the University of the South, Sewanee, Tenn.

26. Bragg to Samuel Cooper, Apr. 9, 1863, Palmer Collection, Western Reserve; Seddon's comments were written on a sheet attached to Bragg's letter.

27. *OR*, vol. 16, pt. 1, 1097–1107.

28. Losson, *Tennessee's Forgotten Warriors*, 101–9; John Euclid Magee diary, Duke University, 105.

29. *OR*, vol. 30, pt. 2, 80, 97, 113, 458–60; ibid., pt. 4, 691–92.

30. Polk to Davis, [Sept. 27, 1863], Dearborn Papers, Harvard University; Polk to Davis, Oct. 6, 1863, Leonidas Polk Papers, Duke University; *OR*, vol. 30, pt. 2, 65–66,

69; Losson, *Tennessee's Forgotten Warriors,* 112–16; J. W. Harris to George Harris, Oct. 13, 1863, Confederate Collection, TSLA.

31. James Longstreet, *From Manassas to Appomattox: Memoirs of the Civil War in America* (Philadelphia: J. B. Lippincott, 1896), 465–66; James Lee McDonough, *Chattanooga: A Death Grip on the Confederacy* (Knoxville: Univ. of Tennessee Press, 1984), 35–37; St. John Richardson Liddell, "Record of the Civil War," Daniel Chevilette Govan Papers, Southern Historical Collection, University of North Carolina.

32. Van Buren Oldham diary, Oct. 29, 31, Nov. 1, 1863, Van Buren Oldham diary, TSLA; Alfred Tyler Fielder diary, Oct. 2, 1863, TSLA; Cheatham to George W. Brent (Bragg's adjutant general), Oct. 31, 1863, Cheatham Papers, TSLA.

33. J[ames] A. Seddon to Cheatham, Nov. 17, 1863, Cheatham Papers, TSLA. Cooper's remarks are on the same sheet as Seddon's, which is attached to Cheatham's resignation letter.

34. *OR,* vol. 31, pt. 2, 658–60; James Longstreet to Cheatham, Oct. 21, 1863, Cheatham Papers, TSLA; Richard I. Manning to his mother, Jan. 17, 1864, Richard Irvine Manning Papers, South Carolina Library, University of South Carolina.

35. Edward C. Walthall to Cheatham, Mar. 17, 1876, and Cheatham to Walthall, Mar. 1876, both in Cheatham Papers, TSLA; Col. W. F. Dowd, "Lookout Mountain and Missionary Ridge," *Southern Bivouac* (Dec. 1885): 399; *OR,* vol. 31, pt. 2, 697, 727.

36. Bragg to Jefferson Davis, Dec. 1, 1863, Dearborn Papers, Harvard University.

37. Bragg to Maj. E. T. Sykes, Feb. 8, 1873, J. F. H. Claiborne Papers, Southern Historical Collection, University of North Carolina.

38. Losson, *Tennessee's Forgotten Warriors,* 133–35.

39. Ibid., 137–40; Connelly, *Army of the Heartland,* 318–21.

40. McWhiney, *Braxton Bragg,* 388–92; Hallock, "Braxton Bragg," 205–06; Elise Bragg to Braxton Bragg, Feb. 15 and Mar. 12, 1862, Braxton Bragg Letters, Barker History Center, University of Texas, Austin.

41. Steven E. Woodworth, *No Band of Brothers: Problems in the Rebel High Command* (Columbia: Univ. of Missouri Press, 1999), 126.

42. The most extensive discussion of the friction between Bragg and his generals is in Connelly, *Army of the Heartland;* Martha [Blackie] to Cheatham, Mar. 30, 1863, Cheatham Papers, TSLA.

43. For an enlightening analysis of how working one's way up the ranks could be beneficial to Civil War generals, see Steven Woodworth's chapter, "Homespun Generals: Nonprofessional Officers in the Confederate Army," in Woodworth, *No Band of Brothers,* 130–57, 173–74.

Grant and Forrest

The Command Value of Calluses

Jack Hurst

Near the end, Confederate Gen. Nathan Bedford Forrest summed up his fifty-six intrepid years and got them about right. They had been, he said, "a battle from the start."[1] But the overtones of his words can be more useful than Forrest ever imagined. They also suggest much of the antebellum experience of the Confederacy's greatest military opponent, Union Gen. U. S. Grant. And they point to an overlooked reason for not only the unexpected military ascendancy of both these men but perhaps the outcome of the war itself.

Forrest and Grant were arguably their respective armies' most successful warriors in the war's Western Theater. There the generalships of both were memorably incubated in such Kentucky and Tennessee battles as Fort Henry, Fort Donelson, Shiloh, and lesser fights. Grant went on to become the soldier all but universally recognized as most responsible for winning the entire conflict, and Forrest was almost certainly the most productive Confederate in the West. When they are compared with their fellow high officers, these two—alone among the conflict's high-ranking generals—are seen to possess a mutual, unique trait. They rose from a grittier level than their comrades of similar or superior rank, men of prominence and cultivation who were supposedly "higher born."

Grant and Forrest had each fought climate and ruin in farm fields. Each had sweated his shirts, blistered his hands, and barked his knuckles battling fate to feed and protect his family. Perhaps most important, the blood in their veins had often pumped swiftly with the stress of survival. Their harder lives and necessary preoccupation with capitalizing on insufficient and imperfect resources had forced each to develop higher degrees of cleverness and adaptability. This common credential made them anomalies in their command hierarchies. It was humble, widely disdained, yet in the end pivotal. Call it calluses.

At first glance, the two men bear no more resemblance than the two vastly different Americas they served. Forrest was born in the slave state of Tennessee, Grant in free Ohio. Forrest stood nearly six feet two inches; Grant, five feet seven inches. Forrest made much of his prewar fortune slave trading on an ultimately mammoth scale. Near the peak of his business he advertised his eagerness to buy African Americans at around $1,000 each in gangs as large as 150 apiece.[2] Grant freed the only slave he ever owned[3] and was hardly more than self-sufficient on the eve of the Civil War.[4]

Forrest was a single-minded, Southern version of the robber barons of later in his century. He was so frugally riveted on insuring himself against a return to poverty that he shunned common pleasures such as whiskey and tobacco.[5] Grant, by contrast, had within him considerably more of the artist—the reader, the writer, and the sketcher.[6] Although unjustly, Grant became nearly as known for the bottle as for battle, and he eventually smoked so many cigars that he died of throat cancer. He logged eleven years in the antebellum military before resigning under an alcoholic cloud.[7] Forrest, before secession, had not been in any army at all. Grant's personality was so understated that a biographer pronounced him unnoticeable in a crowd even in uniform.[8] Forrest exuded charisma and had a temper that was explosive and sometimes homicidal. Whereas Forrest had become rich by the war's eve, Grant had escaped abject poverty only by taking a job clerking for his father.

But a second look at the two is rewarding. Each man was about forty years of age when the war began. In an era when horsemanship was all but a male necessity, each was recognized as an exceptional rider: Forrest as an officer of the Memphis Jockey Club[9] and Grant as the setter of a long-standing jump record at West Point.[10] Grant and Forrest were both lucky in 1861 not to have already stopped a bullet, Grant having participated in most of the battles of the Mexican War and Forrest repeatedly surviving knife and pistol mayhem on the southwestern frontier. Grant looked so at home under fire that a Mexican War comrade called him a "man of fire."[11] Forrest, in the words of a fellow Confederate officer, probably personally killed more enemies than any leader of men since Richard the Lionheart.[12] He consigned thirty Federals to eternity with his own hands.[13]

Most important, both Grant and Forrest rose from closer to their society's bottom than its top. Forrest was the son of a Tennessee blacksmith;

Grant, of an Ohio tanner. Forrest's father died when Forrest was fifteen, after losing his family's 180-acre Tennessee farm and moving its members to leased hill land in northern Mississippi.[14] Grant's father plied the bloody, smelly business of tanning animal hides before expanding into a leather-goods business. Forrest, his family's firstborn, worked from dawn to dark with oxen, horses, mules, and hand tools to feed his siblings and widowed mother. He once split rails for fifty cents a hundred to earn his way home from Texas.[15] Grant from boyhood supplemented the family income working with horses and mules—and he was so adept at it that neighboring farmers and timber-men continually employed him to break the animals and/or use them for pulling, plowing, and hauling.[16]

Both Grant and Forrest had much, if small-scale, antebellum experience in the leadership of men. Grant had served for eleven years as a low-level army officer, and Forrest had shepherded slave gangs along the roads of the western South for more than a decade. Grant was captain of a company when he resigned from the prewar army in 1854.[17] Forrest's slave-trading firm became the largest in Memphis, which was that grisly trade's most bustling center west of the Appalachians and north of New Orleans. Forrest had agents or satellite offices from St. Louis to Vicksburg. During the 1850s his enterprises apparently extended from northern Kentucky[18] to Texas,[19] and advertisements for his slave-trafficking firm appeared from the southern Atlantic Coast[20] to southwestern Dixie.[21]

The extent to which both men knew life at the bottom cannot be overstated. Grant, in shabby clothes, had peddled firewood on St. Louis street corners to keep his family eating; he sold his pocket watch for $20 one year to give them a Christmas.[22] Forrest doubtless amused fellow members of the Memphis city council with his proposed solution to the town's stray dog problem; he said he knew a Mexican who would lasso the mutts for ten cents apiece.[23] His initial election to the council came after an incident rife with overtones of the Old South's least savory elements. He gave crucial testimony in the trial of a fellow slave merchant who had murdered another over the seamiest of transactions. The killer claimed the dead man, a Forrest friend who died receiving care in Forrest's own house, had deliberately sold him a free African American, who afterward recovered his liberty in court.[24]

Such experiences, seamy or not, proved invaluable to both men as Civil War generals. There seems an obvious correlation between the facts that they were the only high officers during the first half of the war who came from their mutual level and that they became arguably the most successful generals in the Western Theater.

Ulysses S. Grant. (Library of Congress)

Each had firsthand knowledge of what was possible and impossible for his men to accomplish physically. Each used every means, including well-developed networks of spies, to gather information[25] because each knew the value of learning all he could about a planned task before beginning it; their previous lives had depended on the accuracy of such knowledge. Having lived where opportunity seldom knocked, each knew the value of capitalizing when it did. Each, therefore, was obsessed with initiative, aggressiveness, persistence, and speed.

Grant graduated from the U.S. Military Academy at West Point. Forrest graduated from nowhere, receiving a total of six months of off-and-on formal schooling in his life. Six months was approximately the same amount that Abraham Lincoln got, but Lincoln had a reverence for books, whereas Forrest's bent was more toward outdoor pursuits, such as horse racing and hunting.[26] One of his few schoolmasters recalled afterward that Forrest was more interested in athletic endeavors than book learning.[27]

Yet Grant and Forrest appear to have held the same general view of West Point. Grant went there reluctantly, his appointment having been wangled by his father, who wanted to avoid paying for the son's higher education. In 1839, Grant took false hope from an abortive move in Congress to abolish West Point because its demise would provide him with a discharge that would not reflect on him as a person or a man.[28] He did not care for his studies at the Point and gave them minimal attention. He preferred reading adventure novels, which he checked out of the campus library,[29] or drawing pen-and-ink sketches, at which he showed talent.[30] Forrest would come to regard West Point with contempt, but he probably had passed out of boyhood before he even heard of it, and had he acquired the necessary preparatory schooling, he had virtually no chance of going there. In the South, such plums were almost totally reserved for rich men's sons. And, anyway, Southern states offered far fewer schools in which poor boys could be educated.[31]

Grant appeared to regard a West Point education as minimally advantageous in the Civil War. Whereas many of his fellow West Pointers sought promotions for men with academy training first, Grant based his recommendations for promotion primarily on an officer's ability to manage troops and fight. During the drive toward Vicksburg, Grant wrote a letter of protest to Abraham Lincoln over plans to promote further one West Pointer, a brigadier general who already had been advanced to supplant a non–West Pointer distinguished in the fighting at Fort Donelson. Grant said the favored one "would scarcely make a respectable Hospital nurse," then went on to recommend instead promotions for seven other officers. Only one of the seven had seen the inside of a West Point classroom, and that one had quit after two years to become an attorney in Iowa.[32] Forrest's contempt for the academy and its theories was more vocal. He once said that, in a fight, fifteen minutes of "bulge"—meaning the upper hand over an opponent—was worth a week of tactics.[33] West Point, at bottom, was established to teach fighting to men who do not know how, and Grant and Forrest, by virtue of their harder lives, already did.

Grant and Forrest exemplified the men in the ranks of their armies more than the men in high command. Grant generally held officers responsible for enlisted men's rules infractions; the officers, he said, were in charge.[34] In Mexico, as a lieutenant, Grant had jumped into a body of water to help his men perform a task there and received praise for so doing from Gen. Zachary Taylor, who became his idol and role model.[35] Similarly, Forrest several times helped his men with their labors, swinging an ax or carrying sacks of supplies across rickety bridges that would not support loaded

Nathan Bedford Forrest.
(Library of Congress)

wagons.[36] Once, confronted with a junior officer who refused to help row a boat because he was not an enlisted man, Forrest slapped him so hard the offender fell from the boat; he then fished him out and told him that if he did not grab an oar he, Forrest, would do it again and let him drown.[37] Forrest also rarely addressed his men in ranks as "Men" or "Troops." He used the more comradely "Boys."[38]

Both men insisted on discipline in their ranks, but administered it by their own individual lights, and their applications of it sometimes varied widely from their era's norms. Both seemed to identify more with the men in those ranks than with their fellow high officers, but neither man was in any way a panderer in the interest of personal popularity.

After President Lincoln's Emancipation Proclamation, it was the officers whom Grant held accountable when some units from southern Illinois tried in various ways to mutiny.[39] And as African American units joined the Union armies, unlike many—probably most—Federal officers of his day, Grant thought every man in uniform should be treated the same, white or black. In a telling incident following the Vicksburg surrender, he backed up a white officer of black troops who retaliated after some of his men and their families had been repeatedly abused by white soldiers. This officer ordered the arrest of two of the offenders and had them whipped—with brush, not a cowhide lash. Despite the outraged reaction of Midwestern newspaper editors, Grant approved the officer's action.[40]

Brush played a significant role in a famous example of Forrest discipline, too. Riding forward into combat at West Point, Mississippi, in 1864, he and Gen. James R. Chalmers encountered a hatless Confederate soldier fleeing the scene. Chalmers later wrote that Forrest jumped off his horse, grabbed some roadside brush, and began beating the soldier with it. He then pointed the white-eyed trooper back toward the front and told him that if he saw him in the rear again, the young man would "not get off so easy."[41]

But upper echelons of the Union and Confederate armies viewed such departures from the military customs of their time with disdain. Each high command was full of men boasting much military and political cachet and cultivation—with superiority complexes to match. But their prewar prominence usually proved to be a millstone, appearing to make most of them fear losing their vaunted reputations. In contrast, such renown as Grant and Forrest possessed—Forrest as a slave trader, Grant as civilian failure and drunkard—they doubtless would have happily shed. Throughout his life, Grant refused to discuss his best-known vice with anybody but his wife Julia and aide and confidant John Rawlins,[42] and Forrest left the slave business in 1860 to become a planter.[43]

Most of the early leaders of both armies would be held in low regard by the war's end, but at the outset they possessed large reputations built on aristocratic or political muscle. Grant's immediate superior, Gen. Henry Halleck, was one of West Point's most respected minds. Grant's subordinates included former congressmen and a governor's son. Similarly, Forrest served under civilian and military representatives of the South's ten thousand richest planter families. This crème de la crème was a tiny fraction of the region's eight million Caucasian residents, but it owned one-quarter of the Confederacy's four million slaves.[44]

The upper classes North and South looked down their noses at presumed inferiors, but Dixie's outdid itself. An infamous 1858 speech by South Carolina Sen. James Hammond, aimed at the Northern working class, breathed contempt for every non-slaveholding laborer. "In all social systems," Hammond intoned, "there must be a class to . . . perform the drudgery of life. . . .

It constitutes the very mudsill of society."[45] Three-quarters of the South's whites did the kind of drudgery the senator derided.[46]

The Southern elite's aversion to thoroughgoing democracy was not just rhetorical; it engineered secession to save slavery, the blood and sinew of its power and pomp. It maneuvered secession ordinances through state legislatures and conventions, which its wealth could control. Except in Tennessee, the question was not put to popular referenda prior to the legislatures and conventions, making it a fait accompli,[47] and Tennessee secessionists waged a vicious pre-referendum campaign to intimidate or expel adherents of the Union.[48]

The makeup of the highest levels of the South's army illustrates the power its elite wielded. During the war, twenty-five Confederates became full generals or lieutenant generals. Just three of the twenty-five were not West Pointers, and two of the three were nationally prominent and/or fabulously wealthy. One, Richard Taylor, was the son of President Zachary Taylor.[49] The second, Wade Hampton, was reputedly the largest landowner in the South, owning property not just in his home state of South Carolina but also vast holdings in Mississippi and Louisiana and hundreds of slaves to work them.[50] The third was Forrest, the onetime non-landowning subsistence farmer who was named a lieutenant general only two months before the war ended. Nearly two-thirds of the South's total 425 generals had West Point or other military training,[51] as did the same proportion of the Union's 583.[52]

At the top, Grant faced the same array of West Point pride, power, and money that Forrest did. His immediate superior, Henry Halleck, although born on a New York farm, had long since enriched and empowered himself as an early corporate attorney in the California Territory.[53] George McClellan, general-in-chief of the Union Army, hailed from an old and wealthy Philadelphia family, and McClellan himself had become one of the prewar nation's leading railroad executives.[54] Don Carlos Buell was a distinguished career army officer.[55] William T. Sherman was the son of an Ohio Supreme Court justice, foster son of one United States senator, and brother of another.[56] John Pope was not just related to George Washington, he was also a nephew of a senator from Kentucky and an in-law of Mary Todd Lincoln.[57] Lew Wallace was an Indiana governor's son.[58]

Forrest and Grant felt uncomfortable in such company, and for good reason. The Southern upper crust ridiculed Forrest behind his back for his coarseness of speech and manner. Some apparently invented faux examples of his labored writing and spelling to try to pass on to posterity.[59] A favorite term that gentlemen-soldiers applied to him—behind his back—seems to have been "vulgarian."[60] He was also condemned as a gambler and, of course, slave trader, sort of the antebellum equivalent of a later era's used-car salesman. Union higher-ups continually brought up Grant's taste for liquor, as if almost nobody in an army drank. In fact, it appears that almost everybody in the high officer corps of the Union Army did drink, especially to build artificial courage for combat. Many, if not most, of these seem to have drunk much more than Grant, who confined his lapses to sporadic sprees. And, unlike many of them, he never felt the need to drink anywhere near a battlefield.[61]

Several Confederate officers overtly avoided association with Forrest. When Gen. P. G. T. Beauregard, claiming to admire Forrest's performance at Shiloh, persuaded him to transfer to the army of Braxton Bragg, two cavalry regiments had to be moved to find three whose colonels would deign to serve under him.[62] Bragg himself first promised Forrest command of his army's cavalry, then reneged and gave that honor to twenty-six-year-old West Pointer Joe Wheeler.[63] Soon afterward, Bragg ordered Forrest out on a perilous midwinter campaign behind Federal lines and, despite having a surplus, refused to issue him arms, ammunition, or other needed equipment.[64] Bragg routinely gave Forrest green units to be trained and largely armed with weapons that Forrest had to capture from the enemy; Bragg then transferred these troops to Wheeler or others.[65] Yet, Forrest used troops whom he had commanded for barely a week to capture a Murfreesboro garrison the size of his own force.[66] Similarly, he used another patchwork unit to wreck Grant's West Tennessee railroad supply line so completely that Grant never used that line again—and, because of the Forrest raid as well as another by Gen. Earl Van Dorn on a Grant supply depot in northern Mississippi, had to change his whole plan for the Vicksburg campaign.[67]

Grant's commander, Halleck, tried frantically to get Grant replaced before and during the Fort Henry-Fort Donelson campaign. Until he began to fear his machinations would be found out, Halleck spread baseless rumors that Grant had returned to his old army habit of hard drinking.[68] Grant's most dangerous subordinate, ex-congressman and Gen. John McClernand, a longtime prewar associate of Lincoln, almost certainly conspired with others to disseminate similar drinking gossip for their own benefit.[69] With all this going on, Grant showed nerves of steel, capturing a Confederate army at Fort Donelson, fighting off disaster at Shiloh, and capturing another Confederate army at Vicksburg. Nonetheless, Halleck shelved him after both Fort Donelson and Shiloh.

What continually allowed Grant and Forrest to defeat their vaunted foes was the creative dogged persistence so necessary to survival on the level of society from which they sprang. Grant had been to West Point and Forrest had not, but neither was bound by its tenets. A bad cliché applies. Grant and Forrest thought outside the box, and the box was West Point's wisdom, especially its seeming overemphasis on defense.

Grant's masterpiece—his capture of Vicksburg, the Confederacy's final fortress on the Mississippi River—flagrantly violated that dogma. He all but cut his army off from its supply bases, first by steaming its transportation vessels irretrievably downriver past rows of Vicksburg cannon and then by throwing his men across the Father of Waters into the interior of hostile Mississippi. After whipping his off-balance foes in five fast-moving, bloody battles stretching across fifty miles of terrain from the river to the state capital at Jackson and then back to Vicksburg, he besieged and starved the Confederates into surrender.[70]

Forrest's greatest victory similarly flew in the face of West Point caution. At Brice's Crossroads in Mississippi, he defeated a far larger Union force by choosing ground where the Federals could employ only a fraction of their men at a time. He then routed and chased them for two days.[71] During the second night, a Forrest trooper pointed out to his general that just ten of their comrades had kept up and that they faced disaster if the Federals turned and fought. Forrest replied that ten Confederates were enough. "Ten good men can whip a thousand in the fix we have them," he said.[72]

Grant and Forrest had each long since learned that the outcome of physical combat depends more on psychology than strength. The most important rule of fighting was to knock an opponent out of a sense of security and then to keep him from recovering it by giving him no rest.

Initiative was, thus, paramount. An opponent must be surprised, pummeled, then pursued "to the wall," in Grant's words. He said one should strike his enemy as early and as hard as possible, continue hitting him, "and keep moving on."[73] Forrest, who had killed men and cowed countless others in personal encounters before the war, was even more specific in his analysis. To a fellow Confederate, he said that humans naturally regarded imminent combat with "horror and consternation," so he tried to make a foe's first sight of a battlefield "as shocking to the enemy as . . . possibl[e]." He did this by refusing to observe the West Point principle of holding a large part of his men in reserve. He would throw "his entire force against them in the fiercest and most warlike manner possible," the fellow soldier quoted him. "He would thus overawe and demoralize them . . . at the very start," and, "with unabated fury," deepen the demoralization "by a constant repetition of blows . . . killing, capturing, and driving them with but little difficulty."[74] If he did not have time to make this eloquent explanation, Forrest had a shorter, homelier one: "Git 'em skeered, then keep the skeer on 'em."[75]

Two of the two men's most important formative experiences occurred within a seven-week period in Kentucky and Tennessee. On December 28, 1861, as a lieutenant colonel, Forrest with three hundred cavalrymen routed and pursued Federal troopers in a "promiscuous saber slaughter" soon praised by Forrest's immediate superior as "one of the most brilliant and successful cavalry engagements" of the young war. That three hundred Confederates could vanquish slightly more than half their number of Federals is hardly remarkable, but the way the untrained Forrest did it is.

Despite being equipped with no rudiment of military education (or much of any other kind), Forrest exhibited formidable martial instincts. He first violated cavalry custom of that era by dismounting some of his men and posting them as sharpshooters. Then he initiated flanking attacks while he himself led an assault on the Federal center. When the center broke, he did not waste time celebrating. Instead, he chased the Union survivors for two miles, his men finding "no difficulty in piercing through [with sabers] every one they came up with" and "leaving many wounded [Federals] clinging to their saddles."[76] The report of Forrest's superior adds a detail that Forrest's own official account does not: that Forrest "was conspicuous for the most daring courage, always in advance of his command. He was at one time engaged in hand-to-hand conflict with 4 of the enemy, 3 of whom he killed, dismounting and making a prisoner of the fourth."[77]

Forrest displayed the same fearsome ability at Fort Donelson seven weeks later. He and his one thousand–plus cavalry opposed the approach of Grant's fifteen thousand troops of all arms along the roads from Fort Henry with such determination that Confederate Gen. Simon B. Buckner, apparently harking back to Forrest's reputed performance at Sacramento, reported that the cavalryman had acted "with his usual gallantry."[78] On the battle's climactic third day, Forrest charged and captured cannons and was stopped only after several hours when his mount was disemboweled by a cannon ball.[79] Finally, he scouted Confederate avenues of escape and then, refusing to surrender, led an exit across one hundred yards of freezing backwater with most of his cavalry and significant numbers of artillerists and infantrymen riding double with his troopers.[80]

Forrest's Fort Donelson steadfastness, though, was eclipsed by Grant's. The Federal general, bearing—unlike Forrest—the burden of supreme command, withstood grinding pressures and numbing reversals in winning a victory that marked him as a singular Union general.

He left his base at Cairo, Illinois, under the cloud of scandalous military charges of drunkenness filed against him hardly a week prior to departure.[81] He could not know, but must have suspected, that his superior—Gen. Henry Halleck—wanted to sack him, and in fact Halleck did wish to; throughout the campaign he tried to get another officer promoted to take Grant's job.[82] In the battle of Fort Henry six days before the beginning of the one at Fort Donelson, Grant's infantry did not arrive until after the fort had surrendered to Union gunboats. All but a handful of the Confederate garrison had fled to Donelson. Grant thus knew that Northern newspapers, as well as his superior, would be underwhelmed.

Grant was therefore in such a hurry to get to Fort Donelson and redeem himself that he obtained only imperfect knowledge of the place before he arrived. Then he found that the Confederate line of trenches stretched more than two miles—from in front of the fort all the way down south of the town of Dover. And, the Confederates were thought to have more men inside these trenches than Grant had outside.[83] He had to call forward the troops he had left behind at Fort Henry to invest the Confederate lines fully. Then, on the second day of battle, the Federal ironclad gunboats, which Grant had regarded as his primary weapon, were all but blown out of the Cumberland River by unpracticed Confederate cannoneers.[84] Finally, on the battle's third day—after Grant left his headquarters to ride several miles north to urge naval officer Andrew H. Foote not to withdraw all the gunboats north for refitting—the Confederates exited their lines in an all-out attack. By the time Grant could get back to his troops, his right had been crushed and thrown back toward his center. Virtually all other officers would likely have either retreated or dug in at the point to which they had been pushed, but Grant did not. Instead, he divined that the Confederates were trying to escape and ordered a charge by his entire army. The charge drove the Confederates back inside their defenses, impelling them to surrender the next morning.[85]

The lesson Grant learned at Fort Donelson was so powerful that he cited it to Sherman at Shiloh at the end of that battle's disastrous first day. Although badly mauled, he said, they could and would attack and win on the battle's second day. Fort Donelson had shown, he explained, that when two armies are fought out, the one that musters the will to launch a final assault will win.[86]

Forrest and Grant fought by feel, not books. They had seen enough life at the bottom, and possessed enough native intelligence, to regard mere theory with caution. Southern cadets at West Point would claim to have been familiar with combat almost from birth, but these were plantation sons who tended to regard it cavalierly. For them it was a matter of dueling and lofty concepts of personal and family honor. Grant, from his familiarity with nose-bloodying country schoolyards before West Point and the Mexican War afterward, and Forrest from his lethal encounters on the streets and back roads of the frontier, could more easily see fighting in the larger, less romantic context it took on in the Civil War. They knew in their bones that defeat meant ruin for their loved ones and their nation.

This attitude showed in their battlefield performance. Wealthy scions of the South and their Northern upper-crust counterparts—a sweat-less class that rarely had to give life-or-death attention to anything—often tended toward sloppiness in such vital activities as reconnaissance, supply, and inspection.[87] Because of their former lives, Grant and Forrest applied themselves to such matters by second nature.

Many might assert that Grant had the advantage over Forrest because Grant had a West Point education, but Grant would very likely disagree. He went there unwillingly, did not like it, and had no ambition to become a soldier.[88] He apparently remained in the antebellum army for eleven years only because he could find no other better- or similarly paying work by which to feed his family. And his pivotal decision in the Vicksburg campaign—to send his gunboats and other watercraft down the Mississippi past Vicksburg's miles of cannon when he knew they did not possess enough power to come back upstream—flew in the face of all West Point teaching. His friend Sherman beseeched Grant not to do it to no avail.[89]

Grant's background, and his army's tolerance of it, gave the Union a decisive edge. The Confederacy's contempt for the similar credentials of Forrest and people like him may very well have cost it the war. Grant gradually moved to the fore of a succession of Union generals who were too self-important, too slow, and too reluctant to attack. Forrest, despite his daunting displays of bravery and brains, was shunned by a chain of command totally dominated by its upper class and by West Point. For its decision makers, Forrest's coarseness, resentment of their slights, and reputation as a slave trader blinded them to his inestimable potential value to their cause. They eventually promoted him all the way from private to lieutenant general, but they rarely, if ever, allowed him input in their councils.

By late 1863, Grant had won at Chattanooga and Lincoln was preparing to order him east to face Robert E. Lee. It is rarely noted, however, that Grant had badly wounded the vaunted Virginian already; his leadership in the West had slashed the supply arteries of Lee's shrinking, star-crossed nation. By contrast, Forrest in late 1863 unintentionally exiled himself to comparative oblivion. His goal was to block the Union's use of the Mississippi River and reclaim it for the Confederacy,[90] but his commander, Gen. Braxton Bragg, first refused Forrest's request for an independent command to do that. Then—having exhausted his patience with the sneers, insults, and manifest ineptitude of his Confederate superiors—Forrest unceremoniously departed them for West Tennessee and northern Mississippi, which turned out from then on to be the war's back roads. He made his exit with quintessentially lower-class directness, one story having it that he vowed to kill Bragg if they ever met again.[91]

Scholars rightly question the judgments of the Confederate high command. Yet, perhaps influenced by its cultivated gentility, they have largely adopted its opinion of Forrest. In the process, they have accepted the Confederate elite's subtle separation of its own virulent but more polished racism from Forrest's. Jefferson Davis and his minions regarded, and helped caricature, Forrest as a cartoonish half-literate who would not follow orders and never could have been more than the peerless independent raider he was. But, the Confederate high command was hardly infallible. Scholars who take its view of Forrest seem not to have noticed that he did not begin the way he ended. He started at Fort Donelson and Shiloh following every order, only to see his blue-blooded commanders squander countless chances for victory. At least as much as his tendencies toward insubordination, it was they, and their sneering incompetence, that drove him to rebellion and resignation—and their Confederacy to its grave.

Andrew Carnegie, the Scotch immigrant who became an international industrial titan after beginning his career in Civil War railroading, later founded free libraries across America to aid the lower classes. He did so, he said, because of their potential to benefit all. "The richest ore," Carnegie asserted, "is oftenest found deep down, and it is in the low stratum of human life that we will find the jewels that will glisten for ages."[92]

The contrasting Civil War fates of Grant and Forrest symbolize the bedrock significance of their war. In it, the Confederacy lost a sincere effort to perpetuate and expand their vision of the Republic. The victorious Union, on the other hand, groped for something higher: an America where more than just propertied white men might enjoy the fruits of liberty. The examples of Grant, Forrest, and others like them also appear not to have been lost on America's military, whose highest ranks are no longer reserved for just sons of the elite. Dwight Eisenhower, the Iowa farm boy-turned-World War II D-Day commander, and Colin Powell, the Harlem-born son of Jamaican immigrants who became chairman of the Joint Chiefs of Staff during the Persian Gulf War, stand as eloquent random examples.

Notes

1. John A. Wyeth, *Life of General Nathan Bedford Forrest* (New York: Harper & Bros., 1899), 622.
2. Frederic Bancroft, *Slave Trading in the Old South* (Baltimore: J. H. Furst Co., 1931), 311, 263–64.
3. John Y. Simon, ed., *The Papers of Ulysses S. Grant* (Carbondale: Southern Illinois Univ. Press, 1979), 1:344, 347.
4. Jean Edward Smith, *Grant* (New York: Simon & Schuster, 2001), 95.
5. Andrew Lytle, *Bedford Forrest and His Critter Company* (1931; repr., Seminole, Fla.: Green Key Press, 1984), 20.
6. Smith, *Grant,* 26–27.
7. Ibid., 87.
8. Bruce Catton, *Grant Takes Command, 1863–1865* (Boston: Little, Brown, 1969), 137.
9. *Memphis Daily Appeal,* Oct. 30, 1859.
10. Smith, *Grant,* 28.
11. Brooks D. Simpson, *Ulysses S. Grant: Triumph over Adversity: 1822–1865* (New York: Houghton-Mifflin, 2000), 44.
12. Wyeth, *Life of . . . Forrest,* 644.
13. Robert S. Henry, *"First with the Most" Forrest* (Indianapolis: Bobbs-Merrill, 1944), 17.
14. Thomas Jordan and J. P. Pryor, *The Campaigns of Lieut. Gen. Forrest and of Forrest's Cavalry* (1868; repr., Dayton, Ohio: Morningside Bookshop, 1977), 18, 34.
15. Ibid., 21–22.
16. Ulysses S. Grant, *Personal Memoirs* (1885; repr., New York: Penguin, 1999), 11.
17. Smith, *Grant,* 86.
18. *Memphis Daily Appeal,* May 24 and May 26, 1857.
19. Jordan and Pryor, *The Campaigns,* 27–29.
20. Bancroft, *Slave Trading,* 263.
21. Ibid., 264.
22. Smith, *Grant,* 91–92.
23. *Memphis Daily Appeal,* July 21, 1858.
24. Ibid., Apr. 7, 1858.

25. For Grant, see the entire volume of William B. Feis, *Grant's Secret Service* (Lincoln: Univ. of Nebraska Press, 2002); for Forrest, see, for example, Deanne Blanton and Lauren M. Cook, *They Fought Like Demons: Women Soldiers in the Civil War* (New York: Vintage, 2002), 70–71; and Jordan and Pryor, *The Campaigns,* 194.

26. Jordan and Pryor, *The Campaigns,* 21.

27. Lytle, *Forrest and His Critter Company,* 14.

28. Smith, *Grant,* 27.

29. Grant, *Memoirs,* 17.

30. Smith, *Grant,* 27.

31. James M. McPherson, *Drawn with the Sword: Reflections on the American Civil War* (New York: Oxford Univ. Press, 1996), 19.

32. John Y. Simon, *The Papers of Ulysses S. Grant* (Carbondale: Southern Illinois Univ. Press, 1967), 7:301–02; Ezra J. Warner, *Generals in Blue* (Baton Rouge: Louisiana State Univ. Press, 1964), 281–82, 278–79, 102, 116, 389, 476, 189.

33. Henry, *"First with the Most,"* 17, 472n21; "Federal Captain Lewis M. Hosea," *Sketches of War History, Ohio Commandery of the Loyal Legion* (Cincinnati: Henry C. Sherick, 1888), 1:81.

34. Simon, *Papers of Ulysses S. Grant,* 7:270–73.

35. Smith, *Grant,* 40.

36. Robert S. Henry, *As They Saw Forrest* (Jackson, Tenn.: McCowat-Mercer Press, 1956), 184.

37. Wyeth, *Life of . . . Forrest,* 508.

38. Henry, *"First with the Most";* Henry, *As They Saw Forrest,* 59.

39. Simon, *Papers of Ulysses S. Grant,* 7:270–73.

40. Record Group 393, Department of the Tennessee, National Archives, Washington, D.C.; Simon, *Papers of Ulysses S. Grant,* 9:23–24, 26–27.

41. Wyeth, *Life of . . . Forrest,* 302–3.

42. Simon, *Papers of Ulysses S. Grant,* 3:271; William S. McFeely, *Grant: A Biography* (New York: W. W. Norton & Co., 1981), 133.

43. Jordan and Pryor, *The Campaigns,* 26.

44. Kenneth M. Stampp, *The Peculiar Institution: Slavery in the Ante-bellum South* (New York: Knopf, 1956), 29–31.

45. McPherson, *Drawn with the Sword,* 48–49.

46. Stampp, *The Peculiar Institution,* 30.

47. Emory M. Thomas, *The Confederate Nation: 1861–1865* (New York: Harper & Row, 1979), 45–56, 93–94.

48. Albert W. Schroeder Jr., ed., "Writings of a Tennessee Unionist," *Tennessee Historical Quarterly* 9 (Sept. 1950): 248; Derek W. Frisby, "The Vortex of Secession: West Tennesseans and the Rush to War," in *Sister States, Enemy States,* ed. Kent T. Dollar, Larry H. Whiteaker, and W. Calvin Dickinson (Lexington: Univ. Press of Kentucky, 2009), 46–66; see also David A. Williams, *A People's History of the Civil War* (New York: New Press, 2005), 55–59, 66–67.

49. Ezra J. Warner, *Generals in Gray* (Baton Rouge: Louisiana State Univ. Press, 1959), xxi.

50. Ibid., 122.

51. Ibid., xx–xxi.

52. Warner, *Generals in Blue*, xx.

53. Ibid., 195–96.

54. Ibid., 290.

55. Ibid., 51–52.

56. Ibid., 441–42.

57. Ibid., 376.

58. Ibid., 535–36.

59. Henry, *"First with the Most,"* 506–7.

60. Bell Irvin Wiley, *The Life of Johnny Reb* (Indianapolis: Bobbs-Merrill, 1943), 338.

61. Smith, *Grant*, 231.

62. Alfred Roman, *The Military Operations of General Beauregard in the War between the States, 1861 to 1865* (1884; repr. New York: Da Capo Press, 1994), 1:402.

63. Jordan and Pryor, *The Campaigns*, 182; United States War Department, *The War of the Rebellion: A Compilation of the Official Records of the Union and Confederate Armies*, 128 vols. (Washington, D.C.: U.S. Government Printing Office, 1880–1901), ser. 1, vol. 17, pt. 1, 420 (hereafter cited as *OR*).

64. Jordan and Pryor, *The Campaigns*, 192, 194; Henry, *"First with the Most,"* 108.

65. Jordan and Pryor, *The Campaigns*, 193–94, 186, 150–51; Wyeth, *Life of . . . Forrest*, 264.

66. *OR*, ser. 1, vol. 16, pt. 2, 722–23.

67. Simon, *Papers of Ulysses S. Grant*, 7:226.

68. *OR*, ser. 1, vol. 7, 595, 598, 600; Simon, *Papers of Ulysses S. Grant* 4:318–19.

69. Simon, *Papers of Ulysses S. Grant*, 3:360, 361, 605, 7:275.

70. Smith, Grant, 234–57.

71. Wyeth, *Life of . . . Forrest*, 400.

72. Henry, *As They Saw Forrest*, 127–28.

73. David Donald and Richard N. Current, eds., *Why the North Won the Civil War* (Baton Rouge: Louisiana State Univ. Press, 1960), 51.

74. Albert T. Goodloe, *Confederate Echoes: A Soldier's Personal Story of Life in the Confederate Army from the Mississippi to the Carolinas* (Nashville: Publishing House of the M. E. Church, 1907), 179.

75. John W. Morton, *The Artillery of Nathan Bedford Forrest's Cavalry, "the Wizard of the Saddle"* (Nashville: Publishing House of the M. E. Church, 1909), 181.

76. *OR*, vol. 7, 66.

77. Ibid., 64.

78. Ibid., 329.

79. Henry, *"First with the Most,"* 55.

80. *OR*, 295–96, 386.

81. Simon, *Papers of Ulysses S. Grant*, 4:111–13.

82. Smith, *Grant*, 151.

83. Simon, *Papers of Ulysses S. Grant*, 4:171–72.

84. Robert U. Johnson and Clarence C. Buel, *Battles and Leaders of the Civil War* (New York: Century Co., 1887), 1:434; Spencer C. Tucker, *Andrew Foote: Civil War Admiral on Western Waters* (Annapolis: Naval Institute Press, 2000), 156; Roy P.

Stonesifer Jr., *The Forts Henry-Heiman and Fort Donelson Campaigns: A Study in Confederate Command* (Ph.D. diss., Penn State Univ., 1965), 253; *OR,* vol. 7, 166.

85. Smith, *Grant,* 156–63.

86. Grant, *Memoirs,* 187.

87. Examples in the Confederate cavalry include Earl Van Dorn and Joseph Wheeler.

88. Smith, *Grant,* 24–27.

89. Lloyd Lewis, *Sherman: Fighting Prophet* (New York: Harcourt Brace, 1932), 271.

90. *OR,* vol. 30, pt. 4, 508–9.

91. Wyeth, *Life of . . . Forrest,* 265–66.

92. David Nasaw, *Andrew Carnegie* (New York: Penguin Press, 2006), 714.

"A Fighting Governor"

Isham G. Harris and the Army of Tennessee

Sam Davis Elliott

Historian Thomas L. Connelly properly observed that more than any other man, Tennessee Gov. Isham G. Harris could claim the distinction of being the father of the Army of Tennessee. As Connelly noted, Harris led his state out of the Union, raised, organized, and equipped "perhaps the best organized state force in the South," and enlisted over 100,000 men for duty. These strengths were counterbalanced with Harris's failure, in Connelly's view, to align properly the state's defenses to anticipate the Federal invasion up the Tennessee and Cumberland rivers.[1] Thanks in large part to Connelly, Harris's part in the formation and early development of the Army of Tennessee is well known. But Harris's role changed with the Federal invasion of February 1862. Blessed with political acumen and a perceptive intelligence, and motivated by the desire that Tennessee be redeemed from Northern occupation, Harris became a frontline governor, retaining his role as the civilian leader of what remained of Confederate-controlled Tennessee and adopting a quasi-military role within the leadership of what eventually became the Army of Tennessee.

Isham Green Harris was born on February 10, 1818, in Franklin County, Tennessee. Successful as a merchant as a young man, he later joined his brother in the practice of law in West Tennessee and became an accomplished lawyer. His father owned a few slaves, and he married into a family of slaveholders. As a Democratic state senator and later United States congressman, he opposed antislavery measures, but was generally not counted among the "fire-eaters" in the 1850s. Harris went into political eclipse in the mid-1850s, his congressional seat gerrymandered away by the anti-

Jacksonian opposition and his rival Andrew Johnson ascendant over the Democratic Party. But effective campaigning for the Democratic ticket in 1856 and Johnson's taking a seat in the United States Senate cleared the way for Harris to be elected governor of Tennessee in 1857, and he was re-elected in 1859. As the sectional crisis deepened, Harris's pro-slavery views intensified, and by early 1861 he was an avowed secessionist. His position as governor allowed him to exercise decisive influence over Tennessee's joining the Confederacy in the late spring of 1861, as the majority of Tennesseans favored resistance to Northern "coercion" against the Confederate states. Elected again in early August 1861 for a constitutionally limited third two-year term, Harris shepherded the state into a war footing.[2]

The situation in Tennessee took a dramatic turn in late January 1862. In the space of a month, the thin Confederate line covering Tennessee's border with Kentucky dissolved with alarming rapidity. Starting with the defeat of a small Confederate army under Gen. George B. Crittenden and Gen. Felix K. Zollicoffer at Mill Springs, Kentucky, on January 19, the rebel positions at Fort Henry on the Tennessee River and Fort Donelson on the Cumberland River fell to Union naval and land forces in mid-February. The loss of Donelson and the capture of the small army that defended it left Nashville indefensible. Confederate forces retreated out of Kentucky, leaving significant portions of Middle and West Tennessee to the advancing Federals. Driven from Nashville, Harris and the Tennessee legislature fled to Memphis.[3]

While Memphis was Tennessee's largest city in 1862, it was not suited to be the state capital. The city was in the extreme southwest corner of the state, and two Union armies and over three hundred miles separated the city from Confederate-controlled East Tennessee. And Memphis was under direct threat from the Federal fleet on the Mississippi, a threat to which it would capitulate in early June 1862. The General Assembly met in Memphis until March 20, 1862, passed a militia law to mobilize "the whole military strength of the state," and then adjourned, never to meet again as a Confederate body.[4]

After the state-formed Provisional Army of Tennessee was turned over to Confederate command in the late summer of 1861, Harris's place in the military hierarchy of the Confederacy was as the civilian leader of a state on or near the front lines. Like other Southern governors, Harris counted on the Confederate military authorities to protect Tennessee from invasion, and worked to raise, arm, and support troops who would facilitate that goal. The crisis of February 1862 brought the governor briefly into close contact with Gen. Albert Sidney Johnston and Gen. P. G. T. Beauregard, and on one occasion he acted as an impromptu messenger between the two, but Harris soon returned to his civilian role. In early April 1862, no longer tied to the Bluff City by the presence of the legislature, Harris took to the field, joining General Johnston and the Confederate Army of the Mississippi.[5]

Johnston and his army gathered at Corinth, Mississippi, massing for a strike on Gen. Ulysses S. Grant's Army of the Tennessee, spread out in unfortified camps across the Tennessee state line at Pittsburg Landing on the Tennessee River. On the western side of the Federal camps was a small log structure, Shiloh Church. A second Federal army, Gen. Don Carlos Buell's Army of the Ohio, was marching from Middle Tennessee to link up with Grant. It was Johnston's intention to strike Grant and defeat his army before Buell arrived. If successful, the disasters that wracked the Confederate West in the first months of 1862 could potentially be reversed. From the standpoint of Harris and the Confederate state government, victory would at least make it conceivable to reoccupy portions of Middle and West Tennessee and recover Nashville.[6]

The Battle of Shiloh proved to be an immensely personal watershed for Governor Harris. In many ways, it defined his role with the western army for the remainder of the war, in that he created for himself a new position within the military hierarchy of the army unlike that of any other civilian. Although consulted by Johnston and Beauregard during the dark days of the previous winter, Harris was not with the army on a steady basis, nor had his relations with those officers become confidential. But the Shiloh campaign for the first time placed Harris on the personal staff of the army commander, and it was an experience that Harris would remember vividly the rest of his life.[7]

Harris was with Albert Sidney Johnston as the Army of the Mississippi massed on April 5 when the commander received a message that the Federal force at Pittsburg Landing was much larger than anticipated. After a moment of silence, Johnston turned to the governor and famously exclaimed, "I will fight them if there is a million of them!" The next day, April 6, Harris was with Johnston as the Southerners made their early morning assault. As Harris later described to Johnston's son, for the most part the Confederate advance that morning was steady, but early in the afternoon, Federal resistance became "obstinate." The opposing forces kept up firing "with great energy" for almost an hour when Johnston remarked to Harris, "They are offering stubborn resistance here. I shall have to put the bayonet to them."[8]

At this juncture, Harris was diverted, for the only recorded time during the war, to engaging the enemy. Gen. John C. Breckinridge rode up and re-

Isham Harris. (Tennessee State Library and Archives)

ported that he had a Tennessee regiment that would not fight. Harris exclaimed, "General Breckinridge, show *me* that regiment!" When Breckinridge indicated the regiment, Johnston said, "Let the Governor go to them." And Harris went and "with some difficulty" got the unit into line. Harris then returned to report his success, even as Breckinridge expressed his fear to Johnston that he could not get the brigade to which the regiment was attached to charge. Johnston promised to help, and again dispatched Harris to the balky regiment. Galloping into the midst of the regiment, the 45th Tennessee, the governor harangued the men with "a few stirring, thrilling words," and drawing his pistol, led them three successive charges against the Federals. With the help of the rest of the brigade, and that of three other Confederate brigades, the stubborn Union line was pushed back.[9]

Miraculously unhurt in the fighting, an elated Harris returned to Johnston's side. Johnston, who had exposed himself to enemy fire during this interval, had barely escaped injury when a Federal bullet struck his boot and ripped off the sole. Perceiving that the Confederate advance had exposed the rebel line "to a raking fire of a battery of the enemy on our left," Johnston sent Harris to order an attack on the Federal guns. Harris galloped away to issue the order, but when he returned, he noticed that Johnston was unsteady in his saddle. Harris reached out to steady the general and said, "General, are you wounded?" Johnston replied, "Yes, and I fear seriously." Harris and another aide guided Johnston and his horse down into a ravine, where they lifted him from his horse and laid him on the ground. W. L. Wickham was dispatched for a surgeon, while Harris held the general's head in his lap. Johnston was insensible for the remaining twenty-five or thirty minutes of his life, his life ebbing away from a severed artery in his leg. Col. William Preston and others arrived just as Johnston expired, making Harris, in the words of Johnston's son, "the faithful comrade who was with him at the last."[10]

With Johnston dead, Harris assumed the duty of informing Beauregard of the army commander's death. As his own horse had wandered off while he administered to Johnston, Harris mounted Johnston's famed thoroughbred, Fire Eater, and rode off to find the general on the other side of the battlefield, near Shiloh Church. When told of Johnston's death, a shocked Beauregard expressed regret, but then briefly discussed with Harris the situation on the Confederate right and the expectation that the battle should continue. Harris then rode away, but returned and stated, "I came here as a volunteer aid to General Johnston; as he has fallen, I no longer have any duties to perform. I intend to remain until the battle is over, and would like to be useful, if there are duties that you can assign me to." Beauregard assented.[11]

Harris was active on the field next day, relaying Beauregard's orders, making speeches to the troops, and observing the tide of the battle. Grant had weathered the fierce rebel assault on April 6, and late that day Buell's reinforcements began arriving. Accordingly, on April 7, Grant attacked, his own severely battered troops reinforced by Buell's fresh men as well as a division from the Army of the Tennessee that was unengaged the day before. Beauregard hoped for reinforcements, but as the day wore on and the exhausted Confederates were pushed back, Harris felt that the army might be endangering its ability to retreat safely by staying on the field too long. The governor expressed that view privately to Beauregard's chief of staff, Col. Thomas Jordan, who soon made a similar observation to the general. Beauregard replied, "I intend to withdraw in a few minutes." Late the afternoon of April 7, the army fell back to Corinth, Harris accompanying Beauregard back to the town.[12]

Shiloh was a bitter personal experience for Isham G. Harris. The trauma of the battle and its result were such that Harris would not revisit the battlefield until 1896, and then only at the urging of Johnston's friends, who wanted him to locate the place where Johnston spent his final minutes. With remarkable memory, Harris was able to identify the spot. As he told Shiloh park historian Maj. D. W. Reed, "The whole subject of Shiloh is a bitter memory which I do not allow myself to talk about or think about when I can help it." Not only had Harris seen Johnston die when victory seemed at hand, Harris's brother, Maj. James Trousdale Harris, an officer in the 15th Arkansas, was killed, as was a nephew, John Clinton Harris.[13]

Notwithstanding these personal blows, Harris stolidly sought duty with Beauregard and provided useful service the next day as the Army of the Mississippi was slowly forced from the field. In his report of the battle, Beauregard mentioned Harris's serving with Johnston, and the fact that Harris subsequently joined his staff. Beauregard wrote that the governor "remained with me throughout the next day, except when carrying orders or employed in encouraging the troops of his own State, to whom he gave a conspicuous example of coolness, zeal, and intrepidity."[14]

Harris proved his usefulness at army headquarters at Shiloh, and with the exception of Perryville, Harris was a trusted member of each successive army commander's staff on every battlefield of the Army of Tennessee—almost to the end of the war. In his report on Murfreesboro, the army's new commander, Gen. Braxton Bragg, commended the governor as a "zealous and efficient laborer in our cause." Accounts show that Harris was an active staff officer for Bragg during the battle of Missionary Ridge and for Gen. John Bell Hood when the Confederates captured the Federal garrison at Dalton in October 1864. Harris was a key witness to the confusion that paralyzed the Army of Tennessee at Spring Hill on November 29, 1864. He carried messages, he brought lunch, and he waited with Bragg in frustration for the attack at McLemore's Cove, in September 1863, perhaps the greatest of the Army of Tennessee's missed opportunities.[15]

As governor of Tennessee, Harris naturally took a particular interest in the troops from that state. Bragg praised Harris in his Murfreesboro report for his aid, "especially with the Tennessee troops, largely in the ascendant in this army." Even if one puts aside Thomas L. Connelly's reference to the governor as the "father" of the Army of Tennessee, Harris certainly had an affinity for and the love of the Tennessee troops in the army. From the time of the retreat from Nashville in February 1862, Harris made speeches to the Tennessee troops on two documented occasions: at Shiloh, and in the maneuvering before the battle of Chickamauga, but very likely also at many other times. After Harris made a speech that "had a good effect for the southern Cause" on April 30, 1862, Gen. William J. Hardee made a specific request two days later for Harris to make another address.[16]

Newspaperman Henry Watterson and Harris became good friends during the war. In his autobiography, Watterson recalled the significance that Harris's appearance held for the Tennessee troops:

> He at no time lost touch with the Tennessee troops, and though not always in the field, never missed a forward movement. In the early spring of 1864, just before the famous Johnston-Sherman campaign opened, General [Joseph E.] Johnston asked him to go around among the boys and "stir 'em up a bit." The Governor invited me to ride with him. Together, we visited every sector in the army. Threading the woods of North Georgia on this round, if I heard it once I heard it fifty times shouted from a distant clearing: "Here comes Governor Harris, fellows; g'wine to be a fight." His appearance at the front had always preceded and long ago been taken as a signal for battle.[17]

At the beginning of the same campaign, a correspondent for the *Memphis Appeal* reported that Harris breathed "the air of home to the [Tennessee] troops." Another correspondent noted some months before that Harris had shared the army's "hardships, privations and dangers" during its previous campaigns. Years later, Gen. William B. Bate observed that Harris exerted "every effort to mitigate the hardships of the soldiers, to supply the necessities of their daily life, and sharing with them the sunshine and storm, the heat and the cold, the joy of victory and the sting of defeat."[18]

Tennessee officers also enjoyed their governor's patronage and support, or at least certain officers did. Writing President Jefferson Davis to urge the promotion of his political ally from Memphis, Col. Marcus J. Wright, Harris held that "Tennessee is entitled to the command of her own brigades as long as she can present good, true and competent men." But, supporting his friend Wright, who happened to be the junior colonel of his brigade, necessarily meant that Harris excluded the claims of others. Col. John H. Savage of the 16th Tennessee Regiment resigned, feeling such a "rule of promotion [was] fraught with injustice and ruin to the service." Savage, a former congressman, concluded that Harris had opposed his promotion, thus becoming an enemy for the rest of Harris's life.[19]

Harris zealously pressed the claims of another and much more famed fellow Memphian, Nathan Bedford Forrest. Harris originally facilitated

Forrest's first cavalry command, and he actually rode with Forrest during a raid he undertook into West Tennessee in the spring of 1864. The capture of Fort Pillow was one of the incidents on that raid (although Harris was not likely present), and Harris was quick to pen a defense of Forrest against the claims that a massacre of Federal prisoners, white and black, had occurred when the fort fell. The admiration was mutual as Forrest was reported in a newspaper to have said, "By God—Harris is a fighting Governor." Forrest's service record indicates that at least with regard to his promotions to major general and lieutenant general, Harris had his say. In the days following the battle of Chickamauga in September 1863, Harris wrote President Davis, urging Forrest's promotion to major general, observing that the Tennessean was "extremely efficient and eminently deserving promotion." Forrest was promoted later that year. In January 1865, Harris again solicited a promotion for his friend, this time to lieutenant general. Forrest was promoted effective February 28, 1865, and in March and April 1865, Harris traveled across the fading Confederacy from Richmond to Mississippi to deliver the promotion personally to the general.[20]

After the fall of Atlanta in early September 1864, disputes between army commander Gen. John B. Hood and his senior corps commander, Gen. William J. Hardee, led to Hardee's assignment to a new command on the Georgia coast. The senior division commander in the corps was Maj. Gen. Benjamin F. Cheatham, a member of a prominent Middle Tennessee family and a hard-fighting veteran of the Army of Tennessee. In the Confederate Army, a corps was properly the command of a lieutenant general. While there was some effort to get a senior officer to take the command, Cheatham eventually took control of the corps, and led it as Hood marched the army into Middle Tennessee. Hood repeatedly sought Harris's aid in promoting Cheatham to lieutenant general, but cooled after the debacle at Spring Hill on November 29, 1864. Harris believed that Cheatham had been improperly blamed for the incident and went to Richmond in March 1865 to urge Cheatham's promotion. Having resigned his command after the army's terrible defeat at Nashville the previous December, Hood was not particularly interested in correcting the record. Cheatham finished the war as a major general.[21]

Correspondence from February 1863 illustrates the significant influence Harris had with Cheatham and others in the army's leadership. In early 1863, the army was under the command of Braxton Bragg, who, in the words of one officer, was "as much influenced by his enemies as his friends and does not know how to control the one or influence the other." Bragg foolishly asked for a vote of confidence from his officers in the aftermath of the battle of Murfreesboro, and did not receive one. When he learned of the situation, Jefferson Davis sent his Western Theater commander, Gen. Joseph E. Johnston, to investigate and report. Johnston traveled to Bragg's headquarters at Tullahoma and spoke with Bragg, corps commanders Leonidas Polk and Hardee, and, significantly, Harris. After summarizing the views of Bragg and his two lieutenants, Johnston reported: "Governor Harris, with whom the general officers converse more freely than with their military superiors, thinks that they want confidence in their commander, but that it is due to the Kentucky campaign, and thinks it is declining." Harris thought the lack of confidence was "not such an evil as would result from the removal of General Bragg." Johnston also noted that Cheatham had stated to the governor that he would not fight under Bragg again, but that Harris thought "he can control that officer and bring him to his senses."[22]

Harris's influence relative to the high command of the Army of Tennessee manifested itself on a number of occasions and transcended his natural desire to advance the careers of his fellow Tennesseans. As Harris thought that the removal of Bragg in early 1863 would be an "evil," he made sure that was communicated to the government through Johnston. Later that year, Harris became alarmed that Gen. John C. Pemberton would be placed in command of the army reassembling after the fall of Vicksburg, and he urged President Davis not to do so. After the loss at Chattanooga in November 1863, Harris wrote a friend that while Bragg was "a much abler and better man than the world is willing to believe, [he] had to a great extent lost the confidence of the officers and men of the army. . . ." Harris then went to Richmond and spent three weeks urging the assignment of Joseph E. Johnston to the command of the Army of Tennessee, which occurred on December 18, 1863. Then, having had a hand in Johnston's promotion, Harris used his friendship with Bragg to urge reinforcements for Johnston so that the Army of Tennessee could mount an offensive into Tennessee, rather optimistically predicting that he could raise thirty thousand new recruits if left in possession of the state for thirty days.[23]

Harris's several trips to Richmond during the course of the war afforded him an opportunity to confer with President Davis personally, as did Davis's three trips to the Army of Tennessee in December 1862, October 1863, and September 1864. Harris also wrote Davis on occasion about conditions in the army. One of the more unique episodes in the history of the Army of Tennessee occurred on the night of January 2, 1864, when Gen. Patrick Cleburne, one of the army's true heroes, boldly proposed to a meeting of most of the high-ranking officers of the army that the Confederates arm slaves to fight for the secessionist cause in return for their freedom. Harris was not present at the meeting, but felt compelled after some reflection to report the incident to Davis, not to impugn the patriotism of the officers in favor of the proposal, but to urge that the matter be hushed up, fearing that public knowledge of the proposal "would produce the greatest possible discontent." Davis agreed, and further discussion of the matter was suppressed.[24]

Throughout the war, Harris burned with the desire to drive the Northern invaders from Tennessee. Albert Sidney Johnston's attack at Shiloh was an effort to restore the losses in Tennessee in the late winter of 1862. Later that year, another opportunity arose. In July 1862, Bragg moved his army to Chattanooga from Tupelo, Mississippi, intending on taking the offensive with a view toward recovering Nashville and Middle Tennessee, and it appears that he consulted closely with Harris in preparation for the move. In late August, over Harris's protest, however, Bragg's desire to support a smaller force marching into Kentucky under Gen. Edmund Kirby Smith sent his army marching into the Bluegrass State, away from Middle Tennessee. Even though Bragg did not invade Middle Tennessee, his move north drew Federal forces from Middle Tennessee, leaving the Federal garrison in Nashville isolated.[25]

Undeterred, Harris turned to the other large Confederate force in striking distance of Nashville: the Confederate forces under generals Earl Van Dorn and Sterling Price that confronted Federal troops in northern Mississippi and southern West Tennessee. Writing Price on September 20, 1862, from Lebanon, Tennessee, about twenty-five miles to the east of Nashville, Harris mentioned that he had left Bragg after the latter's victory at Munfordville, Kentucky, on September 17. Harris relayed that the Federal garrison at Nashville was isolated, "which I have no means of dislodging until you can reach there. General Bragg confidently expects your army to reach Nashville very soon and drive the enemy from that city, and my hopes of its early redemption from Federal oppression are based upon your army." Price responded on September 28, indicating that he had intended on advancing to Nashville, but that military necessity required that he join forces with Van Dorn. While Price promised that the combined force would "at once proceed northward," it instead proceeded to launch a failed attack on Federal troops at Corinth the first week of October, essentially removing it from Harris's plans.[26]

Abhorring the vacuum left by the Federal withdrawal from Middle Tennessee, Harris and his fellow Confederate Tennesseans filled the country outside the city with irregular cavalry. Harris appointed Gen. S. R. Anderson as commander of the state forces in the area, in an effort to coordinate the various and sundry horsemen harrying the Federals. They succeeded in cutting off the city from resupply for a period of fifty days, but as the garrison's commander, Gen. James S. Negley later stated, the garrison did not suffer much more than "inconvenience." The railroad line from the base at Chattanooga was slowly rebuilt back to La Vergne, within a few miles of Nashville, while Harris vainly continued his appeal for regular Confederate troops. Eventually, Negley attacked the rebels at La Vergne on October 7, inflicting a sharp defeat on Anderson. Forrest arrived and took command later in October, and eventually Gen. John C. Breckinridge's division was diverted from Knoxville, but except for a probe of Negley's lines on November 4, no further attempt was made on Nashville.[27]

In the end, Harris's efforts to influence Bragg, Price, or the authorities at Richmond to make a direct attack on Nashville in the fall of 1862 were unsuccessful. In the words of historian Thomas Connelly, Harris had "without any authority assumed a quasi-military command in the Murfreesboro area." Putting aside the question of Harris's authority, which he certainly would have disputed as commander-in-chief of Tennessee's state forces, the governor's efforts to recover Confederate losses in Middle Tennessee showed his determination and organizing ability, and while Nashville was not recaptured, much of Middle Tennessee was recovered. While Bragg returned from Kentucky in late October 1862, disappointed in the tepid response of the populace to his efforts to raise troops, he found that Harris, Anderson, and Forrest had recovered the country between Chattanooga and the environs of Nashville, and that Breckinridge's division was camped at Murfreesboro. Harris had effectively taken advantage of the absence of Federal troops to reassert control of a large portion of Middle Tennessee.[28]

Harris's untapped military abilities manifested themselves on a number of occasions. In March 1863, it was reported in a Tennessee newspaper that a ranking officer opined that Harris's dispatches "evince a clearer military sagacity than those of any one connected with the army of the West." A friend recalled that in late July 1864, Harris was present at army headquarters in Atlanta when a scout reported to Gen. John B. Hood that a column of Federal cavalry under Gen. George Stoneman was heading toward Macon, Georgia. Hood refused to believe the report, but Harris correctly surmised that the scout was correct. And anticipating that Harris might be relieved of his gubernatorial duties by an election in Confederate-held Middle Tennessee prior to the opening of the Chattanooga campaign in the late summer of

1863, Bragg wrote President Davis and suggested that the chief magistrate consider a military appointment for Harris, enthusiastically stating that "if I had a vacant Brigade I should gladly recommend him for it." Unfortunately for the governor, while elected, the successor could not take office under the state constitution unless he could be qualified in the presence of a majority of the members of the legislature. Therefore, his military talents could only continue to be employed in an indirect fashion.[29]

Appropriately, several of Harris's various roles with the Army of Tennessee manifested themselves during its final campaign into Tennessee in November and December 1864. As he had stated in his letter to Bragg in March 1864, Harris hoped that the Army of Tennessee's invasion of Middle Tennessee would raise troops for the Confederate cause. Harris issued a proclamation that called on Tennesseans to "arise" to drive the Yankee invader from the state, and newspapers published his prediction that the now-skeletal Tennessee regiments he raised at the first of the war would be "filled." As he had with Albert Sidney Johnston, Braxton Bragg, and Joseph E. Johnston, Harris acted as an aide to John Bell Hood in the field and, in particular, was a witness to the failure at Spring Hill. On December 15 and 16, 1864, Federal Gen. George H. Thomas launched the counterstroke that drove the much-reduced Army of Tennessee from the outskirts of Nashville. The defeated Confederates retreated south, and on December 18, Hood debated whether or not to try to hold the line of the Duck River during the winter. The next day, Forrest appeared and urged Hood to retreat further south behind the line of the Tennessee River. Demonstrating his clear military judgment, Harris spoke up and concurred with the cavalryman. And finally, as the retreat was ending, the governor again filled his role as correspondent with President Davis, writing him on Christmas Day to endorse Hood's performance during the campaign. If the effort to achieve promotion for Cheatham in the wake of the Spring Hill affair is added to the mix, the Army of Tennessee's last foray into the state that gave it birth was essentially a microcosm of its "father's" continuing role with the army.[30]

While other "war governors," on both sides, could possibly claim that they did much to mobilize the resources of their state to contribute to the war effort, Harris alone had a record of service in the field that rivaled that of many soldiers. As Bate observed after Harris's death, the governor was the Army of Tennessee's "inseparable companion from beginning to end, and heard its first reveille and its last tattoo." While a bit of memorial hyperbole might be expected from an old comrade and political ally, Harris's unique role with the army was contemporaneously recognized by Nathan

Bedford Forrest, an authority on fighting. There were many "war governors," but Isham Green Harris's role with the Army of Tennessee made him the Civil War's only "fighting governor."[31]

Notes

1. Thomas L. Connelly, *Army of the Heartland: The Army of Tennessee 1861–62* (Baton Rouge: Louisiana State Univ. Press, 1967), 25–45.

2. Sam Davis Elliott, *Isham G. Harris of Tennessee: Confederate Governor and United States Senator* (Baton Rouge: Louisiana State Univ. Press, 2010), 2–85.

3. Connelly, *Army of the Heartland,* 86–142; Stephen D. Engle, *Struggle for the Heartland: The Campaigns from Fort Henry to Corinth* (Lincoln: Univ. of Nebraska Press, 2001), 53–98, 108–12.

4. Robert H. White, *Messages of the Governors of Tennessee* (Nashville: Tennessee Historical Commission, 1959), 5:369–72; Harris to Jefferson Davis, Mar. 24, 1862, Harris Papers, Tennessee State Library and Archives.

5. Elliott, *Isham G. Harris,* 82–99; William Preston Johnston, *The Life of Gen. Albert Sidney Johnston* (New York: D. Appleton & Co., 1879), 506; United States War Department, *The War of the Rebellion: A Compilation of the Official Records of the Union and Confederate Armies,* 128 vols. (Washington, D.C.: U.S. Government Printing Office, 1880–1901) (hereafter cited as *OR*), 7:895–96; Alfred Roman, *The Military Operations of General Beauregard,1861–1865* (New York: Harper & Brooks, 1883), 1:506; Harris to A. S. Johnston, Apr. 1, 1862, Fort Donelson/Lloyd Tilghman Files, Eleanor S. Brockenbrough Library, Museum of the Confederacy.

6. O. Edward Cunningham, *Shiloh and the Western Campaign of 1862,* ed. Gary D. Joiner and Timothy B. Smith (New York: Savas Beatie, 2007), 91–114.

7. Elliott, *Isham G. Harris,* 103–6, 295.

8. Johnston, *The Life of Gen. Albert Sidney Johnston,* 569–70, 610–11; Harris to William Preston, Apr. 6, 1862, ser. 1, Box 13, Folder 140, Shiloh National Military Park Archives (this document is a typescript of a letter Harris wrote that evening, kept in William Preston's pocket notebook, now in the National Archives). It should be noted that the main body of the Confederate Army in the west fought at Shiloh and Perryville as the Army of the Mississippi, and assumed its more well-known name as the Army of Tennessee in November 1862.

9. Johnston, *The Life of Gen. Albert Sidney Johnston,* 611, 613; "Gen. Albert Sidney Johnston," *Confederate Veteran* 3 (Mar. 1895): 86; *Memphis Daily Appeal,* Apr. 9, 1862; Cunningham, *Shiloh and the Western Campaign of 1862,* 268–73.

10. Johnston, *The Life of Gen. Albert Sidney Johnston,* 613–14; Harris to William Preston, Apr. 6, 1862, Shiloh National Military Park.

11. Johnston, *The Life of Gen. Albert Sidney Johnston,* 615–16; Roman, *The Military Operations of General Beauregard,* 1:297, 506, 537.

12. *OR,* vol. 10, pt. 1, 387, 594; Elliott, *Isham G. Harris,* 112–13; Connelly, *Army of the Heartland,* 173–75; Thomas Jordan, "Notes of a Confederate Staff Officer at

Shiloh," *The Century Illustrated Monthly Magazine* 29 (Nov. 1884–Apr. 1885): 633–34; Roman, *The Military Operations of General Beauregard,* 1:533.

13. D. W. Reed to Basil Duke, July 20, 1906, ser. 1, Box 13, Folder 140, Shiloh National Military Park Archives; Elliott, *Isham G. Harris,* 111, 294–95.

14. *OR,* vol. 10, pt. 1, 390.

15. Isham G. Harris, Compiled Service Records of Confederate General and Staff Officers, and Nonregimental Enlisted Men, M-331, National Archives; *OR,* vol. 20, pt. 1, 671, 38; ibid., pt. 3, 984; ibid., 39, pt. 1, 717–21; ibid., vol. 6, 107–9, 113–17; "Battle of Chattanooga," *Athens (Ga.) Southern Banner,* Dec. 16, 1863; Harris to James D. Porter, May 20, 1877, in Benjamin Franklin Cheatham, "Lost Opportunity at Spring Hill—General Cheatham's Reply to General Hood," *Southern Historical Society Papers* 9 (Oct., Nov., and Dec. 1881): 524, 532; Harris to Mrs. General Ewell, Mar. 7, 1864, George Washington Campbell Papers, Library of Congress.

16. *OR,* vol. 20, pt. 1, 671; W. J. McMurry, *History of the Twentieth Tennessee Regiment Volunteer Infantry, C.S.A.* (Nashville: The Publication Committee, 1904), 203; *OR,* vol. 30, pt. 3, 581; Ann York Franklin, comp., *The Civil War Diaries of Capt. Alfred Tyler Fielder, 12th Tennessee Regiment Infantry, Company B, 1861–1865* (n.p., 1996), 48; Roy to IGH, May 2, 1862, Harris Papers, TSLA.

17. Henry Watterson, *"Marse Henry": An Autobiography* (New York: George H. Doran Co., 1919), 1:80–81.

18. (Atlanta) *Memphis Appeal,* May 9, 1864; (Atlanta) *Knoxville Register,* Oct. 14, 1863; *Congressional Record,* 55 Cong. 1 sess., 1898, 3171.

19. Harris to Jefferson Davis, Nov. 30, 1862, in Marcus J. Wright, Compiled Service Records of Confederate General and Staff Officers, and Nonregimental Enlisted Men, M-331, National Archives; Savage to S. Cooper, Feb. 4, 1863, in John H. Savage, Compiled Service Records of Confederate Soldiers Who Served in Organizations from the State of Tennessee, M-268, National Archives; Elliott, *Isham G. Harris,* 135. The Compiled Service Records of other Tennessee officers, such as Alexander P. Stewart and John C. Brown, also bear endorsements from Harris.

20. Elliott, *Isham G. Harris,* 156, 180; *Macon Daily Telegraph,* May 5, 1864; *Atlanta Southern Confederacy,* June 15, 1864; Harris to Jefferson Davis, Sept. 24, 1863, Petition to Jefferson Davis, Jan. 3, 1865, and other materials in Nathan B. Forrest, Compiled Service Records of Confederate General and Staff Officers, and Nonregimental Enlisted Men, M-331, National Archives.

21. Christopher Losson, *Tennessee's Forgotten Warriors: Frank Cheatham and His Confederate Division* (Knoxville: Univ. of Tennessee Press, 1989), 2–4, 195–97, 215; *Terry L. Jones, ed., Campbell Brown's Civil War: With Ewell and the Army of Northern Virginia* (Baton Rouge: Louisiana State Univ. Press, 2001), 169–71.

22. W. W. Mackall to his wife, Sept. 29, 1863, W. W. Mackall Papers, Southern Historical Collection, University of North Carolina; Steven E. Woodworth, *Jefferson Davis and His Generals* (Lawrence: Univ. Press of Kansas, 1990), 196–98; Thomas L. Connelly, *Autumn of Glory* (Baton Rouge: Louisiana State Univ. Press, 1971), 77–86; *OR,* vol. 23, pt. 2, 624.

23. Harris to Davis, Aug. 12, 1863, Haskell M. Monroe Jr., James T. McIntosh, and Lynda Lasswell Crist, eds., *The Papers of Jefferson Davis* (Baton Rouge: Louisiana State

Univ. Press, 1997), 9:341; *OR*, vol. 31, pt. 3, 842–43; ibid., vol. 52, pt. 2, 516; Harris to Mrs. General Ewell, Mar. 7, 1864, George Washington Campbell Papers, Library of Congress; Harris to Bragg, Mar. 6, 1864, Bragg Papers, Western Reserve.

24. Connelly, *Autumn of Glory*, 40, 241, 318–19, 469; *OR*, vol. 52, pt. 2, 595, 608; Harris to Davis, *The Papers of Jefferson Davis*, 10:177–78.

25. *OR*, vol. 16, pt. 1, 120, 261–62, 710–11; ibid., vol. 16, pt. 2, 740, 760; Grady McWhiney, *Braxton Bragg and Confederate Defeat in the West* (1969; repr., Tuscaloosa: Univ. of Alabama Press, 1991), 1:266–67.

26. *OR*, vol. 16, pt. 2, 858; ibid., vol. 17, pt. 2, 715; Peter Cozzens, *The Darkest Days of the War: The Battles of Iuka and Corinth* (Chapel Hill: Univ. of North Carolina Press, 1997), 118–25, 159–279.

27. *OR*, vol. 16, pt. 1, 258, 261; ibid., vol. 16, pt. 2, 878, 888, 891, 997, Elliott, *Isham G. Harris*, 123–26.

28. Connelly, *Autumn of Glory*, 14–15.

29. *Chattanooga Daily Rebel*, Mar. 18, 1863; "Gov. Harris at the Close of the War," *Confederate Veteran* 5 (Aug. 1897): 402–3; Bragg to Jefferson Davis, Aug. 7, 1863, *The Papers of Jefferson Davis*, 9:322; Elliott, *Isham G. Harris*, 146–47.

30. *New York Times*, Dec. 25, 1864; *Macon Daily Telegraph*, Dec. 9 and 31, 1864; Harris to C. T. Quintard, Dec. 29, 1894, Quintard Papers, Duke University; Sam Davis Elliott, ed., *Doctor Quintard, Chaplain C.S.A. and Second Bishop of Tennessee: The Memoir and Civil War Diary of Charles Todd Quintard* (Baton Rouge: Louisiana State Univ. Press, 2003), 200–201; Harris to Jefferson Davis, Dec. 25, 1864, The Papers of Jefferson Davis, 11:248–49.

31. *Congressional Record*, 55 Cong., 1st sess., 1898, 3171; *Atlanta Southern Confederacy*, June 15, 1864.

Revisiting the Heartland from War to Reconstruction

An Afterword

BENJAMIN FRANKLIN COOLING

Make no mistake: war is hell, quoting William Tecumseh Sherman, who apprenticed in Kentucky and Tennessee on his way to military fame. It is death and destruction, disease and suffering attached to what meager glory and honor we may think attends such sacrifice to God and Nation, Banner and Cause. The people of Tennessee and Kentucky discovered this from 1861 to 1865. Yet, today we continue to wallow in Patriotic Gore (Edmund Wilson's phrase) by way of Civil War memory, commemoration, and self-inflicted veneration of reenactment of carnage. While always doubting Civil War statistics, even simple unofficial tallies in Frances Kennedy's edited Civil War battlefield guide for significant engagements in Kentucky and Tennessee number over 160,000 casualties for killed, wounded, and captured.[1] These statistics suggest two things. The Civil War and Reconstruction were, after all, America's fiery trail to true nationhood as they were also for Tennessee and Kentucky and their residents (citizens or not) in a national union. The statistics also suggest the impact of combat on participants and how military action forever changed the lives of survivors and the landscape, much less the dead.

The saga of our Civil War is mainly about people in the final analysis. Chapters in this volume suggest what Abraham Lincoln and others termed "a people's war." The saga is about generals and politicians and the common folk (in uniform and not). War and Reconstruction marched across lives regardless of gender, ethnicity, age—and even species. Animals and things, even the landscape itself, were locked in this people's conflict—lest we forget that fact. We would do well to study this whole symbiotic relationship when trying to fathom the forces of danger and destruction, success and failure across the upper heartland.

Nearly a generation ago I posited, perhaps presumptuously, that events in Tennessee and Kentucky determined the outcome of the Civil War. I suggested in two succeeding volumes how a legacy from the very first military events in these states reflected lost opportunities and unrequited dreams that might have avoided much of those casualty statistics but instead merely prolonged a brutal and costly struggle. That struggle extended past the carnage symbolized by Franklin and aftershock of the war's most decisive battle at Nashville, extending into what we call "Reconstruction" with ramifications even unto Reconciliation.[2] Chronicling Kentucky and Tennessee in those three volumes convinces me of a holistic paradigm that we fail to appreciate even after our twenty-first-century experiences in Afghanistan, Iraq, Vietnam, and the Balkans toward the end of the last century. Conflict actually begins long before the combat phases called war, and embraces vague terms like "stabilization," "reconstruction," and "nation-building" all intermingled in time and place. Even though the venerable journalist-scholar Stanley Horn may have half convinced us earlier that Nashville was the decisive battle of the Civil War, I would add Henry and Donelson. The latter set the course that concluded with the former, although war is never over—until it is over.[3]

One wonders today with the Sesquicentennial and political disquietude in Washington and across the nation whether critical components of the Civil War era linger even past the civil rights era, which supposedly eclipsed the fundamental reason for the war in the first place. One surely can wonder about that interval of thirty-four months of continued bloodshed between the upper heartland episodes of Henry-Donelson and Franklin-Nashville to answer whether violence ever burns itself out in the hearts and minds of man despite the futility of resolving much of anything by war. Certainly Kentucky and Tennessee in the early 1860s illustrated how war in various forms involved a certain military determinism every day, month, and year until the conflict there simply burned itself out. This may explain the continuing flood of military history by various Civil War cognoscenti.[4]

From Kentucky-born war presidents Abraham Lincoln and Jefferson Davis to lesser, although nonetheless influential, politicians (witness Sam Elliott's insightful chapter on Tennessee's Confederate Gov. Isham G. Harris in this volume) and Volunteer native generals like Benjamin Franklin Cheatham and Nathan Bedford Forrest (represented by insightful comments from Christopher Losson and Jack Hurst), the sister states held the key to the training and development of a generation of leaders spawned from citizen soldiery as well as professionals useful to regional and national development in war and peace. Tennessean Alexander P. Stewart was yet another, an unsung corps commander whose professional devotion to duty but lack of pretension may still shroud him from modern appreciation.[5] Tennessee and Kentucky also held the fate for more controversial figures like Don Carlos Buell and Braxton Bragg (protagonists on at least one battlefield of the sister states). Stephen Engle's explanation of a Union general whose experience with handling military affairs in the upper heartland shows that modernization of war and politics clearly had passed him by. Earl Hess's and Losson's separate explanations of Buell's unpopular Confederate opponent in the middle period of the war (who many believe lost the heartland) underscore the role of personal misfortune in this dark and bloody ground.

If we accept the premise that somehow everything in war relates directly to military affairs, then these chapters help us to understand the thirty-four months between the Union Army-Navy victories at forts Henry and Donelson and John Schofield's Franklin achievement and George H. Thomas's follow-on at Nashville over what surely must be the Confederacy's epitome of poor luck, John Bell Hood. A continuing litany of bloodshed and destruction not just from main force operations but also thanks to growing partisan or guerrilla warfare and eventually pure brigandage filled that period. Dashed hopes and dreams of both military and civilian participants, the dogged persistence and resistance to invasion by the secessionist-persuaded, the occupation and societal breakdown from perhaps poorly implemented actions by both national and residual state governments under the guise of civil-military relations can be sensed from chapters in this volume. Moreover, the unquenchable thirst for resources in modern war led Confederate and Union authorities to tap white males and liberate their black counterparts in quantity and extent heretofore unenvisioned, hence they were unprepared for the result.

What role did Kentucky and Tennessee play between campaigns and battles by the armies and their generals? Easily remembered are battlefields from Mill Springs to Shiloh, Richmond and Perryville, Stones River and Chickamauga-Chattanooga—epic moments in the Confederacy's elusive quest to place its western frontier on the Ohio River and the Union's counter-drive to eliminate enemy armies, occupy and redeem territory in rebellion, and restore the Union. We can gaze today at their silent landscape as Sacred Ground. Yet, what of the thousands of acres that witnessed a different kind of spatial relationship to these shrines? Was not this landscape also part of the conflict requiring military involvement either as part of economic warfare or genuine concern about another people that transitioned any themes from mystical Union or defense of Southern homeland? Battles and irregular operations moved the Upper South to humanitarian liberation and ersatz emancipation or defense of human property that even yet defies clarity. Hearts and minds were hardened via persecution, depredations, property confiscation, theft, and atrocities by representatives of the state in the gray area between home and fighting front, something of an ungovernable no-man's-land.[6] Even fields of strife mostly now lost to us for preservation and remembrance like Barboursville, Ivy Mountain and Paducah in Kentucky or Bean Station, Campbell's Station, Chattanooga, Columbia, Dover, Fort Henry, Fort Sanders, Johnsonville, Memphis, Murfreesboro (not Stones River, although most of that too), Nashville, and Wauhatchie, plus obscure crossroads, river fords, and front yards of rural dwellings factor into the account.[7]

Studying the interludes between battles and campaigns can also highlight something so sublime as to be lost in the glories of battlefield—the ever suppressed story of logistics and support of field operations. Here Tennessee and Kentucky played an indispensable role, a support role in which the logistical trail of armies often outnumbered the bodies brought on line of battle. Cities like Louisville, Lexington, Bowling Green, Paducah, Clarksville, Nashville, Memphis, and Knoxville became vital for political and economic control and perpetration of the war effort of the armies and navies in the field. Smaller towns and hamlets became "strategic hamlets" (in the parlance of the Vietnam era) for territorial and population control while camps and stations, fortified posts and supply dumps from Camp Dick Robinson to Johnsonville to a rejuvenated Union Fort Donelson reflected this other face of warfare in America. For these reasons, fascinating "what-ifs" emerge from Michael Toomey's exploration of that stillborn and less appreciated Union move to take East Tennessee in 1861, opening the eventual avenue that became a line of communications for Ambrose Burnside's Knoxville campaign in 1863 and, to some degree, a postwar railroad effort reflected by the Cincinnati Southern line. Brian McKnight hints at an almost mystical presence of the Cumberland Gap in strategic implementation that never quite vaulted that key location to the front rank in war. Maybe both sides subliminally realized that nostalgic appreciation of the Wilderness Road, which had opened the Old Northwest to ancestors in an emerging nation, was not truly worth bloody sacrifice in major battle.

We are left—even a century and a half after these military events—with focus and proportionality. Did the celebrated death of Confederate Gen. Felix Zollicoffer at Mill Springs divert fundamental recognition that the Union victory there under George H. Thomas (notwithstanding Buell's invertebrate leadership) broke the deified Albert Sidney Johnston's Confederate defense line from Columbus, Kentucky, on the Mississippi to Cumberland Gap in the Appalachians? More importantly, as historian Kent Masterson Brown observed elsewhere, "never, after Mill Springs, would Kentucky form the western and northern frontier of the Confederacy." The ultimate irony should be that it was Thomas, not Grant, who inaugurated and established his own bookends of major combat in these states with Mill Springs and Nashville![8]

Yet, the supreme irony surely emerges via Wiley Sword's chapter on the "Gettysburg of the West"—Franklin. This epic orgasm of carnage (surpassing even Pickett's destruction at Gettysburg) creases the seam between leadership and followership, valor and stupidity that in both cases produced disastrous results for the Confederacy. It once more epitomizes America's fascination with disaster, bloodshed, and "what-ifs" of tragedy. Sword is a master of emotions, a Shakespearean conveyor of tragedy that will always epitomize the bloodiest of the battles for the heartland. Apparently forgotten to us, however, is the arguably more fascinating and brilliant maneuver campaign of the war, the June 1863 Tullahoma, Tennessee, operation. Here, a much maligned William S. Rosecrans drove an equally maligned Braxton Bragg out of Middle Tennessee at a fraction's cost in human capital that we normally associate with the war. To Tullahoma participants themselves, events at Gettysburg and Vicksburg held no candle to that parry and thrust between the Army of the Cumberland and the Army of Tennessee (the names themselves indicative of kinsmen at war in the upper heartland). Nobody has ever satisfactorily explained why veterans, descendants, and contemporaries have glided past this story to more sanguine fields and excessive casualty lists. All along, have we been praising and venerating the wrong warhorse of Mars?

Stop for a moment and examine this unsung Tullahoma campaign undertaken in late June 1863 in Rutherford and Bedford counties, Tennessee. Even the victor was perplexed when his achievement—at a cost of scarcely six hundred Federal casualties (in contrast to 25,000 Union and 28,000 Confederates at Gettysburg and Vicksburg's estimated)—went unnoticed in Washington. "You do not appear to observe the fact that this noble army has driven the rebels from Middle Tennessee," Army of the Cumberland's

Gen. William S. Rosecrans vented to Secretary of War Edward M. Stanton on July 7, 1863. He chided that distant Washington officials should not overlook "so great an event because it is not written in letters of blood." Justifiably, his achievement fully equaled Gettysburg for result if not quite reaching the lofty place in reopening the Mississippi River to trade and commerce that kept the Upper Midwest in the war.[9] Of course, even then, the latter really awaited capture of Port Hudson, Louisiana, five days later to complete the transaction. Still, Tullahoma cleared the upper heartland in a less costly fashion, thus completing opportunities that Union arms seemingly had squandered ever since Grant's groundbreaking winter success at opening the Tennessee and Cumberland valleys in the winter of 1862.

Rosecrans's careful planning and preparation in defiance of predictable prodding from Washington to attack Bragg, and his superb execution despite inclement weather, reflected the Tullahoma campaign's success in a nutshell. All winter of 1863 after Stones River, "Old Rosey" (as he was known) and Bragg had faced one another as the Confederate leader entrenched a "Duck River line" from Shelbyville to McMinnville. Bragg expected a reverse Stones River whereby Rosecrans and the Federals would attack his defenses. Key positions at Liberty, Hoover's, and Guy's gaps in the knobs in the Highland Rim section of the Cumberland foothills were guarded by infantry and artillery while the static situation enabled Bragg to detach reinforcements to break Grant's siege at Vicksburg. By June 25, with Washington's displeasure at inaction mounting, Rosecrans feinted at Episcopal bishop and Confederate Gen. Leonidas Polk's position at Shelbyville to the west and sent three corps storming the gaps on the other flank. Bragg's cavalry, including those under Forrest and Wheeler, performed insignificantly in uncovering the Federal moves. Significant action took place at Hoover's Gap, where Yankee mounted infantry, sporting repeating rifles personally purchased and supplied by brigade commander John Wilder, drove off defenders in a heavy rainstorm. George H. Thomas's corps then held the position and Bragg realized too late that Rosecrans's turning movement had cost him Middle and East Tennessee. He withdrew behind the Tennessee River at Chattanooga, thus opening everything south of the Duck River to north Georgia and northern Alabama as well as eastward from the Cumberlands to final Federal advance. All this at minimal human cost!

Of course the result was lost upon everyone with the subsequent Chickamauga- Chattanooga and Knoxville campaigns when Rosecrans suffered ignominious defeat and banishment to Missouri and a new team of Grant and Sherman joined Thomas to defend Chattanooga, while Ambrose Burnside held on in East Tennessee. Chickamauga's 34,500 casualties, Chattanooga's nearly 13,000 additional losses, and East Tennessee's various engagements fed in several thousand more to make Tullahoma a child's play in comparison. Surely worth greater consideration than that given just by professional military schools as a case study in the military art, Rosecrans had sought to avoid another costly Stones River. Successive generations seem to have missed that point. Historians have treated this significant campaign only as a prelude to subsequent carnage. Perhaps it was because Rosecrans was not Grant, Sherman, or Thomas. Or perhaps it was not bloody enough to seem worthwhile.[10]

Confederate aversion to talking about the Tullahoma reverse was understandable—victory at Chickamauga was more memorable. Still, at least one rebel brigadier was impressed. South Carolinian Arthur Middleton Manigault felt that "This campaign of General Rosecrans, lasting not more than two weeks, was, I think, the most brilliant of the war, and although no battle was fought, his skillful maneuvering of Bragg out of Tennessee (for although Chattanooga and a strip of the state along the river, as well as East Tennessee, were still in our possession, yet all the most fertile and more wealthy portion of the state was lost to us), even though he never before or afterwards did anything, ought to stamp him as an able general." Thomas Connelly, the redoubtable modern chronicler of Bragg's Army of Tennessee—while at great pains to explain lackluster performance up and down the rebel chain of command—declared that "probably such precious ground had never been bought so cheaply by the Federals." Overall, Tullahoma seemed bland to other participants like Brig. Gen. W. H. Lytle, commanding the first brigade of the 3rd Division, Twentieth Corps. He officially reported on July 6 that there no casualties, but that "it need hardly be stated" that nearly the entire march from Murfreesboro was conducted in a rainstorm "probably without precedent in these latitudes," and that consequently the roads were mainly impassable.[11]

Still, said Lytle, it gave him great pleasure to report that his officers and men "endured their extraordinary exposure and fatigue with the utmost cheerfulness; that there was little or no straggling on the march, and our one matter of regret—that the enemy was not met in force." More personally, however, four days later he wrote to a fellow officer at headquarters that "the news is indeed most glorious so far thus far." It seemed to Lytle "that the Confeds are 'goner up,' so at least the *dawn begins* to *break*." Such varied comments contrasted with a tragic note in a letter to his sister on the Fourth of July wherein he recounted: "to my great regret during the skirmish a poor little boy was accidentally shot dead by one of our sharpshooters." He had run out from a cabin to repair a fence, was mistaken for nearby Confederates by his gray garb, and his father had always been a Union man. As their column marched by, a sister cried out from upstairs with tears streaming down her cheek, "'*Hurrah for the Union,* but oh you have killed our dear little Freddy.'" The bereaved father did not censure Lytle's men, rather swearing "vengeance on the rebels who had thus been the cause of his disaster." "Such is war," decided the brigadier.[12]

Union participants remembered the Tullahoma period more for Fourth of July celebrations and victory announcements from Gettysburg and Vicksburg. German-born Constantin Grebner of the 9th Ohio recalled firing salute cannon, soldiers' camp games, and patriotic songs, and food was in short supply as commissary wagons were stuck north of the flooded Elk River and the bridges had been destroyed by Bragg's retreating men. Another participant, Gen. William Passmore Carlin, offered another reason why Tullahoma resonated so little then and later. True, Middle Tennessee was again given up to the Union Army, he observed, but that fact "we learned to our cost, was not a cause of congratulation." Writing retrospectively, Carlin commented that "it only rendered necessary other campaigns requiring long and difficult marches over mountains and river, in pursuit of the enemy, and other battles under still greater disadvantages." Truth was, he said, this constant retreating of the Confederates "never did us any good, though our people and our armies accepted it as a certain measure of success." What his side most needed "was to meet the enemy's army as near as possible to our base of supplies." Every retreat made by their opponents "rendered it necessary to call for more troops, more supplies of every kind, and increased our distance from our bases, every mile of which had to be guarded with forts, blockhouses, cannon, and troops." Since Rosecrans could not prevent Bragg's retirement, "to follow him became a necessity, cost what it might in treasure, men, and time."

As the respected Federal Gen. David Stanley subsequently explained, Tullahoma failed in its main object—the destruction of Bragg's army—through an act of Providence. Providence, rain, or simply slow pursuit, Bragg escaped, crossed the Tennessee River, and occupied Chattanooga, "the same point from which he had departed eleven months before with the object of invading Kentucky." To a jaded Carlin and perhaps other Yankee veterans of the campaign (some at least from Kentucky and Tennessee), "we had recovered all the territory that Buell held a year before, which had been lost by the necessary retrograde movement of Buell's army, caused by

Bragg's strategic march into Kentucky." Tullahoma, like other military activities, faded into a monotonous recitation of seemingly constant traversing through these states between battles.[13]

While we recognize terrain features as vital to military operations, have we forgotten the role that navigable streams, highways, and railroads preeminently played in the movement of wartime goods and armies? The young rail lines like Louisville and Nashville, Nashville and Chattanooga, Memphis and Charleston, Nashville and Decatur, and Memphis Branch were pressed into service by the military, guarded and disrupted by the military, as well as managed and developed for war by the military. The same for steamboat traffic and overworked roads, fields left destitute or depleted by the armies—the Upper South's infrastructure was damaged by war. How can we of the urban interstate culture today even relate to such occurrence?

Over forty years ago, Anglo-American historian Marcus Cunliffe wrote eloquently on this virtually forgotten hedge against the tyranny of central government and professional standing military. He perceived three sectional military characters distinct to the New World—the Southern chevalier, the Northern rifleman, and the pacific Quakers.[14] One might wonder what happened to this Quaker or pacifistic dimension in the sister states' experience. But Aaron Astor has seized upon the militia tradition in two key Upper South cities to suggest how prewar society in those locales prepared for and contributed to the war's coming. The fruits of that system underpin other chapters and suggest inadequacies of the system—political, military, and organizational—for coping with a full spectrum of modern civil war. Scott Tarnowieckyi depicts Kentucky's Green River country in the next step of transformation from peace to war and one incapable of restraining descent to near-anarchy on the Kentucky home front that became virtually more occupied Union territory despite its professions of loyalty.

Tricia Hoskins's dissection of Kentucky's most destabilized and secessionist-prone section or "the Purchase" beyond the Tennessee River ties to another "war within a war" discovered by historians only relatively recently. But a short distance across the state line, Tennessee Unionism labored to survive in an environment every bit as virulently bloody, costly, and disruptive as any true civil war, and Derek Frisby elevates that topic in the best tradition of Richard Current, William Freehling, and Robert Tracy McKenzie.[15] Wars of survival between "tories" (Unionists), rebels (secessionists), and bushwhackers (banditti, flotsam and jetsam from armies, as well as homegrown patriotic defenders of hearth and home) were as bloodily "knife to the hilt," Black Flag and "no quarter" as anything experienced on the battlefield. Merely suggesting examination of a "people's war" through local or neighborhood study points to a new post-Sesquicentennial history that awaits exploration. It is a history that bridges war and reconstruction yet remains irretrievably linked by violence, brigandage, guerrilla-ism, and organized military actions, and suggests another provocative topic—the role of Kentucky and Tennessee African Americans in the military context.

Their role not only cuts across the three principal Union military invasion routes that traversed these states, but further unites treatment of civil-military relations in occupied territory. Equally important, African American military participation linked liberation and emancipation through racial, economic, and political intersection, bridged the secession-war-stabilization and reconstruction paradigm, and provides causative explanation of the difficult and turbulent postwar adjustments in Kentucky and Tennessee (as elsewhere).[16]

The hard fact that both sides needed and used human and animal resources promiscuously in war should come as no surprise to anyone. Perhaps unappreciated by a post–civil rights, casualty-averse generation of Americans today, humanity was a necessary resource in the absence of later machine technology transformed for war. The Confederacy made the black slave labor conversion from peacetime economic to wartime logistical support more naturally given legal, societal, and exploitative dimensions of its Peculiar Institution. From the start, black Confederates undergird the military and civilian Confederacy in the upper heartland like elsewhere. Supporting forces in the field—maintaining Southern industry and transport, feeding the Confederacy, and tending its agrarian underpinnings—were part of the fabric of the war effort. Mixed success came with contracting for slave labor to build Middle Tennessee's protective forts when crop harvest beckoned owners. Later, these owners moved such valuable property beyond the reach of the invading enemy, which was dislocating for the economy but acceptable for wealth protection. Putting them in organized uniformed ranks and armed for war was not.

The Union, on the other hand, had little compunction about attacking Confederate sinews of war despite laws, customs, and regulations to the contrary and the Lincoln administration's avoidance of alienating slaveholding but loyal Unionist Southerners. Ersatz liberation conflicted with maintenance of legal slavery when every unit in blue went south of the Ohio and Potomac rivers. Racial animus aside, stern necessity—not necessarily humane—attended the role for African Americans as the war progressed. This became readily apparent with all the predictable attendant difficulties in Kentucky and Tennessee. It affected not only the conduct of the war but the subsequent peace.

In a sense, Kentucky and Tennessee bonded over the economic and social dimensions of human enslavement. Ninety percent of the Volunteer State's slave population of 275,719 could be found in Middle and West Tennessee (central avenues for Union invasion). Kentucky slaveholders, totaling 38,645, outnumbered those of other loyal border states combined. They owned 225,483 slaves or 20 percent of the Bluegrass State's population. Thus, a half-million human beings—private property—became a pawn for both sides, but a game-deciding knight for the Union on the chessboard of the war in the West. And the issue would be settled by national policy in Washington, state actions in the region, and among roustabouts on wharves, women and children in holding camps like Dick Robinson, and—most of all—in military camps and battlefields because the Union openly recruited, enlisted, and loosed black males as part of its armies of conquest and subjugation. The story is far more idiosyncratic and poorly appreciated than hinted at in the myriad studies of emancipation.

Progression from legal slavery to legal contraband to ersatz freedom to wartime emancipation to military support and subsequently to armed unit enlistment substituted private exploitation for public service. What commenced in the Mississippi Valley as well as in Middle and West Tennessee from late 1861 onward cracked the Confederacy's backbone—economy, society, and polity—fully as much as what transpired on battlefields. As large numbers of slaves escaped from bondage and sought shelter with Union forces, the fracturing of the Confederacy began. It was handmaiden to a legacy going forward from forts Henry and Donelson, culminating with the black troops of Gen. James Steadman helping to win with their blood at Nashville, fighting alongside the boys in blue. Pragmatic Union authorities looked to freed black people to help gain their salvation through contractual rather than bonded service. They soon found that unending warfare and unsubdued Confederate whites, as well as unceasing casualty figures, dictated that alternate sources be found for cannon fodder. So, winning freedom through armed service became part of the post-1863 emancipation bonding of white and black in the United States voluntary military service. The appearance of second-class citizenship accompanied the process. Kentucky and Tennessee blacks and whites alike contributed to this process.

Recruiters like U.S. Adj. Gen. Lorenzo Thomas and Maj. George L. Stearns, Military Gov. Andrew Johnson, Kentucky Unionist Col. Frank Wolford, and Gen. Stephen Burbridge were part of the turbulent African American military story. But so, too, were loyal-claimant slaveholders like George Browder of Christian County, Kentucky, and, of course, the ever-inflammatory Bedford Forrest and the Fort Pillow drama. White officer–led African American units, organized at locales from Memphis, La Grange, Pulaski, and Lafayette in West Tennessee to Clarksville in the middle part of the state, led the vanguard. Their service as depot, railroad, and bridge guards freed up white Northern volunteer units to go die for Uncle Sam. Rear-echelon chores ultimately involved the test of combat as when Confederate cavalry raiders like Forrest and Joe Wheeler—not to mention the ever-present pestilence of partisan guerrillas and race-hating flotsam from both armies ravaging the countryside—tested black mettle. As major armies burned out most of the Upper South, sending many rebellious whites southward beyond the lines and Unionist counterpart refugees scampering to protective urban sanctuaries for survival, the war zone had so corrupted Tennessee's prewar society and disrupted normal affairs anyway that the presence of United States Colored contingents alongside white Northern—even local volunteer—military units simply became part of the new norm to disturb almost everyone.

Matters in Kentucky, however, were something else, and they changed drastically on February 24, 1864. Disruption of slavery had already begun, but the law still stood. Any black male wishing to enlist in army service had to slip away to Clarksville, Tennessee, or even across the Ohio. Stevedore, railroad construction, even road repair, provided contracted labor for escaped males. Hospital work for females was the principal lot for those who fled bondage. Then on that date, the Enrollment Act, coupled with the previous year's national conscription act, opened floodgates with unanticipated consequences. Slaves, even of loyal owners, became eligible for the draft, and the hue and cry from irate white Kentuckians reverberated to Washington and threatened the state's continued allegiance to the national Union. Black Kentuckians—like their brethren elsewhere—responded enthusiastically with their feet. The formality of gaining owner approval for enlistment was soon forgotten by recruiters and slaves alike. The late-war recruitment, training, and deployment in anti-guerrilla and dissident suppression operations, as well as General Burbridge's ill-fated expedition to Saltville in southwestern Virginia (which included the 5th and 6th U.S. Colored Cavalry as well as white Midwestern units), led to combat that became racially enflamed, resulting in Fort Pillow–like atrocities. All told, however, Kentucky's two cavalries, four heavy artilleries, and seventeen African American regiments contributed to the war effort in the region and beyond. But the whole question of the militarization of Southern blacks provided an unfortunate bridge to postwar difficulties in both Tennessee and Kentucky.

Wartime armies create destruction. One Illinois soldier wrote his mother from La Vergne, Tennessee, at the start of the Tullahoma operation, describing how the town "has suffered the extreme rigors of war." It is burned to the ground, he commented, except for three buildings used for hospitals. It was here that the great battle of Stones River had commenced. Now, "all around us lay the remnants of wagon trains which the rebels burned and the decayed remains of mules and horses, while little piles of bricks and crumbled masonry are significant of the terrible fate and swift destruction that overtook a rebellious city." "It's a terrible sight to contemplate," he concluded, and though it was "just retribution," he could not help "feeling sad at the fate of the misled inhabitants, once happy and joyous as those of our Northern villages, now exiles, with no home on earth."

Two years later an Illinois soldier updated the picture at Tullahoma for his cousin. Most of the people "in this part of the world" have fled either north or south, "and if they ever return they will find a sorry looking place, fields gone, plantations destroyed, buildings burned, their slaves freed, and in short "everything is entirely 'gone up' with only white trash left as ignorant as the heathen theirselves [*sic*]" walking the streets. Half the people one meets, he asserted, are "2/5 Negroes & the rest mostly American citizens of African descent." About the same time, on the Nashville battlefield, a New York soldier toured a land covered "with dead horses and bones of all kinds," but apparently there were no human remains, which he presumed were buried. He picked some flowers from a private cemetery caught up in the maelstrom and dispatched them to his sister "to press them and lay away for me." Such memories and impressions joined what Confederate propagandist Adalbert Volk, postwar Northern observer John T. Trowbridge, and modern historians like Megan Kate Nelson and Lisa M. Brady have recently rediscovered. There was an unsettling blend of reality mixed with propaganda and subsequent Lost Cause hand-wringing about Southern landscapes, natural and human-made, at the end of the conflict.[17]

Gen. William H. Lytle took the portraiture still further. Writing to a friend at the height of the Tullahoma operation, Lytle looked to a benevolent solution to the conflict. "Without any impropriety, and in consonance with practices in other wars," Mr. Lincoln "ought to proclaim an amnesty to all rebels who would lay down their arms and return to their allegiance," and all states or parts thereof that "would proceed at once to elect members of Congress," excepting perhaps the arch leaders of the rebellion—"though even as to such men as Jeff Davis, Slidell, Mason and others, on the principle that it is well to have a giant's strength but not to use it *like* a giant." Such a lenient display "might be the one most befitting a mighty nation which has crushed out the most formidable rebellion in history." By war's conclusion, Lytle decided that "the South will have been punished seriously enough God knows." "Her fields desolated, her people impoverished, her pride humbled, her currency worthless rags, and the blood of her best and bravest shed in vain," a magnanimous and humane policy toward the vanquished "after this overwhelming display of the power of the Federal Gov't" would "be more dignified, would exalt us in the eyes of all foreign states, and would render easier the task of restoration of good feeling between the sections when the war is over," he advanced. Meanwhile, however, "the work so well begun is to be vigorously pushed, without giving the enemy time to 'get his wind' or rally, until his great armies are completely routed, scattered and dispersed." Both the potential of a Tullahoma operation to accomplish such a goal and a more beneficent national policy by the United States government were not to be.[18]

The diversity of the Upper South's martial experience contributed to a different trajectory. Death and destruction enflamed senses as social revolution forced psychological adjustments when Kentucky and Tennessee boys on both sides returned home. In many ways this transition for the veterans merged the mainstream of camp and combat memory with the wartime experience they learned about back home. For as many "who wanted to forget," there were just as many who wanted to "forget, hell!" A postwar Kentucky and a "restored" Tennessee should provide fascinating chapters in how military combat affected the postwar peace in these states. The boundaries are limitless for a new generation seeking post-Sesquicentennial answers and unsatisfied by synthesized accounts. A generation ago, Austin Peay State University professor Richard Gildrie painted a word picture of Clarksville, Tennessee, at the end of the war. The town had escaped major battle, yet witnessed the alarms of partisan raids, military occupation, and suppression of civil liberties and had seen her native sons depart for battle. It had watched the social and economic revolution involving liberation and enlistment of African Americans as well as refugee departures and influx of squatters and carpetbaggers. Gildrie quoted from a July 1865 issue of the Clarksville *Chronicle* about how the newspaper now wished to see people resuming their former avocations, business reviving, and "the channels of trade reopened." "We want to see discord superceded by peace, and demoralization corrected by honest industry." The editor desired "Judges superceding Commandants of Posts, and the soldier giving place to the citizen."

Gildrie noted how Federal troops had yielded the courthouse to civil authority in May, how local avid secessionist Nannie Haskins youthfully reveled in the whirl of "soldiers coming and going all the time," and how Pvt. William Dorris of the 83rd Illinois occupation unit stationed at Clarksville cited a religious revival spirit. Dorris also jotted down rebel soldiers returning "amid peace and quiet" and how a traveling circus had attracted some three thousand war-weary people to the fairgrounds. Even one notably irascible local chronicler had gone to church for the first time since December 1862, Dorris cited, offering a sign of stability returning to the locale.[19]

Clarksville soon had its first mayor since the beginning of the war, and the lucrative tobacco market ("the basis of local economy") reopened in October with the first steamboat shipments to New Orleans since 1861 departing in December. Rail traffic on the Memphis Branch of the Louisville & Nashville Railroad was restored in September 1866. Fifteen new businesses were incorporated by the state legislature, although mostly controlled by "unconditional Union men." And herein lay the rub. Any identification as an ex-Confederate hindered a large segment of the population from regaining assets and livelihood. The outlet of state and local politics offered one avenue for a return to power for such Fort Donelson veterans as Tennessee Gen. William A. Quarles, who after the war became prominent in the state senate. It would take time, something contemporaries termed "redemption," and a multitude of hard feelings, hard policies, even seeming retrogression from social progress that years of reconciliationist words, deeds, and literature would hide. "Life was beginning to make sense again in the town" in 1865, suggested Gildrie. Yet, was it?[20]

Nature soon healed the landscape, yet the work of economic historian Paul F. Paskoff raises questions. Heavy losses of animal and human labor power, but not farm equipment, reflected the war's cost in crops lost, livestock taken, and property destroyed. "Neglected farms, roads and paths overgrown with weeds, and almost no business of any kind being carried on" in Kentucky suggest it was the countryside, not areas of habitation, that were the problem at the end of the "military" part of the conflict. So we should be left with unanswered questions and unbounded curiosity about what it was really like in Kentucky and Tennessee when the guns fell silent.

Gildrie included a subtle coda. Private Dorris and his comrades left Clarksville by steamer on June 25, 1865. Their departure mixed sadness with elation, suggested Gildrie. There were reunions, but "some men came home to find their female relatives had married Yankees and left." As Gildrie remarked, "some family ties were forever broken." Possibly this is a story best left to a third volume, one that would treat the tale of Reconstruction.[21]

Notes

1. Frances H. Kennedy, ed., *The Civil War Battlefield Guide* (Boston: Houghton Mifflin, 1996), inter alia.

2. Benjamin Franklin Cooling, *Forts Henry and Donelson: The Key to the Confederate Heartland* (Knoxville: Univ. of Tennessee Press, 1987); Benjamin Franklin Cooling, *Fort Donelson's Legacy: War and Society in Kentucky and Tennessee, 1862–1863* (Knoxville: Univ. of Tennessee Press, 1997); Benjamin Franklin Cooling, *To the Battles of Franklin and Nashville and Beyond: Stabilization and Reconstruction in Tennessee and Kentucky, 1864–1866* (Knoxville: Univ. of Tennessee Press, 2011); and Benjamin Franklin Cooling, "After the Horror: Kentucky in Reconstruction," in *Sister States Enemy States: The Civil War in Kentucky and Tennessee,* ed. Kent T. Dollar, Larry H. Whiteaker, and W. Calvin Dickinson (Lexington: Univ. Press of Kentucky, 2009), 338–62.

3. See Stanley F. Horn, *The Decisive Battle of Nashville* (Baton Rouge: Louisiana State Univ. Press, 1956), Preface.

4. Supporters of the seminal meaning of the war in the West may be found with recent studies such as Earl D. Hess, *The Civil War in the West: Victory and Defeat from the Appalachians to the Mississippi* (Chapel Hill: Univ. of North Carolina Press, 2012), and Stephen D. Engle, *Struggle for the Heartland: The Campaigns from Forts Henry to Corinth* (Lincoln: Univ. of Nebraska Press, 2001), building upon earlier works such as Thomas Lawrence Connelly, *Army of the Heartland: The Army of Tennessee, 1861–1862* (Baton Rouge: Louisiana State Univ. Press, 1967); Thomas Lawrence Connelly, *Autumn of Glory: The Army of Tennessee, 1862–1865* (Baton Rouge: Louisiana State Univ. Press, 1971); and even John Fiske, *The Mississippi Valley in the Civil War* (Boston: Houghton, Mifflin, 1900), for instance.

5. See Sam David Elliott, *Soldier of Tennessee: General Alexander P. Stewart and the Civil War in the West* (Baton Rouge: Louisiana State Univ. Press, 1999).

6. See Stephen V. Ash, *Middle Tennessee Society Transformed 1860–1870: War and Peace in the Upper South* (Baton Rouge: Louisiana State Univ. Press, 1988), and Stephen V. Ash, *When the Yankees Came: Conflict and Chaos in the Occupied South, 1861–1865* (Chapel Hill: Univ. of North Carolina Press, 1995).

7. Kennedy, *The Civil War Battlefield Guide,* 459–60.

8. See Kent Masterson Brown, "Mill Springs, Kentucky," in *The Civil War Battlefield Guide,* ed. Frances H. Kennedy (Boston: Houghton Mifflin, 1996), 50. The guide as a whole provides a useful tracking device for sorting important western skirmishes and battles.

9. See United States War Department, *The War of the Rebellion: A Compilation of the Official Records of the Union and Confederate Armies* (Washington, D.C.: Government Printing Office, 1880–1901), ser. 1, vol. 23, pt. 2, 522; ibid., ser. 1, vol. 23, pt.1, 402–3.

10. Cursory coverage in Matthew Forney Steele, *American Campaigns* (Washington, D.C.: Byron Adams, 1909), vol. 1, Lecture 20; Peter Cozzens, *This Terrible Sound: The Battle of Chickamauga* (Urbana: Univ. of Illinois Press, 1992); David A. Powell and David A. Friedrichs, *The Maps of Chickamauga: An Atlas of the Chickamauga Campaign, Including the Tullahoma Operations, June 22–September 23, 1863* (New York/El Dorado Hills: Savas Beatie, 2009); and W. J. Wood, *Civil War Generalship: The Art of Command* (Westport, Conn.: Greenwood, 1997), 86–110, contrasts with better recognition in Michael R. Bradley, *Tullahoma: The 1863 Campaign for the Control of Middle Tennessee* (Shippensburg, Pa.: Burd Street Press, 2000); Michael R. Bradley, "Tullahoma: The Wrongly Forgotten Campaign," *Blue and Gray Magazine* 27, no. 1 (2010–10); Steven E. Woodworth, "Braxton Bragg and the Tullahoma Campaign," in *The Art of Command in the Civil War,* ed. Steven E. Woodworth (Lincoln: Univ. of Nebraska Press, 1998), 157–82.

11. Ruth C. Carter, ed., *For Honor, Glory and Union: The Mexican and Civil War Letters of Brig. Gen. William Haines Lytle* (Lexington: Univ. Press of Kentucky, 1999), 178–81; Connelly, *Autumn of Glory,* ch. 6, esp. p. 133.

12. See, for example, Paul M. Angle, ed., *Three Years in the Army of the Cumberland: The Letters and Diary of Major James A. Connolly* (Bloomington: Indiana Univ. Press, 1996), 74–114; Charles E. Willett, ed., *A Union Soldier Returns South: The Civil War Letters and Diary of Alfred C. Willett, 113th Ohio Volunteer Infantry* (Johnson City, Tenn.: The Overmountain Press, 1994), 27–28; Leland W. Thornton, *When Gallantry Was Commonplace: The History of the Michigan Eleventh Volunteer Infantry, 1861–1864* (New York: Peter Lang, 1991), ch. 14; Mark W. Johnson, *That Body of Brave Men: The U.S. Regular Infantry and the Civil War in the West* (Cambridge Center, Mass.: Da Capo Press, 2000), 358–71; Kirk C. Jenkins, *The Battle Rages Higher: The Union's Fifteenth Kentucky Infantry* (Lexington: Univ. Press of Kentucky, 2003), ch. 6; Nathaniel Cheairs Hughes Jr., ed., *The Civil War Memoir of Philip Daingerfield Stephenson, D.D.* (Conway, Ark.: UCA Press, 1995), ch. 9; R. Lockwood Tower, ed., *A Carolinian Goes to War: The Civil War Narrative of Arthur Middleton Manigault* (Columbia: Univ. of South Carolina Press, 1983), ch. 4, esp. 76–77; John Watson Morton, *The Artillery of Nathan Bedford Forrest's Cavalry* (Nashville/Dallas: Publishing House of the M. E. Church, South, 1909), ch. 9; James M. McCaffrey, *This Band of Heroes, Granbury's Texas Brigade, C.S.A.* (College Station: Texas A&M Press, 1996), ch. 4; John D. Fowler, *Mountaineers in Gray: The Nineteenth Tennessee Volunteer Infantry Regiment, C.S.A.* (Knoxville: Univ. of Tennessee Press, 2004); Norman D. Brown, ed., *One of Cleburne's Command: The Civil War Reminiscences and Diary of Capt. Samuel T. Foster, Granbury's Texas Brigade, CSA* (Austin: Univ. of Texas Press, 1980), ch. 2; Nathaniel C. Hughes, ed., *Liddell's Record: St. John Richardson Liddell, Brigadier General, CSA* (Dayton, Ohio: Morningside, 1985), ch. 12.

13. Robert I. Girardi and Nathaniel Cheairs Hughes Jr., eds., *The Memoirs of Brigadier General William Passmore Carlin U.S.A.* (Lincoln: Univ. of Nebraska Press, 1999), 92; Constantin Grebner, *"We Were the Ninth:" A History of the Ninth Regiment,*

Ohio Volunteer Infantry April 17, 1861, to June 7, 1864, ed. and trans. Frederic Trautmann (Kent, Ohio: Kent State Univ. Press, 2009), 130–31; David Stanley, "The Tullahoma Campaign," in *Sketches of War History 1861–1865: Papers for Delivery to the Ohio Commandery, Loyal Legion of the United States, 1880–1890,* ed. Robert Hunter (Cincinnati: Robert Clarke, 1888), 3:181.

14. Marcus Cunliffe, *Soldiers and Civilians: The Martial Spirit in America 1775–1865* (Boston: Little, Brown, 1968).

15. Richard Nelson Current, *Lincoln's Loyalists: Union Soldiers from the Confederacy* (Boston: Northeastern Univ. Press, 1992); William W. Freehling, *The South versus the South: How Anti-Confederate Southerners Shaped the Course of the Civil War* (Oxford/New York: Oxford Univ. Press, 2001); and Robert Tracy McKenzie, *Lincolnites and Rebels: A Divided Town in the Civil War* (Oxford/New York: Oxford Univ. Press, 2006).

16. William Dobak's official army history of the United States Colored Troops is a concise but comprehensive method for exploring this topic. See William A. Dobak, *Freedom by the Sword: The U.S. Colored Troops 1861–1867* (Washington, D.C.: United States Army Center of Military History, 2011), ch. 6–9 and 12. Also indispensable to this topic are Ira Berlin et al., eds., *Freedom: A Documentary History of Emancipation, 1861–1867,* ser. 2, *The Black Military Experience* (Cambridge/New York: Cambridge Univ. Press, 1982), in toto; Ira Berlin et al., eds., *Freedom: A Documentary History of Emancipation 1861–1867,* ser. 1, vol. 1, *The Destruction of Slavery* (Cambridge/New York: Cambridge Univ. Press, 1985), ch. 5, 8; Ira Berlin et al., eds., *Freedom: A Documentary History of Emancipation, 1861–1867,* ser. 1, vol. 2, *The Wartime Genesis of Free Labor: The Upper South* (Cambridge/New York: Cambridge Univ. Press, 1993), ch. 3, 6; and Ira Berlin et al., eds., *Free at Last: A Documentary History of Slavery, Freedom and the Civil War* (New York: The New Press, 1992), ch. 6.

17. Megan Kate Nelson, *Ruin Nation and the American Civil War* (Athens: Univ. of Georgia Press, 2012), esp. 65, 77, 78–79,103, 135–37, 147, 148, 149, 150; Lisa M. Brady, *War Upon the Land: Military Strategy and the Transformation of Southern Landscapes During the American Civil War* (Athens: Univ. of Georgia Press, 2012); John T. Trowbridge, *The South: A Tour of Its Battle-Fields and Ruined Cities* (1866; repr., New York: Arno, 1969); Jennifer Cain Bohrnstadt, ed., *Soldiering with Sherman: Civil War Letters of George F. Cram* (DeKalb: Northern Illinois Univ. Press, 2000), 45–47; Letters, William H. Green to his sister, Mar. 18, 1865, and Lee Anderson to his cousin Nelson, Mar. 22, 1865, both author's collection.

18. Carter, ed., *For Honor, Glory and Union,* 181–82.

19. Charles M. Winters, ed., *Historic Clarksville: The Bicentennial Story, 1784–1984* (Clarksville, Tenn.: Historic Clarksville Publishing Company, 1983), 77.

20. Ibid.

21. For some suggestions, see Benjamin Franklin Cooling, "Bluegrass and Volunteer—Sister States or Enemy States," *The Register of the Kentucky Historical Society* 10, nos. 3 and 4 (Summer/Autumn 2012): 439–80.

Contributors

AARON ASTOR is Associate Professor of History at Maryville College in Maryville, Tennessee. He is the author of *Rebels on the Border: Civil War, Emancipation, and the Reconstruction of Kentucky and Missouri, 1860–1872* (2012) and *The Civil War along Tennessee's Cumberland Plateau* (2015). He has also contributed several articles to the award-winning *New York Times* "Disunion" series dealing with such topics as guerrilla warfare, battles, and campaigns in the Western Theater, popular politics, emancipation and race, and regional identity in Kentucky and Tennessee. He is currently working on a book project that examines the 1860 presidential election as a grassroots phenomenon across the United States.

BENJAMIN FRANKLIN COOLING is Professor of National Security Studies at The Dwight D. Eisenhower School for National Security Strategy and Resource Strategy, The National Defense University in Washington, D.C., and a distinguished Civil War historian. His many publications include *Jubal Early: Robert E. Lee's "Bad Old Man"* (2014), *The Day Lincoln Was Almost Shot: The Fort Stevens Story* (2013), *To the Battles of Franklin and Nashville and Beyond: Stabilization and Reconstruction in Tennessee and Kentucky, 1864–1866* (2012), *Fort Donelson's Legacy: War and Society in Kentucky and Tennessee, 1862–1863* (1997), *Jubal Early's Raid on Washington: 1864* (1995), *Symbol, Sword, and Shield: Defending Washington During the Civil War* (1991), and *Forts Henry and Donelson: Key to the Confederate Heartland* (1988). His current project focuses on resourcing the Civil War.

W. CALVIN DICKINSON is Professor Emeritus of History at Tennessee Technological University in Cookeville. He has published dozens of articles and books, his most recent of which are *Tennessee: State of the Union* (2012), coedited with Larry Whiteaker, *Soldiers, Spies & Spartans: Civil War Stories from Tennessee* (2011), *Rural Life and Culture in the Upper Cumberland* (2004), coedited with Michael E. Birdwell, *Tennessee Tales That Textbooks Don't Tell* (2002), and *Bibliography of Tennessee History,*

1973–1996 (1998). He is also coeditor of *Sister States, Enemy States: The Civil War in Kentucky and Tennessee* (2009).

KENT T. DOLLAR is Associate Professor of History at Tennessee Technological University in Cookeville. He is the author of *Soldiers of the Cross: Confederate Soldier-Christians and the Impact of War on Their Faith* (2005) and coeditor of *Sister States, Enemy States: The Civil War in Kentucky and Tennessee* (2009). His current project examines the religious interest of both Union and Confederate soldiers during the early months of the Civil War.

SAM DAVIS ELLIOTT, an attorney and historian who works and lives in Chattanooga, Tennessee, has published several works on the Civil War, including *Soldier of Tennessee: General Alexander P. Stewart and the Civil War in the West* (1999), *Doctor Quintard, Chaplain C.S.A. and Second Bishop of Tennessee: The Memoir and Civil War Diary of Charles Todd Quintard* (2003), and *Isham G. Harris of Tennessee: Confederate Governor and United States Senator* (2010). His current project is a biography of John C. Brown.

STEPHEN D. ENGLE is Professor of History at Florida Atlantic University in Boca Raton. He is the author of several books, among them *Yankee Dutchman: The Life of Franz Sigel* (1993), *Don Carlos Buell: Most Promising of All* (1999), *Struggle for the Heartland* (2000), *The American Civil War in the West* (2001), and together with Gary Gallagher, Bob Krick, and Joseph Glatthaar, a text entitled *This Mighty Scourge of War* (2003). His most recent publication is with David Coles, *A Yankee Horseman in the Shenandoah Valley* (2012), and his latest work, *Gathering to Save a Nation: Abraham Lincoln, War Governors, and Preserving the Union,* explores the relationship between Lincoln and the loyal governors during the war.

DEREK W. FRISBY is a faculty coordinator for the College of Liberal Arts and Office of International Affairs at Middle Tennessee State University in Murfreesboro and has authored several articles on the American Civil War. His research examines the effects of occupation and reconstruction, and he has a work in progress on guerrilla warfare in West Tennessee. As an associate professor for MTSU's Global Studies and Cultural Geography program, Dr. Frisby leads numerous courses on campus and abroad to study the cultural influences of warfare and public memory.

EARL J. HESS holds the Stewart W. McClelland Chair in History at Lincoln Memorial University. He has authored many articles and nineteen books, mostly on Civil War subjects. Among his publications are *Kennesaw Mountain: Sherman, Johnston, and the Atlanta Campaign* (2013), *The Civil War in the West: Victory and Defeat from the Appalachians to the Mississippi* (2012), *Into the Crater: The Mine Attack at Petersburg* (2010), *In the Trenches at Petersburg: Field Fortifications & Confederate Defeat* (2009), *The Rifle Musket in Civil War Combat: Reality and Myth* (2008), *Pickett's Charge—The Last Attack at Gettysburg* (2001), and *The Union Soldier in Battle: Enduring the Ordeal of Combat* (1997).

PATRICIA A. HOSKINS is Assistant Professor of History and College Historian at Limestone College in Gaffney, South Carolina. She has published articles on the Civil War, and her current project focuses on the Civil War, Reconstruction, and memory in the Jackson Purchase region of Kentucky.

A retired journalist (Maryville–Alcoa *Daily Times,* Nashville *Tennessean,* Philadelphia *Inquirer,* and Chicago *Tribune*) living in DeKalb County, Tennessee, historian JACK HURST has written at length about the Civil War. His publications include *Nathan Bedford Forrest: A Biography* (1993), *Men of Fire: Grant, Forrest and the Campaign That Decided the Civil War* (2007), and most recently *Born to Battle: Grant and Forrest: Shiloh, Vicksburg, and Chattanooga* (2012). He is currently working on another book on the Civil War era.

CHRISTOPHER LOSSON lives and teaches history in St. Joseph, Missouri. He is the author of *Tennessee's Forgotten Warriors: Frank Cheatham and His Confederate Division* (1989). He has contributed sketches to several publications, including the *Encyclopedia of the Confederacy, The Tennessee Encyclopedia of History and Culture,* and the forthcoming *Mississippi Encyclopedia.* His current research projects include a study of the Civil War in the Yazoo-Mississippi Delta and of Nashville's role in postwar Confederate memorialization efforts and Lost Cause ideology.

BRIAN D. MCKNIGHT is Associate Professor of History and Founding Director of the Center for Appalachian Studies at the University of Virginia's College at Wise. He has authored numerous articles on the Civil War and two books: *Confederate Outlaw: Champ Ferguson and the Civil War in Appalachia* (2011) and *Contested Borderland: The Civil War in Appalachian Kentucky and Virginia* (2006).

WILEY SWORD, a distinguished Civil War historian, has published numerous works on the conflict, including *Shiloh: Bloody April* (1974), *Embrace an Angry Wind: the Confederacy's Last Hurrah, Spring Hill, Franklin, and Nashville* (1992), *Mountains Touched with Fire: Chattanooga Besieged, 1863* (1995), *Southern Invincibility: A History of the Confederate Heart* (1999), and *Courage under Fire: Profiles in Bravery from the Battlefields of the Civil War* (2007). He has been nominated for the Pulitzer, Parkman, Bancroft, and Western Heritage prizes.

SCOTT A. TARNOWIECKYI is Associate Professor of History and chair of the Social Sciences Department at Weatherford College. His specialty is the Civil War in Kentucky. He has delivered numerous conference papers on various aspects of the war in the Bluegrass State and his current research project is on the Civil War in the lower Green River country.

Currently Associate Professor of History at Lincoln Memorial University, MICHAEL TOOMEY is the former Curator of History for The East Tennessee Historical Society and the former managing editor of *The Journal of East Tennessee History.* He has authored of several articles on various topics in American history.

Larry H. Whiteaker, Professor Emeritus of History at Tennessee Technological University, has written extensively on the Civil War as well as on nineteenth-century America. Among his books are *The Individual and Society in America* (1979), *Seduction, Prostitution, and Moral Reform in New York, 1830–1860* (1997), and *Tennessee: State of the Union* (2012), coedited with W. Calvin Dickinson. He is also coeditor of *Sister States, Enemy States: The Civil War in Kentucky and Tennessee* (2009).

Index